IS BIRDSONG MUSIC?

MUSIC, NATURE, PLACE
Sabine Feisst and Denise Von Glahn

IS BIRDSONG MUSIC?

Outback Encounters
with an Australian Songbird

HOLLIS TAYLOR

WITH A FOREWORD BY PHILIP KITCHER

INDIANA UNIVERSITY PRESS
Bloomington & Indianapolis

This book is a publication of

INDIANA UNIVERSITY PRESS
Office of Scholarly Publishing
Herman B Wells Library 350
1320 East 10th Street
Bloomington, Indiana 47405 USA

iupress.indiana.edu

The paper used in this publication
meets the minimum requirements of
the American National Standard for
Information Sciences—Permanence
of Paper for Printed Library
Materials, ANSI Z39.48–1992.

Manufactured in the
United States of America

Library of Congress
Cataloging-in-Publication Data

Names: Taylor, Hollis, author.
Title: Is birdsong music? : outback
    encounters with an Australian
    songbird / Hollis Taylor ; with a
    foreword by Philip Kitcher.
Other titles: Music, nature, place.
Description: Bloomington ; Indianapolis :
    Indiana University Press, 2017. |
    Series: Music, nature, place
Identifiers: LCCN 2016059600 (print) |
    LCCN 2017000757 (ebook) | ISBN
    9780253026200 (cloth : alk. paper) |
    ISBN 9780253026668 (pbk. : alk. paper) |
    ISBN 9780253026484 (e-book)
Subjects: LCSH: Birdsongs—Australia. |
    Butcherbirds—Behavior—Australia.
Classification: LCC QL698.5 .T39 2017
    (print) | LCC QL698.5 (ebook) |
    DDC 598.159/40994—dc23
LC record available at https://lccn.loc.gov
    /2016059600

1 2 3 4 5   22 21 20 19 18 17

For Jon

CONTENTS

Foreword by Philip Kitcher   ix

1. An Outback Epiphany   1

2. Songbird Studies   19

3. The Nature of Transcription and the Transcription of Nature   53

4. Notes and Calls: A Taste for Diversity   84

5. Song Development: A Taste for Complexity   112

6. Musicality and the Art of Song: A Taste for Beauty   147

7. Border Conflicts at Music's Definition   180

8. Facts to Suit Theories   209

9. Too Many Theories and Not Enough Birdsong   235

10. Songbirds as Colleagues and Contemporaries   257

Acknowledgments   283

Notation and Supplement Conventions   289

List of Audio Tracks   291

List of Abbreviations   295

Glossary   297

Bibliography   305

Index   333

FOREWORD

Philip Kitcher

M ore than a century has elapsed since Darwin taught the world about the continuity of life. Part of his message, more prominent in the *Descent of Man* than in the *Origin of Species*, affirms a connection between our own species and the rest of the animal kingdom. Yet, as the late Stephen Jay Gould once remarked, when we learn of our evolution from *apes*, we should also recall that we evolved *from* apes. Besides the continuity, there are also differences.

But what exactly are those differences? Are there important kinds of things we can do from which other animals are debarred? Or is it all a matter of degree? Perhaps for any characteristic or capacity that prompts us to swell our chests with pride, there's a nonhuman species anticipating us. For anything we can do, maybe another animal does it to a lesser degree—or simply in a different way. And sometimes better?

Darwin's picture of life has revived, even intensified, the perennial human quest to explain just what it is that makes us different. Scholars complete the sentence "No other animal species can . . ." in many different ways. We have all heard some popular answers. "Humans use tools; other animals don't." "We can talk; they can't." Moreover, the subsequent debates are familiar. Jane Goodall observed chimpanzees stripping leaves from tree branches to fish for termites. Does that count? Is it sufficiently "creative"? Many kinds of animals employ sounds or gestures for purposes of communication. Some—parrots, chimps—can be taught to use human languages. Do these findings warrant attributing linguistic abilities to species other than our own?

Then there's music. It's a wonderful human achievement, one that enriches our lives. Some people think it played a pivotal role in the evolution of human language. A much-admired play opens by characterizing it as "the food of love." Yet, of course, the natural world is full of organized sound. Humpback whales emit patterned clicks, gibbon calls produce focused notes, frogs give rhythmic calls. And even though bees don't do it, birds do.

In fact, birds do it *magnificently*. For centuries, poets have celebrated the beauties of birdsong. Musicians have been inspired to imitate the phrases created in a dawn chorus or a nocturnal serenade. Olivier Messiaen was only the most famous—and possibly the most dedicated—composer to incorporate birdsong into his works. Yet, despite all the fans and the fanfare, skepticism persists. Charming, mellifluous, inspiring it may be. But birdsong can't count as *real music*.

Why not? Probably the most popular reason for thinking that taking birdsong to be music is simply for the birds stems from long-discarded ideas. Many people suppose the vocalizations of birds to be instinctive, matters of running some innate program. Birds have evolved to make a species-typical pattern of sounds in order to attract mates. Come springtime, they perform by rote.

Amateur ornithologists, especially those with sensitive ears, can cite innumerable cases by way of refutation. Hollis Taylor is a professional ecologist specializing in avian behavior (especially vocal behavior), and her ears are surely as keen as any ever to absorb hours of birdsong. After a long career as a violinist, composer, jazz performer, ethnomusicologist, and avant-garde musician, she has become captivated by the vocal talents of a particular bird species: the pied butcherbird, so named for its habit of seizing smaller birds and mammals and storing its food by impaling its prey on twigs. As she puts it, she has fallen in love with "a convict." Her book is the decisive rebuttal of dismissals of avian creativity. It is a gift to our species and a mitigating plea on behalf of another, the principal target of her research.

Birds may sing to attract mates. They may learn a species-typical pattern around which they weave their songs. But, as Hollis's extensive fieldwork shows, their creativity is extraordinary. They may sing for hours on occasions on which advertising to potential partners seems entirely irrelevant. They absorb sounds from the ambient environment into their songs, using them as cues or directly imitating what they hear. Anyone who is inclined to assimilate these activities to some blind instinct or some mechanical program should ponder whether our own musical efforts might merit a kindred explanation. Don't some musical masterpieces have obvious functions? Composers write to celebrate a royal marriage or to honor the deity, songs are sung to woo, and dance music offers opportunities of closer contact. Are the processes of composition rooted in the pleasurable sounds we hear?

Scientists investigating birdsong have joined the consensus among bird lovers. They concede that vocalization isn't always geared to biological functions and recognize that species-typical patterns are learned and often varied. But now pooh-poohing avian creativity and condescending to the birds come in new forms. "To be sure, they can make some apparently musical gestures, but *human* music is distinguished by its . . ." The list of Truly Important Musical Features with which the sentence ends has many entries. We can improvise; they can't. We can transpose; they can't. We can sing duets and trios; they can't. And so on and on and on. Perhaps the list makers should be worried by the inability of many people to do the things they emphasize—and in some cases very few people have the "essential capacity." But, as Hollis demonstrates in example after example, such dismissive claims are thoroughly mistaken. It turns out that the birds *can*.

Her aim is not primarily to *refute* but rather to *include*. Trained as a musician and as a field ecologist, gifted with absolute pitch, and sensitive to the requirements of rigorous collection of data, she brings together the insights of different perspectives. Modestly—too modestly, I think—she characterizes herself as "not a scientist." Her basis for the judgment is her sense of emotional engagement with the birds she studies. By that criterion, Jane Goodall would be denied the title—and so too, I conjecture, would many of the field ethologists who have followed in her wake. Hollis Taylor may have begun as an artist and a humanist. She has also become a scientist, or, to use an older term, a "natural philosopher."

Although the pied butcherbird is her true love, she also surveys other Australian birds. Her conception of music is also catholic: she includes far more than the "Western canon," or the narrowed version of it (Bach to Mahler) that figures in most standards for evaluating birdsong. She is admirably reflective in considering alternative ways of representing birdsong—although her own transcriptions and analyses using standard (Western) musical notation are high points of her powerful argument. Above all, she is inclusive in her sources. The descriptions of her fieldwork sites that punctuate her discussions convey a vivid sense not only of place but also of the people with whom she has engaged. She celebrates the contributions to research of ordinary folk, and her recollections are filled with sincere respect and humane gratitude.

For me, the greatest delights of this book come in the passages describing her musical interactions with the birds she studies. Hollis, the distinguished professional violinist, casts herself as an apprentice, to learn from the birds. In a memorable vignette, she tells how her teachers, after making music with her for a while, became frustrated by the limitations of a mere beginner. Humbly, she takes birds' musical contributions as they are, without thinking of "improving" them. She feels no temptation to force their performances in any preferred direction. One musician, human and also humane, has discovered new players and new possibilities. She sits down to learn from them.

In doing so, Hollis invites her readers to reconceive the debate about human exclusivity and the charge that birdsong isn't "the real thing." Over half a century ago, Alan Turing, mathematician, code breaker, and architect of the digital computer, proposed a test for marking another boundary. Machines, he suggested, count as intelligent if they produce behavior indistinguishable from a human performance. A program might pass the test by conversing with us as if it were a human interlocutor. By the same token, animals might count as musicians if human musical professionals can make music with them. Hollis's (re)compositions for the violin of essentially unaltered transcriptions bring birds' songs—*their music*—to our appreciative ears. As this book and especially the recordings accompanying it show, the pied butcherbird passes a "Turing test" with flying colors.

A brilliant and sensitive musician-scientist has broadened the community of music makers. We should all be grateful.

Philip Kitcher is John Dewey Professor of
Philosophy at Columbia University.

IS BIRDSONG MUSIC?

CHAPTER 1

An Outback Epiphany

WOGARNO STATION, Western Australia, 13 April 2001: Drought has set its oven on slow bake. This autumn, they must assign acres to a sheep rather than sheep to an acre. On our drive up the five-mile dirt track to Lizard Rock, a sacred Aboriginal site, we pass a cinnabar lakebed frosted with cracked salt. Round a bend, a nonsensical white pile on the left vies for our attention: "bone dry" made manifest in the stacked remains of starving sheep, shot during the last drought. I can't take it in.

At noon, several hundred people crowd onto an ancient ironstone outcropping to hear my concert. I marvel that they could all find the place. The canopy erected to protect me and my violin from the sun barely manages. I'm a hostage to brightness and heat: head spinning, ears hissing, lights shooting in my eyes. The devil's box suffers Dante's Inferno.

Back at the homestead, the flash and rumble of a flock of galahs (*Cacatua roseicapilla*) cut across the sky. Wheeling in unison, they seem to say: "Look at us—we're pink, we're grey, we're pink again. Look!" On landing, their metallic "chirrink-chirrink" mixes with the windmill's creak and slurp. A few of the parrots ride it like a Ferris wheel. Others abseil down the stays of the homestead's radio mast, beak on wire. The raucous squawking from these party animals intensifies when one galah ups the ante: a flapping of wings during descent produces several mad circles around the wire. Copy-galahs are quick to follow. Let's twist and shout.

I wander about, collecting grass fishhooks in my socks. Haphazard tin sheds and aging fences, inventions of necessity encouraged to stand for yet another season, masquerade as one-of-a-kind designs. I'm photographing weathered wooden posts coifed with curls and tangles of charismatic wire when I feel a nudge on the back of my leg. It's Macca, the border collie pack leader. Apparently, he intends to chaperone me on my investigations. I always appreciate local knowledge.

He's quite attentive, but after a while I begin to wonder if Macca is just looking for a way to pass time, or if I am a personality so lacking in self-confidence as to appear sheepish. A border collie stare cannot be ignored, nor can it be appeased by tossing a stick or a snack. I feel *object* to his *subject*. When we arrive back where we began, he and the other dogs succeed in roping me into a game that takes three forms and switches from one to another for no obvious reason: kick the ball, stare at the ball, or stare at Marmalade, the cat. I'm trying to grasp the rules of the game, wondering whether Kick-and-Stare is all that happens for an hour and if I'm being a good sport or just a pushover, when out of the blue I hear a leisurely, rich-toned phrase. It's a jazz flutist in a tree. An explosion of sound in another tree answers—a long, bold rattle descends sharply and swiftly, and a duet ensues—no, a trio. Twenty otherworldly seconds pass: low, slow, and enticingly familiar. I had no idea birds sang in trios.

"It's the pied butcherbird," Eva explains to me later. "They get their name from snatching other birds' babies right out of a nest. Then they'll wedge their prey into the fork of a tree or skewer it on a broken branch. And they attack people's eyes," she warns, "so some folks wear hats with eyes drawn on the back to confuse the birds."

I notate several irresistible melodies, later writing in my travel journal devoted to this, my first trip to and across the Australian continent: Enchanted. Hard to put together this songster's name and savage reputation with this angelic voice. Won over by blue notes, hip riffs, and syncopated chimes, I've fallen head over heels for a convict.[1]

Figure 1.1. Pied butcherbird at Wogarno Station, Western Australia. Photograph by Chris Tate (2008). Used by permission.

Hearing these birds was an epiphany, but my partner, Jon, and I only heard one other pied butcherbird during our trip.[2] When stopped at the Western Australia/Northern Territory border, we offered up our grapes to the quarantine officer, but he didn't want them—officers only collect from traffic headed in the opposite direction. Just then, a pied butcherbird who was perched atop the welcome sign tilted back their head, opened their bill, and puffed out in song: a born performer who turns on for an audience—or so we told ourselves. Again, I grabbed my journal and notated some phrases.

When we arrived back in Sydney two months later, pied butcherbirds were still on my mind. Disappointingly, commercial recordings of them were scarcely available. On returning to Paris, I put my hasty notations away. After that, the few times I came across them, I bumped up against the same notion: while the birds' phrases had inspired the composer in me, I was not so interested in "improving" them. I wanted to know more

precisely what these birds were up to. It seemed that something extraordinary was transpiring in their songs, and though my memory of them was
fading, the enchantment remained.

I followed my hunch four years later as a doctoral candidate researching
pied butcherbird vocalizations. Since I had spent the previous thirty years
of my career as a practicing musician and not an academic, I plunged into
my research with the naive expectation that there would be no resistance
from the natural sciences or musicology and that it would be a relatively
simple task to bring them together in the course of my investigations—
this in spite of scientist C. P. Snow's influential lecture-cum-book *The Two
Cultures*, which details what many assume to be a truism: a difference in
methodologies and a notable absence of dialogue between the sciences
and the humanities.[3] I needed a home base from which I could, if not
unite them, at least navigate between the two, a place where the musical,
personal, anecdotal, scientific, philosophical, and environmental could
sit beside one another and keep polite, even good, company . . . a place
where I could ask what turns out for some to be an impolite question: Is
birdsong music?

I initially thought the question, while good, failed to be the most pressing one. My newfound passion saw me probing how to best describe, il-
luminate, and celebrate pied butcherbird vocalizations. *What* did that bird
sing? My enthusiasm also went to other questions: What can musicians
tell us about birdsong that no one else could? What might birdsong tell
us about the human capacity for music that nothing else could? I found a
place where I could ask all of these questions and where the birds could
guide me in determining both answers and further questions.

THE FIELD OF ZOÖMUSICOLOGY

Enter zoömusicology (which I pronounce "zoh-uh-musicology," not "zoomusicology"), a rapprochement and partial remedy to this historical disciplinary tension—but also the source of new tensions. As the study of
music in animal culture, zoömusicology allows for unapologetically bringing musicological tools and ways of knowing to the project, for honoring
painstaking long-term field observation (well-known in ethnography and
the natural sciences), for giving a place to thick description and the ma-

teriality of the experience of music, and for allowing the exceptional and mysterious to play a part in shaping a species' depiction.[4] With no standardized methodology or fixed research questions, work under this umbrella is best considered a mixed-methods, multiperspectival field rather than a discipline.[5]

Given my broad topic and readership, I will at times define terms that may seem self-evident. For instance, while for some, "animal" refers too narrowly to mammals only, others find the term too general for the wide variety of species under this label. Although "earth others," "animal others," "nonhuman" and "more-than-human" have currency, I find them unsatisfactory. I want a word that emphasizes kinship over difference, so "others" and "nonhumans" do not fit the bill. The meaning of "more-than-human" is not immediately apparent and only appeals to a handful of specialists. "Creature," "kin," and "critters" are fine but too awkward for regular use, while "wild community" omits the domestic contingent. This brings us back to "animal," and although humans are of course animals in denotation if not connotation, I will employ the word (with respect and wonder) to signify what most of us assume it to mean: any member of the kingdom Animalia other than a human being. That said, I will spend most of my time dwelling not on generic animals but on individual birds and their achievements.

The musical properties of animal sounds have many champions. "It is probable that in the artistic hierarchy birds are the greatest musicians existing on our planet," proclaimed composer Olivier Messiaen.[6] His teacher Paul Dukas had advised students "to admire, analyze and notate" birdsong, and Messiaen passed this example on to his own students, most notably composer François-Bernard Mâche.[7] Although Mâche is often credited with coining the word *zoomusicologie* in 1983, biologist and musicologist Péter Szőke apparently preceded him, writing in 1969 about Jesuit polymath Athanasius Kircher's "zoomusicological representation of the cock-crow." In addition, Szőke and Miroslav Filip used the term "ornithomusicology" in a 1977 article, following on the heels of an article Szőke wrote in Hungarian in 1963 in which he employed *ornitomuzikológia*.[8] Nevertheless, it is Mâche who has eloquently and meticulously given zoömusicology its initial theoretical, and to some extent methodological, underpinnings.

Although he does not straightforwardly define zoömusicology, Mâche devotes a long chapter from his monograph *Music, Myth and Nature* to the subject. Several sentences could be read as, if not definitional, at least foundational. For instance, he writes, "If these manifestations from the animal sound world are presented to the ears of musicians, it is possible that they will hear them differently from ethological specialists," drawing attention to the signal importance of a musical ear in the study of sound. He encourages us to regard animals' sonic gestures beyond their assumed social functions and to drop the scare quotes around animal music that signal a metaphor rather than the real thing.[9]

Mâche opens a path of analysis among the songs of the sedge warbler (*Acrocephalus schoenobaenus*) and Blyth's reed warbler (*Acrocephalus dumetorum*) and Stravinsky's repetitive yet unpredictable rhythms in *The Rite of Spring* and *Les noces*, and he links the arithmetical procedures of the skylark (*Alauda arvensis*) to the "chromaticisms of durations" favored by Messiaen. A comprehensive grasp of the Western canon also allows Mâche to draw a comparison between the marsh warbler's (*Acrocephalus palustris*) syntactical procedure of elimination and a Beethoven recapitulation, wherein the thematic material is typically reduced to its core, which he also compares to a Debussy theme left suspended in silence.[10] In addition, Mâche understands avian deployments of repetition as essential tools of invention rather than as fill-ins due to a lapse of imagination.

While in this monograph he sometimes writes "musics" in the plural, in a later volume Mâche makes a case for music to be thought of as a singularity.[11] He argues in both books for the linkage of all music and musical capacities. In tracing the musical archetypes and kinds of organization known in human music to birdsongs, he notes that the same solutions crop up, prompting him to conclude that the origins of music must have a fundamental basis in the biology of all living beings. Efforts to slow down a birdsong and speed up a whale song produce remarkably similar results and are just one example in support of his thesis.

Whenever I am in Paris, Mâche and I meet to pour over my latest batch of pied butcherbird recordings and to discuss my analytical results and challenges. His studio is filled with birdsong transcription notebooks—at least one for every letter of the alphabet, he tells me. Early in my research, upon hitting the roadblock of making "scientific" measurements on the one hand, and capturing the essence of a song on the other, I sought his advice. He urged me to first trust my ear, then measurements. Recalling that he used to make his transcriptions too precise, rendering them nearly illegible to other people, he tells me that these days, he simplifies.

Zoömusicology finds a kindred spirit in poet and ornithologist K. C. Halafoff, whose analysis of a superb lyrebird's (*Menura novaehollandiae*) song divides avian sounds into three categories: tonality items (those of definitive pitch); percussion items; and indefinite sounds. In his view, the lyrebird's vocalizations qualify as essentially tonal and are therefore a suitable candidate for conventional notation. Halafoff's side-by-side comparison of Stravinsky's *Symphonies of Wind Instruments* (1920) and a portion of lyrebird song stands out for the use of analytical terms like "introduction," "main theme," "exposition," "recapitulation," "bridge," and "coda" that identify a close structural resemblance of music by Stravinsky and the lyrebird.[12]

While analogies with Western classical music give birdsong credibility in some corners, zoösemiotician, composer, and musicologist Dario Martinelli underlines the importance for zoömusicology of crafting a definition of music without a Euro-, ethno-, or anthropocentric bias.[13] Like him, I am suspicious of definitions, given their cultural constructedness. The inescapable challenge for zoömusicology, however, is that it depends on the human analysis and valorization of the aesthetic qualities of animal sounds and our assignment of cultural meaning—all analysis transpires within the limits of our perception. Besides, to date, few studies of the aesthetics of animal sounds exist to compare and contrast solely within that system. So until a more expansive cross-species database flourishes and "the ultimate referent" is just one among many, a comparison with human music and our sense of musicality seems inevitable (hopefully one carried out in the most culturally neutral and inclusive way possible).

Quite understandably, Mâche privileges those birds who sing best to his ear. "Of some 8700 species of bird, around 4000 or 5000 are songbirds. Of these, 200 or 300 are of special interest to the musician through the variety of their signals," he estimates. "It may be said *en passant* that this is a ratio 50–100 times higher than that of professional musicians in relation to the total population of France."[14] Along these lines, I have not fully risen to Martinelli's challenge to focus on a bird's own concept of music rather than being fixated on comparing it to our musical taste.[15] To lure me in, pied butcherbirds had to strike parallels with my own sense of musicality.

People with an interest in zoömusicology often begin their comments with, "I'm not a zoömusicologist, but . . ." Some feel they have not yet contributed to the field, some conduct their work under a different label, and others are simply not fond of the term. Because the word is an unfamiliar one, I may identify myself as a zoömusicologist, a field musicologist, or an ornithologist. In the words of entomologist E. O. Wilson, "Every species is a magic well. . . . Humanity is exalted not because we are so far above other living creatures, but because knowing them well elevates the very concept of life."[16] I believe zoömusicology can help us know a bird musician well.

RELATED FIELDS OF INQUIRY

Other fields of inquiry have similar interests, and although not all of them have sought formal recognition as disciplines or subdisciplines, they are at minimum scholarly trademarks. George List frames ethnomusicology as "the study of humanly produced patterns of sound, sound patterns that the members of the culture who produce them or the scholar who studies them conceive to be music. Since the definition includes the words 'humanly produced,'" he adds, "bird song lies without the province of ethnomusicology."[17] Despite keeping animals at arm's length, ethnomusicology has relevance for zoömusicology in a number of parameters. For instance, beyond the tall, hand-wringing order of defining "music," which includes the debate of "music" versus "musics," ethnomusicology has participated in a search for or a distrust in (depending on the era and researcher) cultural universals. In this, the tyranny of ethnocentrism is always close at hand. How can we be anything *but* ethnocentric as we attempt to position ourselves in the world? Granted, when accompanied by a belief in the intrinsic superiority of one's own culture and an aversion to others' cultures, this "ism" is problematical.

Both fields require adapting a notation system to an unknown culture (typically an oral tradition characterized by some to be "primitive"), exploring a range of critical and methodological tools, and acquiring recording expertise, all the while developing disciplinary multilingualism and navigating cross-cultural borders—and how to explain the function and meaning of music in relation to cultural practices? Then there are the practical parallels: attending to personal safety in the field ("A dead journalist is not a good journalist," a war correspondent once told me), taking notes constantly, assembling a sizeable corpus, and funding sustained observation. The process is usually slow, painful, and, at least initially, filled with discouragement and setbacks.

Back home at the desk, the production of a detailed monograph is the classic fieldwork outcome, but ethnomusicologists' and zoömusicologists' commitment to whom they study extends beyond the theoretical worlds of texts and publications. Maintaining reciprocal friendships with field informants and fulfilling inherent obligations of responsibility and advocacy extends, in some cases, to contributing to habitat conservation. Then, up from the desk and into the concert hall, where researchers from both fields may commit to performances and exhibits while sharing authorship with their participatory partners. Political considerations range from overcoming Western and "high art" bias to being perceived as a threat by some music departments.

Ethnomusicology has served us well in answering questions on the scope of musicality and in enacting a gradual change in the conception and reception of music outside the West. Calling any human culture's music primitive, or *not* music, is now passé, like plastic bags, fur coats, and sun tanning. Zoömusicology is still positioned in the margins, so it may sound the wrong way round, but in theory (if not in practice), musicology is a subset of ethnomusicology, and both are subsets of zoömusicology.[18]

Music's other "-ologies" and "-istics" are hybrids, several with an overlap with zoömusicology: the psychology of music, biomusicology, acoustemology, and bioacoustics.[19] Many artists and scholars now focus on sound/music's potential relevance in environmental issues, with several fields purporting activist goals: ecomusicology, environmental ethnomusicology, acoustic ecology, and soundscape ecology. It remains to be seen how terms describing these nodes of interest will endure—which will find the widest acceptance, which will be subsumed into others, and which will fade altogether—and how their core agendas will evolve. While a number of these fields contain researchers with similar concerns to zoömusicology's, there currently is no synonym for the word, and aside from ornithomusicology (which, aside from ignoring nonavian species, sees scant activity under its rubric), no other field has as its chief concern the analysis of animal sonic constructs as music. Short of being subsumed into musicology, there seems no other place for work like mine to lodge itself, and I am content with the term "zoömusicology."

Can birdsong research by a zoömusicologist contribute to scientific progress? Is it possible to excel at both science and art (a fair question, Leonardo excepted)? My work does not react to an agenda set by science. It benefits from many of its knowledge claims and methods even as it remains suspicious of others. For instance, I avoid interventions designed to provoke pied butcherbirds to sing. While such a program might produce new questions, generate valuable findings, and supply evidence that bears on my current questions, I believe the best results for this species will come from paying fierce attention to birds in situ, rather than in a laboratory. I am not looking for explanations of hardware that require placing our bird musicians in a cage or "harvesting" their brains. There is no normal behavior or ecological validity for a captive pied butcherbird.

Following on remarks that Aldo Leopold, founder of conservationism in America, delivered to the Wildlife Society in 1940, I am not a scientist. I disqualify myself at the outset by professing loyalty to and affection for pied butcherbirds.[20] Although I avidly read scientists' publications, I never minimize my own knowledge. The musician in me is determined to follow the word "kinship" wherever it takes me. I am not alone. Mâche portrays the pied butcherbird as "a kind of colleague," while composer David Lumsdaine recorded a pied butcherbird in 1983 whom he still describes as "the Buddha of Spirey Creek."[21]

Musical analysis strives to understand the creative process in question. My critical positions of both insider (a fellow musician) and outsider (from another species) perhaps run counter to one another—but when it comes to making music, I wondered how far apart our two species dwell and how much mediation I would have to do. Cast as an intruder and eavesdropper on pied butcherbirds' scene, I held out hope that my physiology and sense of musicality would be similar enough to theirs to allow me entrance into their musical lives. I sensed early on that these birds could revolutionize the way we think about birdsong, human exceptionalism, and the core values of music. Pied butcherbirds were to be neither my laboratory equipment nor my informants—they would become my teachers. What follows depicts how I proceeded and what I have learned.

FIELDWORK PREPARATION

How I hear birds in the field is deeply influenced by a lifetime of musical experiences, which I began formally at age six on the piano. Three years later, I added the violin and knew I had found my calling. Early in my portfolio career I branched out from classical music into music learned largely via the oral tradition, including South Indian classical music, Texas and bluegrass fiddling, several Caribbean genres (including Afro-Cuban music and the Dominican Republic's merengue), and pop music. I played jazz in Paris clubs for two years, then traveled throughout Eastern Europe and Morocco while a resident of Budapest, collecting and transcribing folk music to use in my (re)compositions. While I make no claim to having mastered all these genres, my ear was accustomed to assessing and notating new musical idioms. I reveled in the insights gained by getting knocked back to square one.

I was also skilled in the outdoors, although quite a different one. Childhood family vacations and a good number in later years were spent camping in the forests of Oregon's mountain lakes. I lived for a year in a camp trailer in and around Yellowstone National Park and Jackson Hole, Wyoming (where I discovered fiddling and began transcribing recordings), and later drove the Alcan Highway north to Alaska. Nothing, however, prepared me for the arid isolation of the Australian outback or for its snakes: twenty-one of the world's twenty-five most venomous snakes live here.

A decidedly ethnographic approach pervades my work because of its scope, because no pied butcherbirds hold territories near where I live (west of Sydney in the Blue Mountains), and because a first-person "lived" experience is routine and even essential for a musician. A colleague once cornered me: What *kind* of ethnography? Seat of my pants, improvising as I went along, intent on figuring out what these birds were up to (and instead running into unexpected variety, complexity, and dynamism), didn't even know the word "ethnography" to begin with—I was a complete imposter. However, this turned out to be archetypal: "Each scholar must develop field methods and techniques of his own, in order to solve his own problems. The notion that one goes into the field in order to comprehend the whole musical culture and to make a truly representative sampling of recordings has had to go by the wayside, as we begin to recognize the enormous complexity of musical cultures everywhere, including even the simplest, and as we begin to accept the fact that cultures are constantly changing and have always been changing."[22]

I corresponded with and traveled to meet people who have welcomed pied butcherbirds into their lives, and my studies benefited from their private recordings, generosity, and insights. Of course, I wanted to make my own recordings as well—to be physically present when the birds were singing. It was crucial to me that I not simply exploit existing data. In organizing my fieldwork, I chose to study free-living individuals in three areas: desert country (Alice Springs, in the continent's arid Red Centre); saltwater country (along the Pacific Ocean, including the Great Barrier Reef, from northern New South Wales up through much of Queensland); and savannah country (in North Queensland). You need good luck, as anyone who has done fieldwork will tell you. While I do not really believe in luck, I very much believe in encouraging it. I had a steep learning curve in front of me, which included figuring out where to reliably find pied butcherbirds, when they sing, how to distinguish them from other black-and-white birds, how to differentiate their song from that of similar songsters, and how to record them and document these recordings in an appropriate manner. My initial budget was such that I slept in my car for months every spring during the first five years of fieldwork. After that, I sometimes had funding to rent a camper van.

The reception-based approach to music supposes we can understand it best by being right in the middle of it.[23] Fieldwork knowledge begins as bodily knowledge, quite different from the abstract knowledge of a laboratory researcher, who can leave out of her account that she has a body: "The first takes personal risks; the second carefully avoids them. The first learns to commit herself in favor of the animal, while the second is above all concerned with her list of publications and citation index."[24] Being with pied butcherbirds in the field has been indispensable to my apprenticeship. The scientific attraction of birds is that they are easier to study than many species. My interest gravitates toward prolonged and careful observation of what birds spontaneously produce with a minimum of intrusion. More and more researchers are realizing that the best information comes from giving animals the most interesting existence, even in controlled settings. Naturally, researchers' positions vis-à-vis their objects change when animals are always available to them. A reversal of roles finds *me* vulnerable.

This volume alternates between my fieldwork and deskwork voices. My outback notes, all penned in situ, serve as neither fluff nor padding; these different registers aspire to a kind of zoömusicology that embeds investigations in the richness of the everyday world. I make no attempt to hide the mundanities, inconveniences, difficulties, and fears (real and imagined) inherent in fieldwork. That said, the hold-your-breath drama of avian phrases delivered in the night air is next to impossible to capture. People project their own fantasy onto my fieldwork. Some are aghast at the thought of being alone in the bush in the middle of the night; others romanticize the freedom, the great outdoors, and the anything-could-happen adventure. Nature! But which "nature" will our excursion take us to?

NATURE/CULTURE OR NATURECULTURE?

All words involve elements of contradiction and inconsistency. They are context and user dependent. Still, "nature" seems especially challenging. Where does nature leave off and culture begin, and where do they overlap, if at all? Scholars increasingly complicate such thorny questions. Novelist and critic Raymond Williams reckoned "culture" to be "one of the two or three most complicated words in the English language," while "nature" is "perhaps the most complex word in the language."[25] In these circumstances, my present goals are modest.

Copernicus and Galileo removed us from the center of the universe four or five hundred years ago. Despite this, in the Enlightenment Descartes consolidated the nature/culture divide, a dualism tightly knit into the underpinnings of much Western thought and discursive space. Reader beware: scare quotes ahead! Does "nature" need to be pitted against "culture" and things human in order to make sense of it? How we imagine the themes of separation and continuity has currency in our assessment of birdsong. For instance, since humans supposedly live in culture, while animals live in nature, we come across claims like "music originates from the human brain rather than from the natural world."[26] The disrupting of such oppositions is a move basic to zoömusicology. Rather than simply remake these binaries, I want to underline connectivity.

Many of us expect we can visit nature on weekends and holidays, while the remainder of our lives is spent in culture. Even so, we understand that this is not the innocent, pristine, and trouble-free "nature" of previous times (if there ever was such a place; it is likely we have trailed our impact around with us wherever we have been). Understandings of "nature" across the ages echo this. Nature has been set not only in opposition to culture but also against itself: nature is order/nature is disorder, holistic/mechanistic, inherited/constructed, pure/evil—all of these reminding us of how fraught the term is.[27] Outside of Western contexts, views of the inherited and the forged are much less polarized.[28] After all, as part of nature, humans dwell on the earth and are subject to its basic principles, with similar requirements as other living beings.

Three other words tag along with nature. "The environment" may stand in for it, but again there is definitional contestation. The environment can mean the sum total of our surroundings—air-water-land-organisms, indoors or out. We can further slice up the term by contemplating either a natural or a cultural environment.

"Landscape" is likewise ambiguous. We impact the landscape, but we cannot ignore how it impacts us. Both how we look and what we see, it may be enchanting or threatening, interior or exterior, a picturesque ready-made or a design problem. Landscape sells: it is an awesome setting for a commercial advertisement. Another shake of a culturally pluralistic kaleidoscope moves us from just the good bits—postcard miniatures, land art, and big land—to Aboriginal Australians' "country," where *every* feature of a landscape is associated with a historical episode or sacred verse in their cosmology and not only those worthy of sightseers' attention.

"Wilderness" is another tagalong, and like the other three, it enjoys place-and-mood brand value. "Big enough to absorb a two-week's pack trip," imagines Leopold.[29] Most Americans do not imagine the outdoors as inhospitable, despite the odd desert, snowfall, and grizzly bear. National parks, open ranges, cowboys—it's a romance, Americans and their wilderness. In all such affairs, you overlook a few things, even obvious ones. Mother Nature or Man versus Nature? The fantasy of being on the land modulates for others to wilderness as an alien place filled with antagonism. I have encountered many Sydneysiders who do not romanticize nature in the least (a curve of beach excepted, of course) and have no inclination to go bush.

Among those who seek to distance themselves from any tinge of nostalgia is philosopher Timothy Morton, who reckons "nature" is merely a mental construct—an anachronism well past its use-by date. He likens the concept to "that other Romantic-period invention, the aesthetic," and recommends dropping the word entirely.[30] Such skepticism relies upon a conceptual maneuver that assumes almost everyone romanticizes nature and then calls for hoisting oneself above the fray. At best, this reflects a Northern Hemisphere, First World perspective. While the catchall term "nature" is problematic, the loss of the term is even more so. Morton's theories and those of the "green postmodernists" posit all meaning and value with an elevated humanity, and this hopeless we've-been-every-where-and-altered-everything attitude pulls the rug out from under environmental protection (perhaps at times unwittingly) and instead justifies continued intrusions and exploitations. A pessimist at heart, I nonetheless want to think bigger than this. Wilderness deconstruction, in title and deed, sets itself at odds with efforts to preserve and rehabilitate our planet's biodiversity.[31]

In the coming outback encounters, my aim is overwhelmingly pragmatic. In this, your author's biography is showing. Sound, and not only vision, shapes our perception of nature, environment, landscape, and wilderness, all of which depend on an embodied encounter rather than on theorists with indoor lives. As Sartre recommends, "Jazz is like bananas—it must be consumed on the spot."[32] "Nature" as a mental product rather than a tangible visceral experience depends upon another author who can sustain such a theme, and perhaps another reader—for I fully trust that mine understands the complexities of the word but nevertheless has his or her bags packed and is ready for the journey to begin.

There *is* an outback. Very little of it is parkland. Much is rugged (but not necessarily awe-inspiring), difficult, and demanding. Towns and regional centers dot the land as well. Let's clear the road of scare quotes. Although nature and culture cannot be neatly pried apart, this does not negate their reality. Our travel navigates the highways and byways connecting the two, with sights and sounds that are unforgettable. The trajectory is first to the birds in their environment (a map of my field sites is available online), then to the analysis of their vocalizations, and finally to the theories that would make sense of them.[33] The stops along the way are nonlinear and occasionally lurch to other songbirds and even altogether different, but perhaps *not* so different, classes. Puzzle pieces were added in fits and starts, and only slowly over the years has a more robust understanding of pied butcherbirds' sound world emerged.

NOTES

1. For more on this trip, see Hollis Taylor, *Post Impressions: A Travel Book for Tragic Intellectuals* (Portland, OR: Twisted Fiddle, 2007).

2. The violinist-composer and author Jon Rose; see "Jon Rose," accessed 7 November 2014, http://www.jonroseweb.com.

3. C. P. Snow, *"The Two Cultures" and "A Second Look"* (Cambridge: Cambridge University Press, 1959/1964). This holds today despite music having occupied a key position in ancient Greek natural philosophy, where the mathematical arts of music, arithmetic, geometry, and astronomy were linked in a fourfold study under the rubric *quadrivium*.

4. This follows on Alan P. Merriam's definition of ethnomusicology as "the study of music in culture" ("Ethnomusicology Discussion and Definition of the Field," *Ethnomusicology* 4, no. 3 [1960]: 111).

5. Ecomusicologists Aaron S. Allen and Kevin Dawe arrive at a similar conclusion for their activities ("Ecomusicologies," in *Current Directions in Ecomusicology: Music, Culture, Nature*, ed. Aaron S. Allen and Kevin Dawe [London: Routledge, 2016], 1–13).

6. Olivier Messiaen and Claude Samuel, *Music and Color: Conversations with Claude Samuel*, trans. E. Thomas Glasow (Portland, OR: Amadeus Press, 1994), 85.

7. Olivier Messiaen, *The Technique of My Musical Language*, trans. John Satterfield (Paris: Alphonse Leduc, 1944/1956), 34.

8. Péter Szőke and Miroslav Filip, "The Study of Intonation Structure of Bird Vocalizations: An Inadequate Application of Sound Spectrography," *Opuscula Zoologica Budapest* 14, no. 1–2 (1977): 18; and Péter Szőke, "Ornitomuzikológia," *Magyar Tudomany* 9 (1963): 592–607.

9. François-Bernard Mâche, *Music, Myth and Nature*, trans. Susan Delaney (Chur: Harwood Academic Publishers, 1983/1992), 97, 114.

10. Ibid.; for Stravinsky, see 116–124; for Messiaen, 127–128; and for Beethoven/Debussy, 134–135.

11. François-Bernard Mâche, *Musique au singulier* (Paris: Éditions Odile Jacob, 2001).

12. K. C. Halafoff, "Musical Analysis of the Lyrebird's Song," *Victorian Naturalist* 75 (1959): 169.

13. Dario Martinelli, *How Musical Is a Whale? Towards a Theory of Zoömusicology* (Hakapaino: International Semiotics Institute, 2002), 103. He has imagined zoömusi-

cology as the study of the "aesthetic use of sounds among animals" (Dario Martinelli, "Symptomatology of a Semiotic Research: Methodologies and Problems in Zoomusicology," *Sign Systems Studies* 29, no. 1 [2001]: 3).

14. Mâche, *Music, Myth and Nature*, 96.

15. Martinelli, *How Musical Is a Whale?*, 98.

16. Edward O. Wilson, *Consilience* (New York: Alfred A. Knopf, 1998), 19, 22.

17. George List, "Ethnomusicology: A Discipline Defined," *Ethnomusicology* 23, no. 1 (1979): 1.

18. See Marcello Sorce Keller, "Zoomusicology and Ethnomusicology: A Marriage to Celebrate in Heaven," *2012 Yearbook for Traditional Music* 44 (2012): 172.

19. For a review, see Hollis Taylor and Andrew Hurley, "*Music* and *Environment*: A Snapshot of Contemporary and Emerging Convergences," *Journal of Music Research Online*, 2015, 1–18. Naming, branding, and owning are arenas of substantial human activity not limited to explorers and academics. Witness heavy metal subgenres like Viking metal, symphonic black metal, pirate metal, and funeral doom. Coining "our" word for "our" group—it's what we do.

20. Aldo Leopold, *The River of the Mother of God and Other Essays* (Madison: University of Wisconsin Press, 1991), 276.

21. François-Bernard Mâche, "The Necessity of and Problems with a Universal Musicology," in *The Origins of Music*, ed. Nils L. Wallin, Björn Merker, and Steven Brown (Cambridge, MA: MIT Press, 2000), 479; and author interview with David Lumsdaine, 5 August 2013.

22. Bruno Nettl, "The State of Research in Ethnomusicology, and Recent Developments," *Current Musicology* 20 (1975): 75.

23. Nicholas Cook, *Music: A Very Short Introduction* (Oxford: Oxford University Press, 1998), 85.

24. Dominique Lestel, *L'animal est l'avenir de l'homme* (Paris: Fayard, 2010), 171, my translation.

25. Raymond Williams, *Keywords: A Vocabulary of Culture and Society* (Glasgow: Fontana, 1976), 76, 184.

26. Anthony Storr, *Music and the Mind* (New York: Ballantine Books, 1992), 51.

27. For a review of the "immensely complex and contradictory symbolic load" carried by the term "nature," see Kate Soper, *What Is Nature? Culture, Politics and the Non-human* (Oxford: Blackwell, 1995), 2. Also see Tim Low, *The New Nature* (Camberwell: Penguin Books, 2003); and Holmes Rolston III, "Does Aesthetic Appreciation of Landscapes Need to Be Science-Based?," *British Journal of Aesthetics* 35, no. 4 (1995): 374–386. Rolston's explication of "environment," "ecology," "nature," and "landscape" is a particularly useful entry point.

28. Anthropologist Philippe Descola claims that despite other ways of imagining "nature" than that of the modern West, people always and everywhere distinguish between the domesticated and the wild, between deeply socialized places and those that develop unaided by human action (*Beyond Nature and Culture*, trans. Janet Lloyd [Chicago: University of Chicago Press, 2005/2013], 33).

29. Leopold, *The River of the Mother of God*, 79.

30. Timothy Morton, *Ecology without Nature: Rethinking Environmental Aesthetics* (Cambridge, MA: Harvard University Press, 2007), 22. Also see Irus Braverman, *Wild Life: The Institution of Nature* (Stanford, CA: Stanford University Press, 2015) for an essay on how the change in nature's conceptualization has impacted conservation practices.

31. See Val Plumwood, "Nature as Agency and the Prospects for a Progressive Natu-ralism," *Capitalism Nature Socialism* 12, no. 4 (2001): 3. A number of authors continue her critique of postmodern green theory, including environmental philosopher David W. Kidner, who claims: "Industrial humanity does not so much 'construct' nature as sweep it aside, replacing it with a quite different system that is hostile to and destructive of nature" ("The Conceptual Assassination of Wilderness," in *Keeping the Wild: Against the Domestication of Earth*, ed. George Wuerthner, Eileen Crist, and Tom Butler [Wash-ington, DC: Island Press, 2014], 13). Also see David W. Orr, *Earth in Mind: On Educa-tion, Environment, and the Human Prospect* (Washington, DC: Island Press, 2004).

32. Jean-Paul Sartre, "I Discovered Jazz in America," *Saturday Review of Literature*, 29 November 1947, 48.

33. See www.piedbutcherbird.net.

CHAPTER 2

Songbird Studies

> Competent authorities have proposed to divide the world, biologi-
> cally, into two parts—Australia and the rest of the world, and they
> have considered Australia the more interesting part.
> —John Albert Leach, *An Australian Bird Book* (1911)

AYR TOURIST INFORMATION BUREAU, North Queensland, 5 October 2006: "Good morning. I'm looking for a town map and information on local caravan parks."

"Here you go. There're two in town."

"Thanks—and by the way, have you heard of the pied butcherbird?"

"Yeah-naaah, you'd never find 'em *here*."

In the two minutes it takes me to study the map, he goes outside and returns to proudly report that he's found a pair. I'm dubious. He works at this park and thinks he knows what these birds look like. How could he have missed them before? He directs me down a path—and yes, they are pied butcherbirds. I record several duets.

This time of year, nighttime fires roar through the fields. Set to kill dry sugarcane leaves, the fires also rid fields of rats and venomous snakes before hand harvesting begins. At 4:00 AM I record a bird at the golf course who trumpets out an earthly yet sublime flourish. Across the road, furious orange flames dance in the inky sky above a white-hot canefield. Afterward, I return to the caravan park to transfer and annotate the audio files, and then it's time to quickly pack up and move on.

My field trips are bittersweet. When I drive for hours, especially if I pass occasional pied butcherbirds on a utility wire or in a dead tree, I inevitably register a twinge of disappointment at not hearing and documenting those birds' songs. This morning, the trip lurches between hurry up and wait due to flood damage and consequent road repairs. At one point while I'm stopped in traffic, a bored lineman slouches on a milk crate tossing stones into a tin can. When I finally arrive at my destination and check in, again I ask, "By the way, do you know if there are any pied butcherbirds here?"

"We've got *heaps* of birds here. Heaps! We feed the lorikeets every afternoon at four; then at night the bettongs come to clean up the leftovers—and there's wine tasting at five-thirty and a barbie [BBQ] at six . . ."

"Great—but the pied butcherbird?"

"The *what*?"

"The pied but-cher-bird."

"I don't know 'em." (I admit I take it a bit personally when locals do not know my star, but I try not to let on.)

"Thief!" is handwritten at the bottom of a wanted poster next to the cash register. The mug shot, photocopied from a field guide, shows a glossy blue-black bird with violet-blue eyes. It's a satin bowerbird (*Ptilonorhynchus violaceus*).

"What's the story with him?" I ask.

"Oh, you're a bird lady! Maybe you can help. He stole the tow pins from a truck last week and left the people stranded for three days until they could get another set. And before that, he took the keys for a motorhome. We'd like to know where he keeps his stash."

Named for the architecturally complex and varied stick structures that they build and decorate, bowerbirds live in Australia and Papua New Guinea. They decorate their wickerwork-like bowers and immediate surroundings, known as display courts, with fruits, berries, nuts, flowers, seedpods, feathers, leaves, pebbles, and shells. Other natural objects might include fungi, ferns, tiny skulls, sloughed snakeskin, and charcoal. Their mise-en-scène may also contain human ready-mades like flip tops, rifle shell casings, aluminum foil, bolts, and clothespins. Broken glass and bottle caps are especially popular, as are drinking straws, marbles, and plastic toys. Keys have reportedly been pinched straight from the ignition of a parked car. Birds assemble hundreds or even thousands of such items.

Australia's ten bowerbird species exhibit disparate color preferences. Satin bowerbirds favor blue, with a secondary preference for yellow, while great (*Chlamydera nuchali*), western (*Chlamydera guttata*), and spotted (*Chlamydera maculata*) bowerbirds choose white and grey objects, sometimes adding green and red into the mix. Future-oriented spotted bowerbirds cultivate a nonfood item, a green fruit (*Solanum ellipticum*) that they eventually harvest to decorate their court.[1]

Bowerbird preferences run to more than tint: shape, size, and texture, as well as saturation and sheen, may all factor into the choices a bird makes when assembling his collection. Birds paint the parallel stick walls of their U-shaped avenue bower with a combination of saliva and natural materials, which they apply with their beak, a stick, or a piece of bark.[2] When displaying to the female, a male will often race about the bower, holding and waving one of his collectibles. Males accumulate decorations as a kind of wealth, and we can speculate that enjoyment is involved, as they will perform decoration and courtship behavior in the absence of any audience.[3]

Bowers are high maintenance. Fading vegetable matter and decorative items robbed by competitors must be replaced. A bird constantly revamps and renovates his structure and fine-tunes its decorations, aided by his inspection from the female's viewpoint. Recent research indicates that great bowerbirds create theaters with "forced perspective."[4] The birds capitalize on the geometry of the displays by placing objects that increase in size with distance from the avenue, the predictable viewing perspective being at the female's entrance, thereby creating the illusion that all items onstage remain evenly sized and that the overall bower's size exceeds what it really is. Renaissance painters manipulated perspective to enhance their compositions, but bowerbirds surely predate this activity by millions of years.

A male bowerbird is a stage director, dancer, and vocalist. In addition to his harsh, far-reaching rattling, churring, and chugging, he is a skilled mimic. He must master aspects of architecture, painting, collecting, decorating, and landscaping. In short, he dazzles. Meanwhile, the female serves as an art critic and tastemaker, contemplating what the other sex has created and confirming the influence of sexual selection. Both sexes participate in value judgments. Females also pick up decorative items. I watched one seize a small green lime, followed by another and another—as if to say to the male, who had been waving a white treasure, I'd like more of *this*. White was soon replaced with lime. While a peacock is born with an innate ability to grow an elaborate tail, a male bowerbird must learn to sing, dance, construct a bower, and execute the other associated tasks required of him in order to achieve aesthetic and functional success. They are not robots, and the results vary.

Whenever I am in the field, I hunt for bowers and ask locals if they can point me to any. Coming across a bower feels like stumbling upon a themed event—a surprise party, a burst piñata, or an elaborate picnic. Similar to my experience with pied butcherbirds, I cannot reconcile what I have seen and heard of bowerbirds with claims like this from anthropologist Alexander Alland Jr.: "True artistic behavior is seen in no species other than *Homo sapiens*. Not even a hint of it occurs in the natural behavior of other species." One might think that given the title of his book—*The Artistic Animal*—the author would be making a case for animal abilities; alas, he finds only traits that are precursors to the real thing. Like me, philosopher Denis Dutton marvels at bowerbirds' extraordinary, stunning, and imaginative inventions: "The only other animal species that does anything like this is the one that, inter alia, constructs elaborate art galleries on the island of Manhattan and elsewhere." A page later, however, he lets drop: "Animals, nevertheless, do not create art." Why? No matter how spectacular, bowerbirds' multimodal activities are not humanly made and the product of human self-consciousness. Neither can I reconcile this passage from psychiatrist Iain McGilchrist: "But there are many things of which they [the most highly evolved animals] show no evidence whatsoever: for instance, imagination, creativity, the capacity for religious awe, music, dance, poetry, art, love of nature, a moral sense, a sense of humour and the ability to change their minds."[5] I can only hope that scholars like Alland, Dutton, and McGilchrist will change *their* minds about animals and creativity.

The caravan park owners think their thief is a satin bowerbird, a species found at our home in the Blue Mountains. That's how I know that they have accused the wrong bird—their thief is the local spotted bowerbird, a pale brown bird with a pink ponytail who is known to prefer shiny display objects like keys. With this wanted poster, the humans won't find their culprit. I think I'll leave it that way.

Local knowledge: 80 percent priceless and 20 percent worthless—although getting things wrong can be telling. As I piece together an account of pied butcherbirds, the question of who knows (birds, scientists, musicians, locals, experts) will regularly occupy me. My narrative is an interspecies one built on being attentive to wide-ranging entanglements.

BIRDSONG BASICS

I set about reading what biologists have discovered about birdsong. Songbirds make up about half of the world's approximately ten thousand bird species, so distinguished because they *learn* their song. Intriguingly, this capacity is rare; our closest primate relatives, for example, are not vocal learners. Even the elaborate song bouts of gibbons are innate. Aside from humans and songbirds, to date, vocal learning appears limited to hummingbirds and parrots (and possibly a few other avian groups), as well as bats, elephants, and some marine mammals (cetaceans and pinnipeds).

A bird's sound-producing organ is not the larynx, as in humans. Rather, birds sing from their syrinx, a vocal mechanism that consists of a valve in each of two bronchi (or air tubes) located just below the junction with the trachea. Membranes in the syrinx vibrate when air passes over them. The singing of two unrelated notes is possible, although most birds either double a note with each valve, use one valve for high notes and the other for low notes, or fail to use one of the valves. The function of the syrinx endures as a complex matter under continuous review, and many issues remain unresolved.[6]

"Calls" and "songs" are not interchangeable terms. Calls are social sounds associated with general maintenance activities. They tend to be shorter and simpler than songs and presumably possess an innate basis. However, most ethologists have moved away from the designations "learned" and "innate," which imply strict boundaries, and have instead enlisted terminology like "inherited tendency," "instinct to learn," and "instinct for inventiveness"—and later "learning preferences" and "song template."[7]

In the 1950s ethologists published their first studies of birdsong learning and development, including some conducted under controlled laboratory conditions.[8] The process of song acquisition typically follows a trajectory from the initial tentative and structurally amorphous notes ("subsong"), to the intermediate stages (called "plastic song" because although the notes exhibit more structure, they remain unstable and highly variable), to the mature adult stage ("crystallized song"); in their vocal development, birds follow stages similar to those of human infants.[9] Learning allows for variety and complexity not possible in innate song. This "cultural transmission" can be vertical (learning from parents), horizontal (learning from members of the same generation), and oblique (learning from unrelated birds of different generations).[10] Song tutoring is possible via tape recordings or mechanical instruments, like the serinette. In fact, designs to encourage singing in caged birds date back to at least the third century BCE.[11] The earliest published manual for training songbirds dates from circa 1700; one is still in print, *The Bird Fancyer's Delight*, used to train canaries, nightingales, starlings, and other birds given to our sense of musicality.[12] All songbird territories, even the simplest cage, are thus a blend of nature and culture.

Birdsongs likely involve the most intricate patterns of motor activity found in animal behavior. Few, if any, avian species are equally ready to acquire new songs at all phases of their life; instead, one or more sensitive periods exist, with most learning accomplished in the first year of life, although some species thrive as open-ended learners. Remarkably, memorization and production are not simultaneous: the long-term memorization and storage of song phrases precede a bird's first rehearsal. For example, in a study of swamp sparrows (*Melospiza georgiana*), ethologists found that explicit rehearsal of learned songs began, on average, 240 days *after* the final exposure to the training song.[13]

Once they had established the basic song-learning cycle, researchers went on to refine their knowledge. Many studies take account of songs as social signals and what these communicate. Birdsong is a biomarker— an indicator of the condition of a living organism. A song may advertise ownership of a territory and the ability and intention to defend it, as well as indicate species and individual identity. Of special interest to a female, a male's song might also denote his health and readiness to breed and provide for offspring. Birdsong is likewise a biomarker for humans, reflecting items of interest and consequence to us. We increasingly understand the distribution of birds as a significant tool for measuring our impact, and a singing bird indicates that the individual is both present and in adequate condition to take time and energy away from activities more basic to survival.

With the advent of their studies, ethologists left behind terms developed over the centuries to describe and analyze music, terms even a non-expert would recognize. It is curious and telling that separate terminology for humans and animals was required. Ethologists' specialist terminology seems arbitrary, complicated, and determined to confuse noninitiates. There is a notable lack of consensus concerning key words, and the few that have been adopted from the field of music are applied unpredictably. Ethologist K. A. Shiovitz counted five terms for "phrase," six for "note" (including "element" and "syllable"), and twenty employed to describe song units, while suggesting standard terms to remedy this Tower of Babel. Nearly two decades later, a study reviewing over eighty definitions of "birdsong" found little agreement on its definition or how to differentiate songs from calls, while another article appealed for unanimity of method as it tallied up twenty-eight song-unit identifications. We can look back to biologist Wallace Craig's commonsense advice decades earlier, that while no ornithologist had framed a satisfactory definition of birdsong, they all knew a song when they heard one.[14]

Females sing much more than is usually acknowledged, echoing the historical invisibility of their female human counterparts; the fact that the bulk of research focuses on Northern Hemisphere birds in the temperate zone, where female birds tend not to sing, encumbers a fuller understanding of their vocalizations.[15] Many Southern Hemisphere birds hold their territory year-round, and female song is more common in the tropics. Females sing solo and in duets and may sing to attract mates.[16] Their repertoire can exceed that of males.[17] Nevertheless, the cliché predominates of birdsong as a contest between rival males or between the salesmanship of a male versus the sales resistance of a female.

Those who dismiss a bird's song on the grounds of functionality neglect the fine print. Reductionist views concerning male singing and birdsong's strictly functional nature derive less from science than from popular receptions and misconceptions of science. Even as ethologists concentrate on questions that can be answered within the methodological constraints of scientific inquiry and theory building, their literature contains numerous asides on the aesthetic use of sound by birds—comments like "[some] birds indulge in a process of improvisation, first memorizing and replicating a theme, and then subjecting it to a series of systematic transformations, as though assuaging an appetite for novelty"; and "but the far more complex songs of versatile songsters [with] large individual repertoires sometimes appear to be so variable as to dramatically violate the requirement of song invariance for species distinctiveness"; and also "as I hear [the song of the Swainson's thrush (*Catharus ustulatus*)] I think of Montserrat singing her aria from Puccini's *Turandot*."[18]

In informal conversation, ethologists' accounts of wonder are often more effusive, so it is not so easy to dismiss the function of song as serving solely for survival utility or reproductive opportunity. Ethologists do not claim to have a corner on what can be known about musicality in songbirds, and there is a noteworthy undercurrent that inventiveness in song could surpass biological necessity. While important work has been conducted, much remains to be discovered. Very few species have been studied in depth, and due to premature specialization, much of what we know still depends on a few disproportionately studied "white rats" of the avian world.[19] As new species are added, fascinating capacities are frequently revealed.

In addition, while science has undoubtedly produced exciting research on animals, laboratory results can be problematic, unable to reflect accurately what happens in the wild, and some have now begun to be questioned. Such studies may merely show what a bird can do in an environment never before encountered in that species' evolutionary history, cautions ethologist Donald E. Kroodsma.[20] Another ethologist sent up an alert that not only did laboratory studies fail to identify key variables in song learning, but they also showed learning patterns that differed greatly from those observed in the field.[21] An additional shortcoming of much current birdsong research must surely be its minimal involvement with the more sophisticated avian singers, which I take up shortly.

Curiously, birdsong study finds itself in the almost exclusive proprietorship of biologists. The songs of birds have long inspired artists, writers, musicians, philosophers, and enthralled listeners from all walks of life. Meanwhile, musicologists, who might well have new perspectives to bring to the study and interpretation of birdsong, have all but avoided the subject. Technological advances like wax cylinders, and later shellac discs and magnetic tape, allowed biologists without musical training or complementary input from musicians to capture and study avian vocalizations. Biologists occupied this undefended territory much as an opportunistic bird might.

Ornithologist and avian recordist Albert R. Brand found birdsong interpretation too subjective. To remedy this, in 1935 he developed a method for photographing avian vocalizations on motion picture film for microscopic study, acknowledging that this, too, was imperfect.[22] Sydney E. Ingraham analyzed films sent to him by Brand, concluding that timbral aspects of birdsong were better analyzed via film than by listening to a record. So enamored was Ingraham by timbre made visual that he speculated on how new musical instruments might be built based on birdsong with "special overtone combinations that would add all kinds of amusing natural effects to our orchestras."[23]

During World War II, Bell Telephone Laboratories introduced the sonogram, or spectrogram, a graphic representation of sound that plots time on the x-axis, frequency (the number of cycles of sound per second, of which pitch is the subjective assessment) on the y-axis, and relative amplitude as a grey scale. Contemporary applications allow for a color sonogram, but grey scale remains standard. Ethologist W. H. Thorpe pioneered its use in birdsong studies in 1950, and since then this graphic representation of sound has been championed in word and deed for its nearly unquestioned objectivity. While sonographic analysis has become de rigueur, reliance on the visual (ocularcentrism) perturbs some. For instance, historian of science Peter Galison is concerned with how a visual culture, with its charts, diagrams, and other images, influences science's bottom line.[24] Can the eye make out relationships and implications in a sonogram without supplementary input from the ear? A birdsong transcription when crafted through repeated listening certainly implies more extensive involvement by the human ear than a sonogram, but not everyone views this as an advantage. One neuroscientist told me he rarely listens to the avian songs he studies. For him, graphic representation has replaced listening, which, along with transcribing by ear, has slipped into a questionable category.

Prior to the sonogram's introduction, ornithologists found the most interesting songbirds to be birds with long and variable repertoires, but with the technical limitations of the sonogram, short, repetitive songs became more attractive objects of research.[25] Another potential shortcoming of visual analysis: the image in the sonogram window can be, and usually is, altered. First, we endeavor to drop a bird's phrases into a receptacle of silence by removing all "unwanted" sound. Then, we further adjust the image, believing the act to be an objectification of perception, until we see what we want. Moreover, the sonogram does not entirely represent what the human (and likely the bird's) ear hears, and the computational basis for a sonogram has not gone unchallenged.[26] In addition, it is impossible to have simultaneously a fine frequency and time resolution—you must preference one or the other. While the sonogram has proven more adept at describing timbre than music notation, portrayals of frequency, time, and structure are parameters that in many cases traditional music notation and analysis remain *better* equipped to identify and interpret.

THE PIED BUTCHERBIRD IN FIELD GUIDES
AND ORNITHOLOGICAL REPORTAGE

Scholarship is north-centric. The recent discovery of the origin of songbirds turned the world upside down: articles citing DNA sequence data implicate the ancient supercontinent of Eastern Gondwana (Australia and Papua New Guinea) as the birthplace of songbirds.[27] Since they predate human arrival, songbirds distinguish themselves as truly indigenous Australians.

The pied butcherbird (*Cracticus nigrogularis*) is a medium-sized songbird (or oscine) belonging to the family Artamidae, which also includes various woodswallows, currawongs, the Australian magpie (*Cracticus tibicen*), and other butcherbirds—the grey butcherbird (*Cracticus torquatus*), which is widespread, and the much rarer black butcherbird (*Cracticus quoyi*) and black-backed butcherbird (*Cracticus mentalis*).[28]

Most dinosaurs disappeared some sixty-six million years ago, but birds are living, airborne dinosaurs. The discovery of *Archaeopteryx* in a German limestone quarry in 1861 was the first of successive fossil discoveries to establish this link. Our last living common ancestor with birds disappeared long before the earliest dinosaur: more than three hundred million years separate people and birds. Not only were birds in place long before humans arrived, but birds' arrival also predates that of intelligent apes. As to the songbird who is our focus, the ancestor of butcherbirds split off from the ancestor of currawongs about thirteen million years ago, but it is not possible to say when after that split the first bird we would call a butcherbird lived.[29]

In 1848 English ornithologist and bird artist John Gould created the earliest written description of the species, accompanied by a color drawing of a pair:

> It often descends to the ground in search of insects and small lizards, which however form but a portion of its food, for as its powerful and strongly-hooked bill would lead us to infer, prey of a more formidable kind is often resorted to; its sanguinary disposition, in fact, leads it to feed on young birds, mice, and other small quadrupeds, which it soon kills, tears piece-meal and devours on the spot; wounded individuals on being handled inflict severe blows and lacerations on the hands of the captor, unless great care be taken to avoid them.[30]

Gould identified a second pied butcherbird species in 1865—the pied crow-shrike (*Cracticus picatus*), which has since been subsumed into the same species classification as *Cracticus nigrogularis*.[31] The two subspecies are virtually indistinguishable. *Cracticus nigrogularis* is found in eastern Australia (my "saltwater country" study area), and *Cracticus nigrogularis picatus* is in the west (my "desert country" study area). The putative contact zone of the two is my "savannah country" study area.[32]

Pied butcherbirds usually hunt from bare tree limbs or power lines, diving down to take their prey at first strike. "Butcher" refers to both their method of killing and the ensuing butcher shop where they store their game. Alternative English names include break-o'day-boy, jackeroo, black-throated crow-shrike, black-throated butcherbird, and organ-bird—when not evoking the flute, vocal metaphors often mention the organ or cornet. The name "butcherbird" comes from unrelated shrike species of the Northern Hemisphere with similar feeding habits, such as the great grey shrike (*Lanius excubitor*), or "murdering pie." I find "butcherbird" an unfortunate choice, a word disagreeable in both connotation and sound and one that fails to take vocal achievements into account.

Pied butcherbirds possess sharply contrasted black-and-white plumage with a black hood and bib. Their blue-grey bill ends in a finely hooked tip, for killing. The size and shape of a bird's beak reveal a lot about them. They hunt, forage, and feed with it, but they also use it for thermal regulation: a large beak increases birds' ability to rid themselves of excess heat. Powerfully built, with a relatively large head, pied butcherbirds' legs and wings, useful for striking in confined spaces like bushes, seem short in comparison. Males and females are generally indistinguishable in the field (monomorphic). Juvenile plumage arrives in a pale brownish grey for the first year; although dull and ill defined, the diagnostic hood and bib appear in brown, echoing the adult's glossy black patterning. Their age span is not well known, with estimates based on too few banded and recovered birds. In combining the records of closely related species like grey butcherbirds and Australian magpies, I would estimate that individuals could live twenty to twenty-five years, perhaps more.

The species is nonmigratory and distributed throughout a fair amount of mainland Australia, as well as several coastal islands, with a notable absence from Tasmania and the driest desert areas and a near absence from the southern coast, including the cities of Sydney west to Canberra, Melbourne, Adelaide, and Perth. Pied butcherbirds display a marked preference for open eucalypt forests, acacia woodlands, and shrublands and have only occasionally been recorded in less open rainforests and mangroves. I have photographed an individual on absolute beachfront, perched on a fence facing the sea and scanning the horizon. They frequent modified habitats like parks, gardens, and farmland. However, when I arrive at such locations, I have no guarantee that the birds will be present. Many a time I have hurriedly retreated from a site where I fully expected to find them— say, where a golf course, park, and cemetery converge—only to discover a bird a mile or two out of town in a small clump of trees or downtown singing on a television aerial at the local liquor shop.[33]

Pied butcherbirds build large, externally rough sticknests in the forks of trees. Dry grass, leaves, and other soft matter line the inside, which will hold a clutch of two to five spotted pale olive or brown eggs. Incubation takes twenty-one days, and the hatchlings spend about thirty more days in the nest before fledging.[34] Immature birds often stay on to help feed and protect the next year's nestlings.[35] While rare in the Northern

Figure 2.1. A pair of pied butcherbirds deliver prey to their nestlings. Photograph by Robert Inglis (2011). Used by permission.

Hemisphere, cooperative breeding is quite common in Australia. At least in some species, group cooperation could be the ancestral behavior and pair bonding a later organizational strategy.[36] Some stories suggest that pieds could interbreed with grey or black butcherbirds.

Aggressiveness is routinely associated with the species, particularly around their nests, and a number of accounts detail attacks on humans. Pied butcherbirds have also swooped me during the nesting season, accompanied by loud calls and beak claps, although on each occasion I escaped before suffering a direct hit. In his field guide, Alan Bell warns: "Like a stern officer of the watch the shrike [butcherbird] makes his rounds, an overbearing and resented presence. He arrives quietly but spurns concealment, 'like a cop on a New York corner,' said an American guest."[37]

Nevertheless, they can become tame when regularly fed in picnic areas and domestic gardens, even entering houses and allowing hand feeding: "In one case a 'Butcher' accepted four chop-bones thrown by picnickers

Figure 2.2. A pied butcherbird at the nest. Photograph by Robert Inglis (2011). Used by permission.

and contrived to hang them all in his larder up aloft."[38] Farmers appreciate them dining on pest species like rodents and grasshoppers; pied butcherbirds, individually or as a group, will also take a lizard or snake. I have watched them feast on exposed insects and worms in freshly plowed fields and mowed lawns and have a reliable report of a pair riding along atop an electric lawnmower.

After praising their "beautiful, clear flute-like piping and lower mellow notes" in her Magnetic Island field guide, Jo Wieneke warns: "Butcherbirds can become very tame in suburban areas but please DO NOT FEED THEM. They prey on sunbirds and increased numbers of butcherbirds will mean fewer sunbirds."[39] Meanwhile, another resident of the island fed her butcherbirds and believed she managed to keep the peace between them and the spectacular yellow-breasted sunbirds (*Nectarinia jugularis*) that frequent her garden.

HORSESHOE BAY, Magnetic Island, 18 September 2007, 2:30 AM: Hoop pines, fringing coral reefs, and fractured granite boulders. I walk for half an hour along the dark shore of one of the island's secluded bays, and then I turn my back to the sea and head over a sand dune (actually several, as I inevitably get lost) toward a concealed cabin. I'll record the resident pied butcherbird until dawn and then pay a visit to eighty-one-year-old Delphine, who volunteered to record her soloist in the weeks before I arrive.

Delphine reported several months before: "I fed the baby [pied butcherbird] 144 termites in one go! I'm dropping back with the feeding as we have had a little rain and so natural food will soon be abundant. Our winter has been so very dry, but I have had such pleasure keeping them safe. Thank you for introducing me to this wonderful time with my little birds."

She indulges her songster, allowing karaoke-style practice: "You see, he likes to sing with the radio. He just adores [flautist] Jane Rutter and sings his little heart out," she tells me. Her recording sounds like what it is—a poor quality, slightly distorted track from a cassette recorder perched on an outdoor windowsill. The radio plays in the kitchen as she washes up. Her bird rejects the standard pattern of phrase-then-silence: the song takes shape as a nearly continuous melody. Our soloist is apparently in rehearsal with one of Mozart's flute concertos. A few well-placed trills, a rarity for this species, make me laugh when I hear the recording.[40]

Mozart, concerto soloist, trills, sound and silence—I will follow up on these apparent overlaps with human music in due course.

THE PIED BUTCHERBIRD VOICE

Positive evaluations of pied butcherbirds' vocal abilities abound. "Many people consider the Pied Butcherbird to be the best singer of all Australia's birds," proclaims the Australian Museum's website.[41] "The Pied Butcherbird is Elgar, a traditionalist, a lover of melodic themes—the opening bars of the *Enigma Variations* are pure butcherbird," judges one auditor.

"The tunes are predictable, their structure self-evident; they know where they are going and take you with them. A few moments' listening and you could sing along, if you had the voice for it."[42] I am not sure I know what comes next, but what does arrive usually makes perfect musical sense to me after the fact.

While pied butcherbirds are often singled out as one of the most accomplished songbirds in Australia, this is strictly anecdotal and not the product of detailed research. Most comments on them refer either to their voice, variously described as rich, mellow, magnificent, and superb, or to their ferocity, or to both: a "beguiling song . . . and the habits of a fiend."[43] Their voice box routinely takes second place to their feeding habits: "Butcherbirds? We hate 'em!" exclaimed two elderly women who had stopped to watch me record at their town park. "What they do to the little birds 'n' that." The black-and-white coloring of the species recapitulates these contrasts. Nothing about pied butcherbirds is pastel. With both song and death in their beak, their public relations manager has her work cut out for her. Sometimes, the flavor of an informant's account tells more about the human animal than the avian songster. The earliest vocal description in ornithological reports dates from 1903, when Thomas Carter wrote, "I heard their beautiful notes . . . I shot them both."[44]

In his 1922 book *Mateship with Birds*, journalist and ornithologist Alec H. Chisholm seeks to portray pied butcherbird vocal timbre:

> I have heard the Magpies singing their love-songs to the morn (and also to the moon) on many occasions, but not even those caroling choruses were sweeter than the concert performance of a quartette of Butcher-Birds rollicking in the bush beside Moreton Bay on a day in October. The notes . . . are indescribably rich and pure, and add a certain gipsy wildness to what is probably the nearest approach made by any Australian bird to the full, rolling tones of a pipe organ. . . . One other memory of the mellifluous voice of this gifted bird belongs to a sub-tropical mountain. . . . A massed array of white Watsonias was flowering radiantly at the edge of the jungle-hemmed paddock, and as the deliberate notes of the pure-voiced birds rose and fell, how perfectly the music seemed to harmonise with the *color* of the white flowers! . . . [T]he melody of these Butcher-Birds got beyond the lyrical, developed a Miltonic fullness, as it were, and merged itself in the challenging purity of the white flowers. Anon, as the sun rose and an element of the garish intruded into the symphony, the notes of the birds took a

slightly *golden* tint, this time approximating to the color of a rich rose that festooned a gateway hard by.[45]

The text registers as old-fashioned, but the awestruck sentiment is valid through the ages. Given such accolades, the lack of studies on their voice is astonishing.

A quick scouting report will help us get our bearings: both sexes sing, including in duos, trios, and larger choirs. They hold a species-wide call in common, and ensemble songs indicate their musical custodianship of many an agreed-upon local tradition. The solo songs of mature birds, however, all differ one from another, partially or entirely. In the spring, nocturnal solo songs may span up to seven hours, especially on moonlit nights, and soloists transform their songs annually. Performances often converge on sonic structures and behaviors familiar in human music, including some features thought unique to it. These avian masters of pattern and timbral diversity excel in taking a motif to the limits of expression via elaborate combinatorial reworkings. In addition, they imitate other species and even mechanical sounds.

This survey of field guides and ornithological reportage complete, what comes next is less a critique of scholarly authority than a simple acknowledgment of the role played by citizen science and other perspectives that we might only source from anecdotes.

ANTHROPOMORPHISM: AN INTERLUDE

We begin in the foyer of Edinburgh College of Art, where I have just delivered a lecture to an environmental humanities research group. When Françoise Wemelsfelder introduces herself to me, my first thought is, What is an animal cognition professor doing at a humanities conference? Quite a lot, as it turns out. She dares to study animals as whole sentient beings. Believing that subjective phenomena require their own descriptors, she has developed a novel methodology that combines qualitative and quantitative evaluation. Wemelsfelder and her collaborators make scientific assessments of affective states (like anxious, relaxed, timid, and bored) via body language, claiming that such demeanors are indeed open to empirical investigation. They then guide carers on how to apply Qualitative Behaviour Assessment toward welfare management of farm, zoo, and companion animals. Her approach boldly pushes aside any fear of anthropomorphism, which usually makes scientists reluctant to discuss subjective qualities like well-being or suffering or, closer to my project, beauty or musicality.[46]

The moment we depart official reportage, and even much before, we must dodge the bullet of anthropomorphism. Comments that speak to the musicality of a bird's song are a prime target for the label—suspected of making a category error, of using words restricted to humans, or of crediting animals with more than we ought. Alternatively, following on cultural musicologist Christopher Small, we could probe and commend how members of one culture or species come to understand (and sometimes even creatively misunderstand) and enjoy the music making of others.[47] In 1917 ornithologist Henry Oldys advised that we ignore anthropomorphism and instead craft the simplest and most plausible interpretation of birdsong: that birds consciously appreciate the musical beauty of their songs.[48]

Is anthropomorphism the result of narcissism or empathy? The concept swims in cultural bias—what is anthropomorphism to one could be accepted orthodoxy to another, and if we had never anthropomorphized, there would be those calling for us to do so. I am not advocating a simple anthropomorphism but one that embraces the full complexities of sameness and difference—one that acknowledges that while we humans are also animals, some animals cross the "divide" in the other direction, producing social identities and remarkable deeds. I take inspiration from Len Howard, the naturalist, violinist, and recluse who immersed herself in the lives and minds of individual birds at her Bird Cottage. Wild birds were allowed to enter and roost as they wished. As a result of her cohabitation and assiduous field notes, she published two bird biographies, *Birds as Individuals* (1952) and *Living with Birds* (1956). Howard's meticulous observations show birds in the fullness of their lives: some are talented, while others are dull, some generous and others greedy, some diligent and others ne'er-do-wells, some faithful and others cheats, some good-natured and others cheerless.

Although her approach is holistic and not musicological, in the final chapter of *Birds as Individuals* Howard summarizes her analysis of the birdsongs she regularly heard, discussing frequent overlaps with human music. She notates songs, including the opening phrase of the Rondo in

Beethoven's Violin Concerto in D Major, op. 61, which a blackbird with "imaginative genius" composed over the course of several days. At one point, she writes, "Bird-song, like all music, impresses." For her, birdsong is unequivocally music.[49]

Who is officially authorized to give such an account of birdsong? The foreword to *Birds as Individuals*, penned by ethologist Julian Huxley, is brief and ambivalent. "Miss Howard will not expect a professional biologist to accept all her conclusions," he declares. "But they [biologists] will be grateful for her facts."[50] Fortunately, hers are not dry facts. Despite the best effort of their authors, dry facts convey *more* than just facts. Metaphor is language's essential anchor, and thin language distances us from animals, impoverishes our understanding of animal abilities, and disguises how songbirds serve the human imagination.

Nature is typically framed as a problem in need of empirical information to be gathered, assembled, and analyzed by scientists. What can contemporary scientists make of an intriguing animal behavior situated outside their methodology or the hypothesis they are testing? Such accounts languish as what philosopher Daniel Dennett termed "officially unusable."[51] Fear of the anthropomorphic label can induce what primatologist and ethologist Frans B. M. de Waal terms "anthropodenial," leading to a systematic underestimation of animal abilities. He urges us to "admit that animals are far more like our relatives than like machines."[52] It is telling that the tendency of ethologists to anthropomorphize increases, not decreases, with their experience in the field.[53]

Science's inability to make use of anecdotal data may keep out embellishment and hyperbole with respect to animal capacities, but it also eliminates rarities, one-offs, and anomalies inaccessible in the laboratory, which, when scrupulously observed and analyzed, are precious evidence. Howard invented a rigorous but personal and unapproved methodology. In deliberating on how to judge her work vis-à-vis other avian research, sociologist Eileen Crist reweights the argument: "The truths yielded through detached, methodologically stringent, and quantitative analyses of animal behavior will distort the realities of animal life, if such analyses are taken to be exclusive truths, or fruit of a singularly privileged perspective."[54] This echoes Wemelsfelder's claim that the scientific method gets it wrong if it turns its back on comprehensive, sympathetic knowing and thus ignores subjective experience in animals.

⁕ Allow me to float an idea: an inability to see ourselves as part of eco-systems puts us at grave risk. Our survival partially depends on real-world anecdotes, anthropomorphism, and other holistic, even generous, reflections on animals. Accounts from everyday folks in everyday language are not so remote from the natural sciences as they might seem. Scholar of literature and science George Levine has described how in Darwin's development of his theory of sexual selection, anthropomorphism performed a valuable service.[55] Darwin argued with a personal voice, wrote in an accessible style, and imbued his science texts with humor, doubt, ambivalence, vivid descriptions, and human-animal metaphors devoid of scare quotes. "It is a mistake for us to read Darwin as if the aesthetic implications of his language were quirky, colourful, whimsical or unintentional," stresses evolutionary biologist Richard O. Prum. "They are a fundamental feature of his theory."[56] Darwin's anthropomorphic language springs from the mental and behavioral continuity he understands between humans and animals, and he made inductive use of anecdotal data to evidence phenomena that were otherwise intractable.[57]

Since ordinary people far outnumber scientists, anecdote, when critically assessed, serves a valuable function in the interpretation of animal behavior—and in assessing unique cases, we recall that the individual is Darwin's unit of selection.[58] The humanities are not alone in recognizing the potential of everyday people to increase animal observations on both geographic and time scales; the natural sciences are beginning to look at how to capture animals in novel contexts and expand their research platform via citizen scientists and volunteers, as well as by means of remote-camera technologies and crowdsourcing.[59] Science is gradually discovering how to nurture and harvest anecdotes previously disregarded in knowledge enterprises. Here, then, come just a handful among many pied butcherbird accounts from popular circles and citizen scientists.

OTHER PIED BUTCHERBIRD TEXTS AND ORAL STORIES

Members of the First Fleet, who disembarked in 1788, found Aboriginal people to be widely dispersed, inhabiting almost every plain, tableland, and valley for at least a part of the year.[60] Aborigines were adept bird hunters and egg collectors, and they played a key role in shaping Australian ornithology, with bird-collecting expeditions to remote areas owing their success to native peoples' ability and willingness to lend assistance.[61] In many cultures, treating certain species as kin is well known, as is attributing to them divine or ancestral status.[62] In Aboriginal society, each person comes from at least one totemic being who assists in delineating the individual's origins and connections with the world, and for some people, the pied butcherbird is their totem.

Bird's voices have a history of being esteemed for their prognosticatory ability, and pied butcherbirds feature in this—likened to a forecaster, indicator, interpreter, or even agent of events. "The pied butcherbird makes fun of people," we learn from the Alyawarr language group. "If there is a man sneaking up on game, it discourages them, 'Nothing, you are hopeless and you won't get any game.' It puts them off so they won't spear anything. 'Apapapapapa,' it laughs." From the Anmatyerr language group, we hear: "A pied butcherbird calls a dead person's name and reminds people about them."[63]

Is there a connection between Aboriginal song and birdsong? Ethnomusicologist Allan Marett believes so, likening dialect changes in birdsong to changes in the music of the Wannga of North Australia. "People use musical structures as markers of relationship to place and then manipulate those in order to differentiate themselves from other people," he explained to me, "so they can perform in a way that says we're really different or we're really similar, depending on which aspects of musical structure they're emphasizing—and birds are doing that."[64]

A 1943 excerpt from mammalogist and explorer H. H. Finlayson also suggests structural similarities between birdsong and Aboriginal cultural traditions (Luritja, in this case): "The songs themselves are arresting. In spite of their almost skeletal simplicity, there is something in them akin to our own music; and the springs of emotion which give them origin are not strange and remote as they often seem to be, to an untrained ear, in much Oriental music. Further, each tiny song is a single rich theme, complete in itself, carried swiftly to a logical conclusion, unweakened by meanderings or side issues. It has all the artistic force of a thing free from flaw."[65] Finlayson's observation of the virtues of Luritja song resonates strikingly with how I might describe a pied butcherbird song.

Staying with the Luritja tradition, in 1911 Lutheran missionary Carl Strehlow paired his literal German translation of a song (titling it "Der Krähen Würger") with a second, more interpretative one. Literary scholar

Brian Elliott later brought them together, offering up an English translation as well. He underlines that the *kurbaru* (pied butcherbird in Luritja)
represents not a mere bird but rather a totemic ancestor.[66] While the lyrics
in this ceremonial artifact refer in part to birdsong, "The Pied Butcherbird" cannot be read within a Western framework; such cryptic texts are
rich and dense and do not give up their meaning in a surface reading by
the uninitiated.

Unfortunately, we have neither a recording nor a transcription, but in
pairing Finlayson's description of Luritja singing with this text, I searched
for insight into how the song might have sounded. The syllabic building
patterns remind me of combinatorial pied butcherbird songs—and might
this ancient name, *kurbaru*, be onomatopoetic of the species' common
three-note call (detailed in chapter 4)? I imagine the millennia that it has
cut across this land; our relationship with these songbirds could be stag-
geringly ancient. I can only wonder if avian vocalizations influenced this
Luritja song's creation or delivery.

If humans got music from birds (a topic well beyond the scope of this
book), we would expect to find cases of human music that resemble birdsong, and here a prospective example comes into view—one that would
refute psychologist of music Géza Révész's assertion that "among the
songs of primitive tribes we find none that is imitative of bird-calls."[67]
We might also add to this refutation Marett's many reports of birds as
song-giving agents and ethnomusicologist Robin Ryan's descriptions of
didjeridoo impersonations in nontribal contexts of growling crocodiles,
croaking frogs, hopping kangaroos, howling dingos, laughing kookaburras, singing night owls, honking magpie geese, squawking emus, and calling brolgas, as well as impressive Aboriginal gumleaf imitations of birds.
Musicologists Milena Petrovic and Nenad Ljubinkovic have identified
animal sound patterns like wolves, roosters, turtledoves, cardinals, cranes,
and horses that they believe are clearly articulated in the motifs of traditional Serbian folk songs. The Kaluli people as reported by ethnomusicologist Steven Feld stands as yet another example.[68] Given the human
proclivity for imitating birds, I would expect at minimum that this has
influenced how we listen and how we make music.

Another Aboriginal narrative takes place west of Alice Springs at Glen
Helen, where a towering red sandstone wall collapses into the Finke River.

Usually just a string of waterholes unless rain has been heavy, this ancient artery is thought to have cut a path here for more than three hundred million years, making it the planet's oldest watercourse. As detailed by John Strehlow (grandson of Carl), Altjira, a benevolent spiritual being, became weary of repeated incursions into his hunting grounds and forbade the totemic ancestors to hunt there. An "*urbura* totem god or Black-throated Butcherbird-man seized a stick and struck the water, saying '*Jerrai!*'—Go away! And it did: the sea retreated to the north and for the first time dry land appeared."[69]

Strehlow also directed me to a story involving his grandfather as reported by ornithologist S. A. White during a 1913 scientific expedition in Central Australia:

> The first night we reached a small soakage where some mission natives were stationed to keep the water open for the stock.... Our attention was drawn to a black-fronted butcher bird (Cractieus nigrogularius) [*sic*], commonly called a "jackeroo," which seemed very tame, and after a while came into the camp for food. One of our boys, Jack, was instructed to ascertain from the natives at the soak why this bird was so tame, and had they made it a pet, and this is what Jack said—"Him Christian bird, that fellow; him go along a church and pray." We remembered that the Rev. Mr. Strehlow told us that there was such a bird at the mission, which would persist in going to church on Sundays, and made such a great noise that the preacher's voice could not be heard, so the bird was banished to the scrub around the soak, and this is how we met with what Jack designated "the Christian bird."[70]

"It's a fantastic story!" exclaimed John Strehlow. "This has to be the only bird ever exiled for going to church."

The Hermannsburg mission is still there, its whitewashed church and various outbuildings shaded by tall river red gums (*Eucalyptus camaldulensis*) and date palms. This insistent bit of traditional German farmhouse architecture is in stark contrast to the surrounding countryside. Four rows of small picnic benches line each aisle of the church. Behind the benches are two more rows made of crude board and cruder legs shaved to a point and stuck in the board. A crucifix and a plaque with hymn numbers hang above the pulpit. When Jon and I visited to record the Ntaria Ladies Choir, they sang several hymns in Aranda, including "Rock of Ages." Their mouths barely opened—two of the women even sang from the *side* of their mouth—but still a huge sound came out, all with their distinctive articulation, gliding tones, and timbre. One could speculate, and I have, that "the Christian bird" enjoyed the choir's singing. The old stone church has excellent acoustics and a pump-style harmonium, which the bird might likewise have appreciated.

I also surveyed children's literature, which of course has an enduring fascination with animals. Although not all stories bring new knowledge on our subject, some undeniably assist in filling out an understanding of this understudied species. The liaisons that pied butcherbirds make with humans can be read as a useful ploy by a children's author, but these birds' propensity to thrive in even difficult environmental situations via such relationships has counterparts in reliable real-world accounts.[71]

Animals and animality also fascinate adults. Especially in the first half of the twentieth century, observations that pied butcherbirds mimic other birds and display a special ability for song that overlaps with a human listener's concept of musicality crop up regularly in periodicals.[72] We read that individual birds possess a wide variety of song phrases, that they sing differently one from another, and that their songs transform over time. Ordinary people have documented for decades what I only recently wrote up.

I wondered why as early as 1939 an article mentioned the protection of pied butcherbirds. Then I came across this:

> He tramps the country roads with his brothers, a team of them; he whistles, perfects bird calls and collects the speckled eggs from the nests for the collection which all country boys had in those days. He makes strong and accurate shanghais from forked sticks and strips of rubber, and owns a sharp and many-tongued pocket knife for these and other tasks. He shoots every butcherbird he sees, for they are cruel and kill the smaller birds, the wrens and finches. He is an accurate shot; the sharp pebble flies straight, smashes the ribcage and crushes the heart. The butcherbird drops, blood dribbling from its mouth, to stiffen in the sun.[73]

More often, however, texts describe the viciousness of pied butcherbirds to the exclusion of ours. I cataloged eight poems on pied butcherbirds that are split between attending to superlative vocal abilities and ferocious hunting prowess.[74] For instance, in the confronting poem "Call Her Butcher Bird," Aileen Kelly (b. England, 1939–2011) probes how we might react to the opposite names "butcherbird" and "Organ Bird" and how these variously invoke, perpetuate, or modify the angel/fiend dichotomy.[75] Eminent poet and passionate environmentalist Judith Wright (b. Armidale, Australia, 1915–2000) finds another way through this antimony: "Whatever the bird is, is perfect in the bird."[76]

The more I come to know about pied butcherbirds, the better I am at evaluating and harvesting information from anecdotal sources. Fellow campers that I meet during fieldwork often pose questions or relate anecdotes. I also conduct regular Internet searches, which have been fruitful on a number of fronts. People have generously sent me audio, video, and written observations. Good-mannered, measured requests do not allow for a "take the recording and run" approach. The best material inevitably arises out of developing personal relationships, and a number of my current field sites are the result of such contacts. In fact, citizen science runs deep and wide in ornithology, with some observers possessing an understanding that equals or surpasses official knowledge. The comments below, unless otherwise cited, are anonymous. First, three citizen scientists weigh in on pied butcherbird ferocity:

> If you've ever done any banding, mist netting—the butcherbirds are very smart. They come in very early, and they sit above the mist nets where all the little birds are being caught, and they'll pick them out of the mist nets.

> Today, I heard Pied butcherbirds mobbing something. It turned out to be a Boobook [owl]. They had injured one eye and broken one wing. I took it to a vet, who did not seem optimistic about the state of the broken wing. It would certainly have been killed by the 5 butcherbirds that were attacking it very savagely. I wonder if these types of attacks are now more common as the owls have less suitable roosting sites available to them and end up roosting in open country where they are easily discovered.

> My wife and I got a free lunch at a local hotel thanks to a pied butcherbird. I had dropped her at the door and had to park quite some distance away. I didn't know there was a baby butcherbird, until one of the parents hit me. Then it was on. I whistled a butcherbird threat call, and both parents attacked. They couldn't put a beak on me once I knew they were there, but neither did I manage to hit them with my fist. The initial

attack had drawn blood, and the pub staff was most solicitous. They explained that they had several times moved the baby away, but it kept coming back—and insisted that lunch was on the house.[77]

Next come stories from ordinary people who describe significant relationships with pied butcherbirds:

I raised three pied butcherbird chicks right here in Charters Towers. The one became a real pet and went everywhere on my shoulder, you know. So, one day I walked into the local pub and ordered it a water. The publican immediately banned me from comin' back. I asked him why. He pointed up at the sign. "No dogs," he said.

The home movie "Butcherbird auditioning to join the band" shows Steve singing and playing guitar while a bird vocalizes at the front door:

On the video of the bird demanding breakfast, you will hear the very worst rendition of *Blackbird* ever. It is a pity that I was strumming the guitar during the filming because it does drown the butcherbird out a bit. However, at the time we thought that the guitar had attracted him. On reflection, I am convinced he was just telling us he was wanting a handout.[78]

I regularly encounter locals who feed pied butcherbirds meat scraps. These people likewise have the sense that the birds reward them with song, or sing for their supper, although this behavior has not been formally studied. Barry feeds the pied butcherbirds at a caravan park in North Queensland where he and they reside:

They generally sit in this tree here. I went away for a bit, and they changed their habit. They'd wait for me to come out. There he is; he's coming. They're all pretty fussy. They won't eat rubbish meat. They won't eat fat. Now that's the fellow. They only eat the best of steak. All day, all day long they come here. Them 'n' the magpies, just all day long. There he goes. He'll go away and hide it now, 'n' he'll come back. Just look up here, you see meat stickin' out of all the little bits, but they still come back.

Knowing who is feeding them assists me in working out why some song-posts are chosen and why some pied butcherbird territories are vigorously defended.

A young bird (still brown-headed) broke her beak, and although the bird could eat, hunting would have been difficult. A human neighbor,

Alan, took on the task of feeding the bird and extended family, as well as recording and filming the group for me.

> Broken Beak gets preferential treatment from me: I throw bread bits down on the driveway as a distraction for the magpies and feed her minced meat from my hand on the balcony—in peace! She follows me from backyard to front and flies so close to my head that I feel her wing-beats. Today, I went up on the roof to readjust the TV antenna—all the b/b congregation came up to lob on the antenna and sing at me! Broken Beak sang for the first time! Only soft and briefly, but she did! I feel like I've been present for another birth![79]

I visited Alan's suburban home the next spring and recorded nearby at the local golf course, since it would have been difficult to find or record "his" birds, and for all I know, his birds *are* the golf course choristers. We kept in touch. Because of the marking, Broken Beak could be followed for vocal and other development and provided me with intriguing listening and viewing over two years' time. When Broken Beak healed, Alan ceased feeding the birds.

Then, there are the curiosities:

> Pied butcherbirds are playful birds; I've seen the young ones play tug-of-war with a stick—and the story goes that a pied butcherbird had copied a postman's whistle; several generations afterwards a young bird had a whistle in its repertoire, although the postie was no longer around, and the bird had never heard it.

> My friend and I stopped at a picnic spot for our morning "cuppa." The birds would regularly be fed by the picnickers, and there were a few magpies nearby as well as the whole butcherbird family. One of the sub-adult Pied Butcherbirds immediately perched on the corner of the table between us and gave a glorious rendition of a *magpie* song! No magpie could have done better! We were absolutely astounded, but he didn't get "paid" for his entertainment.

> In defence of the nest one alone usually attacks, but both take part sometimes, one usually in front and one behind. They seem to have

a reasonable amount of intelligence, as shown when attacking boys.
When boys are throwing stones or holding a stick above their heads the
Butcherbirds do not attack, but when they relax for just a moment they
are immediately attacked.[80]

In measuring aspects of stories such as these against my fieldwork results, the accounts stack up credibly. Intuitions are shared across a wide
variety of observers and usually coincide with my own. This typically
excluded knowledge represents far more than misinformed, excitable,
or arbitrary anecdote, and only intellectual contortion could incline us
to disregard it. While occasional anecdotes, even quite elegantly worded
ones, do not match with what I hear in a bird's song, the *sum total* of them,
brought together to talk to one another, undoubtedly enhances our understanding of the species. We are watching birds and vice versa.

My work breaks basic ethological tenets, drawing on rare occurrences,
singular free-living animals, a musician's hunch, and bodily judgments.
We have no more honest way to appraise another than by direct comparison to our own sense of time, weight, size, scale, distance, velocity,
loudness . . . and once we begin such a list, we must expect to encounter
parameters where we fail to keep pace. Anthropomorphism crops up. So
does theriomorphism, which cognitive scientist and philosopher Roberto
Marchesini sees as the projection, attribution, or incorporation of animal
traits into human beings and human culture. He believes that close observation and imitation of animals has led to the adoption of animal behaviors in a number of human cultural practices like yoga and the martial
arts, reflecting an ethology that dates back to prehistory.[81] You could say
that theriomorphism guides my practice as a violinist/composer, since I
incorporate avian vocalizations into my performances.

Plenty of other "isms" tag along with anthropomorphism.[82] With so
many conflicting understandings of it and so many spin-off terms in circulation, anthropomorphism emerges as a hotspot of dissent. We must
be onto something. What's at stake? The universal validity of the scientific method in animal studies by a dispassionate, dislocated observer.
Of course, like composing and making music, science is also haphazard
and messy. It is only onstage, or at the stage of verification and writing
up, that we all put on our best clothes and hide the mess. Although some
might disavow it, when offstage, scientists regularly make use of anthro-

pomorphism.[83] In addition, although it is worthy of much of the respect it commands, the scientific method cannot stand in for all knowledge for all time. Along with new efforts in the natural sciences to harness everyday people, I want to open the window a bit wider to quality reportage. Zoömusicology can bring together an assortment of people in order to broaden the field of inquiry and tell the fullest pied butcherbird story possible.

NOTES

1. Joah R. Madden et al., "Male Spotted Bowerbirds Propagate Fruit for Use in Their Sexual Display," *Current Biology* 22, no. 8 (2010): R264–R265.

2. Females will nibble on the paint, suggesting that it might function as a chemical sexual signal rather than a visual one (Benjamin D. Bravery, James A. Nicholls, and Anne W. Goldizen, "Patterns of Painting in Satin Bowerbirds *Ptilonorhynchus violaceus* and Males' Responses to Changes in Their Paint," *Journal of Avian Biology* 37, no. 1 (2006): 77.

3. Clifford B. Frith and Dawn W. Frith, *Bowerbirds: Nature, Art & History* (Malanda: Frith & Frith, 2008), 25. Also see Hollis Taylor, "A Taste for the Beautiful," in *Esthétique et complexité—II: Neurosciences, évolution, épistémologie, philosophie*, ed. Zoï Kapoula, Louise-José Lestocart, and Jean-Paul Allouche (Paris: Éditions CNRS, 2015), 181–187.

4. John A. Endler, Lorna C. Endler, and Natalie R. Doerr, "Great Bowerbirds Create Theaters with Forced Perspective When Seen by Their Audience," *Current Biology* 20, no. 18 (2010): 1679–1684; and Laura A. Kelley and John A. Endler, "Illusions Promote Mating Success in Great Bowerbirds," *Science* 335, no. 20 (January 2012): 335–338.

5. Alexander Alland Jr., *The Artistic Animal: An Inquiry into the Biological Roots of Art* (Garden City, NY: Anchor Books, 1977), 24; Denis Dutton, *The Art Instinct* (New York: Bloomsbury Press, 2009), 8–9; and Iain McGilchrist, *The Master and His Emissary: The Divided Brain and the Making of the Western World* (New Haven, CT: Yale University Press, 2009), 127.

6. For discussions on the syrinx, see Crawford H. Greenewalt, *Bird Song: Acoustics and Physiology* (Washington, DC: Smithsonian Institution Press, 1968); Neville Fletcher, "Birdsong Science," *Australian Science* 27, no. 9 (2006): 35–37; and Daniel N. Düring et al., "The Songbird Syrinx Morphome: A Three-Dimensional, High-Resolution, Interactive Morphological Map of the Zebra Finch Vocal Organ," *BMC Biology* 11, no. 1 (2013): 1–27.

7. W. H. Thorpe, "The Learning of Song Patterns by Birds, with Especial Reference to the Song of the Chaffinch *Fringilla coelebs*," *Ibis* 100 (1958): 557; Peter Marler, "The Instinct to Learn," in *Language Acquisition: Core Readings*, ed. P. Bloom (Cambridge, MA: MIT Press, 1994), 591, 614; and Peter Marler, "Three Models of Song Learning: Evidence from Behavior," *Journal of Neurobiology* 33 (1997): 503.

8. See O. Koehler, "Der Vogelgesang als Vorstufe von Musik und Sprache," *Journal of Ornithology* 93, no. 1 (1951): 3–20; and W. H. Thorpe, "The Process of Song-Learning

in the Chaffinch as Studied by Means of the Sound Spectrograph," *Nature* 173 (1954): 465–469.

9. The basic notions clearly laid out in these classic studies continue to be relevant and built upon. See, for example, Thorpe, "The Learning of Song Patterns"; W. H. Thorpe, "Further Studies on the Process of Song Learning in the Chaffinch (*Fringilla coelebs gengleri*)," *Nature* 182 (1958): 554–557; Peter Marler and Susan Peters, "Structural Changes in Song Ontogeny in the Swamp Sparrow *Melospiza georgiana*," *Auk* 99 (1982): 446–458; Peter Marler, "The Instinct to Learn," in Bloom, *Language Acquisition*, 591–617; and Peter Marler, "Three Models of Song Learning," and Dietmar Todt, "Learning to Sing," in *Nature's Music: The Science of Birdsong*, ed. Peter Marler and Hans Slabbekoorn (Amsterdam: Elsevier Academic Press, 2004), 80–107.

10. Alejandro Lynch et al., "A Model of Cultural Evolution of Chaffinch Song Derived with the Meme Concept," *American Naturalist* 133, no. 5 (1989): 634.

11. "Bird Instruments," *Grove Music Online, Oxford Music Online*, accessed 7 November 2014, http://www.oxfordmusiconline.com.

12. See, respectively, J. F. R. Stainer, "Singing Birds," *Musical Times and Singing Class Circular* 40, no. 680 (1899): 671; and Stanley Godman, ed., *The Bird Fancyer's Delight* (Mainz: Schott, 1717/1955).

13. See Peter Marler, "Birdsong: The Acquisition of a Learned Motor Skill," *Trends in Neurosciences* 4 (1981): 88; Peter Marler and Susan Peters, "Long-Term Storage of Learned Birdsongs prior to Production," *Animal Behaviour* 30, no. 2 (1982): 479; and Peter Marler, "Song Learning: The Interface between Behaviour and Neuroethology," *Philosophical Transactions: Biological Sciences* 329, no. 1,253 (1990): 109.

14. See Kenneth A. Shiovitz, "The Process of Species-Specific Song Recognition by the Indigo Bunting, *Passerina cyanea,* and Its Relationship to the Organization of Avian Acoustical Behavior," *Behaviour* 55 (1975): 133; David A. Spector, "Definition in Biology: The Case of 'Bird Song,'" *Journal of Theoretical Biology* 168 (1994): 373–381; N. S. Thompson, K. LeDoux, and K. Moody, "A System for Describing Bird Song Units," *Bioacoustics* 5 (1994): 267–279; and Wallace Craig, *The Song of the Wood Pewee* Myiochanes virens Linnaeus: *A Study of Bird Music*, vol. 334 (Albany: University of the State of New York, 1943), 169.

15. See W. John Smith, "Singing Is Based on Two Markedly Different Kinds of Signaling," *Journal of Theoretical Biology* 152 (1991): 248; and Katarina Riebel, "The Mute Sex Revisited: Vocal Production and Perception Learning in Female Songbirds," in *Advances in the Study of Behavior*, ed. Peter J. B. Slater (Amsterdam: Elsevier Academic Press, 2003), 49–86.

16. For an overview of female song and duetting, see N. E. Langmore, "Functions of Duet and Solo Songs of Female Birds," *Trends in Ecology & Evolution* 13, no. 4 (1998): 136–140; and Michelle L. Hall, "A Review of Hypotheses for the Functions of Avian Duetting," *Behavioral Ecology and Sociobiology* 55, no. 5 (2004): 415–430.

17. Eleanor D. Brown and Susan M. Farabaugh, "Song Sharing in a Group-Living Songbird, the Australian Magpie, *Gymnorhina tibicen.* Part III. Sex Specificity and Individual Specificity of Vocal Parts in Communal Chorus and Duet Songs," *Behaviour* 118, no. 3–4 (1991): 270–271.

18. Marler, "Birdsong," 92; Michael J. Boughey and Nicholas S. Thompson, "Species Specificity and Individual Variation in the Songs of the Brown Thrasher (*Toxostoma rufum*) and Catbird (*Cumetella carolinensis*)," *Behaviour* 57, no. 1–2 (1976): 65; and Luis F. Baptista and Donald E. Kroodsma, "Foreword: Avian Bioacoustics," in *Handbook of*

the Birds of the World, ed. Luis F. Baptista and Donald E. Kroodsma (Barcelona: Lynx Edicions, 2001), 11.

19. Luis F. Baptista, "Song Dialects and Demes in Sedentary Populations of the White-Crowned Sparrow (*Zonotrichi leucophrys nuttalli*)," *University of California Publications in Zoology* 105 (1975): 1.

20. Donald E. Kroodsma, "Ecology of Passerine Song Development," in *Ecology and Evolution of Acoustic Communication in Birds*, ed. Donald E. Kroodsma and Edward H. Miller (Ithaca, NY: Cornell University Press, 1996), 4.

21. Michael D. Beecher, "Birdsong Learning in the Laboratory and Field," in Kroodsma and Miller, *Ecology and Evolution*, 61.

22. See Albert R. Brand, "A Method for the Intensive Study of Bird Song," *Auk* 52 (1935): 40–52; and Albert R. Brand, "Why Bird Song Can Not Be Described Adequately," *Wilson Bulletin* 49, no. 1 (1937): 14.

23. Sydney E. Ingraham, "Instinctive Music," *Auk* 55, no. 4 (1938): 615.

24. Peter Galison, *Image and Logic: A Material Culture of Microphysics* (Chicago: University of Chicago Press, 1997), xix. This shift of focus from ear to eye in birdsong studies finds a correlate in those who privilege the score above the sonic experience in Western classical music.

25. Rachel Mundy, "Nature's Music: Birds, Beasts, and Evolutionary Listening in the Twentieth Century" (PhD diss., New York University, 2010), 195.

26. Neil J. Boucher, Michihiro Jinnai, and Hollis Taylor, "A New and Improved Spectrogram," paper presented at the 19th Congress of the Australian Institute of Physics, Melbourne, Victoria, 5–9 December 2010.

27. Scott V. Edwards and Walter E. Boles, "Out of Gondwana: The Origin of Passerine Birds," *Trends in Ecology & Evolution* 17, no. 8 (2002): 347–349; Per G. P. Ericson et al., "A Gondwanan Origin of Passerine Birds Supported by DNA Sequences of the Endemic New Zealand Wrens," *Proceedings of the Royal Society B: Biological Sciences* 269 (2002): 235–241; and Janette A. Norman et al., "Speciation Dynamics in the Australo-Papuan Meliphaga Honeyeaters," *Molecular Phylogenetics and Evolution* 42, no. 1 (2007): 80–91.

28. P. J. Higgins, J. M. Peter, and S. J. Cowling, eds., *Handbook of Australian, New Zealand & Antarctic Birds* (Melbourne: Oxford University Press, 2006), 7A:8.

29. Tim Low, e-mail message to author, 17 September 2014. Also see Tim Low, *Where Song Began: Australia's Birds and How They Changed the World* (Melbourne: Viking, 2014).

30. John Gould, *Birds of Australia* (London: Author, 1848), 2:plate 49.

31. John Gould, *Handbook to the Birds of Australia* (Melbourne: Lansdowne Press, 1865/1972), 180–182.

32. Anna M. Kearns, Leo Joseph, and Lyn G. Cook, "A Multilocus Coalescent Analysis of the Speciational History of the Australo-Papuan Butcherbirds and Their Allies," *Molecular Phylogenetics and Evolution* 66 (2013): 941–952.

33. Environmental philosopher Thom van Dooren has usefully complicated "habitat," reminding us that it is much more than a specific environment (*Flight Ways: Life and Loss at the Edge of Extinction* [New York: Columbia University Press, 2014], 151). A habitat is relational—a storied place replete with multispecies assemblages and multiple meanings. My utterly partial chronicle of any one place prevents me from looking at it and pronouncing with any degree of certainty, "Pied butcherbirds will be here."

34. Higgins, Peter, and Cowling, *Handbook*, 7A:523–524.

35. A. Robinson, "Helpers-at-the-Nest in Pied Butcherbirds, *Cracticus nigrogularis*" (PhD diss., Griffith University, 1994).

36. See James A. Nicholls et al., "The Evolution of Cooperative and Pair Breeding in Thornbills *Acanthiza* (Pardalotidae)," *Journal of Avian Biology* 31, no. 2 (2000): 165–176; and Gisela Kaplan, *Bird Minds: Cognition and Behaviour of Australian Native Birds* (Clayton South: CSIRO Publishing, 2015), 8.

37. Alan Bell, *Common Australian Birds* (Melbourne: Oxford University Press, 1956/1969), 90.

38. Alec H. Chisholm, *Bird Wonders of Australia*, 6th ed. (Sydney: Angus and Robertson, 1934/1965), 233.

39. Jo Wieneke, *Birds of Magnetic Island* (Queensland: Author, 2002), 13.

40. The trill in figure 4.3 (example 1) is from this recording, and the bird's continuous singing concurrent with this flute concerto makes for a compelling listen. Trills from bird and flute often coincide, and there is a sense that the bird is singing in the same key.

41. Australian Museum, "Birds in Backyards: Pied Butcherbird," accessed 29 June 2011, http://www.birdsinbackyards.net/species/Cracticus-nigrogularis.

42. Kay Milton in Mark Cocker and David Tipling, *Birds and People* (London: Jonathan Cape, 2013), 369.

43. Don Watson, "Society of Birds," *Monthly*, December–January 2007–2008, 18.

44. Thomas Carter, "Birds Occurring in the Region of the North-West Cape," *Emu* 3 (1903): 90–91.

45. A. H. Chisholm, *Mateship with Birds* (Melbourne: Whitcombe & Tombs, 1922), 164–166.

46. Françoise Wemelsfelder, "The Scientific Validity of Subjective Concepts in Models of Animal Welfare," *Applied Animal Behaviour Science* 53 (1997): 77. Also see Kenneth M. D. Rutherford, Ramona D. Donald, and Alistair Lawrence, "Qualitative Behavioural Assessment of Emotionality in Pigs," *Applied Animal Behaviour Science* 139 (2012): 218–224; and Clare Phythian et al., "Inter-observer Reliability of Qualitative Behavioural Assessments of Sheep," *Applied Animal Behaviour Science* 144 (2013): 73–79.

47. Christopher Small, *Musicking* (Hanover: Wesleyan University Press, 1998), 12.

48. Henry Oldys, "The Meaning of Bird Music," *American Museum Journal* 17 (1917): 127.

49. Len Howard, *Birds as Individuals* (London: Collins, 1952), 182, 184.

50. Julian Huxley, foreword in ibid., 10. Also see Eileen Crist, "'Walking on My Page': Intimacy and Insight in Len Howards' Cottage of Birds," *Social Science Information* 45, no. 2 (2006): 205.

51. Daniel C. Dennett, *The Intentional Stance* (Cambridge, MA: MIT Press, 1987), 250.

52. Frans B. M. de Waal, "Darwin's Last Laugh," *Nature* 460 (2009): 175; and Frans de Waal, "Are We in Anthropo-denial?," *Discover* 18, no. 7 (1997): 52, respectively.

53. Lorraine Daston and Gregg Mitman, "Introduction: The How and Why of Thinking with Animals," in *Thinking with Animals: New Perspectives on Anthropomorphism*, ed. Lorraine Daston and Gregg Mitman (New York: Columbia University Press, 2005), 7–8.

54. Eileen Crist, "Darwin's Anthropomorphism: An Argument for Animal-Human Continuity," *Advances in Human Ecology* 5 (1996): 33.

55. George Levine, *Darwin Loves You: Natural Selection and the Re-enchantment of the World* (Princeton, NJ: Princeton University Press, 2006), 226.

56. Richard O. Prum, "Aesthetic Evolution by Mate Choice: Darwin's *Really* Dangerous Idea," *Philosophical Transactions of the Royal Society B: Biological Sciences* 367 (2012): 2255.

57. Crist, "Darwin's Anthropomorphism," 35.

58. See ibid., 69. Also see Eileen Crist, *Images of Animals: Anthropomorphism and Animal Mind* (Philadelphia: Temple University Press, 1999); and Hollis Taylor, "Anecdote and Anthropomorphism: Writing the Australian Pied Butcherbird," *Australasian Journal of Ecocriticism and Cultural Ecology* 1 (2011): 1–20.

59. See, for instance, Julie Hecht and Caren B. Cooper, "Tribute to Tinbergen: Public Engagement in Ethology," *Ethology* 120, no. 3 (2014): 207–214.

60. Geoffrey Blainey, *Triumph of the Nomads: A History of Ancient Australia* (Sydney: Sun Books, 1997), 92.

61. John M. Peter, *Some Indigenous Names of Australian Birds* (Hawthorn East: Birds Australia, 2006), 7.

62. Philippe Descola, *The Ecology of Others,* trans. Geneviève Godbout and Benjamin P. Luley (Chicago: Prickly Paradigm Press, 2013), 84.

63. See Alyawarr Language Group, *Things That Birds Let You Know About,* poster published by the Central Land Council, the Australian Institute of Aboriginal and Torres Strait Islander Studies, and the Alice Springs Desert Park, undated; and Anmatyerr Language Group, *Things That Birds Let You Know About,* poster published by the Central Land Council, the Australian Institute of Aboriginal and Torres Strait Islander Studies, and the Alice Springs Desert Park, undated.

64. Author interview with Allan Marett, 5 January 2013. Also see Allan Marett, *Songs, Dreamings, and Ghosts: The Wangga of North Australia* (Middletown, CT: Wesleyan University Press, 2005).

65. H. H. Finlayson, *The Red Centre: Man and Beast in the Heart of Australia* (Sydney: Angus and Robertson, 1943), 91. I will refrain here from mounting a postcolonial critique of "Oriental."

66. Brian Elliott, "Jindyworobaks and Aborigines," *Australian Literary Studies* 8, no. 1 (1977): 50.

67. G. Révész, *The Introduction to the Psychology of Music* (London: Longmans, Green and Co, 1953), 225.

68. Marett, *Songs, Dreamings, and Ghosts;* Robin Ryan, e-mail message to the author, 1 June 2014; Milena Petrovic and Nenad Ljubinkovic, "Imitation of Animal Sound Patterns in Serbian Folk Music," *Journal of Interdisciplinary Music Studies* 5, no. 2 (2011): 101–118; and Steven Feld, *Sound and Sentiment: Birds, Weeping, Poetics, and Song in Kaluli Expression* (Philadelphia: University of Pennsylvania Press, 1990).

69. John Strehlow, *The Tale of Frieda Keysser, Volume I: 1875–1910* (London: Wild Cat Press, 2011), 953.

70. Capt. S. A. White, *Into the Dead Heart: An Ornithological Trip through Central Australia* (Adelaide: Friends of the State Library of South Australia, 1914/1998), 108–109.

71. See Ada Wood, "A Friend in Need," *Queenslander* (Brisbane, QLD), 12 January 1928, accessed 22 June 2011, http://nla.gov.au/nla.news-article22942929, 44; Dorothy Wall, "Blinky Bill Grows Up," a Project Gutenberg of Australia eBook, 1934, accessed 30 June 2011, http://gutenberg.net.au/ebooks04/0400571h.html; and Donna Brink Reid, *A Butcherbird Story* (Bassendean: Access Press, 2000).

72. See, for example, W.C.T., "The Butcher Bird," *Cairns Post* (QLD), 27 September 1930, accessed 22 June 2011, http://nla.gov.au/nla.news-article41054145, 9; Eureka, "Feathered Minstrels of the Bush: The Butcher Bird's Song," *Sydney (NSW) Morning Herald,* 13 February 1939: Women's Supplement, accessed 22 June 2011, http://nla.gov.au/nla.news-article17555296, 18 Supplement; and Thorny, "Outdoor Australia: Songbirds

of the Bush: A Varied Repertoire," *Sydney (NSW) Morning Herald*, 23 April 1940: Women's Supplement, accessed 22 June 2011, http://nla.gov.au/nla.news-article17668184, 14 Supplement.

73. Shirley Walker, *Roundabout at Bangalow* (St. Lucia: University of Queensland Press, 2001), 52. Also see Geoffrey Cousins, *The Butcherbird* (Crows Nest: Allen & Unwin, 2007).

74. See Reginald Godfrey, "Poems & Rhymes: In the Bush," *Register* (Adelaide, SA), 17 October 1925, 4; E. M. England, "A Butcherbird at Dawn," *Brisbane (QLD) Courier*, 3 May 1930, 20; Francy de Gryys, "Butcher Birds," *Outrider* 3, no. 1 (1986): 147; Harold Gascoigne, "A Butcherbird Sings," in *Our Friends the Birds* (Bribie Island: Bribie Laser Type & Print, 1991), 18; John Kinsella, "Rapt," in *The Hierarchy of Sheep* (Fremantle: Fremantle Press, 2001), 73; Francis Duggan, "The Pied Butcherbird," 8 January 2008, accessed 20 June 2011, http://www.poemhunter.com/poem/the-pied-butcherbird; and Robert Adamson, "Pied Butcher Bird Flute Solo," in *The Golden Bird* (Melbourne: Black, 2008), 262–263.

75. Aileen Kelly, "Call Her Butcher Bird," *Poetry Monash* 36 (1992): 9.

76. Judith Wright, *Birds* (Canberra: National Library of Australia, 2003), 1.

77. Chris Watson, interview with the author, 12 August 2011; Andrew Thelander, e-mail message to birding-aus@birding-aus.org, 3 July 2014; and Sydney Curtis, interview with the author, 5 August 2006.

78. Steve Bell, e-mail message to the author, 4 September 2013.

79. Alan Turpie, e-mail message to the author, 6 July 2009.

80. Helen Horton, e-mail message to the author, 6 September 2006; Robyn Howard, e-mail message to the author, 21 February 2005; and Alister Cameron, "Pied Butcher-Bird," *Sunbird: Journal of the Queensland Ornithological Society* 2 (1971): 78.

81. Jeffrey Bussolini, "Recent French, Belgian and Italian Work in the Cognitive Science of Animals: Dominique Lestel, Vinciane Despret, Roberto Marchesini and Giorgio Celli," *Social Science Information* 52, no. 2 (2013): 200, 201.

82. For *egomorphism*, see Kay Milton, "Anthropomorphism or Egomorphism? The Perception of Non-human Persons by Human Ones," in *Animals in Person: Cultural Perspectives on Human-Animal Intimacy*, ed. John Knight (Oxford: Berg, 2005), 255. For *generic anthropomorphism* versus *specific anthropomorphism*, see Pamela J. Asquith, "The Inevitability and Utility of Anthropomorphism in Description of Primate Behaviour," in *The Meaning of Primate Signals*, ed. Rom Harré and Vernon Reynolds (Cambridge: Cambridge University Press, 1984), 143, 139. For *mock anthropomorphism* and *neoanthropomorphism*, see John S. Kennedy, *The New Anthropomorphism* (Cambridge: Cambridge University Press, 1992), 9, 157, respectively. Some have proposed the term *multimorphism* to describe a less-biased way to situate our thinking about the multiple circles and lines that link the human and nonhuman. Levine has emphasized the term *zoömorphism* (*Darwin Loves You*, 197), also a familiar concept to philosopher of science Vinciane Despret, who is concerned with the social dynamics of how we are transformed by our kinship with animals (*Que dirait les animaux, si . . . on leur posait les bonnes questions?* [Paris: Éditions La Découverte, 2012]).

83. See Bernard E. Rollin, "Anecdote, Anthropomorphism, and Animal Behavior," in *Anthropomorphism, Anecdotes, and Animals*, ed. Robert W. Mitchell, Nicholas S. Thompson, and H. Lyn Miles (Albany: State University of New York Press, 1997), 125–133.

CHAPTER 3

The Nature of Transcription and the Transcription of Nature

No notation is a transparent representation of music; or, to put it the other way round, all notations are a blend of conformance, complementation and contest.
—Nicholas Cook, *Analysing Musical Multimedia*

LAMINGTON NATIONAL PARK, Queensland, 22 June 2005, 5:00 AM: I'm scrambling across a steep cliff track behind lyrebird expert Sydney Curtis. My small flashlight and I are barely up to navigating this cold, damp rainforest. We've come for the winter breeding, and thus singing, season of the Albert's lyrebird (*Menura alberti*). Curtis has been recording this individual, nicknamed "George," annually since 1984. Lyrebirds are powerful singers who, although they have their own territorial song, are best known for their mimicry of other species. Primarily ground-dwelling birds, they are understandably cautious, which explains why Curtis wants us in place well before sunrise. We stop at what he identifies as one of the bird's display platforms: trampled vines that George has modified to serve as a stage. Curtis places a microphone above it, attaching a long cord, and then we back off. I position myself behind a tree.

George begins in the distance, and after nearly an hour, he approaches the platform near us. An Albert's lyrebird is variously chestnut, red, orange, cream, and grey in body, complemented by a spectacular black, white, and silver tail. This hugely elongated appendage consists of a pair of long, broad feathers; another pair of ribbon-like plumes; and a dozen lacey, filamentous feathers.[1] When he arrives at his platform, George suddenly erects his tail over his head, partially spreads it like a fan, and begins to sing. The ethereal effect is à la Loïe Fuller, a theatrical play of light and shadow complete with flowing "veils." His head is in constant motion as he rocks his body from side to side. He mimics a number of avian species and other sounds. Lyrebirds are known to mimic wings beating, feathers rustling, feet thumping, bills snapping, frogs calling, and even people talking at a distance (as well as mechanical sounds when kept in captivity).

After about ten minutes, George moves his tail farther forward, enveloping himself. This heralds the dance section of his multifaceted performance. First, he balances himself on several crisscrossed vines. It's not apparent which of these "high wires" he should grab onto; none appear stable to me, but perhaps that is as it should be. He stretches a wing and curls it down. Then he grabs a vine and taps it against another. The immediate stage décor is vibrating vines and leaves set a-shimmer. This in turn shakes the vegetation in all directions of the understory, making for an enthralling spectacle.

Curtis describes how such a simple act, amplified by nature's available technical resources, can impact a wide area: "The effect can be quite surprising. The vines are thin and pliable; the movement is transmitted from one vine to another and along them to the surrounding screening vegetation. One meter away in one direction a small branch of a shrub will move up and down; perhaps a meter or so above it some leaves will shake; three meters away in another direction a large leaf will start to oscillate, and so on."[2]

Next, all mimicry ceases as George prances from foot to foot while jiggling his tail. Instead, he vocalizes clicks and clacks reminiscent of boomerangs and clapsticks, or castanets or even tap dancing. "Gronk!" George then alternates sections of his unmetered "gronking" song with synchronized singing, dancing, and drumming on the platform: "whoa-whap-whap, whoa-whap-whap." George performs in strict $\frac{3}{4}$ time. Other Albert's lyrebird populations may choose two, four, five, or even six beats to a bar, with all the males in an area adopting the same meter. Albert's lyrebirds in effect accompany their song with a homemade musical instrument—birdsongs are seldom so strictly measured.[3]

When done, George thrusts his tail feathers behind him and departs the partially concealed platform. Facing our direction, he gives a shake and heads off to his next platform. And *great* George's multimedia performance was. A photographer who invested eleven years before successfully filming George characterized the spectacle as "an Aboriginal corroboree dance" and George's demeanor as "dancing with all the showmanship of a Broadway entertainer."[4]

As Curtis and I walk back, I notice that even when the sun rises, competition for light is intense in the thick canopy. The cool temperate rainforest sports a mix of ancient, immense individuals: gnarled Antarctic beech (*Nothofagus moorei*), Moreton Bay figs (*Ficus macrophylla*) whose buttress roots seem to melt into the trunk and ground, a few hoop pines (*Araucaria cunninghamii*), and various eucalypts. We pass red-necked pademelons (*Thylogale thetis*), forest-dwelling marsupials who are grazing on leaves and mosses. Later, while warming up over coffee, Curtis asks, "I don't suppose you'd be interested in my correspondence with Olivier Messiaen, would you?"

CURTIS AND MESSIAEN: THE BIRDSONG TRANSCRIPTIONS

Responding to my keen "yes," Curtis proceeded to recount how, in a relationship that to that point had gone unreported outside his own circle, he had written to the composer in 1981 about lyrebird mimicry. Aware that Messiaen employed birdsong in his compositions, Curtis wanted to enlighten him about an avian corollary: lyrebirds who incorporated *human* music in their vocalizations. He sent a cassette, which he titled "Lyrebirds for Olivier Messiaen," containing his original recordings of the two species of lyrebird plus a letter of explanation on how the mapping of one musical language onto another is a cross-species practice.[5] He was rewarded with an enthusiastic and gracious thank-you letter from Messiaen. Curtis promised to send me a copy of the same recording, which he did, accompanied by this letter:

Dear Hollis,

The English, anxious to unload their convicts, established a colony in Australia in 1788. For our bicentennial celebrations, the French Government sponsored a visit by Olivier Messiaen to supervise performances of his works. And of course by Yvonne Loriod as well: in addition to being his wife, she could play the piano parts. . . . I thought that it was well-known that Messiaen was greatly interested in birdsong and that he used it extensively in his compositions. But as the time for his visit approached, there was no mention at all in the considerable publicity of any move to let him hear Australian birds, despite his never having visited this continent before. I had corresponded with him about birds and sent him some lyrebird recordings, so I wrote to point out that he would be here during the lyrebird season and I could arrange to have him taken to hear them if he wished.

His reply was most enthusiastic. He had thought that because he would be here in winter, no birds would be singing. I had given him hope. He immediately instructed the ABC to alter his itinerary so that I could take him to hear an Albert's Lyrebird and wrote to me that he was quite willing to leave his hotel at 4:00 AM if necessary to get to the lyrebirds at dawn. (A 5:00 AM start sufficed.) And the ABC finally got the message and arranged for him to hear Superbs—which had an important consequence.

When he died, Mme. Loriod-Messiaen, in replying to my condolence letter, said that his last major work, commissioned by the New York Philharmonic, was *Éclairs sur l'Au-Delà*, which he had been working on for four years. Sadly, he didn't live to hear its premiere in November 1992. It has 11 sections, and one is entirely devoted to the Superb Lyrebird. . . "*et ceci grace a vous*," she wrote. A comment I treasure.

I've never thought of perfect pitch in that way before. Until now, I've simply thought that a person with that wonderful facility could identify any note on the diatonic scale that they heard played. But birds (with some exceptions) don't sing on that scale, and I wondered how Messiaen could reproduce those in between frequencies so accurately. I still wonder how he notated them.

All the best,
Syd[6]

Messiaen did not hear George. Curtis took him to nearby Witches' Falls National Park, where a lyrebird roosted close to a fairly level part of the walking track. "I was able to get us into position before the lyrebird started calling from his roost—they start before there's much light at ground level," Curtis recalls. "His wife was operating a little recorder, and I held the torch [flashlight] while Messiaen notated."[7]

Messiaen's birdsong notebooks are housed in the Fonds Messiaen of the Département de la musique at the Bibliothèque nationale de France. Some two hundred *cahiers de notation des chants d'oiseaux* survive, totaling approximately ten thousand pages. In addition to music notation, the *cahiers'* marginalia incorporate comments on timbre, musical mood, tempo, and proposed orchestration, as well as Messiaen's personal reaction to the natural world. I contacted pianist and Messiaen scholar Peter Hill to acquaint him with Curtis's story. With Hill's assistance, we uncovered copies of six transcribed pages devoted to the Witches' Falls National Park outing. Three pages were done in the field; the other three are marked "second notation" and are apparently the result of a later transcription from the field recording.[8]

The composer was open about transcribing from his own field recordings. He felt that his second notations from the tape recorder were "more exact but less artistic."[9] Neither did he hide the fact that he listened to commercial ornithological recordings; for instance, he admitted to doing so in his interview with journalist Claude Samuel.[10] That he transcribed from these, however, is a matter he was less than open about.

No recordings from Messiaen's personal collection, neither commercial ones nor his own, are housed in the archives.[11] *Oiseaux exotiques* (1955–1956) is his first composition containing birdsong sourced in part from recordings, and musicologist Robert Fallon speculates that Messiaen may have changed the names of North American birds that he transcribed from a recording to conceal the composition's debt to it.[12] Perhaps his personal collection was never transferred to the archives for a similar reason. A portion of Messiaen's birdsong transcriptions from his *cahiers*, along with his analyses and examples from his compositions, are featured in volumes 5/1 and 5/2 of the *Traité de rythme, de couleur, et d'ornithologie*. The first is dedicated to the birdsong of Europe (France in particular), while the second attends to birdsong of the world. In these 1,300+ pages, I find no mention that any of his notations are transcribed from a recording.

Much ink has been spilt concerning Messiaen's use of birdsong in his compositions. At times he would transfer every nuance of his transcription into a piece, such as the nightingale he notated at Saint-Germain-en-Laye, who figures in the final phrases of the opening piano cadenza of

Réveil des oiseaux (1953). Other times, the composer intervened to a greater or lesser extent, especially in the later works, where dramatic flair, artistic license, and transformation surface regularly.

Music transcription entails the subjective and the reductive. Composer Béla Bartók held that "the only really true notations are the sound-tracks on the record itself."[13] Of course, this ignores technology's varying ability to capture and reproduce sonic properties, magnified by shellac's deficiencies of scratch and click, tape's propensity for wow and flutter, and so on. Listening cannot be classified as an objective act, and neither a recording nor a sonogram may be deemed an unassailable fact.

Messiaen's comments concerning his transcription accuracy and authenticity ping-ponged, sometimes complicated by a lack of clarity on whether the subject was composition or transcription. He clearly was addressing the latter when he told Samuel: "I'm the first to have made truly scientific and, I hope, accurate notations of bird songs."[14] There are those who, ignoring the totality of the composer's comments on accuracy and authenticity, romanticize his ear and cling to the mythology of a "truly scientific" Messiaen transcription. Contradictory statements by scholars, much like Messiaen's own, abound and acknowledge the difficulties of authenticity while, often in the same sentence, insisting on the composer's meticulousness—as if, should his birdsong transcriptions be found wanting, such a discovery would diminish his compositions. Like me, other musicologists are wary of claims of accuracy *chez* Messiaen, insisting that our attention should be on his compositional outcomes.

In browsing any number of books and articles containing birdsong notation from the nineteenth and early twentieth centuries, "quaint" might be the first word that springs to mind—the notations would look at home on a wine label or a greeting card. A simple phrase is typically formed almost entirely with quarter notes and eighth notes; set in $\frac{3}{4}$ or $\frac{4}{4}$ time; and floated on a page filled with, depending on the author, learned observations, sentimental text, or a mix of the two. Arriving on the heels of this, the visual appearance of Messiaen's detailed avian transcriptions, paired with his esteem as a composer, is difficult to dismiss and surely influences our appraisal of them. They look, in a word, *accurate*.

Is transcription accuracy germane? Fallon reasons that it is, not for proving or disproving issues of authenticity or for recovering the original birdsong, but for understanding the composer's "aesthetic of representation."[15] While in my work accuracy and recovery are highly relevant, it seems that composers' birdsong transcriptions can best be read as reflecting the priorities, interests, and enculturation of the individual rather than as proposing to be a scientific fact. Messiaen's birdsong transcription leans toward the prescriptive, a conclusion that I arrived at after studying his notations of three Australian birdsong cassettes.[16] I began with nineteen assorted Australian birdsongs on a cassette titled "Pour Messiaen," which Curtis sent to him in 1989. The composer transcribed most of these, along with the majority of birds from a 1977 cassette recording of Australian birdsong (*Bird Calls of the Inland*) of limited release that, like the Curtis recording, was likely unknown to musicologists, and those from a 1987 Jean C. Roché commercial release.[17]

My method was simple: transcribe the recordings; put both Messiaen's transcription and mine into a music notation program; export them as an audio file; and drop the audio into a sonogram and waveform application, along with the actual bird model. Mine conformed quite reasonably to the model. Messiaen's transcription was another story, and I was able to confirm with new precision what has long been suspected: that he did not wait until the moment of composition to transform the birdsong he notated. He actively and methodically established his creative presence at the moment of transcription, as evidenced by significant deviations from the recording in matters of pitch (allowing for a difference in tape speed), rhythm, dynamics, and portamentos. Sometimes, Messiaen disregarded notes or other elements of a song, while other times he included notes or other details not in the birdsong model. We had different goals.

Another dissemblance: since birdsong dictation must be accomplished at speed, I cannot reconcile Messiaen's omission of noteheads on repeated notes, indicating haste, with the time he then took to notate even slow birdsongs in sixteenth and thirty-second notes with their multiple "flags." I could speculate that thirty-second notes were Messiaen's nod to the fleeting nature of birdsong, but if he turned his back on the full range of rhythmic values available to him, ignoring eighth notes when he marked the tempo *lent*, something else must have been in operation. The look of a transcription can influence more than the reader. Musicologist, composer, and conductor Erhard Karkoschka maintained that notation systems influence both the act of composing and the thinking of musicians: "The aural image of a musical work in every epoch is characteristically related to its visual configuration."[18] For Messiaen, very short note values were pertinent because he would rely upon them in his score (consistent with the busy, complex look of the day that was modernist practice), favoring them decidedly over eighth notes or longer values.

Bartók's folk music transcriptions also aspired to contribute to scholarship. In his essay on compound (asymmetric) meters entitled "The So-Called Bulgarian Rhythm," he writes about the conflict between his enculturated transcription template and the material at hand:

> When I first saw these unfamiliar rhythms [$\frac{5}{16}$, $\frac{7}{16}$, $\frac{8}{16}$, and $\frac{9}{16}$] in which such fine differences are decisive, I could hardly imagine that they really existed. But then I seemed to remember that in my own collection of Rumanian material I had come across similar phenomena, but at that time had not dared—if I might put it that way—to take note of them. Among my old phonograph notations there were dance melodies which, with a perfectly clear conscience, I had noted down in $\frac{4}{4}$, in steady quarter-notes (or perhaps not with a perfectly clear conscience, because I had written on my notations: "the ends of the bars are drawn out in gipsy fashion").[19]

Bartók's 1951 monograph, *Serbo-Croatian Folk Songs*, features detailed transcriptions, a systematic arrangement, and analysis, all of which would be of interest to a Bartók scholar.[20] As I thumb through the book, however, I can imagine others who might draw on these pages, including composers, performers, ethnomusicologists, choreographers, and anthropologists—it's user-friendly. While detailed, it does not overwhelm with a sheer mass of information. George Herzog notes in his introduction that Bartók imagined the collector's and the composer's tasks and responsibilities as completely distinct. Bartók believed that the collector should gather and disseminate the material faithfully and exactly as he heard it, without any patronizing edits.[21] To be fair, "exactly" is subjective and best imagined less as a discrete end point and more as rest stops along a continuum. Having asked provocatively, "Why do birds sound like birds, but Messiaen's birds sound like Messiaen?" composer Alexander Goehr answers the question in his chapter "The Messiaen Class." Recalling that although Messiaen pretended he was simply transcribing birdsongs, "in reality it hardly mattered musically which particular bird he thought he was transcribing; his inventiveness and supreme musical personality revealed itself in the way he set down his transcriptions."[22] Messiaen's transcriptions suggest that he dealt with the tasks of collecting and composing as interwoven and interdependent components, unlike—or at least less like—Bartók, who attempted to separate the activities.

I feel strongly, as did Bartók, about keeping my transcriptions and (re)compositions of them as separate as possible. Of course, the transcriptions bear my fingerprint and benefit from the familiarity that comes from performing them, but I am open to all the acoustic efforts of a bird and not simply those I might use in a composition. My transcriptions sit first and foremost inside birdsong analysis, not inside composition.

MUSIC NOTATION MECHANISMS

As I began to imagine the graphic outcomes of my research, I explored what, if anything, I might find to supplement conventional Western notation. The cultures of China, Korea, Japan, and Europe have been particularly notation-prone.[23] The earliest music notations in China predate 100 CE.[24] Intriguingly, one anonymous fourteenth-century Chinese textbook fails to offer up explicit symbols. The *Great Treatise on Supreme Sound* describes the *gesture* required to produce a sound. The movements of animals are called upon to provide the metaphor for lute students: "an emaciated crow . . . pecking at the snow," "the nonchalant flick of a carp's tail," and "a sacred turtle emerging from the water." To produce a harmonic, one should touch a string lightly, like a "white butterfly fluttering at flower level."[25] The treatise goes beyond rich descriptions of hand motions and sound qualities; it also serves as a window onto Chinese modes of thinking, including an acceptance of parallels in even diverse contexts, an approach to learning by awareness, the role of instinct, and the importance of the mind-body link in performance. This prompts me to wonder what the West's notation might tell the Chinese about us.

Both the vocal and instrumental traditions of Japan have been preserved in part-books. Rather than represent pitch, the instrumental books combine fingerings with mnemonics to help the reader recall the melodic contour and ornamental nuances; rhythm is not indicated, although dots correspond to when each time-marking instrument plays.[26] In this, the part-books resemble many efforts at birdsong transcription. Hopefully, future scholarship will tell us more in particular about the notation of birdsong beyond the West.

My whistle-stop tour had many other visits but soon forced me to acknowledge a bias: my notation goals were pitch- and rhythm-centric. Mine was a nuts-and-bolts approach. Thus, the flamboyant, colorful, and unconventional but also vague and idiosyncratic shapes of the West's neumatic notation had nothing to offer me.[27] As recent as the late Middle Ages (ca. 1270–ca. 1410), works based on birdsong could scarcely be notated due to the lack of sub–half note rhythmic values; notational innovation was required to represent what was already being performed by vocalists in the oral tradition.[28]

The West's visual analogue of music has been reasonably stable since shortly after the invention of the printing press (music began to be printed ca. 1480) and is widely embraced.[29] Composer and musicologist Gardner Read is not the first to challenge the stock axiom that music is the international language, which he dismisses as "myth perpetuated." However, in his manual on modern notation practice, he does not entirely forgo the concept of *universality*. It is not musical sounds, he believes, but their *written symbols* that cross borders and languages with ease—specifically, conventional Western musical notation.[30] While it often does serve as a lingua franca, this codification, with its fixed tones and durations, has the potential to impede musical possibilities even as it opens others up. Notation acts as a filter—it is a bouncer at the door deciding who and what get in and who and what stay out. Nonetheless, my search ended where I began: I find it difficult to resist or improve on this technology, which efficiently carries large amounts of universally understood information.

Although fundamentally static, Western notation does not go uncontested. The twentieth century saw new notation systems come and go in fits and starts, often reflecting the priorities of individual composers rather than being proposals for new universal systems. Scrolling animated notations of canonic Western art music are now commonplace on the Internet—these flip the score from performer's tool to audience's polychromatic entertainment. Most of what is written about notation comes from specialists, including post–World War II avant-garde and electronic composers, who considered the subject from the perspective of reform in their movement away from exact pitch and rhythm structures toward the independence of material structures best suited to graphics, and from ethnomusicologists, who faced the issue of whether to render the music of their study areas in conventional notation.

MUSIC NOTATION IN ETHNOMUSICOLOGY

Ethnomusicological notation focuses on descriptive outcomes over prescriptive ones. Otto Abraham and Erich M. von Hornbostel published a comprehensive treatise in 1909 on how to transcribe traditional, or "exotic," music, urging that deviations from standard notation be kept to a minimum.[31] Many ethnomusicologists have split the difference, pairing their notations, with no or only slight modifications, with supplemental text or graphics while also cautioning against new inventions that could only appeal to a handful of specialists, as well as against notating small pitch deviations that might make the notation too dense.[32]

Similarly, ethnomusicologist and social anthropologist John Blacking employed conventional notation for his analysis of the musical life of the Venda people, contenting himself with pitch values near enough for practical purposes. Although Blacking held birdsong at arm's length in his definition of music, I can imagine replacing "Venda music" with "pied butcherbird song" in his statement that Venda music is "systematic and logically organized, but not necessarily like any other musical system." In addition, his discussion of how musical capacities reside in deep structures in the mind and body waiting to be brought out strikes a parallel with ethologists' discussions of a bird's song template and predisposition to learn.[33]

Four eminent ethnomusicologists notated a Hukwe song with bowed accompaniment for a 1964 symposium. A cursory glance at the results finds nearly as much separating as uniting them.[34] A transcription will always be a hit-or-miss affair, omitting perhaps important details while prone to the introduction of elements from the transcriber's own musical experience to fill in the gaps. With a limited sample, a commitment to laborious work is not interchangeable with direct and prolonged contact in the field. Was it a skilled and representative performance? Was it microtonal or simply out of tune? Nuanced knowledge arrives by working with a sizeable quantity of material, and the more variable a style, the more intimate the familiarity required in order to evaluate and notate. Ethnomusicological grappling with notation continues to this day, trailing behind it issues of accuracy, legibility, flexibility, utility, and idiosyncrasy.

Musicologist Kofi Agawu turns the tables on Read, arguing, "The *problem* of notation is a universal one." He makes the case that our current system suffers inadequacies even for Western art music, since it entails translating actions, reading codes, deciphering signs, and, ultimately, subjectivizing meaning.[35] Whatever is not described must be transmitted externally via a teacher or a supplement. Does it show more regard for African music, or pied butcherbird song, to drop it into standard music notation or to create a wholly new notation style for it? Agawu holds with the former, and his supplement paired with conventional Western notation echoes my inclination. To invent a new notation is to exoticize, to build on difference, while to place the music being scrutinized in conventional notation is to bring it into "a sphere of discourse that is enabled by a distinguished intellectual history and undeniable institutional power," Agawu believes.[36] Ideology and politics can infiltrate the seemingly neutral act of notation.

A transcriber faces the challenge of where to settle on the spectrum from the essential to the detailed in a number of parameters, and this range of choices broadened substantially with the advent of recordings. Jaap Kunst, who coined the word "ethnomusicology," puts the entire field in debt to the gramophone.[37] Recordings provide more than just a second check on the ear; they provide an opportunity for the collection of a vast amount of data and for deep familiarity with the subject. On the other hand, recordings allow researchers to content themselves with deskwork rather than fieldwork, as well as to shelve recordings and postpone analysis. The drawback to postponement is that insights gained from ethnomusicological (or zoömusicological) study could alert researchers to a pressing need to collect additional material while still possible.

As for the artifact itself, whether in the form of cylinder, disc, tape, or file, the recording is now perceived from many, some even hostile, viewpoints. On the one hand, for electronic and pop cultures the recording is accepted as the music, score, performance, *and* representation, arriving in a complete bundle. On the other hand, performers of improvised music may maintain skepticism about a recording not being "the real thing" but simply one snapshot frozen in time, and thus in terms of a transitory medium like music, a partial or even false representation—instead, you had to be there. For jazz, the contradiction is striking, since recordings have documented transformations from its beginnings in a way not possible on the written page. We can transcribe a recording, but we are documenting a sound twice removed from its source. No transcription is faultless in execution or ideal for every situation. Nonetheless, music notation is a powerful meaning-producing, connection-making heritage technology in search of a project, and pied butcherbird song is such a project.

BANKSIA GREEN CAMPGROUND, Myall Lakes National Park, New South Wales, 18 March 2013, 3:22 AM: A seven-note pied butcherbird fanfare awakens me. I know the drill—get up, grab the gear, and head out—but it's absolutely quiet again. I also know what the notes were. I could sit up and write them down, which is my instinct, but I have trained myself to only notate when I have a backup recording so I can double-check my work. I settle for experiencing the event without distraction.

TRADITIONAL AND INNOVATIVE METHODS OF BIRDSONG NOTATION

The story of birdsong notation reads quite differently from conventional notation's near-exclusive monopoly in Western music practice. In representing birdsong, people went in a multitude of directions. Some notated pitch, while others did not; some notated exact pitch, while others notated only relative pitch, or approximate pitch, or merely pitch contour. Some documented exact pitch in the field but did not present it in their unpitched graphics (withholding ledger lines), while others placed all phrases in the same key for comparison purposes. Both enthusiasts and specialists have notated birds' vocalizations, chiefly with the purpose of elevating birdsong to the status of music or of assisting in the identification of birds by their voice, but also of analyzing song. Many methods are graphic and do not require the user to read music.

Spoken/written syllables saw a similar plethora of outcomes. John Bevis distinguishes between onomatopoetic "bird words," which consist of the closest possible phonetic equivalents to the sounds bird make (nonsensical syllables like *widdock-waur* and *pi-weer pi-wee*), and mnemonics, which are composed of existing words like "swee-eet swee-eet peachy peachy" or "are you awake? me too."[38] They have at times been adopted as the popular name for a bird, like "bobolink." Nonsense syllables in English, however, can be problematical because of the language's nonstandard pronunciation. Since both nonsense and meaningful syllables are memory tools for birdsong identification and even some "nonsense" phrases contain recognizable words, I refer to all syllables, nonsense or not, as "mnemonics."

In this free-for-all, most methods overlap in at least some parameters. I will devote the lion's share of my attention to a few key examples. Anathasius Kircher was perhaps the first European to present transcriptions of birdsongs in his 1650 musicological monograph, *Musurgia Universalis*. In an oft-reproduced engraved plate, a nightingale, rooster, hen with her chicks, cuckoo, quail, and parrot share the page with notations of their songs. The five-line staves lack clef signs, he notates rhythm but suggests neither time signatures nor tempos, and he represents timbre via mnemonics (figure 3.1).[39]

Composer William Gardiner's 1832 monograph *The Music of Nature* features short, rudimentary transcriptions of animals and bears an ambitious subtitle: *An Attempt to Prove That What Is Passionate and Pleasing in the Art of Singing, Speaking, and Performing upon Musical Instruments, Is Derived from the Sounds of the Animated World.* He would have us believe that whereas sound derives from the natural world, it is left to humans to make something of it.[40]

Birdsong boosterism motivated a number of birders to write monographs.[41] They believed song was the best way to identify birds or to interest the public in them, and so these volumes take the form of field guides, even if the voice and notation remain the primary focus. The 1896 publication of naturalist Charles A. Witchell's *The Evolution of Bird-Song, with*

Figure 3.1. Anathasius Kircher's transcriptions from *Musurgia Universalis* (see Eggington, "Anathasius Kircher").

Observations on the Influence of Heredity and Imitation placed him far ahead
of his contemporaries with a serious (though somewhat flawed) inquiry
into song learning, variation, mimicry, musicality, and the evolution of
birdcalls and songs. He combined mnemonics and simple conventional
notation with text detailing nine years' surveillance of Britain's wild birds.
However, he only notated the simplest phrases and did not fix pitch.[42]
While these early monographs identify birdsongs as music-like, none offers up a truly sophisticated birdsong transcription—one that takes full
advantage of the notational apparatus and that could serve as the basis
of analysis, for instance. I can only guess what these writers might have
produced had they had access to birdsong recordings.

The new and diverse systems proposed in the early decades of the twentieth century zigzag between a user-friendly approach and a scholarly one,
depending on the goal, although naturalist F. Schuyler Mathews managed to accomplish both. He believed birdsongs could be notated despite
their complexities. In addition to the nuanced textual descriptions of each
species' song in his 1921 *Field Book of Wild Birds & Their Music*, Mathews
employs conventional notation, adding mnemonics as needed. He clearly
privileges notation, proclaiming, "We will be scientific, and when the bird
. . . sings G sharp we will not hunt around for a syllable to represent it, but
put it on the musical staff where it belongs!"[43]

In *Songs of the Birds* (1923), zoölogist Walter Garstang begins with the
timbre of each bird's voice, assigning syllables to the sounds as appropriate; he then casts the syllables into a poetry-like rhythm. The jizz of
Garstang's birdsongs lies in their tone color and gesture—witness his
willow warbler: "Sip, sip, sip, see! Tee, tew, wee, tew! Witty, witty, wee-wee,
weetew!"[44] It's Kurt Schwitters! In fact, Garstang's mnemonics come in
the same decade as the artist's famed sound poem *Ursonate* (1922–1932).
Schwitters broke words down into syllables and letters reminiscent of
the combinatorial sonic abilities of birds that many ornithologists were
attempting to describe. It comes as no surprise, then, that an update on
this Dadaist sonata in primordial sounds animates it as a conversation
between two birds.[45]

Writer, historian, and ethnologist Johannes C. Andersen is a scholar
worthy of zoömusicologists' emulation. His 1926 monograph reviews New
Zealand songbird literature and includes his field notes gleaned from years

Example 3.1. Excerpts from Johannes C. Andersen's transcription of a chaffinch (*Fringilla coelebs*) on line 1, a tui (*Prosthemadera novaeseelandiae*) on line 2, and a bell-bird (*Anthornis melanura*) on line 3 (*Bird-Song and New Zealand Song Birds*, transcriptions drawn from pp. 91, 127, and 158, respectively).

of painstaking observation. The attention to detail in both his music notation and supplement are exemplary, and the book is dated in the best sense of the word (example 3.1). While avoiding sentimental or naive anthropomorphism, his language reminds us of how eminent natural historians used to write up their field notes: his similes and metaphors concerning timbral elements that defy notation ring like a bell and pop off the page, much like his birds do. For instance, he strikes a number of comparisons with New Zealand's tui (*Prosthemadera novaeseelandiae*): (1) "I could think of no similar sound excepting the hypothetical sound of a bell through a kazoo, suddenly muted as it struck the *e*"; (2) "as if the note popped like a cork from a bottle"; (3) "like the occasional jangling irregularities of inexpert bellringers"; (4) "the song could only be likened to a light and liquid fall of music from the bell of a convolvulus"; (5) "like the snapping and intermittent whirring of clockwork, as though his musical-box had been undergoing seasonal repairs, and was being tested principally as to its mechanism."[46]

Proposing a diagrammatic system of birdsong identification in 1935 that "anyone can learn," entomologist and ornithologist Aretas Saunders believed that fluctuations in pitch and time in his local birdsongs made them

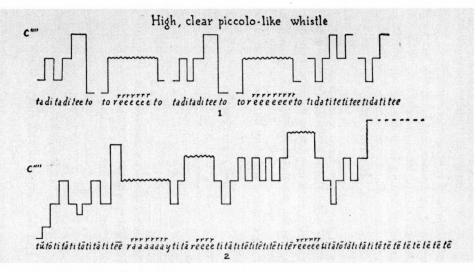

Figure 3.2. Aretas Saunders's transcription of a winter wren (*Nannus hiemalis*) song (*A Guide to Bird Songs*, 118).

unsuitable candidates for conventional music notation.[47] He combined a system of lines, dashes, and squiggles—a musical shorthand of sorts—with mnemonics (figure 3.2). His complicated devices involve up to four sounds and symbols for each vowel, which seems as difficult to learn as music notation while less precise, at least for songs with tonal aspects available to the human ear in the field. Saunders's system never took hold in a substantive way, and soon the sonogram would capture much of what he and others were attempting to describe—cast in a more positive light, the sonogram is a mechanized refinement of Saunders's system.

These monographs with birdsong notation have counterparts in a number of early twentieth-century articles in music journals—but also in ornithological ones.[48] This reminds us that a well-rounded education at that time included the ability to read and write music notation. While music literacy has ceased to be a prerequisite skill even in the music departments of some Western universities, the skill can be easily and quickly acquired. Having taught it to children and adults through the years, I do not think of this as specialist knowledge. A case in point: "I grew up in a very messy household," an audience member told me after I lectured. "One of my mother's forms of procrastination was to listen to the pied butcherbird and then say, I have to go and write this down. I've got lots of songs that have been written by Mum based on this. [Midway through whatever chore], she had to stop everything, and I can remember seeing clothes half hung and the basket still outside."[49]

Since notation is somewhat ineffectual in expressing timbre, those who focused on this aspect sought other solutions. Ornithologist Richard Hunt bemoaned the "each man for himself" jargon, arguing in 1923 that a codified terminology was sorely needed. Toward this end, he proposed a list of "bird sound designations," some of them mnemonic ("chip," "meow," and "quawk") and others descriptive ("drawl," "explosive," and "grasshopper-like").[50] At about five hundred in number, the list is long, and the concept largely relies on those Northern Hemisphere birds whose songs sound more like human speech than human music. At this same time, Andersen was finding his own words to describe the timbral outcomes of his New Zealand birds and notating them as well.

By the mid-twentieth century, efforts to elevate birdsong to the status of music begin to read less like a crusade and more like scholarly discourse. With the sonogram only just coming into use in the 1950s, researchers continued to find themselves drawn toward conventional notation, much of it skillfully crafted.[51] Biologist Loye Miller stands out for his commitment to notation. In putting down eleven phrases of the western meadowlark (*Sturnella neglecta*) in 1952, he concluded that the result was "a mere 'black and white still' of a rainbow-colored fountain of sound that defies capture and imprisonment, but the record does aid the memory."[52] We may linger on how at that time an ornithological journal allowed a UCLA professor of biology to incorporate both notated birdsong and text describing his deep engagement with a species.

Though scarcely acknowledged in the Anglophone world, composer Heinz Tiessen's systematic transcriptions and analyses of the vocalizations of the common blackbird (*Turdus merula*) see an attention to rhythmic detail that exceeds Messiaen's. *Musik der Natur* (1953) benefits from readings in ornithology as Tiessen follows the thematic development of phrases, with speculative harmonic analysis of them, over seasons and years by his musician-birds, regularly drawing parallels between their themes and works of Western art composers.[53]

Example 3.2. Excerpts from Olavi Sotavalta's transcription of a Sprosser nightingale (*Luscinia luscinia*) song ("Analysis of the Song Patterns," 9).

Zoölogist Olavi Sotavalta published an analysis of the complex song patterns of two Sprosser nightingales (*Luscinia luscinia*) in 1956. Guided by absolute pitch (the ability to identify a tone's pitch without an external reference pitch), his notations also surpass Messiaen's in detail and are paired with straightforward graphs, charts, tables, and textual description, none of which requires extensive insider knowledge of his system (example 3.2).[54] I find it intriguing but not surprising that Sotavalta made conventional notation an integral part of his scientific analysis.

A classic study of song development in the common blackbird by pianist and ornithologist Joan Hall-Craggs includes sonograms but also two conventional transcriptions.[55] The pairing of the two made an impression on me, even if she made no attempt to visually correlate them. As late as 1966, W. H. Thorpe, the leading songbird ethologist of the day, felt justified in eschewing sonograms and instead notating the duets of the tropical bou-bou shrike (*Laniarius aethiopicus*).[56]

The constant jockeying between the desire for simplicity of method, with its resultant lack of detail, and the need to formulate a more comprehensive, but demanding, system continued to increase. Something had to give. *Birds of North America: A Guide to Field Identification* (1966) by Chandler S. Robbings, Bertel Bruun, and Herbert S. Zim was the first field guide to offer sonograms, followed a decade later by Poul Bondesen's

Example 3.3. Péter Szőke's transcription of a hermit thrush (*Catharus guttatus*) song (Szőke, Gunn, and Filip, "The Musical Microcosm of the Hermit Thrush," 434).

North American Bird Songs—a World of Music (1977).[57] The sonogram, however, received a challenge from scientist and musicologist Péter Szőke, whose study of the intonation structure of bird vocalizations declared the algorithm used in the fast Fourier transform (FFT) to be inadequate for pitch. He claimed the sonogram was never designed with the primary goal of revealing the musical properties of birdsong. Szőke is also critical of the "foredoomed experiments of primitive musical transcription of bird voices" such as those of Kircher and even Tiessen, whom Szőke labels a "romantic" who merely relied on his naked ear and thus crafted superficial transcriptions that miss most of the goings-on. For instance, Szőke reckons he can find ten to twenty times the number of musical elements in the song of a chaffinch that are lost to the human ear unless the birdsong is significantly slowed down.[58] He pairs his detailed conventional notations with frequency graphs produced by a machine designed by his coauthor, Miroslav Filip, in a process of "sound microscopy" that slows down birdsongs by up to thirty-two times.[59] Such extreme deceleration could produce sound artifacts not present in the original, resulting in accurate transcriptions from somewhat inaccurate sources. Nonetheless, Szőke's transcriptions are impressive (example 3.3).[60]

Example 3.4. An excerpt from David Hindley's transcription of a nightingale song ("The Music of Birdsong," 30).

Other transcribers also slowed down their recordings in order to craft highly detailed transcriptions.[61] Composer David Hindley's supplemental text betrays his sensitivity to the nuances of sound's materiality in a comparison of how a nightingale changed the timbre of his voice much like an organist might toggle stops "to provide an 'edge,' a nasal quality," in what is almost a spectralist's approach (example 3.4).[62] A musician analyzing a bird's song offers essential insights not generally gleaned from contemporary ethologists' reports.

Hindley also participated in "salvage musicology."[63] The New Zealand huia (*Heteralocha acutirostris*) became extinct circa 1907 after overhunting, likely because of their long, metallic, bluish-black tail feathers, which were much in demand by milliners, museums, and private collectors. With only a few references—written descriptions and whistled imitations—Hindley reconstructed the song, which he then set into a synthesized composition that included the sonic background of the huia's territory on New Zealand's North Island.[64]

While all systems have adherents and detractors, this survey of traditional and innovative methods of birdsong notation closes with some clear winners and losers. The losers are, by definition, personalized systems that failed to become institutionalized: graphics, syllabic mnemonics, bird sound characterizations, or any combination of these. Nevertheless, these ad hoc systems, along with the pencil, remain relevant to individuals: "I don't have Finale [music transcription software] on this laptop, so I can only describe how I would notate your sample Butcherbird. First, it's mostly a diminished chord, all minor thirds except one full tone step (4th to 5th note), though it doesn't sound diminished immediately—maybe because of that one step. Of course, there's the universal birdy-glissando at the high note. Second, the di-dit-dah at the end could be notated by a quintuple: $\frac{1}{5}, \frac{2}{5}, \frac{3}{5}$, di-dit-dah, repeated."[65]

The winner is the sonogram. In a sense, the sonogram has come to serve science much the same way conventional notation has served music—as a universal graphic instrument. The runner-up is the supplement, which is typically textual but may even incorporate pertinent elements from the losing systems. Another winner is my smart phone app, which puts the sounds of most Australian birds at my fingertips. Its win, however, is artificial. Much like a television screen, the app's connection to reality is tenuous, framed, and constructed. We are not getting the whole story when we hear one or several individuals stand in for the entirety of a species' vocal culture.

Another loser: conventional Western music notation, which has completely fallen out of favor with ethologists. However, in the coming pages, I will make a case for the use of this marginalized but powerful technology, along with musicology's analytic apparatus, in at least some birdsong studies. Especially when linked with technologies like sonographic analysis, waveform analysis, and other software systems designed to manage the acquisition and analysis of large amounts of data, music notation has significant contributions to make in birdsong research. Taking techniques and ideas from one field into another invigorates them both, and the cross-fertilization of sonograms into musicology and music notation into the natural sciences fits that bill.

THE NOTATION AND ANALYSIS OF PIED BUTCHERBIRDS

This chapter comes full circle, arriving back at Messiaen. At least eight pied butcherbird transcriptions appear in his *cahiers de notation des chants d'oiseaux* (my collection is possibly incomplete; there might be others). The composer was diligent in naming each bird's entrance in his scores, allowing us to track the pied butcherbird in his final completed work,

Éclairs sur l'Au-Delà. The species has the unique distinction of supposedly appearing in three movements: IV, VIII, and X. "As the sole bird to be heard in the tenth movement, it is also the last bird to be heard in the work," explains musicologist Christopher Dingle.[66] However, the "soloist" in the tenth movement is actually a pair of grey butcherbirds from a Curtis recording. In this, Messiaen's transcription and composition match one another but correspond poorly with the grey butcherbird model. Again, the composer seemingly only transcribed those song elements that interested him in compositional mode: rhythm and pitch match partially, but the essence of the song to this auditor would be the long vivid ascending and descending glissando rattles, which were not captured in his notation. In the other two movements, Messiaen drew on the species call and song motifs that he identifies in the score as belonging to a pied butcherbird, although I am unable to trace these exact motifs back to any of his transcriptions in my possession.

Recordings have made obsolete the "preserve for posterity" imperative in birdsong transcription. I consider notation a form of analysis, one that offers a deep musical engagement. The products of notation can be what ethnomusicologist Charles Seeger identified as either a blueprint or a report—mine are often called upon to be both, but never at the same time.[67] The "report" serves as the basis of my analysis. My violin performances of pied butcherbird song are based on the "blueprint," where I allow myself the (re)composerly freedom to adjust the notation to my and the instrument's needs and sensibilities.[68] Each outcome informs and improves the other.

Technology can help us with things that we grasp intuitively and by ear; it can flesh out hunches. I double-check the pitch of each note in the sonogram window, but in matters of uncertainty, I defer to my ear and musical sensibility for the final decision (I have absolute pitch). This aligns with Bartók's observation that "having the best material equipment is not enough: the equivalent intellectual equipment is just as important."[69]

In my early days of fiddling, dull basic versions of tunes filled the few available books. No fiddler played like this. I had to transcribe recordings to find out the real sonic story. Too basic a transcription makes for an incomplete one; a transcription can always be simplified later. That said, increasing the intricacy of detail beyond a certain point does not reliably improve accuracy or after-the-fact analysis, and finding the balance point between the two remains a challenge best taken up by a human, not a machine.

Many musicians and musicologists have registered struggles with transcription, which is on the wane.[70] Ethnomusicologist Marin Marian-Bălaşa captures the current state of affairs: "Difficult transcriptions impress no longer, and, as we can often see, comfortable, intellectually effortless listening is more appealing to everybody."[71] However, I am not in "everybody's" clutches. If we put contemporary comfort aside and demand a deeper encounter, transcription will bestow rewards on both its maker and its reader. I admit that even with years of notating diverse musical genres, I find transcription an intense, laborious, and repetitive process full of doubting, returning, and revising. Such a twisting course does not devalue a transcription but improves it. A sonogram, in contrast, takes mere seconds to make. You never expect to pin down a musical object and fix it for all time; it is, like a bird's song, dynamic and transitory.

The appendix catalogs notational abbreviations and other conventions for my birdsong transcriptions. The most challenging aspect is portamento—often mistakenly called a slur or a glissando, which implies production on an instrument with fixed semitones, like a piano or a harp. Portamentos complicate an analysis of the relational aspects of pitch that normally would ensue in Western music after identifying individual notes, from intervals to melodic contour, scales, and tonality—these key components of typological research fade or vanish.[72]

Automatic music notation may play a part in future birdsong research, but for now it has little to contribute in studies of free-living birds. The primary difficulty is the "intrusion" of the biophony (other animals' sounds), the anthrophony (human sounds—in this case, detritus like airplanes, vehicles, and other mechanical noises), and the geophony (nonbiological natural sound like wind, volcanoes, waves, rain, lightning, and avalanches).[73] It is not easy to capture a clean signal of a single individual. Filtering a recording can leave artifacts that then appear on the automatic music notation, which also founders when it comes to birds' noisy sounds, rapid notes, high pitches, microtones, and portamentos. In addition, even basic rhythmic groupings easily comprehended by a musician often exit automatic music notation looking like chicken scratchings.

Since notation impacts what we examine and what we potentially overlook, a supplement was crucial for the additional items I could track and questions I could follow. Of course, even a supplement will not capture all remaining elements, and any analysis will be incomplete. In mine, I follow items of interest to ethologists, others of interest to musicologists, and all of interest to me. While it is principally a measurement and classification document that relies on information already in the notation, some entries require returning to the original recording, like the start time and duration of each phrase and the interphrase interval, or tacit; "silence" post–John Cage is not a straightforward concept, although I must at times draw on the word. I consider such unvoiced gaps as musical components of the song. In the supplement, I also measure the duration of a rattle or trill and compute its pulse rate, as well as perform analysis, labeling phrases with letters and numbers when appropriate, that might reveal patterns and connections.[74]

This supplementary analysis also draws on and codifies field notes taken from the end of each recorded track, where I announce the night's and morning's proceedings. These observations range from how many birds sang to how many songposts a bird took up, and from which other species were present to whether the pied butcherbird was mature or immature, as well as whether I saw the bird or not. I also record the date, time, place, GPS reading, weather, time of sunrise, moon phase, and habitat. What is happening stage left and right in the stereo mix may require comment—the choreography of who was in which microphone and how that modulated during the course of the recording.

Each graph or code has advantages and disadvantages, merits and limits. I stop short of claiming that notation can capture the value of all musical cultures, human or animal. The fear that notation could provoke an overemphasis of the musical qualities in a bird's song is of scant concern here, since human listeners so readily hear pied butcherbird songs as music.[75] New methods for data collection will hopefully shed light on the structural rules surrounding memorization and retrieval of large amounts of sonic information and the decisional processes inherent in complex animal communication, but some birdsong analysis is artisanal work.[76] Mine is an integrated approach of conventional Western notation in partnership with sonograms and a supplement, all mediated by a trained ear, albeit one trained in human genres. The goal is to strike a balance and not to merely pile up additional analytical tools. Notation is my go-to gizmo. With it, when I hear birdsong, I connect it first not to theory but to other birdsong, to human song, and to internote relationships. My position is not anti-theory; I simply want theory that connects to real-life engagements—to things sounded and heard. The notations in the coming chapters show the way one resolute listener has heard particular pied butcherbird vocalizations and has represented what she heard.

NOTES

1. P. J. Higgins, J. M. Peter, and S. J. Cowling, eds., *Handbook of Australian, New Zealand & Antarctic Birds* (Melbourne: Oxford University Press, 2001), 5:129.

2. H. S. Curtis, "The Albert Lyrebird in Display," *Emu* 72, no. 3 (1972): 83. My reconstruction of the event is indebted to this article and to Glen Threlfo, *Albert Lyrebird: Prince of the Rainforest* (DVD, Canungra, QLD: O'Reilly's Rainforest Guesthouse, 2004).

3. H. S. Curtis, "Messiaen Meets Menura—Part 2," *AudioWings* 12, no. 1 (2009): 6. Regrettably, researchers have yet to follow up on this remarkable ability. Also see H. Sydney Curtis and Hollis Taylor, "Olivier Messiaen and the Albert's Lyrebird: From Tamborine Mountain to Éclairs Sur L'au-Delà," in *Olivier Messiaen: The Centenary Papers*, ed. Judith Crispin (Newcastle upon Tyne: Cambridge Scholars, 2010), 52–53; and Taylor, "Can George Dance? Biosemiotics and Human Exceptionalism with a Lyrebird in the Viewfinder," *Social Semiotics*, 2016, 1–17, accessed 18 September 2016, http://www .tandfonline.com/doi/abs/10.1080/10350330.2016.1223115?tab=permissions&scroll=top.

4. Michael Snedic, "Longing for Lyrebirds," *BBC Wildlife*, September 2008, 68, 69.

5. For more on the mystery of flute-mimicking lyrebirds, see Vicki Powys, Hollis Taylor, and Carol Probets, "*A Little Flute Music*: Mimicry, Memory, and Narrativity," *Environmental Humanities* 3 (2013): 43–70.

6. Sydney Curtis to the author, 14 August 2005. Thus it was that Curtis became one of three ornithologists to take Messiaen birding during his 1988 six-week tour of Australia.

7. Sydney Curtis, e-mail message to the author, 4 March 2013.

8. *Cahier* #23159.64–66 and *cahier* #23161.40–42, respectively.

9. Peter Hill and Nigel Simeone, *Messiaen* (New Haven, CT: Yale University Press, 2005), 208.

10. Olivier Messiaen and Claude Samuel, *Music and Color: Conversations with Claude Samuel*, trans. E. Thomas Glasow (Portland, OR: Amadeus Press, 1994), 93.

11. Peter Hill, e-mail message to the author, 4 February 2013. If Messiaen's personal collection of birdsong recordings is housed in his archives, it has yet to be cataloged and made available to scholars.

12. Peter Hill and Nigel Simeone, *Olivier Messiaen: Oiseaux Exotiques* (Farnham: Ashgate, 2007), 28, 32; and Robert Joseph Fallon, "Messiaen's Mimesis: The Language and Culture of the Bird Styles" (PhD diss., University of California, Berkeley, 2005), 211.

13. Béla Bartók and Albert B. Lord, *Serbo-Croatian Folk Songs* (New York: Columbia University Press, 1951), 3.

14. Messiaen and Samuel, *Music and Color*, 97.

15. Robert Fallon, "The Record of Realism in Messiaen's Bird Style," in *Olivier Messiaen: Music, Art and Literature*, ed. Christopher Dingle and Nigel Simeone (Aldershot: Ashgate, 2007), 115.

16. Hollis Taylor, "Whose Bird Is It? Messiaen's Transcriptions of Australian Songbirds," special issue, *Twentieth-Century Music* 11, no. 1 (2014): 63–100.

17. *Bird Calls of the Inland*, recorded by Harold and Audrey Crouch (cassette, South Australian Ornithological Association, 1977); and *Les plus beaux chants d'oiseaux*, recorded by Jean C. Roché (CD, Auvidis Tempo A6117, 1987).

18. Erhard Karkoschka, *Notation in New Music: A Critical Guide to Interpretation and Realisation*, trans. R. Koenig (London: Universal, 1966/1972), 1.

19. Benjamin Suchoff, *Béla Bartók Essays* (Lincoln: University of Nebraska Press, 1976), 44–45.

20. Bartók and Lord, *Serbo-Croatian Folk Songs*.

21. Ibid., xi. In a similar vein, Bartók wrote: "It is not enough to collect melodies for purely artistic reasons in order to later select only those with musical value. The primary considerations should be purely scientific: all melodies still in circulation should be collected, regardless of their artistic attributes" (Suchoff, *Béla Bartók Essays*, 4).

22. Hill and Simeone, *Olivier Messiaen: Oiseaux Exotiques*, 4; and Alexander Goehr and Derrick Puffett, *Finding the Key: Selected Writings of Alexander Goehr* (London: Faber & Faber, 1998), 50–51.

23. Ian D. Bent et al., "Notation, I: General," *Oxford Music Online* (Oxford: Oxford University Press, 2007–2014), accessed 16 January 2014, http://www.oxfordmusic online.com.

24. Hugo Cole, *Sounds and Signs: Aspects of Musical Notation* (London: Oxford University Press, 1974), 6.

25. François Jullien, *The Propensity of Things: Toward a History of Efficacy in China*, trans. Janet Lloyd (New York: Zone Books, 1999), 113, 115–116, 116, respectively. Also see Kenneth J. DeWoskin, *A Song for One or Two: Music and the Concept of Art in Early China* (Ann Arbor: Center for Chinese Studies, University of Michigan, 1982), 125.

26. William P. Malm, *Music Cultures of the Pacific, the Near East, and Asia* (Englewood Cliffs, NJ: Prentice-Hall, 1977), 195.

27. By the middle of the fourth century CE, neumatic notation had supposedly expanded to over 1,600 various signs, symbols, and letters (Gardner Read, *Music Notation: A Manual of Modern Practice* [New York: Taplinger Publishing Company, 1969/1979], 5). A number of other systems of letters, heavy dots, small curved lines, diamond shapes, and squared-note forms gradually found their way onto staves (and some still do). Staff lines were added and taken away; some were colored.

28. See Elizabeth Eva Leach, *Sung Birds: Music, Nature, and Poetry in the Later Middle Ages* (Ithaca, NY: Cornell University Press, 2007), 119, who summarizes the research of Anne Stone.

29. Two significant developments shifted Western notation toward a codification of practice. First, in the eleventh century the scholar-monk Guido of Arezzo systematized clef signs and the number and arrangement of staff lines. The invention of the printing press both expedited the printing of music and slowed to a near halt the evolution of notation, which might have continued to change if not standardized by the printing press (Read, *Music Notation*, 23).

30. Ibid., 3.

31. Otto Abraham and Erich M. von Hornbostel, "Suggested Methods for the Transcription of Exotic Music," *Ethnomusicology* 38, no. 3 (1994): 427.

32. See, for instance, Helen H. Roberts, "Melodic Composition and Scale Foundations in Primitive Music," *American Anthropologist*, n.s., 34, no. 1 (1932): 102; Mervyn McLean, "A Preliminary Analysis of 87 Maori Chants," *Ethnomusicology* 8, no. 1 (1964): 41–48; and Monique Brandily, "Songs to Birds among the Teda of Chad," *Ethnomusicology* 26, no. 3 (1982): 381.

33. John Blacking, "Tonal Organization in the Music of Two Venda Initiation Schools," *Ethnomusicology* 14, no. 1 (1970): 4, 1, 2, respectively.

34. Robert Garfias, "Transcription I," *Ethnomusicology* 8, no. 3 (1964): 233–40; Mieczyslaw Kolinski, "Transcription II," *Ethnomusicology* 8, no. 3 (1964): 241–251; George List, "Transcription III," *Ethnomusicology* 8, no. 3 (1964): 252–265; and Willard Rhodes, "Transcription IV," *Ethnomusicology* 8, no. 3 (1964): 265–272.

35. Kofi Agawu, "The Invention of 'African Rhythm,'" *Music Anthropologies and Music Histories* 48, no. 3 (1995): 390, emphasis added.

36. Ibid., 390, 392–393.

37. Jaap Kunst, *Ethnomusicology* (The Hague: Martinus Nijhoff, 1974), 12.

38. John Bevis, *Aaaaw to Zzzzzd: The Words of Birds* (Cambridge, MA: MIT Press, 2010), 113.

39. See Timothy Eggington, "Anathasius Kircher," in "Anathasius Kircher, *Musurgia universalis*, 1650," accessed 19 January 2016, https://www.reading.ac.uk/web/FILES/special-collections/featurekircher.pdf. Also see "Anathasius Kircher, *Musurgia universalis*," accessed 20 January 2016, https://standrewsrarebooks.files.wordpress.com/2013/04/kircher-musurgia-bird-song.jpg.

40. William Gardiner, *The Music of Nature: An Attempt to Prove That What Is Passionate and Pleasing in the Art of Singing, Speaking, and Performing Upon Musical Instruments, Is Derived from the Sounds of the Animated World* (London: Longman, Orme, Brown, Green, and Longmans, 1840).

41. See James Edmund Harting, *The Birds of Middlesex: A Contribution to the Natural History of the County* (London: John Van Voorst, 1866); and Simeon Pease Cheney, *Wood Notes Wild: Notations of Bird Music* (Boston: Lee and Shepard, 1892).

42. Charles A. Witchell, *The Evolution of Bird-Song, with Observations on the Influence of Heredity and Imitation* (London: Adam and Charles Black, 1896).

43. F. Schuyler Mathews, *Field Book of Wild Birds & Their Music* (New York: Dover Publications, 1921/1967), xvii.

44. Walter Garstang, *Song of the Birds* (London: John Lane the Bodley Head, 1923), 44. Stanley Morris is another ornithologist who proposed mnemonics (*Bird Song: A Manual for Field Naturalists* [London: Witherby, 1925]).

45. See the two online versions of "Kurt Schwitters Ursonate" listed in the bibliography. Sound colors were also the focus of Gladys Page-Wood. In her unpublished manuscript (written between ca. 1927 and 1932), she used colors to express timbre, including differing shades of blue for whistled notes, and indicated micro-intervals by adding two, three, or four lines within the existing five-line staff. See Trevor Hold, "The Notation of Bird-Song: A Review and Recommendation," *Ibis* 112, no. 2 (1970): 160.

46. Johannes C. Andersen, *Bird-Song and New Zealand Song Birds* (Auckland: Whitcombe & Tombs Limited, 1926). Chapters from this book are available from *Transactions and Proceedings of the Royal Society of New Zealand 1868–1961*. Text quotes are from 118, 123, 124, 128, 130.

47. Aretas A. Saunders, *A Guide to Bird Songs: Descriptions and Diagrams of the Songs and Singing Habits of Land Birds and Selected Species of Shore Birds* (Garden City, NY: Doubleday & Company, 1935/1951), front cover. In 1938, while studying the Kirtland's

warbler (*Dendroica kirtlandi*), zoölogist and trained musician Harold H. Axtell paired
Saunders's shorthand with Brand's film soundtrack, concluding, "Although the human
ear is a relatively imperfect recording device, it does pick out the essentials." Axtell's
mnemonic renderings of birdsongs ran into the hundreds ("The Song of Kirtland's Warbler," *Auk* 55 [1938]: 481–491).

48. See Charles N. Allen, "Bird Music: Songs of the Western Meadow-Lark," *Century
Illustrated Monthly Magazine* 36 (1888): 908–911; Charles N. Allen, "Songs of the Western Meadow Lark (*Sturnella neglecta*)," *Auk* 13, no. 1 (1896): 145–150; L. Belding, "Songs
of the Western Meadowlark," *Auk* 13, no. 1 (1896): 29–30; Henry W. Oldys, "Parallel
Growth of Bird and Human Music," *Harper's Monthly Magazine* 105 (1902): 475; and
Hans Stadler and Cornel Schmitt, "The Study of Bird-Notes," *British Birds* 8, no. 1
(1914): 2–8. Also see W. B. Olds, "Bird-Music," *Musical Quarterly* 8, no. 2 (1922): 242–
255; Alexander Brent Smith, "The Blackbird's Song," *Musical Times* 63, no. 953 (1922):
480–481; Lucy V. Baxter Coffin, "Individuality in Bird Song," *Wilson Bulletin*, June 1928,
98–99; Edward R. G. Andrews, "Bird Songs," *Musical Times* 71, no. 1,047 (1930): 446;
and Ludwig Koch, *Memoirs of a Birdman* (London: Country Book Club, 1956).

49. Fiona Burless, interview with the author, 14 November 2015.

50. Richard Hunt, "The Phonetics of Bird-Sound," *Condor* 25, no. 6 (1923): 202,
206–208. Also see William Rowan, "A Practical Method of Recording Bird-Calls,"
British Birds 18, no. 1 (1924): 14–18; D. S. Falconer, "Observations on the Singing of the
Chaffinch," *British Birds* 35, no. 5 (1941): 98–104; and M. E. W. North, "Transcribing
Bird-Song," *Ibis* 92 (1950): 99–114.

51. Heinz Tiessen, *Musik der Natur* (Passau: Atlantis Verlag, 1953). Professor Dr. A.
Voigt's field guide provides detailed description of the vocalizations of 305 bird species,
along with behavioral information. He mixes up mnemonics, symbols (dots and dashes
of varying heights, thicknesses, and spacings), and notations, often drawing on all three
in order to best describe the songs and calls in question (*Exkursionsbuch zum Studium
der Vogelstimmen* [Leipzig: Verlag Quelle & Meyer, 1950]).

52. Loye Miller, "Songs of the Western Meadowlark," *Wilson Bulletin* 64, no. 2 (1952):
106–107.

53. Tiessen, *Musik der Natur*. Blackbird phrases are the basis for many Tiessen
compositions, beginning with the Septet, op. 20 (1915). In his archives, one transcription
folder is entitled "Amseln" (blackbirds), in which he compiled 312 phrases from 1909
to 1945. The first page is a hand-drawn map of his trips around Berlin and beyond. The
product of a calligraphy pen, each phrase is identified with a location and date.

54. Olavi Sotavalta, "Analysis of the Song Patterns of Two Sprosser Nightingales,
Luscinia luscinia," *Annals of the Finnish Zoological Society "Vanamo"* 17, no. 4 (1956): 2.

55. Joan Hall-Craggs, "The Development of Song in the Blackbird," *Ibis* 104, no. 3
(1962): 277–300.

56. W. H. Thorpe, "Ritualization in Ontogeny. II. Ritualization in the Individual
Development of Bird Song," *Philosophical Transactions of the Royal Society B: Biological
Sciences* 251, no. 772 (1966): 354.

57. Chandler S. Robbings, Bertel Bruun, and Herbert S. Zim, *Birds of North America:
A Guide to Field Identification* (New York: Golden Press, 1966); and Poul Bondesen,
North American Bird Songs—A World of Music (Klampenborg, Denmark: Scandinavian
Science Press, 1977). Bondesen's monograph sees a rare interdisciplinary meeting of the
natural sciences and music: he draws terminology from the discipline of music and ap-
plies it to sonograms.

58. P. Szőke, W. W. H. Gunn, and M. Filip, "The Musical Microcosm of the Hermit
Thrush: From Athanasius Kircher's Naive Experiments of Musical Transcription of Bird

Voice to Sound Microscopy and the Scientific Musical Representation of Bird Song," *Studia Musicologica Academiae Scientiarum Hungaricae* 11, no. ¼ (1969): 431, 427.

59. Szőke and Filip, "The Study of Intonation Structure." Szőke hails from the Hungarian ethnomusicological school of Bartók and Kodály.

60. Szőke, Gunn, and Filip, "The Musical Microcosm," 434.

61. Brian James, "The Rhos Blackbirds—1980–89," *Wildlife Sound* 6 (1990): 42–45; and David Hindley, "The Music of Birdsong," *Wildlife Sound* 6, no. 4 (1990): 25–33.

62. Hindley, "The Music of Birdsong," 30.

63. Rugula Burckhardt Qureshi, "Other Musicologies: Exploring Issues and Confronting Practice in India," in *Rethinking Music*, ed. Nicholas Cook and Mark Everist (Oxford: Oxford University Press, 1999), 317.

64. David Hindley, *Lifesong: Amazing Sounds of Threatened Birds* (cassette, Cambridge: Mankind Music, 1992), liner notes.

65. Alan Powers, e-mail message to the author, 29 June 2011. Also see Alan Powers, *Birdtalk* (Berkeley: Frog, Ltd., 2003).

66. Christopher Dingle, *Messiaen's Final Works* (Farnham: Ashgate, 2013), 143.

67. Charles Seeger, "Prescriptive and Descriptive Music-Writing," *Musical Quarterly* 44, no. 2 (1958): 184.

68. See, for example, Hollis Taylor, *Riffingbirds* for solo violin (Wollongong: Wirripang Press, 2009). Works for other instrumentations include Hollis Taylor, *Bird-Esk* for string quartet (Wollongong: Wirripang Press, 2009); and Hollis Taylor, *Cumberdeen Dam V & T* for solo bassoon (Wollongong: Wirripang Press, 2009).

69. Suchoff, *Béla Bartók Essays*, 10.

70. See, for example, Doris Stockmann, "Die Transkription in der Musikethnologie: Geschichte, Probleme, Methoden," *Acta Musicologica* 51, no. 2 (1979): 204–245; and Jason Stanyek, "Forum on Transcription," special issue, *Twentieth-Century Music* 11, no. 1 (2014): 101–161.

71. Marin Marian-Bălaşa, "Who Actually Needs Transcription? Notes on the Modern Rise of a Method and the Postmodern Fall of an Ideology," *World of Music* 47, no. 2 (2005): 22.

72. Of portamentos, Craig observed, "The slur itself is a unit. For it is not just any slur; it is a perfectly definite slur which is repeated again and again" (Wallace Craig, *The Song of the Wood Pewee* Myiochanes virens Linnaeus: *A Study of Bird Music*, vol. 334 [Albany: University of the State of New York, 1943], 164). Frederick R. Burton encountered difficulties in notating Native American songs with portamento, bemoaning the "vagueness" (*American Primitive Music* [New York: Moffat, Yard and Company, 1909], 22), and Bartók also found such notation challenging (*Béla Bartók Studies in Ethnomusicology* [Lincoln: University of Nebraska Press, 1997], 1).

73. Musician and wildlife recordist Bernie Krause coined these terms in *Wild Soundscapes: Discovering the Voice of the Natural World* (Berkeley: Wilderness Press, 2002), 152.

74. I document ascending and descending octave leaps, arpeggios, instances of transposition, the widest ascending and descending leap of a song, and the highest and lowest pitch in a song. I also track the presence of calls, mimicry, timbral effects, certain recurrent intraspecific note combinations, and more.

75. See Charles W. Dobson and Robert E. Lemon, "Bird Song as Music," *Journal of the Acoustical Society of America* 61, no. 3 (1977): 888.

76. See, for instance, Michael Weiss et al., "The Use of Network Analysis to Study Complex Animal Communication Systems: A Study on Nightingale Song," *Proceedings of the Royal Society B: Biological Sciences* 281 (2014): 1–9.

CHAPTER 4

Notes and Calls

A Taste for Diversity

> The unifying theme in the primatology done by women has been
> their high likelihood of being skeptical of generalizations and their
> strong preference for explanations full of specificity, diversity, com-
> plexity, and contextuality.
> —Donna Haraway, *Primate Visions*

YUNGABURRA, North Queensland, 8 June 2005: Now-extinct volcanoes
shaped the Atherton Tablelands. These wet tropics are as far north as I
intend to travel on my first recording trip. I head out just before 4:00 AM,
listening for anything that might be a pied butcherbird. I've still only heard
a few, so I am hoping I will recognize their voice. The morning is far from
stellar. Finally, at 6:50 AM a trio of birds flies out of a tree one by one. They
announce themselves with the same three-note flourish and then . . . nothing. I follow them for an hour—not a sound. A total waste of a day, or so I
think. We shall return to this Yungaburra trio.

I finish out the morning with more amenable creatures. The Tablelands are home to over a hundred mammal species, including thirteen
endemic to the region, like Lumholtz's tree-kangaroo (*Dendrolagus lumholtzi*)—yes, *tree*! Primarily folivores (leaf-eaters), they are extremely hard
to spot. They cannot curl their long, pendulous tail around branches, so
the instructions suggest that you look way, way up and pin the tail on the
. . . well, tree-kangaroos are actually heavy-bodied (the largest rainforest
marsupials), but by the time they have reached the heights, you just look
for a grey basketball with a tail. I was lucky to glimpse one in the shadows
during her brief foray on the ground.

Another iconic species here is that oddest of creatures, the platypus. This semiaquatic mammal lays leathery eggs in a nesting burrow on the bank of a creek. Their fur coat is waterproof, and their wide, flat tail is multipurpose. They have webbed feet with sharp claws, and the male has a toxic spur on his hind leg. More than forty thousand electrosensors in their soft, tubular bills aid these agile swimmers in finding and feeding on aquatic insects, fish, frogs, crustaceans, and worms. After peering into Peterson's Creek for a good length of time, I notice slow concentric ripples in the water. Then a platypus surfaces. Improbably constructed and impossibly cute—small wonder that the platypus is featured on the reverse of our twenty-cent coin and is the animal emblem of the state of New South Wales. However, my thrill is short-lived; I'm brooding about pied butcherbirds, who are barely singing right now. I've come at the wrong time. I begin to doubt my entire trip, my project even. There are just too many things I don't know.

When I began later to analyze my eventual recordings, no how-to field manual in zoömusicology awaited me. In fact, my field looked more like a vacant lot. I began nudging things along, conscious I was operating on guesswork—although hopefully the inspired guess. Rather than beginning on the level of songs, I began with a detailed look at the most basic kinds of sounds pied butcherbirds make.

BASIC NOTE STRUCTURE

Imagining each species with its own repertoire of characteristic sounds—those available to their anatomy, suitable to their purposes, and pleasing to them—I tallied basic pied butcherbird note types, a level of analysis facilitated by the graphic illustration of a sonogram. A note is a discrete sound unit, whether modulated or not, represented by a continuous trace on the sonogram. (Since sound must be heard to be truly understood, throughout the text a 🔊 indicates an audio track, often paired with a sonogram and/or notation, that is available online; see www.piedbutcherbird.net.)

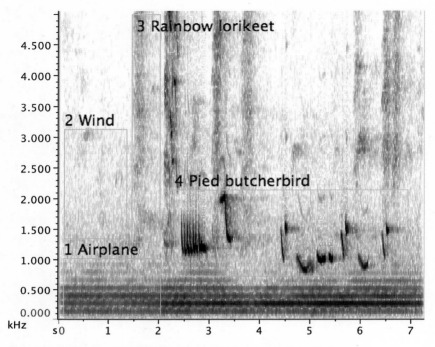

Figure 4.1. A pied butcherbird competing with a busy acoustic basket.

As in Western music notation, time in a sonogram is represented horizontally, and frequency vertically. Although the relative intensity of the sound (its amplitude) is indicated by depth of shading, waveform analysis can better isolate this component. The sonogram displays the entire acoustic basket as it unravels. In the case of a pied butcherbird phrase in figure 4.1 (◀ AUDIO 1), the bird is competing with a small airplane in the low register, wind in the trees in the midrange, and boisterous rainbow lorikeets (*Trichoglossus moluccanus*) in the mid- to high frequencies.

Figure 4.2. (*facing*) A representative series of basic note types of the pied butcherbird. Line 1: #1: a very short note (about 0.02 sec) with stable frequency; #2: a longer note with stable frequency; #3: an ascending note; #4: a descending note; #5: a note that descends, then ascends; #6: a note that ascends, then descends. Line 2: #7: a very short, swiftly ascending note; #8: a very short, swiftly descending note; #9: an apparent simultaneously produced double note from one bird; #10: a note that begins simply and is made more complex. Lines 3 and 4: #1–6: complex tones that sound harsh, buzzy, or "noisy."

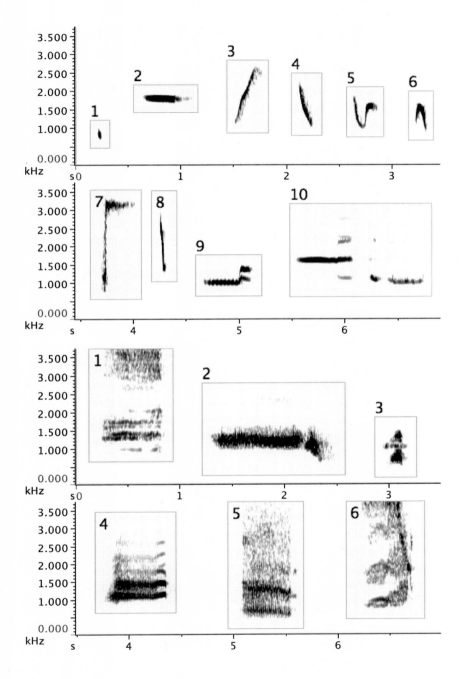

I need to filter out these sounds, or simply pick phrases with less acoustic competition, so we can go in for a closer look at pied butcherbird notes.

The first two lines of figure 4.2 (◄» AUDIO 2) detail a representative series of basic note types, all of which are common, except very short, swiftly ascending notes. On line 2, sound #9 (at 4.0 sec) shows an apparent simultaneously produced double note from one bird. Meanwhile, sound #10 (at 4.4 sec) seems to begin simply enough, but my colleague—engineer and acoustician Neil Boucher—finds complexities of wobulation (a frequency that wobbles around a center point) in the first "simple" note, followed by more complexities as another tone is added, affecting what we hear. In fact, Boucher finds "a whole zoo of inter-modulation frequencies" in some pied butcherbird notes, while in others a bird deliberately produces harmonics "by arranging a non-linearity in the vocal tract."[1]

Although few empirical studies have been conducted to date on the systematics of avian pitch, it seems that in at least some birds their hearing is acute in both low- and high-frequency ranges; they are able to discriminate the songs of other species, even at the level of individuals, with precision; and their acoustic acuity and temporal discrimination are often better than those of humans.[2] Thus, a "discrete pitch" is a messy, complex arrangement, and even what we think we hear as pure is not straightforward. A more in-depth study of note morphology might clarify techniques that pied butcherbirds use to build diversity and how the sound of a note evolves over time. Lines 3 and 4 (◄» AUDIO 3) detail complex tones where the energy is distributed at multiple frequencies. These can sound harsh, buzzy, or "noisy."

SHORT, REPEATED NOTES

Birds build signal diversity with a variety of short, repeated notes that demonstrate exquisite vocal control, ostensibly produced near the physical limitations of a bird's vocal system (◄» AUDIO 4). Six deserve detailed description and are launched in a sonogram. Sound #1 (figure 4.3, line 1) is a trill, uncommon in pied butcherbird songs. This is Delphine's Magnetic Island bird from chapter 2 who sang concurrently with a Mozart flute concerto. The rarity of the trill tempts me to suggest that the bird learned this technique from the classical music regularly played on the radio, but

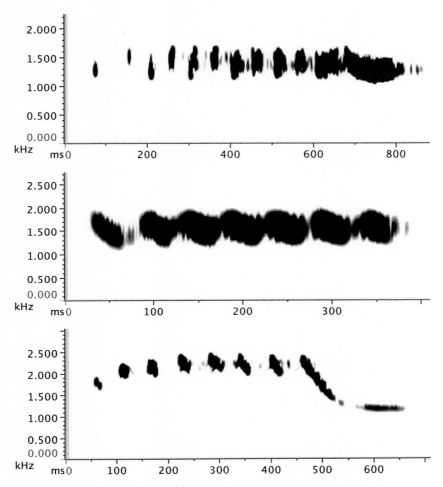

Figure 4.3 (*above and following page*). Pied butcherbird short repeated notes. Line 1: a trill; line 2: a quasi rattle; line 3: a rattle that ascends, then descends; line 4: a noisy *prew*-sounding rattle; line 5: a hollow-sounding rattle; and line 6: a laughing-sounding rattle.

I cannot prove this. Sound #2 (at 1.6 sec; figure 4.3, line 2) is a quasi rattle (or QR, where the pulses fail to completely separate to the ear and on the sonogram). The remaining examples are rattles, a repetitive sequence of short pulses not unlike a tremolo. Rattles may ascend or descend or both (like sound #11 at 12.2 sec; figure 4.3, line 3) and may be delivered on a

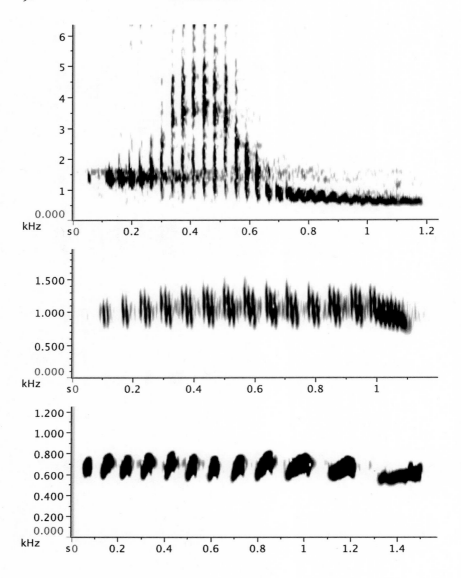

number of pitches. Rattles vary in duration and pulse rate and bring to mind tone colors like hollow, laughing, gurgling, or noisy. Notice the complex, ultranoisy rattle in sound #16 (at 18.4 sec; figure 4.3, line 4)—this aggressive *prew* and the other noisy rattles find pied butcherbirds performing complex gestures that in contemporary music we would label an "extended technique." A hollow-sounding rattle figures in sound #17 (at 20.0 sec; figure 4.3, line 5), and a laughing-sounding one in sound #20 (at 24.7 sec; figure 4.3, line 6). I could fill page after page with further examples of rattle prowess. As with the sounds to follow, these are assembled from a number of birds, and no individual would be expected to have all of these in their repertoire.

TIMBRE

Many features or qualities fit under the umbrella of timbre. These include pitch and amplitude, which can affect timbre even though they can be spoken of separately. Timbre carries information about a sound's source and the environment that it has traveled through. In addition to "flute," "cornet," and "organ," "liquid crystal" is a frequent metaphor for pied butcherbirds' tone colors. I met a camper who fondly described a vocalist back home in Queensland: "It sounds like the boy soprano's voice rising over the top of the choir." One listener was reminded of "a piano-tuner harmonizing notes," while Alec Chisholm summed it up as "a glorious gipsy warble." In his survey of musicality in Australian songbirds and with the human's standard as his measuring stick, philosopher Charles Hartshorne described the pied butcherbird as "the true 'magic flute,' the perfection of musical tonality coming from a bird." He adds, "I doubt any European will have heard anything so richly musical from birds."[3] Pied butcherbirds have even more timbral tricks than these.

Notes may call to mind mnemonic syllables. The falsetto phrases of friarbirds (sometimes called leatherheads) are prime examples of such constructs. Friarbirds deliver long, repetitive chatterings like "more tobacco, more tobacco, more tobacco" and "I've got red hair, I've got red hair." Unlike friarbirds, pied butcherbirds usually deliver only a syllable's worth of mnemonics, so unless a bird repeats the same mnemonic syllable, the surrounding notes will sound like pure whistled tones. ◀) AUDIO 5 highlights some of pied butcherbirds' strikingly different tonal qualities that suggest mnemonic syllables. They sound to me like #1: *bip*; #2: *bop*; #3: *tap*; #4: *top*; #5: a double *tik*; #6: *tok*; #7: *took*; #8: *tonks*; #9: *tonks* followed by *tooks*; #10: *chip*; #11–12: double *chops*; #13: four *che-omps*; #14: *che-omp*; #15: *ch-ch-chow-oh*; #16–17: *woop*; #18–19: *wows*; #20–21: a rattle *wow*; and #22: *wow-ow*. Because there is no evidence that birds sing exact equivalents to human vowels and consonants, the syllables are highly subjective, part acoustics and part psychoacoustics. Mnemonics' key value is to indicate a change in timbre, and the syllables ring truest when coined by each human listener.

I mark very swift upward or downward frequency sweeps with "ES" in my notation, underlining the electronic signal that they call to mind. The faster the delivery or the steeper the frequency rise/drop, the more heightened the effect. ◀) AUDIO 6 details notes suggesting analog synthesizer signals: #1–4: swift upward frequency sweeps; #5–8 (from 3.0 to 5.2 sec): swift downward frequency sweeps; and #9 (at 5:3 sec): a note of almost constant frequency interrupted by three swift, downward frequency sweeps. The diversity and complexity found in these sonic events continue in an inventory of pied butcherbird calls.

CALLS

A bird's call possesses syntax, which refers to its structure, and also semantics, which refers to its meaning. Birds will call to indicate pleasure or distress, aggression or alarm; there are calls for feeding, nesting, flocking, contacting, greeting, mobbing, flying, and more. Information gleaned from calls can be social, environmental, identificational, and/or locational. Any vocalization at minimum conveys the message: I am me, I am a pied butcherbird, and I am here—excepting calls and songs intended to be ventriloquial in nature.

Figure 4.4 / ◀) AUDIO 7 details a variety of calls. In sound #4 (at 7.8 sec), a mature bird approached me at an outdoor restaurant and begged for food; after eating her fill of my handout, the beggar flew with the leftovers to a tree above me and wedged them between the V of two branches. Sometimes birds deliver nonvocal mechanical sounds, which are not technically a call. Pied butcherbirds favor beak claps: "Most savage in their attacks are the Butcherbirds, that dive on the goshawk, clattering their beaks like machine-gun fire," notes feminist and environmentalist Germaine Greer at her South East Queensland reclamation project.[4] The literature does not recount, nor do my experiences indicate, that this species makes use of other nonvocal physical sounds, like beating wing feathers or drum-

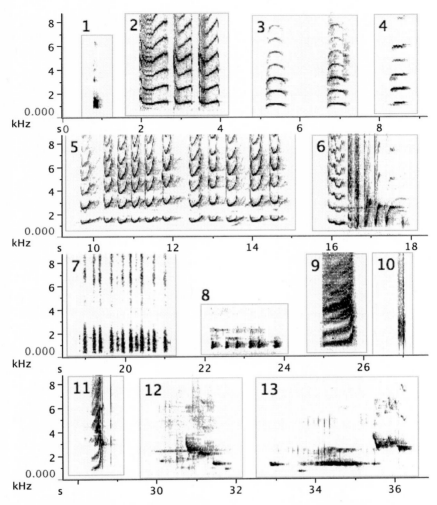

Figure 4.4. Pied butcherbird calls: #1: a call from an adult approaching the nest with food; #2: a food-begging call from a nestling; #3: a food-begging call from an immature bird; #4: a food-begging call from an adult; #5: food-begging calls from several immature birds; #6: a food-begging call and beak claps from nestlings; #7: a bark-like call from an adult in competition for food; #8: another bark-like call from an adult in competition for food; #9: a scolding call given to a cat; #10: two beak claps delivered in quick succession given as a sign of aggression to an Australian magpie; #11: a swift, steep, complex-sounding *zip* and a pair of beak claps; #12: song notes and beak claps from a group of pied butcherbirds; #13: song notes, beak claps, and a species call (described below) from a group of pied butcherbirds.

ming with beaks or tools. Some calls, especially food begging (#2–6 from 1.4 to 23.0 sec) and cat scolding (#9 at 29.4 sec) ones, are largely defined by their harmonics, which appear as stripes above the fundamental.

Most pied butcherbird alarm calls are sourced from a multipurpose call, which my informants have variously identified as a flight, contact, separation, advertising, dominance, mutual recognition, mobbing, and "I am a pied butcherbird" call. The call's meaning is not innately fixed and re- quires interpretation by the birds. Since it lacks a single motivational basis, I coined the term "species call."[5] This call is delivered across the continent by birds separated both geographically and historically and is diagnostic for the species: a pied butcherbird can be identified by it, whether or not the bird has been sighted (this assumes that another species is not mimick- ing the pied butcherbird). Depending on how many notes it is composed of, the call has been referred to with the mnemonic "eight-two-two" (if delivered as three notes), or "eight twenty-two" and "por-rk-it-tee" (if four notes). Often a species call is preceded by long squirty *zips* up to the call notes, and the *zips* may even be delivered by themselves. The call's tessi- tura is an octave higher than the standard singing register, in the seventh octave, and this is crucial to its identification.[6] These are the notes deliv- ered in flight by the Yungaburra trio.

Subsequently, I have analyzed over three hundred species calls re- corded between 1968 and 2015 from around the country. A surprising amount of plasticity in the call emerges, with individuals finding count- less opportunities to put their personal spin on the motif. They may vary it in the following ways:

- *Number of notes*: from one to five, with three or four clearly favored;
- *Pitch range*, excluding introductory notes: from C^7 to $A\sharp^7$, with F^7 to G^7 favored;
- *Pitch contour*: ascending, descending, stable, bowl (down-up), arch (up-down), up-down-up, down-up-down, and up-down-up-down; bowls and arches may be lopsided;
- *Note morphology*: ascending, descending, stable, bowl, and arch;
- *Rhythm*: from evenly paced to swung, like "wait for me" or "have a cup of tea";
- *Tempo*: from very slow to very fast;

- *Tone quality*: from nasal and complex to pure sounding, flute-like tone colors, with the harmonic partials appearing as very strong to very weak stripes;
- *Introductory notes*: from none to a very short note of stable pitch, to a steep, swift, and complex *zip* or two, to other complex sounds;
- Zip *direction*: typically ascending but very occasionally descending;
- Zip *portamento length*: typically, about eighteen semitones, but as short as nine and as long as twenty; and
- *Pitch relationships of adjacent notes*, excluding introductory notes: typically, small intervals of one to three semitones, but ranging from microtonal to leaps of nine semitones.

In this and subsequent analyses and discussions, the reader will notice my reliance on words like "typically," which is not due to caution or in order to guard myself from an anomaly that might someday be discovered. This lack of straightforward pronouncements stems from my current knowledge of exceptions, elaborations, and inventions, not to mention surprises and mysteries. Perhaps the species call works like this: the bird begins with an innate call (or sketch of it, since it is apparent that immature birds have to rehearse in order to sing these notes clearly) and expands the call via learning experiences, singing capacities, and aesthetic preferences, as well as a possible need to personalize it for identification or other purposes.

◄) AUDIO 8 details species calls from ten individuals, with an emphasis on comparing variation in pitch and melodic contour, while example 4.1 / ◄) AUDIO 9 highlight the varying number of notes, from one to five. When notations also have outcomes as sonograms or audio, the first "bar," for instance, is understood as synonymous with the first sound sample. ◄) AUDIO 10 focuses on introductory notes: #1–2 (at 0.4 and 2.0 sec) are very short notes of stable pitch; #3–4 (at 4.2 and 5.6 sec) are complex ascending *zips* delivered by themselves; in #5 (at 7.0 sec) each note is complex and steep; #6 (at 10.0 sec) is a descending *zip*; and #7–11 (at 11.5, 13.4, 15.3, 17.4, and 19.2 sec) contain other complex, "noisy" introductory notes.

With so many flexible parameters, an archetypal call fails to emerge; nonetheless, due to its elevated pitch and relative simplicity, the call is easy to identify. Some individuals sing more than one version; truncation

Example 4.1. Pied butcherbird species calls composed of from one to five notes.

is common. My conclusion is that while any delivery of this call by a pied butcherbird is immediately recognizable, the possibilities for alteration and innovation are nonetheless vast. The call could serve as a signature or password for an individual or group. I wonder if any part of the call carries more information than the rest. For instance, the beginning of each note (the *attack transient*—the first few milliseconds, as opposed to the rest of the note's envelope—the sustain and decay) could carry key identifying features or other important information, as it does in musical instruments.

ALICE SPRINGS TELEGRAPH STATION, 16 November 2007, noon: Alice Springs is the country's most inland town. Upon his 1855 arrival in Stuart, Charles Todd changed the town's name to that of his wife, although it was and still is known as Mparntwe in Aranda. Todd had been put in charge of construction of a massive Overland Telegraph Line, which he brought to completion in 1872. There would be eleven repeater stations in the nearly two-thousand-mile overland route that linked Adelaide to Darwin and continued via underwater cable to Great Britain. Of those that remain, several have been converted into museums; the Alice Springs Telegraph Station is the crown jewel, with its restored brick buildings and manicured green lawns set in the midst of an otherwise arid habitat. To reconstruct the livestock yard, weathered posts have been gathered from a now-deceased four-foot fence and tilted against a square frame of rails. I am greeted by a bunch of aging, lounging chums all leaning into a photo, a thousand stories awaiting whoever can decode them.

Indoors, a telegraph key sits on a table, while a recording of Morse code plays. Another room houses a piano that bumped up on the Old Ghan railway from Adelaide in 1870, making the final haul at rail's end on the back of a camel. Two other uprights have also retired here. I pry them open and look inside, finding all three in various stages of distress. A small termite mound inside the camel piano crowds its inner workings, echoing the hump of the beast of burden that transported it. Outside, an extended family of pied butcherbirds actively engages in song throughout the day. Suddenly, a call for reinforcements goes out, and from the alliances they make with other species, a number of other birds join them to protest the arrival of a wheeling flock of black kites (*Milvus migrans*). The pied butcherbirds rely almost exclusively on the species call.

This kite mobbing can be heard in ◄) AUDIO 11. I have also heard western bowerbirds deliver credible mimicry of pied butcherbird species calls when a whistling kite (*Haliastur sphenurus*) flew overhead. In ◄) AUDIO 12, an Australian raven (*Corvus coronoides*) is the mobbing subject. Several species calls are delivered an octave lower than the standard call and remind me of trumpet charges—the cavalry is coming! Long squirty *zips* up to the call notes are prominent in both. Some individuals appear to issue only *zips*. The effect is loud, brassy, and boisterous. Both examples contain beak claps delivered as a rapid pair. In ◄) AUDIO 13, a possum is the focus, as evidenced by the loud hisses emitting from the dense cover of a tree. "The butcherbirds were the ones that always told us when the pythons were coming out," explained a Brisbane resident. "You'd be in the house, and you'd just hear it [unrelenting species calls], and you'd go, 'Oh my God! There's a snake somewhere.' We'd always find one, on the clothesline or hanging off a tree, or whatever."[7]

Humans are not immune from bouts of interspecific aggression, as evidenced in ◄) AUDIO 14. Escalating beak claps and *zips* from a group of about eight birds convinced me to exit their territory. Young birds were no doubt in the nest. I sneaked back and hid behind a tree but was straightaway threatened by a bird who landed on the trunk just above my head and uttered a harsh *zip*. I swiftly complied.

Currawong, boobook, and koel come to mind as Australian birds named with a word resembling their call. Might an onomatopoeic name for pied butcherbirds based on the species call be found in any Aboriginal languages? I examined the thirty known names for them from as many languages, but the search was inconclusive. The names range from two to five syllables, begin variously on one of two vowel or nine consonant sounds, and are notoriously difficult to pronounce simply by reading the anglicized spelling. No commonality emerges, which is not surprising: the variety of the pied butcherbird species call would discourage a codified onomatopoeic naming.[8]

"Work it out, work it out, work it out!" insists a friarbird.

CALLS IN SONG

The differences between calls and songs are sometimes portrayed as clear-cut, but in practice the distinctions are not so easily demarcated. Although pied butcherbirds lack species-typical song phrases, examples of apparent reworkings of the species call delivered as a motif in solo and ensemble songs are plentiful. If I were to place the species call at one end of a continuum and a pied butcherbird song phrase at the other, we would find many points along the way, with some vocalizations quite challenging to position. The blurring of call and song begins when the species call is answered by a song phrase, or vice versa. In ◀) AUDIO 15, the species call prompts a song phrase in response, while in ◀) AUDIO 16, a song phrase precedes the species call.

The species call is an example of a theme that is not so idiosyncratic that it cannot be easily integrated into other phrases. In multi-individual examples, the motif hovers in a border territory between call and song. Some contributions seem entirely free, similar to the interjection "amen" in a Southern Baptist church meeting. Examples of the "call" in solo song particularly cause me to wonder whether this flexible motif, able to suggest and carry so many types of information, actually shifts and becomes information-free. On the other hand, these could be cases of birds crafting pleasing ways to announce their identity. Whether delivered in solo (example 4.2 / ◀) AUDIO 17) or ensemble songs (example 4.3, where upward and downward note beams serve to separate the birds' contributions / ◀) AUDIO 18), the boxed motif supplies contrast and balance; it seems a coherent part of the musical statement, a call become song, or call-in-song. We see why the definition of song elements has been so challenging to ethologists.

I want to consider in depth one solo song with the species call motif. In example 4.4 / ◀) AUDIO 19, the bird delivers the motif via an additive

Example 4.2. Species calls from six different sites as motifs in solo songs.

Example 4.3. Species calls from five different sites as motifs in ensemble songs (two or more birds).

Example 4.4. Pied butcherbird species call notes incorporated in three phrases of one individual's solo song.

process (the expansion and contraction of small musical cells or modules) as two, three, and then four notes. In the interest of simplicity, I have not notated minor portamentos. The other motif with which it is paired repeats exactly in the second phrase and is truncated in the third (consisting only of the final three notes, which are placed at the end of the phrase as well, with the final note repeated—as if, having deleted the first half of the motif, the phrase length would be too short without a concomitant lengthening elsewhere). This truncation underlines the alternation of a descent from F^6 to D^6 that inverts an octave higher in an ascent from D^7 to F^7. Notice also the octave leap from D^6 to D^7 each time as the bird moves from the lower motif to the species call motif. A fuller discussion of octaves vis-à-vis animals and humans will occupy us in chapter 6; for now, I simply note how these phrases can be fruitfully described by Western musicological apparatus—these techniques are familiar ones.

Thus, the call regularly undergoes manipulation that points to a bird's capacity to categorize, personalize, and employ it as a call but also to a musical imagination able to redeploy it in song.[9] The sheer diversity found in species calls-in-song offers a helpful set of data when it comes to transposition. Despite neuroscientists often crediting transposition as an area of primate exceptionalism, both mature and immature pied butcherbirds regularly transpose species call motifs when placed in song.[10] On the other hand, transposition is apparently unknown in some human music.[11]

Only one other motif seems to be held in common by many pied butcherbird individuals in several states, causing me to suspect that birds commonly subject the species call to yet another treatment to build singing performances. In this case, they revise the call down an octave to the standard tessitura and reduce the tempo. This typically two-note motif, articulated short-long, usually descends by a minor second (SLD2) from $F\sharp^6$ to F^6. The short-long articulation is also common on other frequencies, and then the intervals are not stereotypical: they can be descending or

Example 4.5. Seven basic variants of the short-long descending second (SLD2) motif.

ascending and even encompass large leaps. Perhaps there exists something akin to an innate template for articulation that at times merges with the archetypal species call.

Seven SLD2 variations from as many individuals feature in example 4.5 / ◄⁾ AUDIO 20. Bar 1 illustrates the archetypal motif, while the much rarer bar 2 reverses the pitch direction. Bars 3–6 exemplify how the SLD2 may expand to three notes, while bar 7 sets out an elegant solution to the problem of how to elaborate two notes: beginning with an octave leap, the motif deflects by the interval of a tritone to a C^6, which Western listeners would likely hear as the dominant tone that leads toward a resolution to the tonic, the F^6.

The motif can be fruitfully examined in other ways. I cast myself as a sonic cartographer in a brief survey of SLD2 variants, tracing them from east to west in and around Alice Springs (all locations are within several hours' drive of one another in a more or less straight line). The examples are presented more as an introduction to the wealth of material that a zoö-musicologist might have at her disposal than as an exhaustive analysis.[12] Example 4.6 plots a single phrase that includes the SLD2 motif (a singer often delivers multiple variants) from each of eight individuals engaged in solo nocturnal songs in 2007. I had hoped that such cultural asset mapping might demonstrate how the SLD2 and other motifs gradually change across space in the trading zone among groups, but in an analysis of this and other motifs, difference was more salient than sameness and individual invention more common than subtle borrowing from a neighbor. "Gradual" simply was not pertinent.[13] Ovals mark the SLD2 motif, but other relationships stand out, notably the ascending octaves in bars 4 and 8 and the inversion of the ascending major third C^6 to E^6 in bar 3 to an

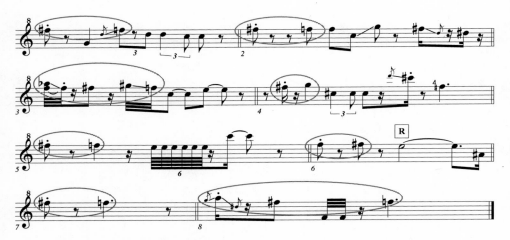

Example 4.6. Mapping the SLD2 motif (in ovals) in solo nocturnal songs from east to west in and around Alice Springs in 2007: #1: Ross River Resort Campground; #2: Trephina Gorge; #3: Jessie Gap; #4: Emily Gap; #5: Ross/Stuart Highways; #6: Gemtree; #7: Ormiston Big Tree; #8: Ormiston Gorge.

ascending minor sixth E^6 to C^7 in bar 5, which all suggest but do not prove some cross-cultural similarity in harmonic implications.

Much like the species call-in-song, a continuum exists for the SLD2 motif. On one end we might place a short and simple two-note motif. Next are phrases with notes inserted on either side of or in between the motif notes (most often after), then on to phrases where the pitches or the articulation (but not both) seem to derive from the SLD2 motif, to "phrases" of just one note—an $F\sharp^6$ of short articulation—or that note followed by completely different material, and finally to phrases with no apparent relationship in pitch or articulation to the SLD2 other than to provide musical contrast and balance. I also traced the SLD2 over time in the same place.

ROSS RIVER RESORT CAMPGROUND, 2007: The three-hundred-million-year-old MacDonnell Ranges stretch out for two hundred miles east and west of Alice Springs. This tilted red rock library of time consists of parallel ridges with dramatic gaps and gorges and contains many features of Aboriginal significance, including ancient carvings and rock paintings. The road from Alice Springs heading out to the East Ranges runs in fits and starts for fifty miles before ending at Ross River Resort. The "highway" alternates between one and two lanes. Drivers must keep a constant watch for oncoming traffic and be prepared to urgently pull off onto gravel shoulders. Forget enjoying the windshield vista. On this road, I'm a pattern and motion detector for vehicles, birds, lizards, cattle, snakes, dingoes, wallabies, brumbies (wild horses), and camels. Much like my zoömusicologist's brief, my driver's task is looking for patterns.

Over one million feral camels (*Camelus dromedarius*) are estimated to roam Australia's deserts. These transplanted ships of the desert are remarkable.[14] In a dust storm, they can close their nostrils. They have hair in their ears, a thick split upper lip for pulling leaves from the prickliest trees and shrubs, and a double row of eyelashes. They store fat, not water, in their hump, which insulates them from the sun. They can go without water for seventeen days and can lose up to 25 percent of their body weight without ill effect. Their padded leathery feet do less damage than the hooves of cattle, sheep, horses, donkeys, and goats, and their habit of browsing on the move means they do not feed intensively in any one area. Twice on this drive I make a hasty exit onto the red dust and gravel so as not to collect a camel with the car.

I reach the end of the bitumen and pull into the resort, which has just reopened after a period of closure. The historic homestead dates from 1898, when it was a working cattle station. The no-frills cabins lack telephones and televisions, and there is no cell phone reception. Instead, low-key camel safaris and horse treks are on offer. I check in at the homestead and then drive across the dry riverbed, passing a few ramshackle outbuildings and a disabled bus with a "Way 2 Go" bumper sticker on my way into the dusty, near-empty campground.

Ross River has a handful of bush stone-curlew (*Burhinus grallarius*)—large, ground-dwelling birds that resemble waders. Curlews' camouflage of grey-brown streaked with buff-white and rufous, with a prominent white eyebrow, serves them well by day when they spend much of their time standing in the shade with heads lowered and eyes half-closed. They feed and sing at night. Their mournful call begins low and softly and builds to a trilled, screeching crescendo. This eerie, high-pitched wailing is an iconic sound of the Australian bush. To my ears, some individuals are particularly gifted, and such is the case with the soloist at Ross River, whose midnight rendition culminates with hauntingly silver tones. Three hours later, I arise for the hoped-for pied butcherbird soloist. At 4:35 AM, a bird begins softly along the cliff-face. The volume increases, but at 4:53 AM the chorister flies down the canyon to continue in a place too distant for my microphones or legs.

These eighteen minutes yielded four SLD2 variants. Notations of phrases containing the SLD2 motif (or related material in the case of 2010) at Ross River Resort Campground in this and subsequent years are available online (www.piedbutcherbird.net). Although they are nonmigratory, the birds are not banded (and, in any case, singing is nocturnal), so I make no claim that these phrases come from the same soloist in different years. I am, however, certain that within each year, the phrases all come from a single individual, since they are my own recordings. Phrases have been arranged in approximate order of increasing complexity, but also in an order that might best provoke comparisons.

HOME IN THE BLUE MOUNTAINS AND BACK TO WOGARNO STATION, 2008: When I began my research in 2005, my supervisor suggested that one year of fieldwork would suffice. Another key advisor, an ornithologist, amended this to "one *good* year of fieldwork—likely the third year." I did need three years, and once those were completed, I still felt the pull to record and be in the field with pied butcherbirds. In the autumn of 2008 (March and April) I visited many of my regular sites, along with potential new ones, to observe and record pied butcherbird vocalizations in a different season. The ensemble singing was abundant. I did not conduct spring fieldwork in Alice Springs, instead spending much of the season writing up my results. I did, however, manage a trip back to Wogarno Station, where my passion for pied butcherbirds had begun. I was able to turn that barely remembered birdsong into my first recordings there and to be reminded of how substantial the Wogarno singing tradition is.

ROSS RIVER RESORT CAMPGROUND, 2009: The campground, like all of us, continues to age. Two trailers with flapping canvas canopies are fenced off at the entrance, and opposite them sits a motorhome affixed with a "Livin' the Dream" bumper sticker. Several rusted half barrels–cum–barbeques are on offer. The grass is tall and dry—whistle-dry, fire-dry, snake-dry. I take a walk on the red-sand track, which shows evidence of cars, shoes, birds, dogs, and kangaroos. When I return, two small but tenacious dogs, barking and growling, chase me into my car. The new campground manager comes to retrieve them.

"Are they going to roam free at night?" I ask.

"Why?"

"Because I'm here to record birds, and I'll be up about three AM. Even if they are tied up, a recording is no good with barking dogs in it, and I don't want to wake up the whole campground."

"I'll put them in the trailer, but I have to tell you that if these dogs worry you, you should be even more concerned about the pack of seven or eight dingoes that we've been seeing around here. One's not a problem, but I'd be quite concerned about you wandering about in the dark with the pack of 'em."

Either the dingoes did not materialize, or they had no interest in me.

The first sixty-six minutes of the two-plus-hour 2009 nocturnal song yielded eleven SLD2 variants. Additive process is at work.

ROSS RIVER RESORT CAMPGROUND, 2010: When I approach the homestead, I see three joeys (baby kangaroos) in the yard, orphaned as a result of "lead poisoning," as the locals call it. Minnie wanders around, while Jacky and Ross hang upside down in cloth bags on the backs of chairs. Indoors, a yellow-faced whipsnake (*Demansia psammophis*), found in the leaf litter out front, is on display. They assure me that while it is venomous, the snake's bite is not fatal. That night, I rise at 3:00 AM. A hunting dingo passes near me in the dark but makes no attempt to interact with me. As soon as the pied butcherbird begins to sing, I sense that my star of previous years is no longer here. The new lead singer, while interesting, is not as inventive or timbrally diverse. Two other soloists remind me of the Australian driving license system, designated by probationary "L" and "P" (learner and provisional) plates. These "L" and "P" singers drop in and out, leaving the dominant singer to complete the morning's task without taking a break.

In 2010 the soloist fails to deliver any short-long articulation in an hour-plus of nocturnal solo song, but the pitches $F\sharp^6$, F^6, and E^6 are structurally significant.

ROSS RIVER RESORT CAMPGROUND, 2011: I go over to tell my neighbors that I'll be departing at 3:00 AM and not to worry should they hear me; from the smell of it, they're preparing beef masala. I settle for a salad. I never cook on my field trips—I cannot spare the time, and it's much too hot. Other than recording a curlew, a dingo, and a boobook owl (*Ninox boobook*), my early start is not rewarded. In 2011 no pied butcherbirds deliver nocturnal solo songs during the four weeks (mid-August to mid-September) that I am in the area. After I depart, I receive an e-mail that they have begun (September 23).

ROSS RIVER RESORT CAMPGROUND, 2012: I've brought my violin along with me, a rarity due to temperature extremes in this high-desert environment. In ten days' time, I'll be giving a concert at the Alice Springs Desert Park as part of Bird Week. Once I feel sure that I have captured what's on offer for nocturnal song (the approximate one-hour solo includes two different short-long articulations that bear no pitch or intervallic relationship to the SLD2) and subsequent dawn chorus ensemble vocalizations, I head to the amenities block. It's the only indoor, and thus shaded, location where I can practice the violin.

    "Unattended children will be given an espresso and a free kitten," or so the sign warns. I tune and put on my mute, propping my music against the back of a washbasin. I limit my warm-up out of courtesy to the other campers and quickly move on to pied butcherbird phrases. After several minutes, the pieds start up again. I know the routine: at this time of day (10:00 AM), they might sing a phrase or two, but then they'll stop. I'm not going to let them interrupt me—but they *don't* stop. After five minutes, I go outside, torn between the birds and my practice session. Seven or eight individuals are spread out amongst towering river red gums. They take turns singing phrases of immediate variety (as opposed to eventual variety), delivering about one a minute. I play each phrase back to them. This call and response goes on and on.

My colleague Jane, who has joined me for two weeks, hears something unusual—so much singing for this time of day—and comes over to investigate, recorder in hand. She catches on immediately and points her microphone at the treetops. I hold my own quite well until yet another pied butcherbird flies in and delivers an impossible phrase that I have never before heard—plus it's long and timbrally difficult to execute on a violin. I mangle the end of it, but they don't give up on me. We continue like this for half an hour. Then I try to get ahead, suggesting one of their phrases for them to repeat after me. Nothing. I try again. No—they won't have a bar of it. We revert to them calling and me responding. I am the birds' apprentice. After another ten minutes, I put the violin away, they stop a few minutes afterward, and Jane turns off her recorder. "This unmusical species comes into our territory and makes so much noise, what with generators, cars, radios, all the yelling, cooking, setting up and breaking down camp. Now, finally, one of them has shown just a bit of promise. What an oddity! Let's check it out." It's only a guess. Is violin playing birdsong? Borderline, they seem to be saying.

🔊 AUDIO 21 documents an excerpt from this encounter.

ROSS RIVER RESORT CAMPGROUND, 2013: In January an overnight fire devastated the campground, causing over a million dollars' worth of damage to the outbuildings, trailers, and water and power supplies. The main homestead, about a half-mile away, survived. Firefighting crews had been there the previous day, creating breaks and putting out spot fires, but the winds shifted in the middle of the night.

When I arrive in September, the campground has begun to be rebuilt. The blackened bottom half of many trees and the charred hills behind the camp are testimony to the fire's ferocity, but this is not the only problem they have struggled with. Alice Springs is in the midst of a feral cat (*Felis catus*) plague. Cats have been present in Central Australia for over a hundred years, having successfully adapted to a variety of habitat types. Adept hunters on the ground, cats will also climb trees to feed on avian eggs and nestlings and even roosting adults. They can apparently survive without drinking, obtaining their fluid requirements from live prey. The tiny Ross River community, consisting of an extended family plus a few others, has killed eighty cats this year alone. One cat's skin hangs on the bare wall—it's immense, about three times the size of a domestic pussycat. "The curlews are all gone—the cats got 'em," the manager, Shane, tells me. "Our other birdlife is way down too, like the galahs. They can't nest successfully in the tree hollows—the cats get up there. Every night we lose stock to 'em. I've been sleeping in the coop to protect my chooks [chickens]."

"Won't the dingoes control feral cats?" I ask.

"Yeah, but for some reason, the dingoes are gone—I know there used to be seven or eight of 'em. Now we rarely see one."

The pied butcherbirds are still at Ross River Resort, and in 2013 a forty-minute nocturnal solo song yielded eleven SLD2 variants.

The SLD2 motif also regularly surfaces in diurnal *ensemble* song at Ross River, also available online. A full accounting of the musical aspects of these songs is more than I can undertake here. In this section, my principal point is that the SLD2 is a cultural meme that underlines the sheer variety and dynamism of songs. The types of creativity brought to bear on the motif include the addition of introductory and coda material, interruption via deflection, timbral decoration (quasi rattles, rattles, a *wow* sound, broad-spectrum notes, and double notes), transposition, and additive process.

The species call-in-song proves to be an easily learned archetype that plays a significant role in shaping pied butcherbird aesthetic practice.

A PIED BUTCHERBIRD SCALE?

Composer, poet, and music critic Henry Tate (1873–1926) was one of the first white Australians to encourage birdsong as an overlooked resource for a composer's toolkit. Believing that birdsong was registered in the national psyche and had the potential to underpin a recognizable Australian music, he suggested that composers move beyond imitation and sonic caricature and instead copy birdsong at the level of repetition, cells, and sequences. He singled out pied butcherbird phrases, which he, like the birds themselves, found "readily combinable with other calls in an artistic ensemble."[15] If we are to judge by what remains of his notebooks, Tate appears to have notated only a few fragments of pied butcherbird song, each a reworking (whether by Tate or the bird is not clear) of the same motif—the species call.[16] He applied the motif to "Morning in the Gully" from his *Suite Joyous*, to *Bush Miniatures*, and to *Symphonic Rhapsody*, indicating that he took his own advice to seek musical material from native birdsong. His prescience in the possibilities inherent in Australian birdsong appropriation is, however, a more significant and enduring legacy than his musical corpus.

I was particularly intrigued by Tate's suggestion that vocalizations might be mined for their scales.[17] He suggested altering the tones of his perceived butcherbird scale by the addition of a minor sixth, linking this to Bartók's practice, derived from Hungarian folksong.[18] As I began my research, I looked forward to confirming or refuting Tate's notion—would it be the Rosetta Stone into pied butcherbird vocal culture? I wanted to be able to state, "This is what they do." I was looking for rules and structure. However, simple membership in this or any other species does not determine all musical outcomes. What I found again and again were individual innovations and dynamic interactions. I would soon discover that pied butcherbirds do not all sing in Tate's or any other scale. Just as the sonic building blocks they draw on—notes, timbres, and calls—achieve a sustained and extraordinary level of diversity, so too do their song phrases.

NOTES

1. Neil Boucher, e-mail message to the author, 4 January 2016; and Neil J. Boucher, "Understanding Avian Sound—It's Not What You Think!," *AudioWings* 15, no. 1 (2012): 8, 10.

2. Thorpe observed, "There is some evidence that the bird's pitch-discrimination is as good as that of human-beings; time-perception characteristics are probably better— perhaps by a factor of 10" (*Bird-Song: The Biology of Vocal Communication and Expression in Birds* [Cambridge: Cambridge University Press, 1961], 62). Also see Crawford H. Greenewalt, *Bird Song: Acoustics and Physiology* (Washington, DC: Smithsonian Institution Press, 1968), 138; Robert J. Dooling, "Auditory Perception in Birds," in *Acoustic Communication in Birds: Song Learning and Its Consequences*, ed. Donald E. Kroodsma, Edward H. Miller, and Henri Ouellet (New York: Academic Press, 1982), 1:95–130; Robert J. Dooling, "Perception of Complex, Species-Specific Vocalizations by Birds and Humans," in *The Comparative Psychology of Audition: Perceiving Complex Sounds*, ed. Robert J. Dooling and Stewart H. Hulse (Hillsdale: Lawrence Erlbaum, 1989), 423–444; and Timothy Q. Gentner, "Temporal Auditory Pattern Recognition in Songbirds," in *Neuroscience of Birdsong*, ed. H. Philip Zeigler and Peter Marler (Cambridge: Cambridge University Press, 2008), 187–198.

3. Anonymous camper; Blanche E. Miller, "Some Birds of Mount Tambourine, South Queensland," *Emu* 23 (1928): 131; Alec H. Chisholm, *Bird Wonders of Australia*, 6th ed. (Sydney: Angus and Robertson, 1934/1965), 71; and Charles Hartshorne, "Musical Values in Australian Songbirds," *Emu* 53 (1953): 118, respectively.

4. Germaine Greer, *White Beech* (London: Bloomsbury, 2013), 301.

5. Hollis Taylor, "A Call of the Pied Butcherbird," *AudioWings* 8, no. 2 (2005): 4–8.

6. All analyses referring to pitches with octave designations, like D^6 or F^7, conform to the Acoustical Society of America system, where the octave number increases by one upon the ascension from a B to a C. (Middle C is C^4.) Archival recordings made on tape are not included in my assessments of pitch due to potential inconsistencies in tape speed.

7. Jodie Solczaniuk, interview with the author, 11 August 2011.

8. See www.piedbutcherbird.net for a table of Australian Aboriginal names for the pied butcherbird.

9. François-Bernard Mâche, *Music, Myth and Nature*, trans. Susan Delaney (Chur: Harwood Academic Publishers, 1983/1992), 154.

10. See, for example, Marc D. Hauser and Josh McDermott, "The Evolution of the Music Faculty: A Comparative Perspective," *Nature Neuroscience* 6, no. 7 (2003): 666.

11. George Herzog, "Do Animals Have Music?," *Bulletin of the American Musicological Society* 5 (1941): 4. A sonogram is available online that shows how an immature bird relies heavily on the species call, delivering it within the familiar pitch range and at a number of lower transpositions. The bird delivers an ascending *zip* (often associated with the beginning of the call) both with and without call notes following it.

12. See Hollis Taylor, "Towards a Species Songbook: Illuminating the Vocalisations of the Australian Pied Butcherbird (*Cracticus nigrogularis*)" (PhD diss., University of Western Sydney, 2008), 1:170–176 for more of this analysis.

13. Ibid.

14. Brought to Australia in 1860 for exploration purposes, camels became the prime means of transportation in Centralia until the 1920s.

15. Henry Tate, *Australian Musical Possibilities* (Melbourne: Edward Vidler, 1924), 20. Also see Roger Covell, *Australia's Music* (Melbourne: Sun Books, 1967), 3.

16. A fuller discussion of his work can be read in Hollis Taylor, "Composers' Appropriation of Pied Butcherbird Song: Henry Tate's 'Undersong of Australia' Comes of Age," *Journal of Music Research Online* 2 (2011): 1–28.

17. Tate, *Australian Musical Possibilities*, 27, 22–23, 27.

18. Ibid., 23–24.

CHAPTER 5

Song Development

A Taste for Complexity

> We can say that life has desires, and we can talk about what these
> desires are: life desires complexity, life wants to join, create, experi-
> ment, do more.
>
> —Deborah Bird Rose, *Wild Dog Dreaming: Love and Extinction*

ARALUEN ARTS CENTRE, Alice Springs, 7 October 2012, 3:00 AM: This
cultural arts precinct is located on the Two Women Dreaming Track, with
seven registered Aboriginal sacred sites and trees of significance, including a three-hundred-year-old corkwood tree in the sculpture garden. Pied
butcherbirds undoubtedly appreciate this tree, as well as the massive river
red gums throughout the property. The soloist that I record here annually
is a favorite of mine, but when the bird begins, the recorder picks up about
equal measures of bird and humans—a young couple is fighting nearby. I
take sides, but only in my mind. The argument is too heated to approach
them and request that they move along. I'll just have to make do. Then, as
if our species could not do any worse, a man wearing a blanket paces back
and forth nearby, giving me a furtive glance from his parallel universe. The
couple's argument begins to get physical, and I wonder if I might have to
intervene when they head my way. I'm torn between them and my recording and worried that my presence could increase the situation's volatility.
Meanwhile, the pacer lies down on the ground next to me, requiring yet
another personal safety assessment—all in a night's work.

Nothing for me is more thrilling, or frightening, than waiting in the
dark for a pied butcherbird to begin singing. Things go bump in the

night—is it a kangaroo or a camel, a dingo or a domestic dog, a human or a family of emu? Snakes can be active nocturnally. While I await my potential soloist, there is always plenty to worry about and time to do it.

Time to think back to remote Cumberland Dam in North Queensland. I had investigated this ghost town the day prior—just a square brick chimney is all that remains, plus a number of bird species, but nary a human, near as I can tell. I rise in the dark and drive half an hour, pulling off at the side of a long gravel road at 2:30 AM. I open the car door—it's a still, moonless night in the savannah grasslands—and quietly pull it toward me without clicking it shut. My goal is always to record an entire song, so I must begin before the bird does, but inexcusably I delay getting out of the car. I'll just sit here for five minutes and gather my resolve, I think to myself. It's more nerve-racking than fidgeting in the green room before a major festival performance. "Five minutes, Miss Taylor." Smack! Someone hits the driver's door. Since it's too late to shut and lock it, I reach for the headlights. My mind would never have pictured what they partially light up: a huge Brahman steer with floppy ears. Perhaps we have startled each other—he's not at all deadly, unless you count a heart attack.

Time also to remember a small green sanctuary with tall trees in suburban Brisbane: fruit bats are squabbling and flapping their opera cloaks overhead. A tall young man ambles toward me in jeans and a stocking cap that covers much of his face. Nobody ambles at four in the morning—you power walk, you jog, you stagger drunkenly. For safety's sake I depart, heading out to the middle of the street near the brightest light until he disappears. In hindsight, perhaps I am the peculiar-looking one, a bird woman passing in the night under a slight fizz of rain.

Time to remember Pine Creek, the Northern Territory. I'm standing in a park when I hear barking dogs approaching and see a flashlight bouncing behind them. What to do—interrupt the recording by alerting the dogs' owner to my presence, or stand still and hope for the best? No need to decide—the dogs are right on me. I plead for their owner to call them off, but I'm the problem for him. He shouts two gruff words, which roughly translate to "What's with you just standing there in the dark?"

Time too to think back to my first trip to Gregory Downs, North Queensland: a long, hot drive ends at the banks of the Gregory River.

Pools of inviting water tempt me to camp right there, but I must stay where I think the birds might sing. There's a problem, though—the campground is littered with broken bottles, plastic sacks, and other garbage, plus there's no toilet. As I look around, I meet a truck driver who calls me "doll" and suggests I camp in front of the toilet block next to his truck and opposite the hotel. I do and crawl in the back of the car to sleep, but it's not the quiet spot I expected—throughout the night, five mining truck engines idle, while crowded cars make regular stops for all to pile out and use the facilities. At about 2:30 AM I depart, driving the side roads in every direction in search of a nocturnal singer. After nearly two hours of back and forth, I finally hear a bird—in the trashed-out campground. I pull in and quickly get out before getting a decent fix on the bird's location, in my enthusiasm breaking a personal rule. I walk so far away from my car that I cannot return to it when growling dogs chase me. Their humans cannot be bothered, locked as they are in a drunken dispute. Since I cannot go back, I keep walking toward the bird, who fortunately moves songposts, possibly in reaction to the raucous dogs, and then again—but wait! Now there's a carload with unknown intentions driving through the campground; they stop, shine their headlights on me, and honk. My heart races as their harassment, or perhaps just curiosity, escalates, and I walk off a bit more. They depart but come back ten minutes later. This time I fight back, gesturing between the tree and my hand-held recorder. I'm not brave— I'm cornered. I cannot return to my car, and I'm going to have to fight for this recording.

Time to remember Bowen, a North Queensland beach town whose white settlement dates to 1861: my route in the dark from the caravan park to where a bird sang the previous spring is well rehearsed. I drive along the beach for two blocks past the Big Mango, the town's thirty-three-foot-high fiberglass promotional grotesque, and turn right at a backpacker accommodation. Talk about poor judges of character—whistles, waves, and fists pumping the air: two still-partying backpackers on the street feel in solidarity with me, or at least with my rented camper van. First block, past the Central Hotel (a bar); second block, past the Cadillac Bar; third block, past the Larrikin Hotel (a bar) and turn left at the Holy Trinity Bar (in truth, the Anglican Church). It's Sunday and a full moon. I sit worrying more about people than whether a bird will sing. I imagine how I will defend my recording and myself. Only last week two policemen interrupted me, but soon I get real characters to fill in the blanks: a security guard pauses to shine his spotlight on my van; a drunk approaches me, cigarette sagging from his left hand, beer can swinging in the right, his untucked flannel shirt and long, wild hair blowing in the wind, but then he staggers off while swearing under his breath; next a young man walks by very close to me with an iPod going full blast. Life rarely unfolds as we expect—it's two magpies that interfere, flying in and perching next to my singer in their I'm-twice-as-big-as-you thuggishness. My singer stops, snaps at them three times in as many minutes, then flies off to resume singing, but not before vocalizing what sounds like a threat. *Bird, interrupted.*

When an individual begins a nocturnal song, often softly and slowly as if warming up, and then comes into full, flute-like voice, and the principal motifs and phrases begin to be transformed by a virtuoso of combinatorial prowess—nothing compares. After several hours, the sun rises, the dawn chorus swells, and I know that the bird and I have both made it safely to the start of another day. That's the happy ending I cling to in the darkness. I would never be out here at that time of night if it were not for the birds— but what prompts *them* to sing at this hour?

SONG TYPES IN THE ORNITHOLOGICAL LITERATURE

Song categories are artificial. The *Handbook of Australian, New Zealand & Antarctic Birds (HANZAB)* details three types of pied butcherbird song: breeding song, day song, and whisper song, although their differences are insufficiently described.[1] Only the dominant male in the territory is thought to sing breeding song, which is delivered nocturnally, but the exact function of this song and the sex of nocturnal singers remain undocumented. *HANZAB* speculates that day song could commence during and overlap with the final minutes of breeding song and might be initiated by the mate of the nocturnal singer.[2] Whisper song for one ornithologist becomes subsong for another: in mature birds, both terms are applied to low-intensity, rambling diurnal singing that bears little or no resemblance to other solo or ensemble song. However, subsong also describes the first attempts of an immature bird.[3] I intend to challenge all of these terms and divisions as definitive indexes of pied butcherbird vocal culture, but first we must take into account how the above conclusions were drawn.

Although *HANZAB* is a recent, multivolume document, certain deficiencies are apparent. Australian birds are not well studied in general, and we see how this applies to pied butcherbirds when encountering the first entries after the rubrics "Social Organization: Poorly known"; "Social Behaviour: Poorly known"; and "Breeding: Not well known." Under "Voice," we read "Quite well known," despite no in-depth, peer-reviewed article or longitudinal study having taken up their song by the time of this volume's 2006 publication.[4] To support and flesh out these three song types, *HANZAB* lists all historical mentions of pied butcherbird vocalizations. The authors are of uneven reliability and expertise, and the bulk of pied butcherbird description derives from inventories by geographic area. Thomas Carter commented in 1903 that settlers occasionally kept pied butcherbirds "for the beauty of their notes," although accounts of birds admired and then taken as specimens or pets cannot be dismissed offhand as issuing from nonspecialists.[5] Nevertheless, none of the reportage except a thesis on helpers-at-the-nest is based on intensive or extensive research into pied butcherbirds. This is not to diminish the value of *HANZAB* collating these accounts in one volume but rather to signal my reluctance to accept these premature conclusions. Instead of building on the received three-song-type premise, I will propose how I believe we might better understand their vocalizations.

There is consensus on certain basic parameters. Preferred song perches for day song are overhead wires, television aerials, or the highest branch of a dead tree (a recurring sight in parched Australia), although reports on whisper song suggest it occurs in a more sheltered position or on a low tree branch. Diurnal vocalizations, including during the dawn chorus, are assumed to be sung by both sexes in either solos, duos, or ensembles. Singing is not constant; while prominent in the dawn chorus, vocalizations are heard less afterward. A number of reports claim that vocalizations are ventriloquial—the birds seem to be able to throw their voices (I follow this up in the next chapter). In short, their habits make them potentially difficult to locate.

E. L. Hyem introduced the possibility of "accent" (or dialect) in the pied butcherbird, a favorite songbird of his, although none lived nearby. In the spring of 1961 he found a nest in an adjacent area where the birds were plentiful, removed three eggs, and placed them in a grey butcherbird's nest. Two birds were successfully reared:

> It had been my hope we would have the pleasure of hearing the beauti-
> ful notes of the pied butcher-bird about the place, at least for a while.
> But things did not turn out that way. When the young birds started to
> call, it was with the voice and notes of their foster parents. The young
> male gave an excellent imitation of the grey male's rollicking song but
> it could be distinguished from the foster parent's partly by the tone
> and partly by an extra note put in at the end. Similarly, the young pied
> female joined in the choruses with the female's part of the "grey's"
> song. . . . Perhaps the performance could be described as "speaking grey
> butcher-bird with a slight pied accent."[6]

This anecdote and others I have collected of Australian magpie and grey butcherbird elements creeping into pied butcherbird song underline how their voice is a learned phenomenon somewhat adaptable to circumstance.

RETHINKING PIED BUTCHERBIRD SONG TYPES

In every way that we might think of pied butcherbird songs, the birds frustrate and collapse our categories with multiple exceptions. Like most artists, they cannot be pigeonholed—they are fluid. Nonetheless, in order to effectively consider their habits and anomalies, I begin by considering songs by time of day—that is, as nocturnal and diurnal. While I only oc-casionally speculate on the motivation of singing or attempt to evaluate its communicatory capacity, I do point out from time to time when I feel a song appreciably exceeds its assumed function.

Nocturnal Singing

Three types of song occur nocturnally. The first two are related: formal solo song and mimicry appended to formal solo song. These correspond to *HANZAB*'s breeding song. The birds also deliver odds and ends that resist categorization: interjections, fanfares, and other soundmarks, which *HANZAB* does not cover.

1. *Formal solo song*. The bulk of nocturnal singing consists of what I describe as formal solo song: a soloist sings *discontinuously*, with an interphrase interval that is as long as or longer than the phrase itself, though birds occasionally take a slightly longer break to feed on an insect. Most phrases are one to three seconds in duration.[7] Unlike for a human singer, no pause to breathe is required, since birds take a number of minibreaths while singing.[8] Although a case could be made that the soloist is listening during this gap between phrases, the unvoiced gap does not simply mark a switch in function from singing to listening. Tacit periods "between" phrases are a musically essential part of phrases, which become a jumble, at least to my ears, when played back with no space in between them—all sense of proportion evaporates. A tacit pause is a considered and musically meaningful choice. The *phrases*, not the bird, need to breathe. Neuroscientific studies have demonstrated that when humans listen to music, the silence between sounds stimulates the most intense brain activity: "When we confront silence, the mind reaches outward."[9] Could this be an intentional ploy by bird musicians? "Interphrase interval" does not begin to describe the magic of sound-and-silence.

Once begun, the song continues until, or even through, the dawn chorus, unless the bird is stopped by heavy rainfall or an apparent threat from another species. Soloists tend not to repeat a phrase; instead, these versatile birds sing with immediate variety. The song might be as short as fifteen minutes or as long as seven hours (such a long performance would inevitably see a few breaks in singing). While some birds remain at the same songpost for the entire song, others take up a number of songposts; one bird had eight in the course of a song. These multiple songposts may be close together and thus pose only a minor problem for the recordist, or they may be so distant that the vocalist can scarcely still be heard and the recording cannot be continued. Birds may or may not sing in flight when moving to another post.

Determining the total number of components in a repertoire is problematic. In the course of a song, a bird might manipulate three to twelve phrase types; if material is added, deleted, combined, or otherwise reworked, especially if the song is over thirty minutes, distinguishing what is a permutation from what is a new phrase type becomes an entirely arbitrary exercise. In addition, birds recorded on consecutive nights may introduce new motifs, or at minimum variants, each evening.

Although the species is not migratory, my search for characteristic phrases or motifs indicates that nocturnal formal songs change from year to year even in the same location. I have recorded at and revisited over one hundred sites, many of which I monitor on an annual basis. No two mature birds to date have solo phrases that all match. Since soloists remain unobserved until near the end of the song (when it begins to be light), or if they are singing near a streetlight or during a full moon, "mature" must be, and is easily, determined by tone quality and consistency of singing. Besides, immature birds rarely attempt more than a few minutes of nocturnal song. Most solo phrases differ significantly from bird to bird, and some neighbors have *no* shared elements.

Although their phrases lack stereotypy, a few mnemonics for them have been proposed. One person heard "'Toll-de-lol-fāh' (the last note long drawn out and of liquid sweetness); then twice and quickly repeated in a lower key—'You chatterbox'; then in a higher key and with very full, rounded notes, and twice repeated—'Sweet after forty.' So charmed was I with the song and appearance of these birds that I determined to secure one to take home with me. . . . I eventually managed to get one from one of the station hands, and my captive has furnished me with many opportunities of study."[10]

During nocturnal formal song, another soloist, or several, may be heard in the distance. When interaction is involved, as there often seems to be, ethologists use the term "countersinging," which may be matched—when a bird preferentially sings a phrase from a common repertoire that best matches what the other is singing—or unmatched—when a bird avoids repeating what the other just sang. In some species, matching a song type immediately after a neighbor has sung it is an act of aggression.

Birds deliver the bulk of formal song in the spring, which is one reason it has been identified as breeding song. However, "spring" in Australia is not straightforward. It has ties to rainfall and food supply and is not just a calendar day or a change in heat or light. My impression is that formal song is sung before, during, and after breeding, with a drop in singing during nesting and before the young have fledged. I am not prepared to assign a function to formal song, although it could have one or more.

The broadcast space is often wide open for pied butcherbird nocturnal vocalists, with the most common interruptions coming from sporadically singing nocturnal birds, as well as from magpies and willie wagtails (*Rhipidura leucophrys*). This is quite unlike the contrapuntal events of the dawn chorus, with its wide range of frequencies, timbres, and sound sources that form the ultimate "surround sound." Feathered choristers compete intensively for their niche in the available broadcasting space and time, with the theatrics of the dawn chorus's sonic story not entirely told by notations, sonograms, or even recordings. Why, then, do some "nocturnal" pied butcherbird soloists choose to sing for, say, twenty minutes right at the dawn chorus, rather than in the twenty minutes just beforehand when the airwaves are not yet clogged? The minute-by-minute tasks facing a bird in the dawn chorus's crisscross patterns are considerable, but by placing a "nocturnal" song at this later time, perhaps a bird avoids what is potentially an increased predatory risk in the near still of night.

WORDSWORTH ROAD, between Townsville and Charters Towers, North Queensland, 28 September 2007, 4:10 AM: My ID reference for birds as often as not harks back to the trespassing names and questionable honor of dead white men. "Wordsworth" is delivering formal song with a regular pattern of sound and silence. While the delivery style is typical, the palette sees strong contrast. A conspecific can be heard in the distance delivering similar, but not identical, phrases. After an hour and three-quarters, Wordsworth abandons formal song with a coda of mimicry, breaking species-specific tendencies such as phrase and interphrase duration, vocal range, and timbre. With a memory bank of ready-mades as building blocks, the bird creates a forty-three-second nonstop sonic tangle that is difficult to unravel (◀) AUDIO 22).

I stay on to record ensemble songs during and after the dawn chorus. At 8:30 AM I pack up and drive down the narrow two-mile road, which dips and rises through creekbeds. About halfway down, I see an olive-colored stick across the road that was not there when I came in. It's about six feet long, and now I see its raised head and flicking tongue. I slow down, but I'm too late. If I brake, I might stop right on it, so I just coast, my eyes on the rearview mirror. The snake has vanished! I've been warned that they can attach themselves to the underbelly of a car and then strike when you open the door. I pull off into grass, convinced that this coastal taipan (*Oxyuranus scutellatus*), one of the world's deadliest and most aggressive, is clinging to my car. If so, the creature would surely get off now—please. However, there will be no closure this morning: in my mind the snake will remain on my car for a good week.

2. *Mimicry appended to formal song.* W. H. Thorpe defined mimicry as "imitation by birds of sounds outside their specifically characteristic vocalisations."[11] A dictionary entry is by design an impoverished way of describing the out-of-the-blue lavishness of avian mimicry when overheard by a human. About 5 percent of formal songs are appended with mimicry, which is usually placed at the song's end or at a point when the bird intends to fly to a new songpost afterward—or at least to take a short break. Birds deliver mimicry in a continuous fashion and at a considerably lower volume than their own phrases. A mimicry coda runs in the order of thirty to ninety seconds.

NEWHAVEN WILDLIFE SANCTUARY, four hours' drive northwest of Alice Springs, 15 August 2010: Owned by the Australian Wildlife Conservancy, these 650,000 acres are set at the intersection of the Great Sandy and Tanami Deserts. The red-dust road into Newhaven is always 4WD only, but this season the drive presents both sand dunes and long stretches of water. Recent heavy rainfall following a succession of drought years is important for plant reproduction, although it poses subsequent wildfire risks. Jon has joined me on this leg of the trip. We stop at the most serious of the watercourses and plan our route, choosing to follow the freshest tracks, with no idea if this ephemeral lake is deeper than when the last vehicle plowed through. Purple-red quartzite mountains, ochre clay pans, iron-red dunes, and pastel salt lakes color our drive in, although it's easier for Jon to steal a view than for me, the driver.

We install ourselves at the basic Newhaven Camp West and take a quick walk around before dark. Later, we're sipping red wine over a twilight campfire when a pied butcherbird sings four phrases about ten minutes apart, each from a different tree. Unfortunately, a guitar "owner" at a nearby campfire has other ideas that are not so well crafted. The bird obliges on the next three evenings as well. This or some other pied butcherbird also supplies me with many hours of nocturnal recordings each morning at 3:00 AM.

3. *Interjections, fanfares, and other soundmarks.* Proclamations like those from "Newhaven" may happen at twilight, just after dark, or even in the middle of the night. They may be delivered singly or as multiple phrases, but they never amount to more than a handful.

Diurnal Singing

The prescribed categories of breeding song, day song, and whisper song also break down in diurnal singing. What to do with a so-called breeding song, which we expect only nocturnally in something approaching spring, when it arrives instead in autumn during the day? In addition, *HANZAB* fails to clarify whisper song while lumping everything else into day song. My experience in the field indicates that diurnal singing may arrive as formal solo song; as ensemble song; as solo subsong, with or without mimicry; and as interjections, fanfares, singing lessons, and other soundmarks. The old ways of discussing diurnal performances fall short of fully describing what the birds are up to.

1. *Formal solo song.* Although most formal song is nocturnal, I have encountered significant diurnal formal songs. A short song of fifteen or twenty minutes' duration might begin just before or at the dawn chorus, complicating the task of identifying it as diurnal or nocturnal. I have never heard a formal song sung after the dawn chorus in the spring. However, some individuals have delivered formal song at midmorning or midday in May and June, considered late autumn and winter months, and with no apparent concurrent nesting activity. My impression is that diurnal formal

songs resemble their nocturnal counterparts in all ways except the time of day and season in which they are sung. Neither has absolute purchase on any of the procedures for crafting and varying song. As with nocturnal formal song, the function of diurnal formal song remains unclear.

2. *Ensemble song.* Recent articles have proposed that female song is both ancestral in songbirds and widespread.[12] Since in pied butcherbirds the sexes are indistinguishable in the field and I am not working with banded birds, I can only speculate on female song. However, a study of the closely related Australian magpie found that "male birds performed less than 5% of solo vocalisations, with females participating in more than 95% of solo vocalisation performances."[13] Whether female pied butcherbirds sing solo songs, and if so how often, is unknown. It is clear that females play a key role in duets and other ensemble songs. For this species, music is a family affair; like the von Trapps, everyone contributes to the sing-along.

Just as in solo song, tracking the repertoire and rules of communal song is not straightforward. My autumn field trips have been the most productive for recording ensembles. Duets range from interchanges of apparently informal timing to remarkably complex, coordinated performances. In human music, a sequential duet where singers take turns so rapidly and with such precision that they form a single melodic line is known as a hocket, paging back to medieval motets, for example, or antiphonal song (ethologists employ this term for birdsong, as do musicologists in describing the call-and-response alternation of an officiant and a choir). The timing of duets is normally such that without visual contact, the contributions do not parse easily, so it is essential that this be annotated by the recordist in the field. When singing, pied butcherbirds also operate on another communication channel: their multimodal display sees them alternating a standard upright posture with raising the bill high and sinking it on the breast, as well as opening or even flapping wings, all of which assist in part identification. These whole-body motor performances enhance the audio and remind us of music's corporeal and haptic dimensions.

Ensemble songs may be repeated, either exactly or with variation, a handful of times before the birds switch to a new one, which may be prefaced by a move to a new tree or other songpost. When the result is not a "tight" hocket but instead a looser ensemble song, a strong sense of collective improvisation may be evoked, like the contrapuntal multisoloing of Dixieland jazz. Unison duets are rare in pied butcherbirds, although input from supernumeraries in trios, quartets, and larger ensembles often sees unison singing of one or more motifs. In this, the pied butcherbird would be a candidate for expanding a human exclusionary zone, since *Homo sapiens* is commonly regarded as the only species to sing in unison.

In addition to the analysis and comparison of ensemble songs, intriguing questions about the relationship between solo and ensemble songs are always in the back of my mind, particularly the reach of a phrase across territories and years. The collectively held repertoire of ensemble songs is more stable than individually crafted productions—ensemble songs are their classics and their *musica franca*. I have analyzed ensemble songs that are almost exact replicas of vocalizations a hundred miles distant. That said, I have detailed how at Ross River changes in ensemble song surface even in a year's time.

3. *Subsong, with or without mimicry.* Since subsong is favored by ethologists, I employ that label, although with reservation. Other terms called on to describe similar vocalizations are whisper song, soft song, quiet song, chatter song, twitter song, short-range song, low-volume song, unobtrusive signals, and undirected song. Neuroscientists Constance Scharff and Jana Petri compare male zebra finches' (*Taeniopygia guttata*) undirected song, which often occurs while birds are alone, to private soliloquizing, another supposed area of human exceptionalism.[14] Whether in the voice of a human or a bird, "whisper" implies a weaker signal, an altered vocal timbre, and a modulation of communication strategy. Amplitude is subjective, and some pied butcherbird subsong does not seem so quiet to me, nor am I yet satisfied that all songs of lower-than-normal volume share a similar context or function. The act of coining a new word implies that another is not available and, more importantly, that the object in question is understood and thus a definition can be supplied. I am not certain that this is the case with subsong.

Both juvenile and mature pied butcherbirds may deliver subsong in the wind, the rain, or the heat of the noonday sun. A bird might sing almost nonstop for fifteen or more minutes, and an interphrase interval is lacking in this *moto perpetuo*. Mimicry is more often present than not and, aside from in formal song, only occurs in diurnal subsong. With no apparent advertising function, it is not clear if subsong is a rehearsal (an étude), or if song is simply its own reward.

4. *Interjections, fanfares, singing lessons, and other soundmarks.* A number of other diurnal contexts exist where vocalizations do not fit neatly into the previous descriptions: when a bird seemingly intends to initiate a duet by singing what is part of ensemble song repertoire but is not answered; when a bird sings one unanswered phrase that seems complete unto itself, as in formal song, and is not part of ensemble song repertoire; when an individual begins to sing what is apparently formal song repertoire but is shortly joined by another bird; and when a recorded excerpt cannot be confirmed as solo or antiphonal, since many recordists begin around the dawn chorus and thus only capture a few minutes of pied butcherbird nocturnal song. In addition, apparent singing lessons differ from other diurnal singing.

The multiple folds of song types open out into methods of description and analysis in the next section as I work my way toward identifying the vocal conventions and preferences of the species.

DESCRIPTION AND ANALYSIS OF FORMAL SOLO SONG

To my mind, here is where zoömusicology really hits its stride. I will consider two songs, one nocturnal and the other diurnal. I made these recordings, a two-hour song and a three-and-a-quarter-hour song, without interruption, and both comprise the entire vocalization delivered by a single bird.[15] In long birdsongs, significant matters of repertoire and organizational structure can be examined, like whether there exists a cyclic, sequential, or other regular order to phrases. In addition, as with the species call, song phrases can be searched for shared elements in neighbors' solo and ensemble songs, as well as for invariable elements in successive years at the same site. What's new, what's disappeared, and what's stable?

A Nocturnal Formal Song

ALICE SPRINGS, Central Australia, 8 October 2006: The previous night on my drive to record elsewhere, I heard a bird where the Ross and Stuart

Highways converge. This evening, I determine to position myself where I think that bird was. At 3:45 AM under a full moon, I turn on the recorder. After a couple of minutes and two distant phrases, "Ross Stuart" flies across the highway into the tree above me and sings for two hours from one perch. I have stumbled onto the box seat. It's a cold desert night, with only occasional traffic, and although several times cars slow, thankfully no one stops. One driver shouts abuse while passing; the bird stops briefly, then resumes. Half an hour into the recording, I hear two other pied butcherbirds, one closer than the other. My fingers become progressively colder, and when the bird stops singing, I must take great care not to drop the recorder as I turn it off.

Sonic material both suggests and winnows down the possibilities for analysis, but I make no claim to arriving without baggage; I come with *many* bags and choose from among them. I walk round and round the topography of each song—hearing it live, rehearing it on a recording, launching it in a sonogram, notating it, refining the notation, taking measurements, marking my worksheets, relistening, sometimes playing it on the violin, making the best of the translational limitations in each medium—and then I walk round again. Certain qualities may be revealed with one strategy, some via another.

In notating Ross Stuart's entire song (555 phrases), I assigned the six phrase types with the letters A–F and the phrase's variants with numbers. One phrase was a hybrid of Phrase A and B, which I identified as Phrase BA (the motif from Phrase B arrives first). I then listed for each phrase the melodic character, total number of variants, range, key intervals, contour, and timbral attributes. The decidedly abridged comments below are a sampling of how I analyze phrases (example 5.1 details Phrases A, B, and C). Ross Stuart's phrases are relatively homogeneous and ambiguous, making the "melodic character of the phrase" mode of description less rich for this individual than for many songsters.

Phrase A has a capriciously modular quality. Ross Stuart alludes to the articulation of the SLD2 motif in many phrase types, and the pitch and

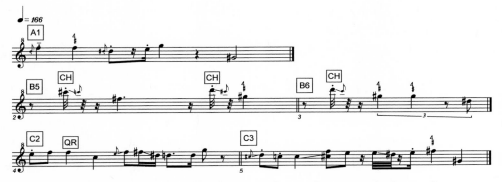

Example 5.1. Selected Phrase A (bar 1), Phrase B (bars 2–3), and Phrase C (bars 4–5) outcomes from the bird Ross Stuart.

articulation come together in Phrase A to form the SLD2 motif, although ascending for this individual rather than the more common descent.

In Phrase B the longer tones are bell-like. Only during traffic noise does a rapid rattle replace an otherwise slow, hollow-sounding rattle heard in some variants. Every motif and gesture seems a potential stopping point. Cognitive musicologist David Huron employs the term "post-skip reversal," replacing composer and philosopher Leonard B. Meyer's "gap-fill" and thus refining our understanding of how "melodies behave according to regression to the mean."[16] In human music, Huron found that the farther the leap moves from the mean pitch, the more likely that the next pitch will be closer to the mean; conversely, if a leap takes the melody toward the mean, then the melody will likely continue in the same direction. It remains to be seen if this holds for pied butcherbird song, but certainly the lack of a post-skip reversal in Phrase B6, with two consecutive descending fourths, is uncommon and commands attention.

In Phrase C two variants (including C3 in bar 5) contain a double note, with the one "voice" rising a perfect fourth while the other rises a minor second. When delivered, it had a strangely ventriloquial quality, as if one of the notes were coming from another individual; since multiple occurrences of this phrase all include this double note, it must originate from the two sides of the one bird's syrinx. Many elements in Phrase C are reminiscent of other phrases, but a perfect fourth (between C^6 and F^6), delivered both descending and ascending, is the defining aspect of this ephemeral phrase.

There is something in an entire performance. If a formal song is really only advertising, then advertising never sounded so good. Very typical of such songs, it begins and ends *pianissimo*, framed by a gradual crescendo and subsequent decrescendo. Phrase truncation and interphrase interval augmentation also contribute to a gradual abatement, bringing closure to the performance. The form has links to a classic bebop jazz solo.

The contour of most phrases is essentially zigzag. Shifting motivic duration and narrow portamentos add interest. Much of the motion is stepwise, almost a sort of doodling, but then suddenly large leaps, more often falling than rising, draw our attention. Many phrases seem subtly cut from the same cloth and are manipulated by way of contrast, addition, subtraction, and substitution. I find no predictable phrase ordering on a small or large scale. No mimicry is present, nor is there a species call, delivered either separately or embedded in a phrase, although the species call derivative (SLD2) is present. Once I turned off the recorder, Ross Stuart signed off with a three-note species call on the pitches G^7–$F\sharp^7$–F^7.

I gathered other songs from Ross Stuart's immediate area, with particular interest in shared material. In Alice Springs and its environs, the SLD2 motif is common. I found similarities in other motifs with nearby birds, but no close matches, as well as similarities in motifs in the same location in consecutive years, but again, no close matches.

A Diurnal Formal Song

NELLY BAY, Magnetic Island, North Queensland, 12 June 2005: I'm five miles offshore from Townsville on "Maggie," the only arid island in the Great Barrier Reef. The island takes its name from Captain Cook's 1770 logbook entry about an apparent magnetic effect on the ship's compass. The previous day a bird was already singing here when I arrived. I recorded for an hour and a half before my feathered protagonist flew off. Today, I arrive earlier. Since a long song is a challenge for batteries, I wait to turn on the recorder until I hear singing or at least see the bird (to solve this, I now travel with two recorders). Thus, I miss the first two phrases, which I quickly sing into the recorder in the interval between phrases. The bigger tree from which the pied sings is a melaleuca, also known as a paperbark; the other is a eucalyptus—and thus my reference name for this soloist: "Two Tree." Beginning just before 10:45 AM, Two Tree sings until 2:00 PM and then flies off.

Then I announced into the microphone:

> Pied butcherbird. No apparent rival when he began. He looked back and forth whenever he was not singing. He began in the left tree; at thirty-nine minutes he moved to the right tree and was in the sun. Just before fifty-four minutes in, he moved back to the left tree and proceeded to fly around to several perches. He had a distant rival, and he positioned his back to where I thought the other bird was. A closer bird came in towards the end and got him started again. He shared the trees at different times with rainbow lorikeets, pied currawongs, and sulphur-crested cockatoos. A blue-winged kookaburra flew in about six feet from me and walked on the ground for a while but never made a sound. With the two conspecific rivals, there were both matching and contrasting phrases. It's probably 85 degrees today on Maggie.

As I recorded, cars drove by, radios went on and off, airplanes flew overhead, and a gardener worked in front of me, spraying herbicide. The following two days, I neither heard nor observed this bird singing, after which I departed the island.

My decision to notate this song reflects a serious underestimation of the complexity of the musical material. As with Ross Stuart, I begin by examining a few phrases that can both elucidate the song and indicate the types of analytical tools I found most effective.

Individual Phrases of a Diurnal Formal Song

Unlike Ross Stuart's relatively homogeneous, ambiguous motifs and phrases, those of Two Tree invite contrasting adjectival descriptions like "magisterial," "exuberant," "playful," "unsettled," "improvisatory," "mercurial," "dynamic," "unyielding," and "kick ass and take names."[17] I initially identified eleven phrase types, assigning each with a letter. However, the sheer combinatorial complexity of this song, with so many hybrid phrases, required me to rethink the efficacy of phrase labeling in this case. Two Tree brings us face-to-face with "the vexed problem of inventiveness in song."[18] I now believe that my initial analysis forced phrase types onto what could be more fruitfully imagined in other ways. For this song, assigning letters on the motif level, rather than on that of a phrase, makes more sense, assuming one has the statistical support to then manage and analyze the data. Therefore, I use "Phrase" advisedly here and with quotation marks.

I begin with the fourth phrase that the bird sang, which I initially identified as the theatrical "Phrase D," which sees 102 variants, including hybrids and rhythmic/rattle variations (example 5.2). The three key components are the whistle motif, rattle motif, and descending portamento motif. The jump to B^6 in this latter motif, which descends via portamento to an E^6, is a particularly satisfying post-skip reversal. Because of the discrete, highly segmented nature of its motifs, "Phrase D" straightforwardly gives up its building conventions. Both prefixes and suffixes, and even both, may be added to the phrase.

An online table clearly demonstrates what causes me to back away from designating phrase types in this song (see www.piedbutcherbird.net). My initial observation was that any of "Phrase D's" three motifs can be present without the other two, although the whistle and descending portamento motif are never delivered without the rattle between them—and up to this point I remained confident that I could label this as a discrete phrase type with variants. However, what if only one of these three motifs materializes, as in bars 12, 449, 784, and many others? Is the result still "Phrase D"? What if only one motif arrives and attached to it are a prefix and suffix with material borrowed from other "phrases"? What phrase is it now? The phrase divisions begin to collapse into one another.

Similar abilities are also in evidence in what I initially identified as the magisterial "Phrase A," which accommodates a number of entry and stopping points. Human memory strategies include combining, or "chunking," items of information so that these can be recalled as a single unit

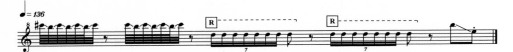

Example 5.2. A typical example of "Phrase D" from Two Tree.

Example 5.3. A partial catalog of "Phrase A" variants. Boxes and lines trace areas of commonality.

in memory. In examining how chunking might be relevant in the avian brain, example 5.3's boxes and lines trace areas of commonality. These are just eleven of the twenty-two variations (motifs from "Phrase A" also appear in other phrase types), presented in the order of the shortest and simplest, rather than in the order delivered, as a window onto the additive process. "Phrase A" variants call to mind the modularity of snap-together beads. With this number of stopping points and small combinatorial units, clearly the bird is not managing the entire phrase as one indivisible package. You could say that these phrases are to the listener both memorable and a "sabotage of memory."[19]

Combinatorial abilities are also in evidence in the playful "Phrase E," whose 110 variants include rhythmic variations and hybrids that again challenge the usefulness of identification by phrase letter and variant number (example 5.4). Constant changes in direction and flexible reiterations emphasize and energize the boxed motifs. The tension generated by repetition with variation creates ambiguity. "Phrase E" sounds like a stuck record. Whether motif boundaries are determined by rhythmic or melodic grouping is unclear. A notable augmentation occurs in several deliveries by way of a trill, as in bar 19. Two Tree is managing a hefty number of alternative choices and displays striking skills in matters of storage and recall, a feat that surpasses what I as a human musician could accomplish.

Two Tree's song calls to mind musical games of the late eighteenth (and into the nineteenth) century, where ready-made motifs were selected by spinning a top, throwing dice, or choosing random numbers. This systematic arrangement of prefabricated materials was known as *ars combinatoria*. Haydn and Mozart were known to participate in such pastimes. With just a few, simple component pieces, a vast number of combinations and permutations open up.[20] The art of combinations was also well known to French mathematician and music theorist Marin Mersenne and before him to Kircher, who in *Musurgia Universalis* (1650) claimed that combinatorics allowed even a novice to acquire compositional skill in a short time.[21] Kircher possessed a musical composing machine: a miniature

Example 5.4. (*facing*) In this partial catalog of "Phrase E" variants, presented in order of increased complexity, one of several alignment points is boxed or traced by lines.

chest of a dozen tiers with 119 drawers. A tiny slat inscribed with music could be pulled from each drawer. Other methods included bars of music inscribed on cards. These "tuneful lotteries" enabled even novices to create "four-part polyphonic church music."[22]

I would stop short of claiming that pied butcherbirds are experts in the mathematics of variability. How, then, to understand their combinatorial proclivity and productivity? In ensemble song, they learn how to piece together snippets of this and that to form a coherent musical statement, and they take this skill into their solo songs, where again motifs and patterns are short, incomplete, or unstable enough to work well in combination. Combinatorics is one way—one *very good* way—to generate new ideas and achieve complexity.

Two Tree is a powerful singer who moves with each phrase, involving the entire body. Likewise, and perhaps related, the vibrant gestural phrases command attention. Most of the 1,123 phrases are delivered at maximum volume, although the lowest notes are softer. Portamento is frequent, and the bird brings a dazzling panoply of timbral effects to bear, including a trill, *wow* sound, *chip* sound, bubbly sound, whistle reminiscent of a telephone ring, and quasi rattle, as well as six rattle types. The rhythmic language of individual phrases fits conventional notation, but only just.

The unequal and unstable duration of motivic segments adds interest. Phrase contour ranges from arch to bowl to ascent but usually betrays zigzag or spiky elements. Cognitive scientist Albert S. Bregman holds that "pitches are very noticeable when they are at the points at which the pitch movement changes its direction, at the peaks and valleys of the melodic contour, or if they are at the ends of phrases."[23] Leaps and sharp switchbacks are rife in Two Tree's phrases. Could these angular phrases be bids to attract attention?

Although not all phrases appear with equal frequency, no obvious hierarchy emerges, especially as a result of the combinatorial nature. The song displays a remarkable balance between predictability and surprise. My intuition is that phrase "order" is largely determined by the desire to create passages of diverse timbre, rhythm, contour, duration, tessitura, and melody that will command, hold, and recommend attention. Transition versatility (the likelihood of successive phrases being different) is extremely high. External factors could demand adjustments and refinements. The unyielding "Phrase K" is a case in point, where the chatterings of a raucous group of rainbow lorikeets or another singing pied butcherbird typically accompanies the seventy-seven deliveries of this phrase—as if to say, I'm not going to be put off my game!

There is neither mimicry nor a species call, either separately or embedded in a phrase. Dynamism pervades the entire song bout. Such an overflow of vigor, virtuosity, and versatility appears to exceed what is necessary for practical purposes. To date, this complexity without apparent meaning has not yet yielded to solution—I have yet to unravel the structural rules of Two Tree's song.[24]

In light of this bird's astounding ability to invent and recombine motifs and phrases, I returned to Magnetic Island in 2006 to record Two Tree, if still living, and other birds to compare with this song. The birds were scarcely vocalizing during my trip, 31 July through 9 August. I was able to record one diurnal singer at Arthur Bay who delivered mimicry in subsong; the only familiar sonic construct was the descending portamento motif from "Phrase D." This motif was also the only 2005 remnant still in the repertoire on my trip to Magnetic Island the next year, in the third week of September 2007. I recorded at three locations; as the songposts were within blocks of each other and in the Two Tree territory as it seemed in 2005, these were likely all the same bird. My diagnostic for Two Tree would be the frequency of use and variety of the rattles and the combinatorial ability as displayed in both variants and hybrids. I do not believe any of these recordings is of Two Tree. Since I was concerned that perhaps Two Tree was poisoned by the herbicide applied directly under these favorite songposts, I corresponded with the head ranger of Magnetic Island National Park and sent him a ninety-page transcription of this song. We both hoped that an appreciation of this bird's accomplishments might assist in the park's environmental management and conservation efforts, which face pressure from commercial and political agendas.

Due to the limited opportunities to record pied butcherbirds on Magnetic Island for comparison purposes, I conducted fieldwork on the mainland. As in the birds in the Alice Springs area, in the birds along the

Flinders Highway between Townsville and Charters Towers, ensemble songs of neighbors showed only minor differences, while the formal song repertoire was markedly individual and changed annually. There was more difference between the nocturnal formal songs of two adjacent soloists than between diurnal vocalizations of groups many miles apart.[25]

Formal songs from the Townsville/Charters Towers area have no motivic overlaps either with Two Tree or with the formal songs from the Alice Springs area, including Ross Stuart, except for those elements associated with the species call: the SLD2 motif and the species call-in-song motif. The disparities between Ross Stuart and Two Tree are largely a difference of degree and not of kind, such as the higher number of hybrid phrases found in Two Tree's song and the multiple iterations of phrases in Ross Stuart's. Two Tree's performance remains the most combinatorial one in my library—other diurnal formal songs are more similar to Ross Stuart's nocturnal formal song.

I suspect that pied butcherbirds deliberately vary their solo song from that of their conspecifics (whether annually or seasonally is unknown) in a search for novelty. I acknowledge that this is a bold supposition. Since soloists often borrow material from ensemble songs, an alternative explanation could be that new phrases are partially formed from these in combination with the previous year's solo phrases, producing a similar outcome. I cannot rule out that the birds do not entirely remember previous years' phrases and must reset and recraft them.[26]

DESCRIPTION AND ANALYSIS OF ENSEMBLE SONG

Duets and other ensemble songs have elements of ritual and dialogue. Ensemble song repertoire changes over the course of a day, and it can be difficult to quantify the number of duets and other ensemble songs, since only some have a fixed form, while others are freer in construction, especially if more than three birds are singing. I have filmed eight birds, seven of which were mature, singing together on a utility pole. A repertoire of four to ten duets and ensemble songs would be the norm, and some motifs might figure in more than one song.

Duets suggest a fascinating array of questions:

Example 5.5. Two pied butcherbirds in a duet.

· Is there a sense of melody and accompaniment?
· What can the birds accomplish together that cannot be accomplished solo?
· Is there unison singing?
· Are there preferred intervals at the hand-off point between birds?
· Is there transposition?
· Is there a seeming tonal center?
· Are the intervals large, small, or a mix?

The phrases in all of the multi-individual songs to come are not merely answers to what preceded them; they are *musical* answers.[27] They make sense to human ears, and they submit easily to analysis as it is broadly understood in the Western tradition. In example 5.5 / ◀) AUDIO 23, a sonogram would miss what the ear picks up: a supernumerary joins a duetting pair and contributes to only two of the motifs (boxed). Parentheses mark notes in the notation from the supernumerary delivered slightly later than the second bird. The ear also notices the doubling of the final *wow*, but in this contribution the supernumerary is in sync with the second bird. It seems likely that the recordist missed the beginning of the fourth phrase. Half-sharp signs indicate this duet's microtonal nature, but what I find most remarkable is the contrast of longish, slow notes from the first bird with the short, repeated notes (except for the *wow*) from the second bird.

Example 5.6. Two pied butcherbirds in a duet singing similar phrases.

In essence, I hear a melody with accompaniment à la Mozart-to-Chopin—
a solo piano work performed instead by duetting birds.

The joint performance in the next duet (example 5.6 / ◀) AUDIO 24)
involves rapid, hocket-like exchanges. The pitch contour (D^6–F^6–G^6) of
motif A is held in common by both birds but with a subtle variation. The
first individual approaches the motion chromatically (line 1, first motif),
while the second individual alternates thirds (line 2, final motif). This
second bird completes both motifs with a steep descending portamento.
Some pitches seem to serve a structural purpose and others an ornamental
one. The capacity to distinguish structural pitches from ornamental ones
is thought to play a key role in humans' perception of melody.[28] Motif B
(from D^6 to C^6 on the bottom staff) is transposed upward by an octave
(becoming D^7 to C^7 on the top staff). It seems such an obvious strategy
that one could miss its potential significance. Readings in neuroscience
and the psychology of music indicate that only certain mammals have a
sense of "octave generalization," which is a special case of transposition
where, in addition to contour, the intervals and chroma (in essence, a note
name of whatever octave) are also preserved. Pied butcherbirds might
assist us in revising our understanding of this capacity, and I tally a number of other octaves in the coming duets. The form of this duet (ABBA)
indicates that both birds are in command of the other's part, although in a
personalized manner. On the same morning, this same pair sang a handful
of other duet types.

The motifs in the next three duets (example 5.7 / ◀) AUDIO 25) cannot
be assigned with certainty. In bar 1, large leaps predominate, including
a descending octave from $D\#^7$ to $D\#^6$ and an F^6 to F^5 descending octave

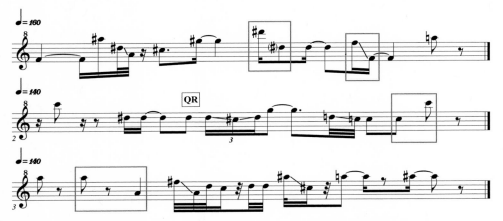

Example 5.7. Bar 1: a duet with large leaps, including descending octaves (boxed); bar 2: a duet that alternates between step-wise motion and large leaps, including an ascending octave (boxed); and bar 3: a duet with a descending octave (boxed) and other large leaps.

Example 5.8. Bar 1: a duet that sees two octave leaps (boxed) between singers; and bar 2: a duet with octaves (boxed) at the hand-off point between singers.

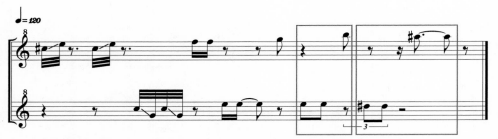

Example 5.9. A duet with contrary motion in the two individuals' portamentos and transposition in the final three plus three notes (boxed).

portamento near the end (both boxed) that both birds seem to sing. Duets in bars 2 and 3 also contain octave leaps that are boxed.

The interval of an octave continues to be highly pertinent at the hand-off point in the next two duets (example 5.8 / ◀) AUDIO 26), indicating at minimum a special appreciation of the octave. In these, I was able to divide the parts onto separate staves.

The final duet (example 5.9 / ◀) AUDIO 27) sees both birds delivering fast portamentos in contrary motion that create timbral interest. The intervals are smaller than in previous duets, and the motif E^6–E^6–B^6 is transposed down a semitone to $D\#^6$–$D\#^6$–$A\#^6$.

Our understanding of ensemble songs and group dynamics would benefit from a zoömusicologist living alongside these bird musicians to regularly document their deliveries.

DESCRIPTION AND ANALYSIS OF MIMICRY

Mimicry is a stimulating topic because of its unexpected vocal results, unclear functional aspect, and link to human music making. Prior to my studies, the literature had tallied twenty-nine bird species whose vocalizations were taken up with relish by the pied butcherbird, as well as a dog barking, a lamb bleating, a human whistling, and a horse whinnying.[29]

ARTHUR BAY, Magnetic Island, Queensland, 6 August 2006: I inch my way down the decaying Radical Bay Road in a four-wheel-drive vehicle. It's more "radical" than "road," with potholes both deep and wide. I pull off at Arthur Bay, where I've been told there's a pied butcherbird and, likely, a death adder (*Acanthophis laevis*) or two waiting in ambush. They camouflage their short, robust bodies and triangular-shaped heads in sand or leaf litter, only exposing a thin, worm-like tail, which they wiggle. One of the planet's deadliest, a death adder possesses the quickest strike and reset of any snake in the world.

A path to the beach cuts past hoop pines, vine thickets, and a mesh of mangrove roots but no apparent death adders. With fractured granite boulders behind me and the sea in front, I sit at the single picnic table eating my lunch—and of course hoping a bird will show up. One does, landing on the table and looking across at me. I assume "Arthur" is hoping for a bite of my food. Then off s/he goes, about seven feet up into the drooping foliage of a casuarina tree (*Casuarina equisetifolia*). I grab my recorder and shotgun mic, which is covered by a grey "fluffy." With wind and breaking waves, I cannot get by without this fake fur windscreen, which resembles a dead cat.

I position myself just below the bird, who tolerates my presence. Arthur sings, but it's not at all what I expect. I'm so accustomed to rich, flute-like songs that when Arthur begins, I'm stunned. While I know in theory that pied butcherbirds are mimics, at this early point in my fieldwork I have yet to hear mimicry live. Arthur is singing falsetto, like a bird of half the size— swift arabesques, squeaks, chips, and chirps, next a gurgle, and now metal-lic sounding. The interphrase interval has disappeared: Arthur sings nearly nonstop for twenty minutes.

Since recording Arthur, I have documented many other mimicking pied butcherbirds, in the process corroborating nine of the twenty-nine bird species that the literature details, as well as a dog and cat and, with expert assistance from Australian ornithologists, adding nineteen avian species to the list, for a total of forty-eight. Four *probable* new avian species and a frog expand the catalog, as well as very credible mimicry of a human voice, a cell phone ringtone, and a car alarm.[30] I now have my own recording of the whinny of a horse. Analyzing mimicry is a laborious process accom-plished via aural and sonographic comparisons of the species in question;

it requires working on a second-by-second basis in order to identify all the sound treasures that pied butcherbirds bring together from a variety of contexts. I have recorded both immature and mature birds eclectically copying material developed by other species. The rate of delivery might be as many as fifty or more motifs per minute, most from other species but a few from the bird's own phrases. The question of whether pied butcherbirds deliver their mimicry in a regular and repeated sequential cycle (like Albert's lyrebirds) or in a less predictable manner (like superb lyrebirds) is to date inconclusive because, whether delivered during the day or appended to formal song, mimicry is rare enough to make assembling enough data from one individual difficult.

In addition, although pied butcherbirds possess a capacity for high-fidelity duplication, they do not necessarily copy an entire motif from the model. They take a shorthand approach: you know the currawong, you know the magpie, and so on, with most of the mimicked species lasting one second or less, which makes identification challenging. Since some material remains unidentified, it is not possible to say whether the birds at times begin an appropriation in the middle of another species' signal. In those models that are identified, pitch conforms to the model. I cannot guess what the sound makers that they mimic have in common, if anything, and why other sounds are rejected.

Mimicry violates most pied butcherbird song conventions: the vocal range extends upward, and some assumed motor constraints in singing ability or affinity are invalidated. One bird sang almost continuously for forty-five minutes before the tape ran out. Exaggerated warbling atypical of nocturnal or diurnal singing can occur. The full-on effect is that of a DJ session.

CONVENTIONS AND PREFERENCES

In my search for underlying pied butcherbird conventions, the species call (a sure diagnostic for this species) stands out, as does tone. Nonetheless, the voice of the Australian magpie, grey butcherbird, and grey shrike-thrush (*Collurincia harmonica*) can be confused with that of the pied butcherbird, partially because the pied can mimic them and, at least in the first two, vice versa. The grey butcherbird's voice sounds higher in frequency, more staccato, and more frantic than a pied's; for pied "economists," every note counts for something. The magpie's complexly modulated sounds tend to be faster, more warbling, and less focused on discrete pitches than a pied butcherbird's. When magpies do sing more pure-sounding notes, phrases often repeat or at least alternate, unlike a pied. Finally, the grey shrike-thrush possesses a melodious ringing voice but likewise sings much more repetitiously than a pied.

Some pied butcherbird phrases have the sense of a finely wrought melody from an ancient contemplative tradition, while others sound pedestrian. Singers may establish and then play with expectation: a regular delivery of symmetrical phrases might be suddenly violated with angular slivers of sound. Combinatorial variants can begin to sound like de novo material. Nevertheless, some stylistic conventions and essential ingredients must be conformed to, whether inherited or learned. A song must be representative yet stand out; it must have cultural efficacy. The nonmimicry singing range typically spans an octave plus a perfect fifth, while extremes of range stretch this to nearly three octaves. In mimicry, genre-fluid deliveries crash through most parameters; then, singing covers nearly a four-octave span. A tally of conventions and preferences excluding mimicry is available online.[31]

I admit that the latitude of pied butcherbird vocalizations makes for a disappointing "summary," but only when considered as my inability to better synopsize their singing. Looked at from their perspective, a song has bounce and ambition. The regular and routine are neither easily summarized nor narrow in scope. I can scarcely distinguish between a highly individualistic song and a transgression. The margins of possible variation are amplified by their exploitation of intra- and interphrase contrast via alternation and opposition, even if no reductive sequential formula for phrase succession or type of contrast emerges. It is rare, however, to encounter rhythmic variations of motifs. How structure is relevant on a performance-as-a-whole basis is also inconclusive.

Instead of building or critiquing grand theories, I have by and large stayed with the small details of what pied butcherbirds do. Where I sought a code and its concomitant decoding, instead I found tendencies and affinities—a continuum of exquisite modifications, elaborations, and intensifications in most parameters. Pied butcherbird vocalists are unique and not merely a kind. Musician and musicologist Franco Fabbri has questioned why "musical events with all the characteristics for working well (satisfying the rules of genre)" may still fail or deteriorate.[32] Even had I "cracked the code," formal and technical rules are never enough to describe a bird's song or an individual bird, a human piece of music or a human. The limits of numbers and words do not signal the limits of our or the avian musical world. Pied butcherbird vocalizations are orderly but dynamic; they are unfixed and reshuffled. If we never untangle how and why they sing, they nonetheless do it perfectly well. While this chapter has meditated on general categories and principles, overarching matters of form and structure, and song repertoire, the next follows individuals as they manipulate complex sound forms, with particular emphasis on mutualisms with the human experience of music.

NOTES

1. P. J. Higgins, J. M. Peter, and S. J. Cowling, eds., *Handbook of Australian, New Zealand & Antarctic Birds* (Melbourne: Oxford University Press, 2006), 7A:522.
2. Ibid.
3. W. H. Thorpe problematized the term *subsong* in 1961 (*Bird-Song: The Biology of Vocal Communication and Expression in Birds* [Cambridge: Cambridge University Press, 1961], 64–70).
4. Higgins, Peter, and Cowling, *Handbook*, 7A:521, 521, 523, and 522, respectively.
5. Thomas Carter, "Birds Occurring in the Region of the North-West Cape," *Emu* 3 (1903): 90.
6. E. L. Hyem, "Butcher Bird Notes," *Wildlife in Australia* 6, no. 1 (1969): 123.
7. Sometimes a "phrase" consists of only one note (around 0.2 seconds). A phrase of 7.7 seconds is the longest coherent phrase in my library (with no pause and no possibility of another bird also singing). The normal rate of delivery when vocalizing maximally could be five to ten phrases per minute; a high rate of delivery would be eleven to twenty-two or more.
8. Marc F. Schmidt and Robin Ashmore, "Integrating Breathing and Singing: Forebrain and Brainstem Mechanisms," in *Neuroscience of Birdsong*, ed. H. Philip Zeigler and Peter Marler (Cambridge: Cambridge University Press, 2008), 115–135. This calls to mind what Jon Rose describes as "Aboriginal Australia's greatest contribution to new music worldwide": the technique of circular breathing (*The Music of Place: Reclaiming a Practice* [Strawberry Hills: Currency House, 2013], 34–35).
9. George Prochnik, *In Pursuit of Silence: Listening for Meaning in a World of Noise* (New York: Doubleday, 2010), 14.
10. Alex. Wm. Milligan, "Notes on a Trip to the Yandanooka District, Western Australia," *Emu* 4, no. 4 (1905): 154–155.

11. W. H. Thorpe, "Singing," in *A New Dictionary of Birds*, ed. A. Landsborough Thomson (London: Nelson, 1964), 744.

12. See, for example, Katharina Riebel, Michelle L. Hall, and Naomi E. Langmore, "Female Songbirds Still Struggling to Be Heard," *TRENDS in Ecology and Evolution* 20, no. 8 (2005): 419–420; J. Jordan Price, Scott M. Lanyon, and Kevin E. Omland, "Losses of Female Song with Changes from Tropical to Temperate Breeding in the New World Blackbirds," *Proceedings of the Royal Society B: Biological Sciences* 276 (2009): 1971–1980; and Karan J. Odom et al., "Female song Is Widespread and Ancestral in Songbirds," *Nature Communications* (2014): 1–6.

13. Emma Rose Roper, "Musical Nature: Vocalisations of the Australian Magpie (*Gymnorhina tibicen tyrannica*)," *Context: Journal of Music Research* 32 (2007): 62.

14. Constance Scharff and Jana Petri, "Evo-devo, Deep Homology and Foxp2: Implications for the Evolution of Speech and Language," *Philosophical Transactions of the Royal Society B: Biological Sciences* 366 (2011): 2125.

15. For the entire transcription and supplemental details for both songs, see Hollis Taylor, "Towards a Species Songbook: Illuminating the Vocalisations of the Australian Pied Butcherbird (*Cracticus nigrogularis*)" (PhD diss., University of Western Sydney, 2008) vols. 1 and 2.

16. David Huron, *Sweet Anticipation: Music and the Psychology of Expectation* (Cambridge, MA: MIT Press, 2007), 83. Also see Leonard B. Meyer, *Explaining Music: Essays and Explorations* (Berkeley: University of California Press, 1973), 144.

17. See David Borgo, *Sync or Swarm: Improvising Music in a Complex Age* (New York: Continuum, 2007), 129. Also see Susan McClary and Robert Walser, "Start Making Sense! Musicology Wrestles with Rock," in *On Record: Rock, Pop, and the Written Word*, ed. Simon Frith and Andrew Goodwin (New York: Routledge, 1990), 277–292, where the authors take up the "kick butt" colloquialism to grapple with how rock music directly affects listeners; the avian application is equally pertinent.

18. Thorpe, *Bird-Song*, 90.

19. Bob Snyder, *Music and Memory* (Cambridge, MA: MIT Press, 2000), 66.

20. Leonard G. Ratner, "*Ars Combinatoria*: Chance and Choice in Eighteenth-Century Music," in *Studies in Eighteenth-Century Music: A Tribute to Karl Geiringer on His Seventieth Birthday*, ed. H. C. Robbins Landon and Roger E. Chapman (New York: Oxford University Press, 1970), 343–363.

21. Eberhard Knobloch, "*Musurgia universalis*: Unknown Combinatorial Studies in the Age of Baroque Absolutism," *History of Science* 17 (1979): 266.

22. See R. T. Gunther, *Early Science in Cambridge* (London: Dawsons of Pall Mall, 1937/1969), 96; and Jamie C. Kassler, *Music, Science, Philosophy* (Aldershot: Ashgate, 2001), 37.

23. Albert S. Bregman, *Auditory Scene Analysis: The Perceptual Organization of Sound* (Cambridge, MA: MIT Press, 1990), 475.

24. "Mantras and bird songs share not only certain structural properties, but also lack of an inherent or absolute purpose" (Frits Staal, "Mantras and Bird Songs," *Journal of the American Oriental Society* 105, no. 3 [1985]: 556). For a discussion on how complex birdsongs remain largely unexplored, see Kazutoshi Sasahara et al., "Structural Design Principles of Complex Bird Songs: A Network-Based Approach," *PLoS ONE* 7, no. 9 (2012): 1–9.

25. This echoes zoölogist Gayle Johnson's studies of grey butcherbirds ("Vocalizations in the Grey Butcherbird *Cracticus Torquatus* with Emphasis on Structure in Male

Breeding Song: Implications for the Function and Evolution of Song from a Study of a Southern Hemisphere Species" [PhD diss., Griffith University, 2003], 290).

26. Birds are known to regenerate neurons in their brains; see Fernando Nottebohm, "The Neural Basis of Birdsong," *PLos Biology* 3, no. 5 (2005): 759–761.

27. This echoes Henry W. Oldys on the antiphonal singing of a pair of song-sparrows (Henry W. Oldys, "Parallel Growth of Bird and Human Music," *Harper's Monthly Magazine* 105 [1902]: 477).

28. Aniruddh D. Patel, *Music, Language, and the Brain* (Oxford: Oxford University Press, 2008), 202.

29. All of these examples are summarized in Higgins, Peter, and Cowling, *Handbook*, 7A:522, except the neighing of a horse, which is described in E. A. R. Lord, "*Cracticus nigrogularis* (Black-Throated Butcher-Bird) as Mimic," *Queensland Naturalist* 12, no. 6 (1945): 119.

30. Australian ornithologists Chris Corbet, Sydney Curtis, Gayle Johnson, Vicki Powys, Carol Probets, Eric Vanderduys, and Chris Watson assisted me in mimicry identification.

31. This understanding was greatly enhanced by a three-day, thirty-hour drive from Alice Springs to Sydney with Constance Scharff, who asked (and answered) questions, took notes, prodded, provoked, and in many other ways large and small assisted me to frame a preliminary pied butcherbird overview.

32. Franco Fabbri, "A Theory of Musical Genres: Two Applications," in *Popular Music Perspectives*, ed. D. Horn and P. Tagg (Göteborg: International Association for the Study of Popular Music, 1982), 61.

CHAPTER 6

Musicality and the Art of Song
A Taste for Beauty

Everyone wants to understand art. Why not try to understand the
song of a bird?
   —Pablo Picasso

MARY CREEK, North Queensland, 2 April 2013: "Hi, welcome to Mary
Creek. You're the first camper of the year. I'm surprised to see you. This
time of year, the snakes come in."

I took a photo of a poor snake today in Mareeba that was run over by a
car. It was still alive, but it could barely move.

"Yeah, it musta had its back broken."

My hostess warms to her subject and begins to rattle off more snakes
than I can remember.

"We have two kinds of pythons, and taipans—they have a red outline
around their eye—and the Eastern brown snake, and the black snake, and
the brown-snouted blind snake—when you find 'em in the toilet, don't
worry when they thrust their head at you repeatedly—they really can't
see you. And of course the pythons aren't venomous, and anyway more
people get bitten by great whites."

Yes, but I'm not surfing; I'm here now.

"You have a torch, don't you? Don't go to the toilet without watching
where you're stepping, including once you get there. The green tree frogs
in the toilet attract the snakes—that's why we have these nice English
lawns—not to emulate them, but to see the snakes. Once I really had to

go, and I went running into the toilet, my pants were half down, 'n' out of the corner of my eye I saw a big python—so just keep an eye out."

I nod in vigorous agreement while biting my lip.

"And this time of year we have lots of figbirds, and the snakes go up the trees and get them for dinner."

I pay up, and she departs after inspecting the toilet block for frogs and snakes. In the distance I can see a dividing line between savannah and rain forest. What a slitheringly beautiful place! It has only cost me $15—I could just leave. No one would know, but I won't allow my fear to get the best of me. With no one else here, recording conditions are ideal. I move the camper van into position, so shaken that I let out the clutch while still in gear. I go to draw some water, ready for a bee to tumble out of the spout but not a spider. She dashes back up. I try to slow her down so I can fill my bottle, but she won't be turned back. I settle on washing up with my bottled water. Two mosquitoes in the van are all it takes to sound like a veritable invasion.

I rise at 5:00 AM and enter the amenities block with a flashlight in my left hand and a headlamp strapped to my forehead, my caution index set on extreme code red. When returning to the van, I drive fifty feet to my recording site rather than walk. No pied butcherbird sings, nor do I see one, and despite the lack of human sonic detritus, the dawn chorus is a washout. At least no snake strikes pay dirt. The sun comes out, but I'm not going back to that amenities block. At the first small town, I stop at the side of the road to brush my teeth. The pied butcherbirds there sing a few snippets, but I'm too late for them. (Note to self: never ignore the town birds.)

The next night, I record in a park next to a small performing arts center. The air is redolent with spring blossoms, mostly sweet, but some seize my throat and lungs. The fly veil serves double duty as a mosquito net. In one phrase, the soloist incorporates what sounds like a transposed motif borrowed from a magpie-lark. Next, a fanfare ends on a descending octave, and then a syncopated phrase displays striking harmonic implications straight out of Western music. The bird has been singing for about an hour when two conspecifics slip out of the concert early to feed on moths and other insects that have collected overnight in the lights under the welcoming arch. I have no idea how the soloist experiences this apparent lack of attention. The bird does not stop. From all my years in jazz clubs, I know the energy an audience brings to a performer and how this would make me feel. Later that day, two of this bird's phrases are still looping in my inner ear.

In cataloging correspondences between human and pied butcherbird music making, I am deeply dependent on my biographical trajectory. Other auditors, particularly from other cultures and species, might perceive matters differently. The best I can do is to consider my responses and those of my informants, as well as reports in archival and contemporary texts. I register both sonic *objects* and *behaviors* with human correlates, discussing some behaviors as I progress and separating out others to consider in the chapter's final section.

Countless songbirds hold traditions not entirely unknown or even marginal in human music. By drawing comparisons in a notated blackbird phrase with both a sea shanty and the Gigue from J. S. Bach's Suite No. 3 in D, Joan Hall-Craggs finds that the bird's ability to balance motifs is as sure as a human's. Patricia Gray and colleagues' transdisciplinary, transspecific approach to music links whale songs, bird songs, and human music; they observe, for instance, that a canyon wren's song incorporates a musical scale bearing close resemblance to the opening of Chopin's "Revolutionary" Étude, op. 10, no. 12 in C minor.[1] Charles Hartshorne also compared birdsong to human music and proposed methods for describing and notating birdsong, claiming that human composers under the same constraint to pen short phrases would be hard-pressed to surpass birds and might do less well.[2] His elaborate formula for rating birdsong stresses field experience, and Hartshorne deemed it crucial to disclose whether he had heard a particular species sing in the wild. He ranked the pied butcherbird as one of the world's top songbirds.

The coming sampler pops the hood on issues of rhythm and meter, pitch and melody, timbre, structure, and virtuosity and stage presence. While not all of the topics are equally relevant for pied butcherbirds, the overlap with some human music genres is substantial.

RHYTHM AND METER

The common wisdom is that birdsongs are rhythmic enough, but their pulse is seldom as regular as in much Western (and other) music with simple, set meters. True to this cliché, pied butcherbird vocalizations possess rhythmic vitality, and although to my judgment there is a strong gestural or kinetic component, the songs are not metronomically rigid or brittle. On the other hand, pied butcherbirds often sing one-pitch phrases with equal temporal spacing, indicating they are capable of evenness of delivery. It is entirely possible that their songs possess complex rhythmic or metric relationships yet to be identified, although the presence of additional singing birds or other events could disrupt pacing and flow. In any case, melody does not depend upon strict meter or rhythmic patterns.

Pied butcherbirds can establish common rhythm and temporal devices like accelerando, ritardando, rubato, triplets and other tuplets, anacrusis, rhythmic tension, and swing in very short compass.[3] Likewise, although another analyst could insist that a regular rhythm must be set up before syncopation can interrupt it, I believe that such regularity can be implied quickly within a phrase or by inference from surrounding phrases. Pulsing rattles and slices of silence, so well known in their songs, also fall under the rhythm rubric. "You know how they never really seem to finish their phrases?" a camper once quizzed me. Phrase endings that seem to end on weak beats ("weak" might be influenced by pitch choices) are common in their sound repertoire, as they are in jazz.

MELODY AND PITCH

Music is not a formula: "First you find the logical way, and when you find it, avoid it" was the advice composer and conductor Will Marion Cook gave to Duke Ellington.[4] Neither scientists nor machines can create a great melody or the *je ne sais quoi* that is the hallmark of great music. However, I believe that some songbirds can, just as some, but not all, humans can. Scientists and machines will likely always struggle in their analysis of music—and if machines someday do replace composers, including songbirds, the most that can be said is that they have not yet.

Example 6.1. A compound melodic line sung by one bird. The lower "part" is boxed. Bars 2 and 5 contain octave leaps from F#^{5} to F#^{6}, and bar 3 contains an octave leap from D^6 to D^7.

Pied butcherbirds create melodic expectancies that often resolve as I imagine they should, which could be tested on human listeners to see if they concur. However, "human listeners" is not a homogeneous group. For instance, a study of German and Chinese folksongs found marked contrasts in interval size and phrase position.[5] How would the pied butcherbird compare? Such studies hark back to the seminal work of Leonard Meyer, who underlined that "rich relationships arise from modest means."[6] To be sure, music is and is about relationships: between sounds, between humans, between birds, and sometimes between birds and humans. Melodic perception depends on the brain making connections within and between limited numbers of components, and although a monophonic melody like a pied butcherbird's can be dismissed for its apparent simplicity, such melodies allow for abundant possibilities of description.

Compound melodic line. Earlier, I described how two or more bird musicians may fuse their melodies into a single line to create a hocket. In another type of melody, a single musician alternates between high and low tones, pulling the melody apart and implying two lines. This Gestalt grouping technique is found in the solo violin works of Biber and Bach. In example 6.1 the song suggests separate lines by means of large pitch jumps. Albert Bregman terms this a "compound melodic line," also referred to as

Example 6.2. "The Singing Lesson," where Bird 1 puts forth a few basic notes (lower staff) while Bird 2 unravels a melismatic cadenza (upper staff).

"implied polyphony" or "melodic segregation."[7] I do not know whether this bird is attempting to imply the presence of two singers or is merely taking full advantage of contrast and balance so typical of pied butcherbird vocalizations.

Melisma. Although they can be vocal gymnasts with a flourish here and an arabesque there, pied butcherbirds are not prone to extreme elaboration by way of melisma unless mimicking. Example 6.2 is a notable exception; the experience left the recordist with the vivid impression that he was witnessing a singing lesson by the bird placed in the upper staff.[8] While the simple notes of the bird on the lower staff are in stark contrast to the over-the-top melismatic decoration of the top bird, it is also conceivable that the individual with these simpler notes was the mentor, giving the other a lesson on taste and elegance.

Chimeric melody. One melody eliding into another forms a chimeric melody.[9] The hybrid phrases of Two Tree in the previous chapter are a case in point. In addition, pied butcherbirds' affinity for combinatorics may merge with their penchant for mimicry. In these chimeric melodies, a motif from an alien species is decontextualized and absorbed into a pied butcherbird phrase rather than delivered with other mimicry. Much like a griffin, that legendary creature with the body, hind legs, and tail of a lion and the head, wings, and forepart of an eagle, such a melody makes for an impossible mixture. Some might argue that only the modern human imagination could produce such a construction.[10] ◄) AUDIO 28–32 detail various chimeric melodies, followed by the copied models, all of which, except ◄) AUDIO 31, were recorded at the same site.

Three pied butcherbird motifs from the same bird incorporate a motif from a peaceful dove (*Geopelia placida*) in ◄) AUDIO 28. The dove model is presented twice (at 3.3 sec and 6.8 sec) to aid assessment. ◄) AUDIO 29 incorporates a low note of a peaceful dove (model at 3.7 sec), and ◄) AUDIO 30 a motif from a noisy friarbird (*Philemon corniculatus*) (model at 2.2 sec). ◄) AUDIO 31 features what sounds like a motif from a grey butcherbird. The closest match is at 4.4 seconds, but in general the pied butcherbird's entire phrase seems grey butcherbird–like, with a fast-paced, almost frantic aesthetic (model at 3.6 sec). There are grey butcherbirds in the territory of this chimeric melodist, but since I did not record them there, this model comes from elsewhere. Finally, one bird whom I recorded at the aptly named Butcherbird Hill mimics a human auditory icon—the alarm signal of a reversing truck—matching it in frequency, duration, and timbre and incorporating it in formal song (◄) AUDIO 32).

Human counterparts are rife. A chimeric melody recalls centonization, when a literary work is put together with selections from other works or when a melody is pieced together from preexisting fragments.[11] Although often applied to Gregorian chant, centonization surfaces throughout the world. In addition, incorporating nonsense syllables into a human song is a trick songwriters use in an attempt to turn a good song into a hit song; chimeric melody could be a pied butcherbird analogue.

Iconic human melodies. Occasionally, pied butcherbird themes and those of humans converge. Ornithologist John Hutchinson reported hearing the opening notes of Beethoven's Fifth Symphony.[12] Another person tallied up the themes from the TV shows *The Beverly Hillbillies* (the eleven notes after "[Come and] listen to a story 'bout a man named Jed") and *F Troop* (the nine notes of "The end of the Civil War was near"), as well as the Schertzinger/Mercer song "I Remember You," made popular in 1962 by Frank Ifield (six notes, including splitting "you-ou" into two notes) and several others.[13] A jazz musician heard an exact rendition of trumpeter and bandleader Dizzy Gillespie's six-note riff "Emanon."[14] An informant reported that his neighbor used to play "La Cucaracha" in his hotted-up car, and one morning he heard the pied butcherbird sing it.[15]

Example 6.3. Fanfares from six different pied butcherbirds.

I have encountered melodic inventions that correspond to Richard Wagner's "Bridal Chorus" from his 1850 opera *Lohengrin* ("Here comes the bride"); Kurt Weill's "Mack the Knife"; a variation on the Tin Man's Arlen/Harburg lament "If I Only Had a Heart" from *The Wizard of Oz* (["When] a man's an empty kettle, he should . . . and yet I'm torn apart"); and Miles Davis's "Freddie Freeloader"—the basic SLD2 motif corresponds in pitch and rhythm but not articulation to the Davis theme. One person noticed a change in a song. "'My' birds seem to have become quite adept at the tune I've termed 'You do something to me,' which they developed from an initial 2 notes to the current 7," he reported. "It's mostly done as a duet these days with one bird whistling the melody and its partner whistling an accompanying 2 notes for each one of the melody in a lower key."[16] Human recognition: if we know it, then it *must* be music. Although iconic human themes are amusing and validating, encountering a compelling but previously unknown theme is equally or more satisfying to me.

Fanfare. A flourish from the brass section, flush with arpeggios and repeated notes—with their cornet-like tone and swift, bold delivery, plenty of pied butcherbird phrases fit this metaphor. In example 6.3 / ◀) AUDIO 33, repeated notes and ascending thirds, fourths, and fifths form arpeggiated chords that call to mind a fanfare.

Accent. An accent is perceptual by nature. A "phenomenal accent" can be sparked by an event of emphasis, intensification, or difference; this is where we find the most obvious examples in pied butcherbird songs.

In canvassing phrases for phenomenal accents, we find them in *sforzandi* (notes with a strong attack transient); in complex, harsh, buzzy, or "noisy" notes; in rattles; in sudden dynamic or timbre changes; in leaps to relatively high notes, like all examples of the species call-in-song; in leaps to relatively low notes; and in long notes, like the two long notes in ◄» AUDIO 32 at 1 second matching the signal of a reversing truck and the second note of any SLD2 motif.

When a phrase consists of only one note, not to mention the first and final notes of each phrase that contains more than one note—and most, of course, do—this creates a "structural accent." Arpeggiated chords and any group of two or more consecutive leaps also produce structural accents. "Metrical accents" depend on a sense of evenly spaced meter being set up, and while some songs lean in this direction, this type of accent is much less pertinent, at least to my ear.

Absolute pitch, relative pitch, pitch processing, and octaves. Birds do not just sing songs; they also receive and interpret songs. Absolute and relative pitch perception, as well as a sense of pitch contour and pitch ratio (interval), have been found in some, but not all, birds studied. European starlings (*Sturnus vulgaris*) possess absolute pitch and show a preference for learning pitch patterns on that basis, while black-capped chickadees (*Poecile atricapillus*) can retain a melody with a change of key—in fact, they are able to transpose their phrases across a wide range of pitches.[17] Relative pitch in other songbirds, including birds who shift their song upward to compete with traffic noise, is now well documented in a number of studies.

Birds are far superior to mammals, including us, in their capacity for absolute pitch.[18] Do pied butcherbirds possess it? Ornithologist Gloria Glass recorded out her bedroom window annually for a decade. These recordings provided me with the opportunity to follow the same individual on multiple days and to follow changing phrases through the years.[19] "I would have the tape recorder set up by my bed and just reach out and press PLAY when the singing started before dawn," she wrote to me. "Then I'd hope our dogs would continue to sleep on."[20] In analyzing hours of daily recordings over a two-and-a-half-week period in 2002, I found virtually imperceptible variation in intonation. Variations in recording technique and environmental conditions, as well as the changing position of the bird vis-à-vis the microphone, would be expected to introduce more disparity than exists among the phrases. Combining this with the knowledge that pitch is often stereotypical in pied butcherbird motifs held in common in both ensemble and solo songs leads me to believe that absolute pitch is the norm for pied butcherbirds. Another explanation could be that the birds rely on muscle memory instead of pitch memory, and in any case without banded birds my results are provisional.

Do pied butcherbirds possess relative pitch? If so, they would be able to transpose their melodies, as black-capped chickadees do, with varying starting pitches for the same melodic contours. Again, my hunch is *yes*. The most obvious instances are the numerous cases of the transposed species call and the species call-in-song, as well as duets with transposition. I also have examples in my archive of transposition in solo songs, but since I do not have a *professional* pied butcherbird in a laboratory where I can ask the individual if transposed motifs are equivalent, I cannot make this claim.[21] In addition, absolute pitch tends, at least in this musician, to work against relative pitch—if I learn something in one key, I can only with difficulty transpose it. I have to force the learned pitches out of my head.

Example 6.4 / ◄ AUDIO 34 show phrases from two individuals with a substantial commitment to octaves. The human brain recognizes the octave as special: tones separated by an octave are heard as essentially the same. Octave generalization has been found in white rats (*Rattus norvegicus*), but this is controversial, and in rhesus macaques (*Macaca mulatta*), suggesting a neural basis for this capacity and not learning.[22] There is no evidence to date for this capacity in avian species—but what are we to make of the abundant octave leaps in both solo and duet singing, including at the hand-off point in a duet? Might these leaps suggest that pied butcherbirds possess octave generalization? In another case, a bird was singing in the presence of a more powerful signal from a magpie-lark (*Grallina cyanoleuca*), whom the pied butcherbird mimicked, transposing the phrase down an octave to a more standard pied butcherbird tessitura. I could speculate that the stimulus equivalence for an octave does exist in the magpie-lark example and in the duet in example 5.6, but I lack enough data to make the case for it. Due to the considerable sexual dimorphism in the voice of human males and females, it makes sense that when we do sing

Example 6.4. An individual sings ascending and descending octave leaps in three consecutive phrases (all of which resolve satisfyingly down a semitone) in bars 1–3. Bar 4 displays descending octave leaps on two different pitch pairs from another bird.

together, we need octave equivalence. The capacity seems less relevant to pied butcherbirds' sonic world.

Microtonality. Instances of pied butcherbird microtonality have clear overlaps with human interests, as in the work of Julián Carrillo, Harry Partch, Alois Hába, and Ivan Wyschnegradsky. Chapter 8 details microtonality in a number of other human cultures.

Just intonation. Violinist Jascha Heifetz was reputed to have said, "I don't play in tune; I merely adjust faster than anyone else can hear." Whether he did or did not (say or do this), it is true that our ears are tolerant, even generous, in matters of intonation. Listeners will round up and down. Pitch may be used expressively as well, and vibrato affects pitch. Except among early music and experimental tuning specialists, the twelve-tone equal-tempered system today prevails in Western music. The system is built on compromise, and among vocalists, string players, and other musicians who are free to do so, pitches that are not drawn from the tempered scale are plentiful. While the twelve-tone equal-tempered scale finds "impure" notes nudged into position, just intonation is built on the "pure" tones of simple ratios, an oversimplification nonetheless ample for our purposes here. I am often asked whether I believe that pied butcherbirds sing in just intonation, the assumption being that with its "natural" ratios, just intonation should be found in nature.

In attempting to address the question, I found that measuring a note was not straightforward. Setting aside portamento notes, already a prob-

Example 6.5. Scalar motion in a pied butcherbird duet (upward and downward stems mark the part separation).

lem, I was advised to measure the spectral peak of more stable notes. However, is the peak frequency the best place to measure a note, or might it be the durational center of the note, or the longest stable part of the note? Granted, reporting the standard deviation of repeated measurements would provide increased credibility, but between my doubts about where best to measure and the preponderance of portamentos in pied butcherbird notes, I did not pursue this avenue of analysis. It remains an appealing topic for research on songbirds with fewer portamentos.

Scales, chords, and tonal center. Scalar passages are not common. When intact scales arise, they often consist of a combination of microtones, half and whole steps, and minor thirds; some notes can be repeated before the bird moves on. Most scalar passages are found in mimicry, and these instances fail to suggest a tonic. Other times, a "scale" is merely an ascending or descending rattle. I have not attempted to construct these after the fact as a chromatic, major, or minor scale or as a mode of whatever type and assign songs a harmonic identity like "key of G." In one rare and compelling example of scalar motion (example 6.5 / ◀) AUDIO 35), a duet sees the movement from B^5 to B^6 accomplished via small intervals. Everything about this says "scale."

To date, many of the solo songs that I have notated include all or most of the twelve notes from the chromatic scale with no meaningful statistical preference, not to mention the complication of portamentos connecting pitch points. This remains consistent with my aural impression that many songs lack a clearly defined tonal center, although a single phrase may imply one. Other songs, however, do indeed display pitched hubs of attraction and repose. In addition, inferred chords are common, accomplished either by arpeggiation in the case of a soloist, or arpeggiation and/ or unison singing in ensemble song. The duet in example 6.6 / ◀) AUDIO 36 is such a case, with an F♯ major chord formed by the initial three notes.

Example 6.6. A major chord outlined in the first three notes of a pied butcherbird duet.

If the purpose of a scale is to provide a tonal center as a reference point, one might question the need for it in those humans and birds with absolute pitch. Neither would require asymmetric scale steps or a clear sense of key in order to navigate the acoustic landscape. Perhaps birds' tolerance for ambiguity is greater than ours. Familiar motifs performed on the customary pitch could suffice as avian perceptual anchor points. So while some pied butcherbird vocalizations do present a set of pitch collections, for others this may be the wrong question.

TIMBRE, A "SOUND," AND *KLANGFARBENMELODIE*

Beyond the tone colors reminiscent of a flute, cornet, or organ, mnemonic syllables, and very swift frequency sweeps presented in chapter 4, timbre and its transformation come together in the overarching "sound" of human musicians, birds, and instruments. Composer Arnold Schoenberg coined the term *Klangfarbenmelodie* in 1911 to suggest how a melody might be formed and perceived through timbral transformation. *Klangfarbenmelodie* hinges on structural relationships that are as a rule principally intervallic instead of being formed solely by a succession of shifting tone colors. The strict understanding of Schoenberg's proposal is that changes of color must occur on a single pitch—we find this in pied butcherbird songs. Other scholars have argued that *Klangfarbenmelodie* merely requires that timbre be used structurally, for instance, via a sudden shift in register that draws our attention, or by a robust emphasis on timbral variety.[23] We also find this approach in pied butcherbirds, where a sound's timbral (rather than pitch) contribution is central and the palette is remarkably wide-ranging, with strong fluctuations in multiple parameters.

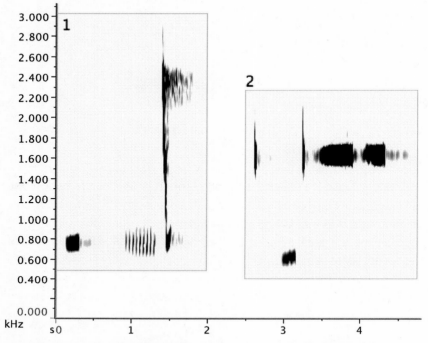

Figure 6.1. Two different pied butcherbird phrases boasting *Klangfarbenmelodie*.

Sound #1 (figure 6.1 / ◀) AUDIO 37 at 0.0 sec) sees a bird following the beginning sustained G^5 with portamento signals, focused again on that pitch, that recall a vintage VCS-3 analog synthesizer. These swiftly ascending repeated notes begin quietly and crescendo slightly but are in stark dynamic contrast to the final note, delivered as a powerful twenty-semitone portamento down to the beginning G^5 pitch. In sound #2 (at 3.5 sec), a bird proposes three distinct colors: a swift, descending semitone portamento arriving at G$\sharp^6$ is followed by a D$\sharp^5$ at the lower limit of the species' range. Such low notes are always softer and timbrally distinct from the notes in the more standard tessitura. The bird repeats the G$\sharp^6$ as a descending portamento and then sings the same pitch twice more—but this time as steady, pure-sounding long tones.

In ◀) AUDIO 38, each of the bird's virtuosic phrases displays clear, bold quality differentiation, at times imparting a feeling of impulsiveness.

Intensification via powerful attacks and steep but rapid ascending and descending portamentos are in evidence, as well as the juxtaposition of pure-sounding notes with noisy ones.

Ensemble singing is also rife with timbral riches, as we have already heard. When looking for a kaleidoscope of colors, the prime exemplar must surely be mimicry (◀ AUDIO 39). Avian forays that are more sound based than pitch based have counterparts in sound art and in the timbral explorations of modernist composers like Luciano Berio's *Sequenzas* for solo instruments and of spectralist composers like Gérard Grisey.

STRUCTURE

Structural relations in birdsong and human music variously manifest from the level of a single note on up to many hours. In this section, I trace how the structuring devices of repetition and variation, ostinato, canon, phrase endings, combinatoriality, and shape and balance play out in pied butcherbird songs. First, however, a word about macrostructure. Whatever a pied butcherbird formal song is, it is not in service to the macrostructures that dominate nineteenth-century Western art music. Although pied butcherbird songs seemingly lack a strict beginning and end, a predetermined length, a set phrase order, and a climax, a formal song does have shape, with its gradual crescendo and eventual decrescendo, as well as the usual truncation of phrases at song's end. The frequent alternation of contrasting themes in rondo form could be compared to avian formal song, but the lack of one principal theme that is regularly returned to (as in a rondo) makes this a weak comparison. I do not claim competence in all musical cultures, but we can look for macrostructural comparisons in non-Western traditions, in improvised music, and in any contemporary or heritage music where cells, stasis, improvisation, free forms, and possibly even free rhythms figure in.

Neither are pied butcherbird ensemble songs without human structural counterparts. Like the music of Anton von Webern, their ensemble exchanges find much happening in a very brief time frame. Human call-and-response activity ranges from Indian classical music to salsa, from African American work songs to military cadences, and from sea shanties to drinking songs. More precisely timed avian hockets find an analogue in Inuit women's finely meshed vocal exchanges.

Repetition and variation. Repetition dominates most music. Over 99 percent of our listening encounters entail music that we have heard before, David Huron claims.[24] These "repeats" occur both within and between works/experiences.

BRUCE HIGHWAY, Queensland: An idle mind is the earworm's workshop—especially when I'm traveling for days on the road. The young man in the camper van next to me only listens to "Stairway to Heaven" three times, but I'll keep it going all evening and crank it up again tomorrow until a traffic sign flashes: "Follow lineman instructions." Soon afterwards I notice, "the Wichita lineman is still on my mind." And later still, just when I'm sure I've put that song behind me, "I think I need a short vaca-uh-tion." The next week, leaving Charters Towers, I tell Jon I'm about to hit the road. I wasn't looking for a pop soundtrack to my life, but an hour later while driving, I had to trace where "Jack, and don't you come back no more, no more, no more, no more" had come from. I pass a fisherman with "Benny" in huge letters on the front of his truck. That's all the prompting required for "B-B-B-Benny and the Jets." And so it goes until I can get a violin under my chin again.

Stuck song syndrome—these scraps of sound that stick in our head and endlessly repeat are tagged *Ohrwurm* (earworm) in German, *musique entêtante* (insistent music) in French, and *canzone tormentone* (tormenting song) in Italian. Whatever the terminology, do they have a counterpart in the avian world? Many a bird's simple, repetitive themes command attention and are easily remembered. Some catchy snippets take me over for the day, while others hook me into including them in my avian (re)compositions. Repetition and memorability are cornerstones in music, including commercial jingles, no matter the species.[25]

Music tolerates, invites, and exploits reiteration. In most genres, we want to predict, *but* we also want to be surprised. Hartshorne's most significant article concerns the monotony-threshold, or limit of tolerance for

Example 6.7. Bars 1–2: two one-pitch phrases from different birds. The first bar sees rhythmic variation on one pitch, while in the second example a bird delivers all seven notes in the same steady rhythm. Bar 3: as part of a pied butcherbird duet, one individual repeats the first motif four times.

repetition, and how this is reflected in a bird's singing rate and transition versatility. He understands the interplay of repetition and variation as music's core challenge.[26] Musicians must engage and reengage the listener's ear to prevent dullness, on the one hand, and chaotic variability, on the other. To produce songs unique yet suitable to the task, pied butcherbirds, like their human counterparts, draw on repetition techniques as "a structuring principle of coherence" yet seek out fresh material to combat aesthetic fatigue.[27]

Repetition can occur at every structural level as a bird transforms familiar phrases in subtle and not-so-subtle ways. Notes can be repeated (the one-pitch phrases in example 6.7, bars 1–2 / ◄》 AUDIO 40 exhibit a slower delivery than a rattle), motifs can be repeated (the duet in example 6.7, bar 3 / ◄》 AUDIO 41), phrases can be repeated immediately or later in the song, and a group of phrases can be (but very rarely is) repeated in sequential order. A musical component can stay the same structurally and yet modulate from a functional or psychological point of view.

Combinatoriality. We associate additive process with minimalist composers like Steve Reich and Philip Glass. The previous chapter followed the combinatorial proclivities of Ross Stuart and Two Tree in solo song, where additive process is also routine. I developed a color chart for its analysis (see www.piedbutcherbird.net). Although initially intended to assist those unable to read standard notation, these charts became quite useful to me, particularly when phrase type is not relevant, since they work on motif and note levels, revealing how avian minimalists go about building a large, rich repertoire.

In another approach to analyzing combinatoriality, we developed a statistical estimate to quantify phrase order. We found that while birds of high repertoire complexity keep interest going by having different phrase types, they avoid confusing their avian audience by placing familiar motifs into their phrases. The metaphor of snap-together beads again pertains. Say the orange bead appears in multiple phrase types (whether at the beginning, middle, or end of a phrase). These orange "beads" will appear regularly and be evenly spaced in these different phrases. As human musicians often do, pied butcherbirds balance complexity by maximizing the regularity of certain elements of their songs.[28]

Ostinato. NELLY BAY, Magnetic Island, North Queensland, 17 September 2007, 5:50 AM: At sunrise, breaking waves mix with a dawn chorus of small tropical birds and insects, underscored by a pied butcherbird who maintains loyalty to a two-note ostinato in the acoustic fabric of an otherwise high-frequency shimmering. As acoustic calling cards go, this pied butcherbird's is all low-hype, high-integrity prog chirp.

In human music, some ostinatos (simple, repeated, and unchanging patterns in the midst of other changing sounds) serve in the background—like the sonic workbenches of ground bass figures or the *lahara* in Hindustani classical music—while other ostinatos are foregrounded—Maurice Ravel's *Boléro* comes to mind. Jazz and blues riffs are ostinatos. Sub-Saharan African music and Afro-Cuban music are also well acquainted with the concept (whether melodic or rhythmic), as are some birds. In the dawn chorus, a grey shrike-thrush (GST) predominates, while a pied butcherbird (PBB) with a delicate, spare aesthetic holds to a two-note ostinato (example 6.8 / ◄) AUDIO 42). The harmonic convergence, with the GST rising a major third above and doubling at the octave, makes for an intriguing pairing.

Canon. Meaning literally "rule," the term *canon* pertains when "one melodic strand gives the rule to another."[29] Counterpoint contributes

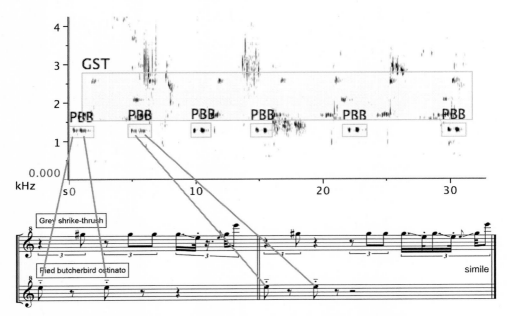

Example 6.8. A pied butcherbird (PBB) sings an ostinato while a grey shrike-thrush (GST) rings out its phrase (music notation takes account of the first 10 sec).

to music's magic, but pied butcherbirds only sing monophonically (an unaccompanied single voice) with occasional doubling—or do they? The timing of countersinging in formal song can be concurrent, alternating, or overlapping. Granted, the *function* of countersinging could be a vocal contest or a sure ploy for getting attention, like playing on a rest beat, but the effect is a highly musical one. Anthropomorphism forbids, but zoö-musicology encourages, speculation on the possibility that creating an aesthetic experience is also part of the function of countersinging, since almost anyone hearing it would think so. Are pied butcherbird phrases formed with the instinct that they must work together harmonically when more than one singer is broadcasting in the acoustic space? Some soloists appear to alter their phrase choices when there is countersinging. Is a bird merely minimizing the competitive background noise through "song asynchrony" or "displacement patterns," as ethologists might character-ize it, or could these emerging and fading phrases from the avian song community have a satisfying musical purpose?[30] While we might assume

Example 6.9. Phrase endings with rhythmic reduction.

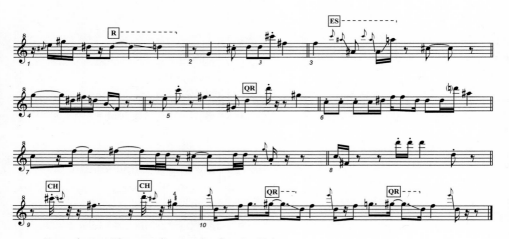

Example 6.10. Phrase endings with a drop in pitch.

that these songs foreground vocal expertise and that harmony is not their essence, to consider a soloist's song independently from a neighbor's is to perhaps drift into a merely functional interpretation—to believe that song is simply a bird taking care of business. I cannot speak to birds' intentions, but countersinging strikes a clear parallel with Thelonius Monk and Charlie Rouse breaking into an improvised canon (or "canonic imitation") on a chorus of "Bemsha Swing."[31]

Phrase endings à la Schoenberg. Schoenberg sees a phrase as possessing a sense of completeness and yet as well adapted for recombination with

Example 6.11. Phrase endings graduating to smaller intervals.

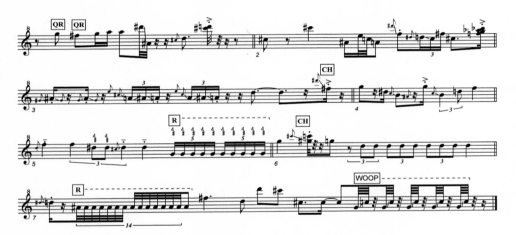

Example 6.12. Phrase endings with other suitable differentiations.

other similar components. He suggests conventions that can facilitate phrases achieving internal cohesiveness and artistic coherence, noting that a phrase ending is typically rhythmically differentiated for the sake of punctuation. A combination of distinguishing features may mark a phrase ending: "rhythmic reduction, melodic relaxation through a drop in pitch, the use of smaller intervals and fewer notes (part and parcel of rhythmic reduction), or by any other suitable differentiation."[32] These are widespread in pied butcherbird song (examples 6.9–6.12). One deserves expanded comment. Example 6.12 details what "other suitable differentiations" might look like *chez* pied butcherbirds. Bars 1–3 each ends with an accent. In bar 1, the bird accomplishes the accent via a large leap and a two-note chord on the final note. Bar 2 is similar, with the accent on an upward leap and a note of wide harmonic content on the final note. Bar 3's accent and large leap are followed by a steep portamento creating a *chip* sound on the final note. A structural accent in the outline of a G dominant seventh chord arrives after a leap in bar 4. Bars 5–7 see extended repetition of the final note. All of these phrases also achieve the rhythmic punctuation upon which the other suggestions are premised.

Shape and balance. Pied butcherbirds and humans often find themselves on the same page in matters of shape and balance. In example 6.13 / ◀) AUDIO 43, a bird embellishes and then revisits $F\#^6$, followed by an octave drop to $F\#^5$; this leap then reverses with an arpeggio ending on $D\#^6$. I hear this phrase as suggesting an F♯ major sixth chord. The E^6 note that follows in the second phrase gives the strong sense that it is the resolution of the $D\#^6$ note, reinforced by the outline of a C major chord, again by way of a leap that reverses. I notate rests here to clarify the imparted sense of shape and balance. Such economy means that each note takes on more importance, structurally and musically, than might normally be the case, and the phrases accord well with my acculturated Western ear in matters of shape and tonality.

Likewise, the spareness in example 6.14 / ◀) AUDIO 44 is musically demanding. The bird on the lower staff sings an ascending and then a descending perfect fourth, with note 2 ($D\#^6$) resolving downward a semitone to note 4 (D^6). The beginning and ending $C\#^6$ in the upper staff heightens this sense of resolution, which ascends by a semitone in the lower staff bird's final D^6. The simplicity of the lower staff sets off the embellishments in the upper staff.

A recording of nocturnal formal song at Lamington National Park, Queensland, began at 5:45 AM (example 6.15, bars 1–4). The alternation between the descending and ascending major thirds is particularly satisfying to my ear, which I hear as movement between an F♯ major chord and a C major chord a tritone away. However, in bar 2 the phrase does not find repose on the C^6 but instead moves ambiguously to a $C\#^6$ and then $D\#^6$. The $D\#^6$ resolves downward a semitone on the first note of bar 3, and the jockeying between the two chords begins again, although bar 4 is truncated. The four phrases are delivered twice intact, and then the bird

Example 6.13. Shape and balance in a pied butcherbird formal song.

Example 6.14. Shape and balance in a pied butcherbird duet.

Example 6.15. Phrases of nocturnal formal song delivered at Lamington National Park at 5:30 AM (bars 1–4), 7:30 AM (bars 5–8), and 9:00 AM (bars 9–11).

begins to transform the material, first repeating bar 4 (the final two notes of line 1) and then exploring other possibilities, including truncation of other phrases. As the song progresses, these basic phrases are delivered "out of order," thwarting my expectation; I notice my brain attempting to rearrange them to conform to my memory and my musical sense of how they should be ordered. While the surprise created by angularity and disproportion after the avian "classicism" is not what I would think to compose, the phrases nonetheless so parallel my sense of musicality that this song features in my (re)composition portfolio.[33]

By 7:30 AM this or another individual at the same location contradicts my personal experience of never hearing a formal song delivered after a spring dawn chorus. However, the phrases are sporadic, and the recordist reports: "A series of solo calls, mostly segments of the dawn song (heard earlier) and occasional distant answering calls. Sounds like a young bird practicing."[34] Again, I hear a sense of proportion and balance so familiar to my ear, including reversals after leaps interspersed with deferred semitone motion (bars 5–7). At 9:00 AM a bird delivers additional isolated fragments that see a further reworking of the themes of leaps and semitone motion, both deferred and contiguous (bars 8–10).

VIRTUOSITY AND STAGE PRESENCE

Virtuosity. A virtuoso amazes, enchants, and seduces us with risk and flair, energy and self-confidence. Chopin had his études, Paganini his caprices, and Hendrix his incendiary version of "The Star-Spangled Banner." Some pied butcherbirds are also elite musicians who set themselves apart through virtuosity. Although mimicry contains the bulk of gymnastic efforts, formal solo and ensemble songs also see noteworthy efforts in this direction.

ETHERIDGE RIVERBED, Greens Park, Georgetown, North Queensland: In 2015 I recorded a bird for five consecutive days. In four of them, this energetic virtuoso of timbral tricks, large leaps, and combinatorics, including two phrases with harmonic implications convincingly paralleling eighteenth-century Western classical music, sang reliably from one songpost. Pull up, point microphone, and wait—it's rarely so simple for me. Day 3 was more typical. I had to go running to stay close as the bird rotated among distant songposts outside the park. Near dawn, the bird flew right over me and landed in a tree ten feet away. I was too close—perhaps for the bird, but definitely for my own sensibility. The signal was so loud that

I had to pull the long-distance "shotgun" microphone out of my hand-held recorder to avoid distortion. I went to the in-built mics. Still too loud. I turned down the input, but what I could not turn down was this virtuoso's high-voltage presence. I took several steps back. The experience was larger than life, much as you might imagine a human soloist, who must project from the stage to the very back of an auditorium, suddenly being right there in your face. It took me back forty-plus years to when I accompanied conductor Walter Susskind to Henryk Szeryng's hotel room to hear a Paganini violin concerto. Szeryng was due to premiere it with the St. Louis Symphony. His virtuoso technique and the loud, luscious sound he made on his Guarneri del Gesù "Le Duc" were overpowering. At one point he said while continuing to play, "Paganini himself said this passage was impossible."

In ◄» AUDIO 45, the first soloist (at 0.0 sec) sings two double notes, followed by a long rattle that morphs into a quasi rattle. The second soloist (at 3.3 sec) sings rapid ascending and descending portamentos. The ensemble song in ◄» AUDIO 46 sees notes varying in multiple parameters and includes a remarkable two-and-a-half-octave descending portamento from near the top to near the bottom of the species' range (from A^7 to E^5). The semitone alternation of the final four notes is also notable—familiar to a Western auditor as a leading tone resolving to the tonic. ◄» AUDIO 47 depicts an even more virtuosic ensemble.

Stage, stage presence, and visual spectacle. A stage or musicians' platform finds correspondence in an avian songpost, whether a tree, utility wire, roof, aerial, or other suitable location. Not just any post will do. Acoustic properties and other environmental factors can affect performance, either constraining or enhancing it. There are issues of comfort and safety. Diurnal singers would be concerned with how best to present their visual displays. Sometimes it is not the music but the commitment and character of the musician coming through. You have to "sell," and some songsters know how to read and work the crowd—they have "it." I have heard individuals take advantage of reverberant spaces like a cliff face and metal constructions like an awning or an arch under a building overhang. From a listener's point of view, "where you are perched/seated" impacts the performance's reception, as it does for humans. Male bowerbirds also consider this aspect.

Ventriloquism. POINT KARUMBA, Gulf of Carpentaria, tropical North Queensland, 27 October 2013: On my drive across the tidal flats toward Karumba, the trees all but disappear, and the horizon thins to a line. While still fifteen miles from the sea, I pass a twenty-inch dead fish on the road. The minute I arrive and get out of the van, I'm self-conscious about committing multiple crimes against fashion. I'm wearing humidity's hot, wet blanket, and my hair has gone from dishwater blonde to dishrag blonde. The view is spectacular, unbroken by swimmers or waders. There's not a soul on the beach, since the local "salties"—saltwater crocodiles (*Crocodylus porosus*)—would quickly eliminate anyone foolish enough to enter the water, as would the marine stingers. Most people are here for the fishing. Trophy-size barramundi, salmon, snapper, and mackerel are regularly taken from the Arafura Sea. Another drawing card this time of year are the linear clouds that stretch for up to six hundred miles. Low and tube-shaped, Morning Glory (or "roll") clouds usually come as one-offs, but this rare phenomenon can arrive in rows of six or more. A sign in the women's amenities block details the proclivities of Graham, a green tree frog. He has full rights here and occasionally even sneaks into the swimming pool. We are warned that we should leave him and his siblings alone and that, if he is sent away, he will return before day's end.

That night, I park at the golf course and head out walking. In due course, I hear several singing birds, all echoing similar themes. However, each time that I close in (I think), like the end of a rainbow, no bird can be found. The singing is brief, and the sound has no known address.

The ability to make sounds seem to come from somewhere other than the emitter occurs in some birds' alarm calls and serves as an effective defense mechanism. Ventriloquism in song could also be such a mechanism, since a bird singing alone in the dark inevitably draws attention—or it could simply be that our large human head and external ears are not efficient at localizing these sounds. With longer songs, I have been successful in finding ventriloquists by heading out in multiple "wrong" directions until

I finally narrowed in on the soloist. While not a quotidian human activity, ventriloquism nonetheless has modified links to human music. The off-stage choruses in Verdi's operas *Il Corsaro* and *Il Trovatore* come to mind, as does the remarkable coloratura soprano Edith Helena, who mimicked the violin with her voice while appearing onstage playing a stringless violin in pantomime to "Intermezzo" from *Cavalleria Rusticana*.[35] Helena's vaudeville act included taking the violin out from under her chin at the end while continuing her singing, to the astonishment of her audience.

MUSICAL ACTIVITIES AND BEHAVIORS

A few final avian activities and behaviors with strong links to human ones need our reflection. A song directed toward a potential mate can be appreciated as a serenade (it's Rod Stewart singing "Da Ya Think I'm Sexy?"). The dawn chorus marks a moment and a place like a town clock or pealing church bells. Mobbing is a protest song. Outdoor concerts may be canceled due to inclement weather. Subsong has links to humming and the quiet, subdued singing termed *sotto voce*. Much like an orchestra, gamelan ensemble, or freely improvised music session, multi-individual birdsongs demand that avian choristers subordinate and integrate their musical personality into the general group. Phrase length in formal solo songs is similar to human phrases, while the overall duration of formal solo songs displays a yearning for expansive content. A list of other mutualisms must surely include vocal contests; rehearsals; warming up; do-it-yourself production; musical activities for certain hours, seasons, places, and situations; musical authority (who has the right to sing at any given time); ergonomic issues; performing for an audience; reactions to poor performances; ambition exceeding competence; building on previous efforts; singer-songwriters; music as a tool for marketing; and singing lessons.

Composition. Pied butcherbirds—they take their own and others' stuff, customize stuff, chop stuff up, add stuff, restuff, possibly stuff up, and recycle. This "acceptance and rejection" of ideas, as well as transformation of them, is consistent with the ability to compose and not merely a "manifestation of their behavioural flexibility," as scholarly language might portray it.[36] More often than not, pied butcherbird vocalizations strike me as an unfolding composition.

Festival music and music camps. Do pied butcherbirds, like humans, go to music camps, have song festivals, or conduct music tourism? In the spring of 2014 I recorded at six new sites along the Ross River Highway east of Alice Springs, each a few miles from the previous. Due to the large number of energetic individual singers of varying abilities at each site and no lone singers in the miles in between, each "camp" had a celebratory feel. I spontaneously wrote up these zones of beauty in my field notes as "music camps." For instance, two main soloists held forth with rolling phrases in the massive river red gums at Bitter Springs Music Camp, with a number of understudies also joining in. Several miles away and across the highway, Trephina Ridges Music Camp had birdsong coming from several different clumps of nondescript trees lining a dry creekbed. Afterward, I wondered if I was simply expressing my enthusiasm for the experience, or if there could possibly be something to it. Some bird species are known to gather in leks for courtship during the breeding season. My speculation here goes beyond this, to wondering if there is a function outside of breeding for these "camps," that of coming together to learn and celebrate singing. At first blush it seems preposterous, given everything I have read about the function of birdsong—but if instead of thinking about it I go back to my sense of it, I come to a different conclusion.

Juvenile singing. Humans do not have a corner on out-of-tuneness, bad tone, or questionable musicality. While such a judgment is subjective, since nearly all of my examples of these come from immature birds, and since this trio of qualities generally arrives together, it seems a safe conclusion. A sonogram depicting the highly variable and poorly defined notes of a juvenile singer in ◀ AUDIO 48 is available online.

Improvisation. The dawn chorus could be considered a large-group free improvisation where avian songsters work across species to create a consensus of impromptu patterns. My focus here, though, is on matters more easily documented in the song culture of specific pied butcherbirds. Improvisation suggests a substantial commitment to in-the-moment decision making that sets it apart from precomposed music. An oral culture is not necessarily an improvising one, but for those pied butcherbirds who do improvise, instantaneous choices are likely drawn from previously rehearsed musical content. While prior planning maintains a degree of invisibility in improvisation, constraints do pertain. As in composition, improvisation sees a musician making choices and balancing the security of something familiar with the specialness of something new. It arrives in a pluralistic scene: from Two Tree's long, sustained process of improvisation shaped by combinatorics to an immature bird's rambling mish-mash, and from dynamic ensemble songs to a sudden montage of alien species appended to a formal solo song.[37]

Music as the production of place. The connection between sound and environment is ancient.[38] Composers have regularly grappled with how to represent a place in their music. Some works seem to merely bear a location's name, while in others *place* is more than an extraneous component: a place may be commemorated, evoked, or propped up. Sound artists and pied butcherbirds are known to sonify their neighborhoods. Ensemble songs and dialects speak to where birds are from, and avian solo songs can be framed as statements of power that register a territory; both have correspondences to a place-making song or a national anthem. Meanwhile, some group agonistic calls bring to mind a military band.

Singing lesson. MALENY, Queensland, 25 March 2013, 6:17 AM: It's autumn, so no nocturnal singing is expected or delivered. The dawn chorus commenced at 5:10 AM, including song from laughing kookaburras, pied currawongs, and eastern whipbirds (*Psophodes olivaceus*). Four pied butcherbirds, two mature and two immature, sang about a dozen varied ensemble phrases from 5:30 to 5:45 AM and then fell silent for thirty minutes while feeding. Now, at 6:17 AM, they begin again, delivering twenty-five varied ensemble phrases. Next, a mature and an immature bird fly up to a utility wire and face each other, inches apart. The immature bird hunches over, as if in complete concentration. The mature bird begins to sing, raising and lowering the bill as the notes require.

Something is noticeably different: rather than singing with immediate variety, the bird repeats each phrase a number of times. The five phrases in this morning's lesson are more difficult than the ones sung earlier. Phrase A, which begins with two extremely low portamentos, sees thirty-seven iterations, each about five seconds apart. Twice, when attention seems to be waning, the apprentice is brought back around with a swift beak snap. The young bird flies off with a shriek but immediately returns. Phrase B (a descending rattle) sees eight iterations, Phrase C (which begins with an ascending octave leap) eleven, Phrase D (which begins with two *chip* sounds and arrives in several truncated forms) thirty-five, and Phrase E (a stationary rattle) five. While a few are intermixed, most come in segregated sections of just the one phrase type. Unlike in a Suzuki class, there'll be no call and response. In this home schooling, the teacher has the floor, and the student is expected to learn by listening. Suddenly, it's a surprise test. After sixteen minutes, the adult flies down to the "butcher shop" and retrieves a morsel. While holding it in the beak, the adult begins a soft barking sound that continues while the immature bird flies down to the tree near the adult. The immature bird sings for over nine minutes and is joined in the end by a second immature bird who also sings. None of their phrases are from the lesson; the phrases are instead from their easier, already mastered repertoire. In the end, the adult swallows the treat and flies off.

Cognitive neuroscientist Stanislas Dehaene asks, "Why is *Homo sapiens* the only species that actively teaches itself? Why is he unique in his ability to transmit a sophisticated culture?"—and Dehaene is not alone in this belief.[39] "Pedagogy: Confined to Humans," begin cognitive scientists David Premack and Ann James Premack. They insist that in pedagogy, the model must observe the novice and judge her, as well as actively intervene to modify her performance, which the authors believe is unknown in animals.[40] However, the teaching just described in the Maleny bird checks off each of their boxes and demonstrates a complex form of knowledge sharing.

The event also meets all of biologists T. M. Caro and M. D. Hauser's requirements for teaching: the teacher has modified his behavior only in a naive observer's presence and has done this at some cost or at minimum without immediate benefit; the teacher's behavior has encouraged and/ or punished the pupil's—both in this case; and the teacher has provided the pupil with experience that assists her to learn this skill more rapidly and efficiently than she might otherwise do.[41] While I find nothing in the literature detailing a mature bird offering to reward a vocal student with food, this is the way the event reads. More stringent definitions of teaching require the teacher to be sensitive to the pupil's changing competence, and here again this singing lesson checks off the box, since the Maleny tutor was singing difficult phrases that the immature birds had apparently not yet learned or perhaps not yet attempted to sing. A photo of this remarkable singing lesson is available online.

This chapter has investigated the musical substance of pied butcherbird songs as they relate to human genres as I know them. Equivalence in every parameter is not my claim. This distillation of their songs lays bare how, though much is familiar, some of what they sing is strange to us. Nonetheless, whether subtle or bold, simple or complex, lyrical or spirited, their vocalizations, while not conforming to any one human genre, sound musical to humans on our own terms. These choristers lead robust musical lives, singing songs that seem to go far beyond what would be necessary for registering an occupation of place and passing along their genes. This review of their success in creating and re-creating a culture with clear and unequivocal links to sonic objects and behaviors in human music now puts us in a better position to contemplate a definition of *music*.

NOTES

1. Joan Hall-Craggs, "The Aesthetic Content of Bird Song," in *Bird Vocalizations: Their Relations to Current Problems in Biology and Psychology. Essays Presented to W. H. Thorpe*, ed. by R. A. Hinde, 376, 377 (Cambridge: Cambridge University Press, 1969); and Patricia M. Gray et al., "The Music of Nature and the Nature of Music," *Science* 291, no. 5,501 (2001): 53. The latter article is an outcome of BioMusic, a think-tank of scientists and musicians formed in 1986 to enhance our appreciation of the environment through music (see "BioMusic," accessed April 22, 2014, http://www.biomusic.org /index2.html). Also see Luis F. Baptista and Robin A. Keister, "Why Birdsong Is Sometimes Like Music," *Perspectives in Biology and Medicine* 48, no. 3 (2005): 426–443; Bernie Krause, *Wild Soundscapes: Discovering the Voice of the Natural World* (Berkeley: Wilderness Press, 2002), 51–62; and Hollis Taylor and Dominique Lestel, "The Australian Pied Butcherbird and the Natureculture Continuum," *Journal of Interdisciplinary Music Studies* 5, no. 1 (2011): 57–83.

2. Charles Hartshorne, *Born to Sing: An Interpretation and World Survey of Bird Song* (Bloomington: Indiana University Press, 1973); and Charles Hartshorne, "The Relation of Bird Song to Music," *Ibis* 100 (1958): 427.

3. I use *swing* here in the sense of a two-to-one subdivision of regular pulses. There are many other understandings and outcomes for swing.

4. Stephanie Stein Crease, *Duke Ellington: His Life in Jazz with 21 Activities* (Chicago: Chicago Review Press, 2009), 48.

5. Daniel Shanahan and David Huron, "Interval Size and Phrase Position: A Comparison between German and Chinese Folksongs," *Empirical Musicology Review* 6, no. 4 (2011): 187–197.

6. Leonard B. Meyer, *The Spheres of Music: A Gathering of Essays* (Chicago: University of Chicago Press, 2000), 56.

7. Albert S. Bregman, *Auditory Scene Analysis: The Perceptual Organization of Sound* (Cambridge, MA: MIT Press, 1990), 464.

8. Recorded by composer David Lumsdaine at Pebbly Beach, Station Creek, New South Wales, 23 September 1983. "'The Singing Lesson': two birds perched side by side on a banksia singing a *solo* song; one sings the fully decorated version of the local dawn solo, the second a more sketchy outline version. A beautiful study of what structure, tuning and melodic decoration might mean to pied butcherbirds" (David Lumsdaine, letter to the author, 2 July 2005).

9. David Huron, *Sweet Anticipation: Music and the Psychology of Expectation* (Cambridge, MA: MIT Press, 2007), 233.

10. See Gary Tomlinson, *A Million Years of Music: The Emergence of Human Modernity* (New York: Zone Books, 2015), 260.

11. Willi Apel, "Cento," in *Harvard Dictionary of Music* (Cambridge, MA: Belknap Press, 1970), 140.

12. P. J. B. Slater, "Sequences of Song in Chaffinches," *Animal Behaviour* 31 (1983): 278.

13. "This ['I Remember You'] is so obvious that even my most sceptical golfing partners have to agree with me. Less frequently, they perform the first lines of 'Money Makes the World Go Around' and 'Whistle while You Work.' Some three weeks ago I heard a Butcher Bird sing perfectly the first two notes of 'You Do Something to Me'—namely, 'You do.' This was all they could come up with until this morning when I heard a bird from outside my home add another two notes, so that we now had 'You do something!' If I tell you that I'd actually been whistling the first line to them after I initially heard the first two notes you could easily be excused for thinking that I'm making it up. Far more likely that they have some capacity to construct songs with which humans can easily identify" (Simon Green, e-mail message to the author, 5 October 2008).

14. "It was a bird in Lismore, New South Wales in 1989" (Freddie Hill, e-mail message to the author, 30 March 2011).

15. Warwick Biggs, author interview, 14 November 2015.

16. Simon Green, e-mail message to the author, 12 May 2009.

17. See Stewart H. Hulse and Suzanne C. Page, "Toward a Comparative Psychology of Music Perception," *Music Perception* 5, no. 4 (1988): 427–452; and Ron Weisman et al., "Absolute and Relative Pitch Production in the Song of the Black-Capped Chickadee," *Condor* 92 (1990): 118–124.

18. Ronald G. Weisman et al., "New Perspectives on Absolute Pitch in Birds and Mammals," in *The Oxford Handbook of Comparative Cognition*, ed. Thomas R. Zentall and Edward A. Wasserman (Oxford: Oxford University Press, 2012), 67–79.

19. Gloria Glass, CD038-CD042, author library.

20. Gloria Glass, e-mail message to the author, 29 May 2006.

21. "Professional" is how Dominique Lestel aptly describes laboratory animals (*Les origines animales de la culture* [Paris: Flammarion, 2001], 394).

22. H. Richard Blackwell and Harold Schlosberg, "Octave Generalization, Pitch Discrimination, and Loudness Thresholds in the White Rat," *Journal of Experimental Psychology* 33, no. 5 (1943): 407–419; and Anthony A. Wright et al., "Music Perception and Octave Generalization in Rhesus Monkeys," *Journal of Experimental Psychology: General* 129, no. 3 (2000): 291–307. For more on octave generalization, see Jeffrey Cynx,

"Auditory Frequency Generalization and a Failure to Find Octave Generalization in a Songbird, the European Starling (*Sturnus vulgaris*)," *Journal of Comparative Psychology* 107, no. 2 (1993): 140–146; Wright et al., "Music Perception"; and Josh McDermott and Marc Hauser, "The Origins of Music: Innateness, Uniqueness, and Evolution," *Music Perception* 23, no. 1 (2005): 29–59.

23. See, for example, Alfred Cramer, "Schoenberg's 'Klangfarbenmelodie': A Principle of Early Atonal Harmony," *Music Theory Spectrum* 24, no. 1 (2002): 1–34.

24. Huron, *Sweet Anticipation*, 241. Also see Elizabeth Hellmuth Margulis, *On Repeat: How Music Plays the Mind* (Oxford: Oxford University Press, 2014).

25. For more on this phenomenon, see Daniel J. Levitin, *This Is Your Brain on Music: The Science of a Human Obsession* (New York: Dutton, 2006), 151; and Oliver Sacks, *Musicophilia: Tales of Music and the Brain* (New York: Alfred A. Knopf, 2007), 41–48.

26. Charles Hartshorne, "The Monotony-Threshold in Singing Birds," *Auk* 73 (1956): 176–192.

27. Arnold Schoenberg, *Coherence, Counterpoint, Instrumentation, Instruction in Form*, trans. and ed. Severine Neff (Lincoln: University of Nebraska Press, 1994), 37.

28. Eathan Janney et al., "Temporal Regularity Increases with Repertoire Complexity in the Australian Pied Butcherbird's Song," *Royal Society Open Science* 3, no. 160,357 (2016): 1–15.

29. Tim Rutherford-Johnson, Michael Kennedy, and Joyce Bourne Kennedy, "Canon," in *The Oxford Dictionary of Music*, accessed 5 April 2014, http://www.oxfordreference.com.

30. Martin L. Cody and James H. Brown, "Song Asynchrony in Neighbouring Bird Species," *Nature* 222, no. 5,195 (1969): 778–780.

31. *Thelonius Monk: The Complete Riverside Recordings*, Riverside RCD-022–2, disc 15, track 8 (1986).

32. Arnold Schoenberg, *Fundamentals of Musical Composition*, ed. Gerald Strang and Leonard Stein (London: Faber and Faber, 1967), 3.

33. Hollis Taylor, *Lamington Plateau* for flute (Portland, OR: Twisted Fiddle, 2008).

34. David Lumsdaine, letter to the author, 2 July 2005.

35. "Edith Helena," accessed 14 April 2014, http://www.tinfoil.com/cm-0503.htm.

36. Trevor Hold, "Messiaen's Birds," *Music & Letters* 52, no. 2 (1971): 114; and Luis F. Baptista and Pepper W. Trail, "The Role of Song in the Evolution of Passerine Diversity," *Systematic Biology* 41, no. 2 (1992): 245.

37. See Hollis Taylor, "Blowin' in Birdland: Improvisation and the Australian Pied Butcherbird," *Leonardo Music Journal* 20 (2010): 79–83.

38. Traditional Australian Aboriginal culture knew no other possibility. For a fuller discussion, see Hollis Taylor and Andrew Hurley, "Music and Environment: A Snapshot of Contemporary and Emerging Convergences," *Journal of Music Research Online*, 2015. Likewise, the Temiar people of the Malaysian rain forest "map and mediate their relationships with the land and each other through song" (Marina Roseman, "Singers of the Landscape: Song, History, and Property Rights in the Malaysian Rain Forest," *American Anthropologist* 100, no. 1 [1998]: 111).

39. Stanislas Dehaene, *Reading in the Brain* (New York: Viking, 2009), 3.

40. David Premack and Ann James Premack, "Why Animals Have Neither Culture nor History," in *Companion Encyclopedia of Anthropology*, ed. Tim Ingold (London: Routledge, 1994), 354.

41. T. M. Caro and M. D. Hauser, "Is There Teaching in Nonhuman Animals?," *Quarterly Review of Biology* 67, no. 2 (1992): 153.

CHAPTER 7

Border Conflicts at Music's Definition

Whoever engages in a musical performance, of whatever kind, is saying to themselves and to anyone who may be taking notice, *This is who we are*, and that is a serious affirmation indeed.
—Christopher Small, *Musicking*

WILLS DEVELOPMENTAL ROAD, North Queensland, 30 October 2013: Dark clouds of red-tailed black cockatoos wheel overhead as I depart Karumba for Gregory Downs. Although paved, the byway rides like a horse in places. Cockatiels, budgerigars (parakeets), and wallabies keep me on high alert with their last-minute swoops and bounds across the road. Sudden braking rearranges the back of the van several times. When I get out to straighten up the mess, the cicadas are so loud, I fear they will damage my hearing. Coming into Gregory Downs (population 40), a sign on the sunbaked macadam reads: "No parking next 1.5km—Emergency Airstrip."

Australia is such a sunburned land that "shade tree" is an oxymoron. Trees have extraordinary rules: grow your leaves small and turn them away from sunlight. For instance, the fork-leaved corkwood's (*Hakea divaricata*) needle-like leaves expose scant surface area through which to lose moisture, while the leaves of the prickly wattle (*Acacia victoriae*) have a waterproof wax coating that helps hold in moisture even on the hottest days. Upon my 10:00 AM arrival, there's not a bit of shade to park in at Gregory Downs (the camper van is not allowed on unpaved roads), so I am forced to take a room. The air conditioning doesn't really cool, but it spits shards of ice onto the bed. Meanwhile, the fan hums: "what'll it be, what'll it be, what'll it be?" and later, "do your best, do your best, do your best." I try to catch the very moment that "and the next one, and the next one, and the next one" morphs into "and the next, and the next, and the next." It has an impressive repertoire. A fellow on the deck next door is crinkling a beer can every twenty minutes and tossing it. The heat gets to you. It's hard to believe I am only a half-day's drive from Karumba, the Arafura Sea, and Graham, the green tree frog, but then. . .

Dear Graham, I see that you are perched front and center on my toilet seat. I note that you have grown dramatically since we last met. The contrast of green and white makes for a fine photo. Your black eyes also contribute to the intensity of your look. While I feel I cannot disturb you, neither can I complete my own tasks. Moments like this make me want to give it all up. Is there space for negotiation? This is the only night of my two-month trip that I have paid for a motel room; having spent the $100, I'm loath to walk down the road to the public toilet, where I'm sure to meet up with your cousins and suffer other indignities. If I sprinkle water on you, will you feel content and meander off for the moment? I also note the gap under the bathroom door and ask that you respect this divide and my right to sleep uninterrupted. Frogs moving about in the dark of night bring to mind mice and snakes. I understand that you are a regular, while I am a transient. While I want to work with you toward a shared resolution, if you come into the main living area, I will feel compelled to remove you. I may attempt this hastily and with less finesse than you would hope for. Whether successful or not, both of us will be disturbed by the effort. I have no training in how to treat you—how delicate or hardy you are. Therefore, I urge you to find a place in the bathroom other than my toilet seat to spend your time, although I will grant that in all likelihood "my" toilet is actually "your" swimming pool; that grates on me. Wading is also fine. I will sprinkle water in the shower and wish you an enjoyable evening. The first flush of the swimming pool is at 3:00 AM. Perhaps that is of no concern to you. Unlike today, this cannot be put off, nor can it be accomplished if you are in the current perch position. Afterward, you may have free run of the place while I am recording birds. I return to take my shower at about seven. Since hot water is involved, I urge you to remove yourself prior to this. Thank you, Graham, for your consideration.

To give Graham time to retreat, I go outside to scout for birds and meet the local dogs. I make it my business to always learn their names and allow them to learn my smell, so that when we meet up in the dark, I am not put out of action. A blue heeler goes for a walk with me. Crushed toads coat the scorched, bubbling pavement, but they aren't Bob's chow. He pulls his wallaby tartare off to the grass and munches on the hindquarters. I hope he'll be around to chaperone me in the night and not off gnawing on roadkill leftovers.

Dear Graham, the photo of you folded in and clinging to the shower wall to the right of the soap holder is also a fine one. I took care in turning on the cold (tepid in these parts) water. You spread out, but your suction-cup toes ultimately could not hold on. Now that you have slid to the bottom of the shower, I'll let you make a dignified escape. I shall return in thirty minutes' time.

Dear Graham, I see you are not deadline-oriented or that the rules are perhaps not mine to set. I did not enjoy this endeavor, me with liquid bath soap in one hand walking into the shower but discovering you still there. I did the best I could when, after much indecision, I poured water into the electric jug (cold water, lest it should fall on you) and pushed the shower curtain halfway into the shower, with me on the outside. It was less than satisfactory, and I was glad when you decided to vacate so I could wash my hair. Perhaps you will find that large cockroach behind the trashcan and have him for breakfast. I don't know why I felt the need to cut my hair after this shower—I thought I was growing it out. Four snips and I'm freed of as many inches.

I arise at 3:00 AM. Graham is not in evidence, nor is Bob around. Instead, Pebbles comes to sit with me in front of the motel room. I relax, knowing this large mutt is on snake duty. Since the tallest trees are right around the roadhouse, I hope I'll get lucky, but it is not to be. The soloist is a late starter who eventually sings for fourteen minutes in a small tree above the diesel gas pump. I weigh it up in my mind: a long and expensive drive, a $100 hotel room shared with Graham, the heat, the stress—for fourteen minutes of song. In the first years of my fieldwork, I referred to formal songs as "long songs"; I subsequently adjusted my terminology to reflect the much shorter songs of recent years.

Departing Gregory Downs, acres of termite "tombstones" line the narrow road on the drive to Burke and Wills Roadhouse. I pass ten pelicans sharing a waterhole with as many cattle (a completely unlikely assemblage in my imagination), and later I startle half a dozen feral pigs at Firey Creek. A kite flies off with four feet of red and white ribbon ripped from the gut of kangaroo roadkill. The long stretch between facilities means most folks make at least a short stop at the Burke and Wills crossroads to fuel up. On arrival, I sit outside on the covered deck with an order of chips and salad. An apostlebird (*Struthidea cinerea*) with a lame leg flies up to beg. These highly sociable birds tend to come in groups of a dozen, and thus the name. I shouldn't, but considering the leg, I take pity and throw a tidbit the bird's way. Immediately, over fifty apostles arrive. What happened to the cliché of a dozen? I've been set up! Harsh "tearing sandpaper" voices demand that I share. People are looking at me. Like everyone of guilty conscience, I do the only thing one can do: I look away, pretending I didn't do it. A helicopter lands, a welcome distraction. A young man climbs out and walks to the bar. Three minutes later, he exits with a case of cold beer under each arm and a sagging bag with six bottles of spirits hooked onto his left elbow. He climbs back in and flies off.

The sign on the amenities block reads: "Please keep Ladies Toilet Door closed at all times as BROWN SNAKES like to visit very often!!" I secure the door and go to bed, much earlier than anyone else. It's difficult to sleep with so many people playing pool and the jukebox roaring. They sing along on the choruses or, rather, shout. The refrain to the current song is "Whiskey for my men, beer for my horses!" I don't hear a thing on the jukebox that can touch what I'll hear at 4:00 AM.

Of course, the toilet door is wide open when I get up in the dark, signaling that women also enjoy their whiskey. There's just a slice of moon. I head to the stockyard across the road, where the soloist sang last season, turn on my recorder, and hope. Wills does not disappoint, singing forty-five minutes of thrillingly combinatorial phrases, including truncation, SLD2, virtuosic leaps and portamentos, species calls-in-song, rattles, low-pitched notes, timbral tricks, and arpeggiated minor chords. This bird's got style. At times, the longer phrases sound crafted on the spot. I'm right underneath Wills, who stays loyal to one songpost for the entire song. I try

not to move and sometimes forget to breathe. Two other pied butcherbirds
are singing in the distance. Near the end, the phrases become much softer,
and Wills caps off the performance with a divertissement: it's mimicry,
with a new sound about every second, including a car alarm. Then, Wills
flies across the road and sings a species call. I don't hear another pied
butcherbird for the rest of the morning.

MIMICRY VERSUS ORIGINALITY

My interest here is to delve deeper into avian mimicry as a way of opening
a discussion on the nature and definition of music. At least one-fifth of
songbirds are vocal mimics.[1] This makes it noteworthy that so few studies
into the capacity have been conducted. Importations and appropriations
occur in a variety of social situations and differ widely among species.
Some birds mimic when stressed. Functional hypotheses propose that
mimicry might assist in foraging efficiency, predator avoidance and defense, communication in dense habitat, song development, mate attraction, recruiting assistance for mobbing—and on it goes.[2] Avian mimicry
is poorly understood, and my own comparative studies of lyrebirds and
pied butcherbirds suggest that a single functional accounting will likely
never serve for all mimicking species.[3]

One wonders what motivates pied butcherbirds, who have a good-sized
repertoire of their own, to incorporate the sonic constructs of others. It is
unknown whether the signal of an alien species, when pasted into formal
song or subsong, refers to that species, merely represents an appreciation
of diverse sounds, or denotes something else altogether. Might it be an
audio diary? Is it neophilia? Could it be a way of detaching a sound from
its use value and branding it "pied butcherbird"? A bolder move might be
to frame mimicry as a hyperintensification of a bird's milieu—as a bird
revealing their inner world at the same time as connecting to their total
environment, sonic and otherwise, and perhaps even to a source of power.
Yes, this smacks of religion—which is often interwoven with music. If
we think of the cave painters at Lascaux as establishing and celebrating a
metaphysical connection to prey and survival, as well as the surrounding

cosmos, can we likewise allow an avian artist such a moment? Asking such a question is impossible for a scientist because at present there is no chance of answering it. A zoömusicologist, having thought the question but also lacking any expectation of an answer, perhaps has a responsibility to blurt it out nonetheless. We cannot overlook that some human cultures believe animals have souls and participate in ceremonies.[4]

On a lighter note, I have wondered if mimicry could be an amused glance at other species—an inside joke. Might mimicry be a narrative, and does it archive any extinct species? "Other orders of being have their own literatures," supposes poet Gary Snyder. "Narrative in the deer world is a track of scents that is passed on from deer to deer with an art of interpreta- tion which is instinctive. A literature of blood-stains, a bit of piss, a whiff of estrus, a hit of rut, a scrape on a sapling and long gone."[5] Detaching a sound from its original function is a process often assumed to be purely human. One assumes this degree of complexity and elaboration would be well beyond what is necessary for survival and reproduction.

Mimicry is equally relevant to understanding the human sound world. Composers are prolific borrowers, from one another and from their own past works; jazz improvisers are fond of quoting themes from both within and without their idiom. Musicians and other artists know mimicry by a myriad of names: imitation, borrowing, quotation, appropriation, brico- lage, pastiche, parody, rescoring, citation, aping, and even plagiarism—I believe it is the ubiquitous basis of music making, while originality is rare and often illusory. A view from musicologist Robert Walser allows us to frame mimicry as "trying on for size" ways of knowing and experiencing other musical cultures, as when J. S. Bach experimented with French and Italian styles.[6] A cover band, a stylistic crossover—whatever the label, the mimetic powers of pied butcherbirds betray their oral absorption of the exterior world. Wills's delivery of a new sound every half-second aligns with a human's imaginative "trying on for size."

Since it underpins human music, I want to keep mimicry (or imitation) sitting at the table.[7] This will take some effort, however, since much dis- course leads us in quite another direction: originality, creativity, and tran- scendent genius are regular and significant markers of value. Philosopher of music and aesthetics Lydia Goehr argues that with the elevation of these concepts in Western art music around 1800, the multiple use of existing, adaptable material through skilled reorchestrating or revising began to fall out of favor, replaced by the rigid concept of a musical work—unique, self-sufficient, and formed in the mind of an elite composer.[8] Works were launched as "high art." This newly minted distinction between utility and aesthetic merit found function, endeavor, occasion, and effect eclipsed by *product.*[9] Thus arises a problem of signal importance for any definition of music vis-à-vis birdsong: Must a bird compose works of genius, or is being an adept mimic and clever remixer acceptable? This is not to deny the inventiveness found in some birdsongs but to highlight the mutable way humans set standards and make assessments.

In addition, the purported shift to embrace notions of originality, creativity, and genius is overly simplistic and by no means universal. Borrowed themes with variations, along with paraphrasing and arranging, continued throughout the nineteenth century by Western classical composers like Brahms and Liszt and into the twentieth by Busoni, Ives, Schoenberg, Webern, and Stravinsky, in what is a very partial listing. Other cultures maintain their music over long periods of time with relatively little change and may not revere original composers. Songs may be received from the spirit world, for instance, and compositional agency or novelty may even be construed negatively. As only one of many ways to think about music, a "rare work of genius" allows us to appreciate an irony: while "geniuses" might be few, thousands mimic them. Imitating and copying are also well known in film, theater, television, and literature, as evidenced by sequels, adaptations, series, and spin-offs.

Issues of authorship and ownership spill over into more than our conceptual orientation; they follow musicians to both the bank and the attorney's office, the way strewn with contentious matters of sampling, hip-hop production, remix, mashup, turntablism and DJ culture, copyright infringement, cover version, piracy, plunderphonia, the commons, and fair use. We assume more and more (and once again) that cultural, and not just natural, resources are ours for the taking. "Plagiarism? Excessive borrowing? The normal creative process?" begins an article on famed classical composer Osvaldo Golijov, known for his "magpie technique of borrowing from various sources and different musical traditions."[10] Reusing and recontextualizing never went away; these techniques are routine in music and birdsong. It is not my intention to claim that we are *only* plagiarists but simply that the practice is well known to artists of all stripes, including Western art composers past and present.

While genius is held up as a mysterious force, the riddle of mimicry is equally mysterious. Moreover, new research indicates that mirror neurons mediate songbirds' imitative powers, linking what is perceived with what is performed; with this new understanding, imitation has been yanked out of the much-disparaged mechanical category.[11] Since mimicry puts pressure on a purely functional rationale for birdsong, perhaps it can assist us in letting go of the assumption that the only legitimate cultural agent is human (or superhuman). Evidence of the postmodern ethos is thoroughly encapsulated in a mimicking pied butcherbird. Drawing seemingly at random on this and that genre, mixing and matching fragments with no regard for species-specific rules, and eschewing the slow development of their formal songs—these moments show pied butcherbirds to be splendid plunderers. Evaluations of imitation, however, may differ markedly depending on whether they address the human or avian capacity. Some ethologists will speak of a copying *error*, rather than an inventive appropriation of motifs from another species' repertoire.[12] Nonetheless, by whatever name, the capacity of vocal learning and copying that we share with songbirds but with no other primates is deeply entwined with our essence, the essence of our music, and the essence of a bird's song. Pied butcherbirds are skillful mimics, and they produce beautiful songs—on that listeners agree—but does that make them musicians or what they produce "music"? If musical analysis of a bird's song with Western musicology's analytic tools can be fruitfully conducted, might this imply that birdsong is music? Of course, our answers will be influenced by how we define our subject.

BUT IS IT MUSIC?

Any attempt to craft a clear and unmistakable definition of "music" is fraught with difficulties. First, one must discard or amend all definitions that fail to make the distinction between music and language. Sound poetry, chanting, rapping, *Sprechgesang*, recitative, tonal languages, and keening occupy the liminal space between the two categories. So do motherese, mantras, and auctioneering.[13] Even if music preceded language, it seems music did not have a visual manifestation until well after language. The predominance of alphabet letters for Western note names again confuses the two.

In addition, although it varies considerably, music of some type is found in all human cultures unless suppressed, so one must take each type into account. Music's meaning both extends across and is constrained by cultures. Most musicologists agree that the quest for musical universals has come up empty-handed. With intraspecies variation rife, with each musical event betraying the participants, materials, traditions, meanings, and functions in that one time and place, ethnomusicologists had to settle for "statistical universals" rather than unambiguous ones, and the search has shifted to areas like music perception and cognition.[14]

Human music's multifunctional nature likely reflects multiple selection pressures, and present-day musical activities may not correspond exactly to earlier uses. Despite a complex evolutionary history and unlikely monogenesis, a definition is nevertheless tasked with connecting to the entire musical experience, addressing key questions like, What does music do? Is music a physical, mental, or ideal object? What does music mean? Perhaps unsurprisingly, musicology lacks a working definition of its subject, so I cannot turn to the discipline's benchmark, *The Grove Dictionary of Music* (subsumed into *The Oxford Dictionary of Music*), for a definition. It does not offer one.[15] Instead, I must patch together proposals from diverse sources with competing and inconsistent interests. Since universals are apparently absent in music, I appear defeated before beginning. However, rather than seeking a "perfect" characterization of music, my search is for what qualities a definition concerns itself with, what a definition tells us about its makers, and, to add one more difficulty, how these play out at the human-animal interface.

Although musicologists have discounted "universal" in the cliché that music is the universal language, I might pose the question, Is music a language? Granted, I only just attempted to distinguish music from language and leave the latter behind while acknowledging thorny borderline cases, but in our logocentric culture, language has a way of entering and reentering the debate through the front or back door, and language conducts the debate. François-Bernard Mâche cautions against the syllogism: "Language distinguishes man, and music is a kind of language, therefore music is a purely human cultural fact."[16] Music is, for him, neither a language nor purely human.

There are a number of nuances in distinguishing music from language. Music's prime purpose *cannot* be communicative in an information-carrying way, argues musicologist Elizabeth Hellmuth Margulis, since repetition is so prolific.[17] Ambiguity is a merit in music, which is not a coded endeavor awaiting our decoding. It favors a rich network of associations over objective content. Like the philosophers Susanne Langer and Stanley Cavell before her, Diana Raffman has written on "musical ineffability," or the verbally inexpressible in musical knowledge.[18] Still others have highlighted the rich but nonetheless nonpropositional aspect of musical meaning, including things social and embodied.[19] With no fixed, unanimous reference, musical meaning is open to interpretation.[20]

As with birdsong and music, so too with birdsong and language: there are calls to do away with speciesism and conduct comparative studies with animals.[21] While this could be a valuable line of inquiry, a danger is that once slotted into the language category for comparison purposes, birdsong will be found deficient. Birdsong will never be fully and richly described if we restrict our comparisons of it to language.

MAPPING TERRITORIAL DISPUTES

Given these challenges, it is small wonder that music's various definitions read like a map of territorial disputes from around the world, both past and present. So vast is music's scope and so numerous, and even conflicting, are its functions that no single explanatory model holds sway. In the coming survey, much will be left out: people and movements are glossed over if not out-and-out slighted. The chapter is an introduction to primary sources and not a substitute for them, since it would take a larger book than this to do them justice.

Human/Animal

The first border conflict I visit is, understandably, the human/animal divide, where the search for a simple declarative sentence to pin down music in the twentieth century and beyond has granted particular appeal to the human cutoff point in music's definition. Music as a uniquely *human* activity is a regular proposition.[22] Igor Stravinsky, for instance, allows that while birdsong, along with a breeze in a tree and a rippling brook, may suggest music or delight us: "They are promises of music; it takes a human being to keep them: a human being sensitive to nature's many voices, of course, but who in addition feels the need of putting them in order and who is gifted for that task with a very special aptitude. In his hands all that I have considered as not being music will become music."[23]

This passage captures the sentiment of many other anthropocentric definitions of our subject. At the expense of giving a more realistic accounting of our ongoing reliance on imitation in all its shades, and by alluding to human (male) brilliance while ignoring avian accomplishments, Stravinsky avoids stripping his music of its mystery. This is a classic example of power brokering à la Western art music. Perhaps it is pushing the story too far to say that birdsong can assist us in mediating binary others—and yet mimicry seems able to both identify and flatten difference. Another potential flattener: Péter Szőke's detailed but little-known transcription of a hermit thrush song. Was Stravinsky only acquainted with "romantic," "foredoomed" birdsong transcriptions? Perhaps.

If music is truly peculiar to humans, when did it begin? For example, did Neanderthals produce music? Archaeologist Steven Mithen credits *Homo neanderthalensis* with musical communication via a musical proto-language but not with music.[24] Like language, the origins of music remain unknown, although there is no shortage of speculation—for instance, Steven Brown's "musilanguage" theory of a joint precursor to speaking and singing.[25]

The refusal to allow birdsong within music's border prompts me to contemplate what criteria a bird's song would need to meet in order to find acceptance. A reasonable definition of music must surely include "bad" music as well as "good," not to mention "good" music performed "badly" and music's equivalent of "outsider art," but this is not consistently the case. At least tangentially, many definitions imply that even the human acoustic object must meet certain aesthetic standards in order to be considered music. Writers like Herbert Spencer and Richard Wallaschek did not hold back in critiquing the sonic constructs produced by "primitive" humans.[26]

Darwin made his thoughts clear, and although we might wince today, most of us have uttered unsympathetic comments about someone else's music: "Judging from the hideous ornaments and the equally hideous music admired by most savages, it might be urged that their aesthetic faculty was not so highly developed as in certain animals, for instance, in birds."[27] Notwithstanding Darwin's praise for birds' aesthetic faculties, the assumption that birdsong is instinctive and unskilled remains widespread. In this, birdsong shares not just with "primitive" humans of yesteryear but also with contemporary human improvisers, who have also been cast as primitive, irrational, untutored, and whimsical.[28] In addition, while many would define music as an exclusively human art, "human" is far from universal in meaning and is often a mere subset. In various times and places, the word has excluded the majority of "humans" (like women, infidels, and certain ethnicities), while, on the other hand, "human" (and especially "person") for some casts a far wider net, taking in spirits, animals, and plants in a permeable and fluid understanding of kinship.

Formalism in Music

The border I am most concerned with here is the human/animal one. Nonetheless, other lines of demarcation are germane to our thinking about music and birdsong. Formalist tenets hold that music makes its own rules and that the only source of music's meaning lies in its internal structural relationships. Nineteenth-century music theorist Eduard Hanslick challenged the doctrine that music's duty is to represent or arouse feelings. He emphasized that music's essence resides in "sound and motion" (also translatable as "tones in motion") and thus invokes a metaphor of music as a kind of kaleidoscope of dynamic patterns that speak to the imagination rather than to the emotions.[29] Although Hanslick was adamant that music is uniquely human, his focus on animated patterns is tremendously appealing, and I take delight in such patterns in birdsong.

Psychologist Edmund Gurney also viewed music as pattern and form, denying any possibility of referential and emotional meaning. In his 1880 monograph *The Power of Sound*, he repeatedly directs us to the musical surface, where the "pure and lofty enjoyment" of the listener is the ultimate test of musical quality.[30] The key word here is apparently "pure," as opposed to "impure" sensorial and emotional pleasure. Gurney is prepared to endure endless contortions in order to keep emotion out of the picture. Another formalist position is that of Leonard Meyer, whose classic 1961 monograph *Emotion and Meaning in Music* understands music as a closed, although meaningful, system.[31] Music *means* itself. His assumption of a value-free, ahistorical viewpoint is a challenging course to maneuver when discussing the psychology of human listeners in time.

In cleaving to the concept of absolute music, some choose to preference music's structure and theoretical basis over its actual sound. In their classic study, musicologist Fred Lerdahl and linguist Ray Jackendoff describe a musical grammar with respect to human music and its listeners, writing: "A piece of music is a mentally constructed entity, of which scores and performances are partial representations by which the piece is transmitted."[32] Practice-oriented musicians find such comments disconcerting.

Music as Evoking Emotion

Birdsong unhooks us from the everyday:

> We were in a very remote part of Carnarvon Gorge, in the Moreton section, over 700 kilometers to get there. You need to carry petrol, so not many people go there. It's where they found some of the earliest remains of tapa cloth and burial sites in these high, ancient sandstone cliffs. We were in this campground on our own, and there was a bit of water in the creek. We both found ourselves waking up after midnight with these amazing songs. I went outside, and there was a full moon and there were layers of mist and there were a lot of trees around, and there quite a few pied butcherbirds, and they were calling. I got back into the tent and listened to these incredibly complex calls [sobbing]. These birds were obviously calling to each other, and motifs were being repeated. Some birds were starting a motif, other birds were finishing it, and I reckon there were at least half a dozen—or there could have been 20.[33]

"Music sounds the way emotions feel," reads one attempt to paper over the divide.[34] Others have more decisively rejected the formalist position of belief in the purely musical, making instead a full-on case for the emotionalist position. Composer Wilson Coker's 1972 survey of whether composers believe that music has the ability to be extragenerically meaningful finds

that a majority do.[35] Musician and musicologist Deryck Cooke argues pointedly that music can *express*, and not simply *evoke*, emotion.[36] *The Language of Music* (1959) details Cooke's controversial lexicon of how to decipher the musical language of Western art music, in which he matches chords, harmonies, and contours with affects. Other scholars, while stopping short of this, have nonetheless weighed in on the primacy of music in inducing and expressing emotion, as have many nonspecialists for whom music is emotion, plain and simple.[37] This orientation, however, typically claims both too little and too much for expressions of emotion. Many musical engagements are memorable without focusing on emotion as the key attribute; meanwhile, musical emotion is far more nuanced than is usually acknowledged, and the categories of emotion currently being studied by music psychologists seem crude and hackneyed. An alternative way to think this through is to acknowledge that some music does have expressing or evoking emotion as its goal, while other performances have goals like getting us on the dance floor or drawing attention to sound and its perception.

Music and the Superhuman

In another line of thinking, while a musical work may not hold its entire meaning within itself, it sources these from the *extra*human or *super*human. For simplicity's sake, I lump together a number of concepts: the metaphysical, the divinely inspired, the mathematical, the perfect, the scientific, the natural (like the properties of sound and the overtone series), and the abstract. All of these universal orders of organization offer the tremendous appeal of one truth.

Pythagoras springs to mind as "high priest" of this category. In the sixth century BCE, he elucidated a system of tuning that brought harmony into correspondence with acoustic phenomena, a result of his discovery that the length of vibrating bodies corresponds to notes of the scale in simple integer ratios. As it turns out, however, the ratios may be simple but must be fudged for the purposes of equal-tempered music. He also described an exquisite relationship between sound and numbers and between sound and mass. His theories about planets and stars link the physical world and the structure of music in the *unheard* "harmony of the spheres."

LEICHHARDT RIVER at the Frank Webber Bridge, North Queensland, 29 October 2013: There's just enough room to pull off and park. It's not an official campground—the closest would be several hours down the road. One experienced recordist notified me that he heard more pied butcher-birds singing at this remote river crossing than at any other place he'd ever visited, so I decided to take a chance. Two vehicles pass in the night. They don't particularly worry me, but at 12:54 AM, I wake up to a slowing car. As it rattles and rumbles past, I lose my nerve. For an hour, I run a list of what-ifs and the various ways I could die. I add "die of fatigue" to the list and put in another forty-five-minute sleep cycle. The next thing I know, I fear I've overslept and missed the proceedings. Unlike usual, it's totally silent: no frogs, no insects, no traffic, no wind, no generators, and no birdsong—nor will there be this morning. The creatures here no longer sing; they've become Pythagoreans.

Nuanced though they are, philosophical distillations concerning music tend to dwell on disinterested contemplation and eternal truths and display minimal concern for the situated and contingent aspects of music making, or when they do, these are the messy parts that get in the way of theory. Toggling between the formal and mathematical aspects of music, on the one hand, and the surface and sensory ones, on the other, results in a dizzying appreciation and depreciation of music. To add one more perspective, some indigenous people claim to listen to the spirits of "apparently inaudible" plants and animals, disturbing an easy reading of who attends to the sounded and who the unsounded.[38] In any case, music cannot be decoupled from real life—from its social dimension, its participatory nature, and its very kick, hook, groove, and guts. Music is engagement rather than distancing and is thoroughly audible. I can only wonder how philosophers might have theorized with a pied butcherbird singing outside their window.

Other themes that champion the overlap of the laws of nature and the laws of music include the universe as a composition, musicians as a priesthood of superindividuals divorced from the world, and music as a transcendent and autonomous natural language. For some, music is the last vestige in the secular world of a connection to the divine. Composers have used mathematical models to generate and extend their ideas, with the separation between pragmatic organizing principles and eternal or absolute principles not always clear-cut.[39]

ALTERITY AND MUSIC'S DEFINITION

Beyond the human/animal partition, the mapping of music and its binary others finds variously drawn boundaries overlaid upon much the same territory. Music/noise, music/nonmusic, music/sound, and music/silence: How much music do we relegate to the other side of the slash in our demarcations? Such divisions and oppositions are at once cultural and acoustical, and many current reviews of music's others do not take animal sounds into account.[40]

Music/Noise

BURLEIGH GOLF CLUB, Miami Beach, Queensland, 7 October 2010: The club has kindly allowed me entry well before opening hours. Nocturnal song eventually gives way to diurnal ensembles, and the birds keep me running around the golf course as they conduct their morning patrols. At 7:00 AM, golfers begin to arrive and tee up. I try to stay out of their way in order to keep them out of my recording. My method is to stare up into the trees as if deeply occupied, even if I cannot see a bird. One golfer cannot resist: "You're bird listening."

"Pardon me?"

"You're *bird* listening."

"Yeah, recording."

"Oh, okay, so when you squeeze that trigger, you. . ." (He speaks right into my microphone to the drowned-out accompaniment of three pied butcherbirds.)

"I don't squeeze it. It's on right now."

"And it doesn't pick up our voices?"

"It *is* picking you up, yes." (Laughter all around—but he "stepped on" the trio.)

Figure 7.1. A pied butcherbird in Miami Beach, Queensland. Photograph by Hollis
Taylor (2010).

From tinnitus to traffic (and golfers to golf balls), the world is filled with
unwanted sounds beyond our control. Noise is interference. Yet musical
instruments have their share of it—the rattling of piano keys, the clicking
of saxophone keys, the scratching and rasping of a bow on strings, and the
squeaking of guitar strings. When placing diverse noises into songs to expand their acoustic palate, pied butcherbirds call to mind Luigi Russolo's
futurists.[41] "Music needs noise, its essential condition," observes Michel
Serres, while "noise has no need of music."[42] In attempts to distinguish
musical material from noise, the discourse often pivots back onto music
as a social construct. Noise is less a matter of intensity of sound than intensity of relationships, believes cultural historian Hillel Schwartz.[43] The
border is unsettled and mutable, with no simple consensus.

Meaning and pattern have a way of surfacing even in noise. From the mid-twentieth century on, "noise music" has been claimed by various sound-based genres and musicians: from death industrial to noise rock, from power electronics to noise pop, and from metal to glitch music. Noise may refer to a high volume level, to tone color (including broadband sounds, feedback, distortion, and static), to structure (formed by indeterminacy or improvisation), and to method of generation (often relying on machines and processes). No longer unwanted, noise is hip.

Music/Nonmusic

Phenomenologist Thomas Clifton does not deny the existence of aesthetic standards but holds that the difference between music and nonmusic lies in the manner and context of the experience, thus directing us to our body.[44] Nonmusical sounds can have quite an effect, for example, calming or startling us. Insomniacs now have commercial options to remedy their condition: rain or thunder, wind or waves, crickets or campfires. Gurney would have been a ready customer, since he found continuous nonmusical sounds to be soothing, whereas musical ones were intolerable when prolonged.[45]

Music/Sound

Perhaps no one stresses music as an audible fact more than Descartes, who begins his *Compendium Musicae* (1618) with the terse statement: "Its object is sound." Music has arrived square in the scientific revolution, having abandoned the unsounded and the divine (and the possibility of describing the world and its workings through music theory) for materiality.[46] These days, sound as an organizing principle (rather than, for instance, verse-chorus or sonata form) is increasingly commonplace, including in popular music like hip-hop. The ease with which many listeners easily transition between music and the sonic sensations of the world at large owes a substantial debt to film music. For its part, sound art has weakened what used to be a compliment to the music side of the music/sound binary. The slash that separates them may imply their link—we mention them in the same breath as a nod to sound art—or the slash may be replaced with "and." Percussionist, composer, and music theorist Chris Cutler, however, cautions against removing the boundary completely: "If, suddenly, *all sound* is 'music,' then by definition, there can be no such thing as sound that is *not* music. The word music becomes meaningless, or rather it means 'sound.' But 'sound' already means that." Instead, Cutler returns us to a particular activity under the rubric of sound, that of a "conscious and deliberate organization within a definite aesthetic and tradition."[47]

"'Music' is judged by the full weight of history and fashion," reckons composer and sound artist Nicolas Collins; "substitute 'Sound Art' and most of these preconceptions fall away."[48] Although sound art has less baggage, I am wary of this reorientation as it pertains to birdsong. On more than one occasion, I have heard, "Yes, birdsong can be amazing, but it's something *else*." Birdsong, like sound and sound art, is subject to shifting valorization, and even some who acknowledge birdsong's qualities prefer that it be categorized in an outlying conceptual domain. Such categorical wrangling gets birdsong nowhere and merely sidesteps its tantalizing qualities and why they affect us.

Music/Silence (and the Night Shift)

BOOTH ROAD near Townsville, North Queensland, 28 October 2012, 2:30 AM: I have recorded at this remote cattle station annually since 2006. Having telephoned the owner on the previous day to confirm my arrival, there was no need for a daytime visit. However, when I pull in, where there is normally an empty field, my headlights reveal free-roaming, barking dogs and a new house. Somehow, these details didn't seem relevant to my host when we spoke. I retreat far enough to encourage the dogs to forget me. I'm listening intently as they quiet down and hoping a bird will also sing somewhere on this tree-lined road. Straining to make out a birdsong is like a hearing test. Then, a noise! Something has hit the spare tire mounted on the back of the car. Next, someone crashes onto the roof, rocking the vehicle. I'm terrified. Game over! I cannot form a narrative of who this intruder is and what he is doing up there. I wait for a chainsaw crazy to begin removing the car roof. Only when the light comes out does the narrative advance: the allied rock-wallaby (*Petrogale assimilis*) is known for amazing agility in leaping up and down rock ledges—add my car to the list. When departing, the creature left telltale traces in the red dust on the vehicle's roof and side.

"The urban animals that live in closest proximity to us listen out for us so intensely, that hearing them is the sound of our own silence, and their silence the sound of our approach," writes author Steven Connor commonsensically.[49] Silence may be an event (or a monograph) unto itself. Others focus on the balance between sound and silence. "Music," Claude Debussy is reputed to have written in a 1906 letter, "is the space between the notes."[50] The music/silence dualism is not an adversarial one. Music needs silence, just as it needs noise. Without an interphrase interval, for instance, the musicality of a pied butcherbird formal solo song founders.

STILL MORE DEFINITIONS OF "MUSIC"

A few final characterizations move us out of formalist, emotionalist, and binary positions; music's embodied, social nature is pertinent in them all. Music is an aide-mémoire for Australian Aboriginal people navigating their country via songlines. For some, like Duke Ellington and Irving Mills, "It Don't Mean a Thing if It Ain't Got That Swing." This remark from composer Edgard Varèse is often repeated: "I decided to call my music 'organized sound' and myself, not a musician, but 'a worker in rhythms, frequencies, and intensities.'" However, this was not his preferred definition. Instead, he extolled the virtues of one proposed by philosopher Józef Maria Hoene-Wroński: "the corporealization of the intelligence that is in sound."[51]

Christopher Small turns his back on music's concepts and objects, entitling his monograph with music's gerund and proposing this definition: "To music is to take part, in any capacity, in a musical performance, whether by performing, by listening, by rehearsing or practicing, by providing material for performance (what is called composing), or by dancing."[52] Small would thoroughly ground "musicking" in the social world.

Recent pluralist perspectives also allow us to escape music's grand narratives, notably (but not exclusively) from feminist philosophers and

musicologists. However, we cannot expect to find a straightforward definition of music from this corner. Such theorists reject institutional and
patriarchal legitimation. One meditation on matriarchal art finds reso-
nance with life in a pied butcherbird singing community, where everyone
is simultaneously musician and spectator.[53] While such discourse has
accomplished the theoretical work of knocking at music's door, even if its
back one, the door has yet to be flung open.[54] Musicologist Susan McClary
has observed that musicology often "remains innocent of its own ideology,
of the tenets with which it marks the boundaries between its value-free
laboratory and the chaotic social world."[55] The most abstract of the arts
has an undeniable occupation in the everyday.

Pied butcherbird song is my "text" and my argument. Despite music's
meanings and values being determined and controlled by some who reject
birdsong as music, I remain optimistic that even the secondhand experience of hearing a pied butcherbird recording has the potential to charm,
disarm, and win over such persons of influence—or at least make them
hesitate.

EVALUATIVE AND CLASSIFICATORY
CORRELATES IN DEFINITIONS OF "ART"

AN ABORIGINAL ART CENTER, Alice Springs, 15 September 2013: Seated
on the concrete floor with a brush and some jars of red paint, the elder
artist is attended by two assistants. When he's ready, they turn the immense canvas for him. The gallery manager tells me that the artist began
with dot painting but found his way into his now-trademark abstract red,
or sometimes blue, squares. Charged with electric energy, the canvas
pulses. Do artists and musicians require proof of training in a major human cultural center to be taken seriously? This artist didn't need to study
in Paris. He doesn't send to New York for his ideas. A pied butcherbird
chorister is no different.

Musicology does not travel its bumpy roads alone. Debates on the definition of "art" traverse similar terrain, grappling with art objects from

cultures outside the West, from "primitives" of whatever time and place, and from other outliers. Asking what kind and class of thing an art object is turns out to be a booming cottage industry for philosophers.[56] Philosopher Stephen Davies speculates that attempts at definitions of music are much less frequent than ones of art because music is so easily identified; evidently, my expedition pales next to the lively and dizzying practice of art world ontology.[57]

Art cannot be defined, according to theorist Morris Weitz, since there are "no common properties—only strands of similarities." His model to facilitate the identification of art objects derives from Wittgenstein's concept of family resemblance. Weitz claims that art is "a decision problem"— we cannot arbitrarily close concepts that are by their very nature open.[58] I subscribe to his suggestion that we can window-shop definitions without buying into them and am sympathetic to his emphasis on similarities and relationships—on the evaluative stance.

Working at the interstices of art and anthropology, Howard Morphy also turns to family resemblance when it comes to objects that sit outside the province of art history. In the value creation process, he finds no justification for a certain conception of art to set itself up as "the de facto category to which all other arts are compared in order to determine the degree to which they are art." Instead, Morphy looks for a broad range of attributes found in works of art. For him, an exhibition could simultaneously focus awareness on and value a set of objects esteemed by another culture and at the same time draw attention to their function in a wider context.[59]

However, attributes of art and institutional needs and interests are in frequent tension, with artworks' *nonexhibited* qualities garnering the lion's share of attention. Philosopher of art George Dickie trusts institutions to make classificatory determinations about and confer status on objects in their domain and encourages institutions to maintain their independence from aesthetic judgment.[60] Here we diverge: I want to be more generous in assessing and according value to the surface, the material, the local, and the outsider. Besides, our appraisals can be easily flipped: the work of graffiti artist Banksy transformed from vandalism/nonart to someone-important-has-championed-it/art. The young Wagner, who wrote out Beethoven's symphonies note for note, finds a corollary in painting students copying canonical works and returns us to the imitation versus originality strophe, while the shift in a viewer's reception of a painting upon discovering that the masterpiece is a fake again underlines the contribution that contextualization makes in our judgments of art. In addition, claims of making classificatory decisions aside, I believe institutions *always* make determinations that are evaluative (the criteria being their own interests and collective pressures). If this is so, the best we can do is admit that the classificatory and the evaluative are practically one and the same, the former being a veiled determination and the latter a more open one. Weitz's decision problem in institutional hands is a problem indeed.

Argumentation that moves me so far away from the art object in its social setting makes me want to quit the art room, taking with me birds, fellow musicians, and, more broadly, artists of all stripes. However, back in the music room, it is much the same: an evidence-based approach is called upon when an easy and obvious critique is at hand—when a simple, "primitive," repetitive, or uninteresting (to a human) birdsong is on offer. Meanwhile, a more complex birdsong will be met with the classificatory process, deployed as a shield to avoid confronting sonic evaluation. Complicating this, musicians are known to take great pleasure in the wayward results of those who do what no trained musician could: we appreciate some musicians precisely for their *lack* of proficiency, like the Shaggs, an American sisters' rock group formed in 1968.

Of music's binary conceptions, some remain useful, while others are being reconfigured, but only the human/animal opposition seems to be drawn without benefit of evaluation. If birdsong is to be met with a classificatory verdict, it remains futile to draw on empirical research like a study that compared not acoustic signals but receivers' responses, finding "birdsong and music engage the same neuro-affective mechanisms in the intended listeners."[61] Neither in such circumstances can cognitive psychologists assist us with concepts of family resemblance and graded membership—nor can zoömusicologists successfully proffer their assessments. A remark from social anthropologist Alfred Gell pushes this point: "It is the way an art object is construed as having come into the world which is the source of the power such objects have over us—their becoming rather than their being."[62] The authority of Western art music to make claims about the entire sonic experience has links with intellectual, economic, and political power. Songbirds find many looking away from vocal accomplishment and instead toward a narrative of progress and exceptionalism, suggesting how value laden and historically situated our *idée fixe* of music is.

This brings us to the unsatisfactory point where, while no single philosophical, scientific, or performance-driven definition of music preponderates, like Cutler, I cannot propose that anything and everything is music. His definition is one of the most successful on offer, but semiologist Gino Stefani takes it a step further, seeking to permit "any type of activity performed around any type of event involving sound" to be described as music.[63] Its broadness allows those who reject it to craft their own more restricted subset without censoring a disparate musical community or event. Most of us would find the definition controversial and excessively permissive. We need a demarcation, but the minute we attempt one, a trespasser shows up. To define music is to invoke cartographic metaphors, where words like "claim," "control," and "separatist movement" scramble to find their time and place. Even the most thoughtful characterization can offend by leaving something out or putting something in. Nonetheless, categories are far from useless at their edges: contact zones can be where we find the most interesting activity.[64] Some artists and musicians, like some wildlife, are edge dwellers. They work on the brink and beyond, rebuffing boundaries' fixed and unbreachable signposts, extravagantly wandering off paths, and overstepping orderly lines. Music is superhuman, music is human, music is the province of *certain* humans—music is what we say it is.

Despite previous chapters having shown an enormous number of shared properties of birdsong and human music, our understanding of songbirds' vocalizations has been severely hampered by premature, lopsided mulling over of hypotheses based on biased and outmoded definitions. It is against this backdrop that I will in the next chapter debunk specific objections to the contention that birdsong is music, building on the premise that nothing about music logically and incontrovertibly leaves birdsong out of the ambit of its definition if our deliberation is *evaluative* and not merely classificatory.

NOTES

1. Andrew M. Hindmarsh, "Vocal Mimicry in Starlings," *Behaviour* 90 (1984): 302.

2. See David S. Dobkin, "Functional and Evolutionary Relationships of Vocal Copying Phenomena in Birds," *Zeitschrift für Tierpsychologie* 50 (1979): 348–363; and Laura A. Kelley, Rebecca L. Coe, Joah R. Madden, and Susan D. Healy, "Vocal Mimicry in Songbirds," *Animal Behaviour* 76, no. 3 (2008): 521–528.

3. See, for example, Jeffrey R. Baylis, "Avian Vocal Mimicry: Its Function and Evolution," in *Acoustic Communication in Birds*, vol. 2, ed. Donald E. Kroodsma, Edward H. Miller, and Henri Ouellet (New York: Academic Press, 1982), 51–83; and Anastasia H. Dalziell et al., "Avian Vocal Mimicry: A Unified Conceptual Framework," *Biological Reviews* 90, no. 2 (2015): 643–668.

4. Musicologist Gary Tomlinson has also contemplated early cave paintings but comes to an entirely different conclusion. He locates the origin of music (and behavioral modernity more generally) in the incremental development of human abstract thinking—in the interaction of biology and culture across deep history. We spent an hour in Sydney listening to and discussing pied butcherbird recordings and have agreed to disagree about birdsong vis-à-vis music—despite seeing music as uniquely human, he nevertheless professed enthusiasm for pied butcherbird vocal culture (Gary Tomlinson, *A Million Years of Music: The Emergence of Human Modernity* [New York: Zone Books, 2015], 289).

5. Gary Snyder, *The Practice of the Wild* (New York: North Point Press, 1990), 112.

6. Robert Walser, "The Polka Mass: Music of Postmodern Ethnicity," *American Music* 10, no. 2 (1992): 198.

7. See Alan P. Merriam, *The Anthropology of Music* (Evanston, IL: Northwestern University Press, 1964), 150.

8. Lydia Goehr, *The Imaginary Museum of Musical Works: An Essay in the Philosophy of Music* (Oxford: Clarendon Press, 1992).

9. Ibid., 152.

10. Daniel J. Wakin, "Musical Borrowing under Scrutiny," *New York Times*, 7 March 2012, accessed 8 October 2013, http://www.nytimes.com/2012/03/08/arts/music/osvaldo-golijov-fracas-over-sidereus-overture.html?pagewanted=all.

11. Ofer Tchernichovski and Josh Wallman, "Behavioural Neuroscience: Neurons of Imitation," *Nature* 451, no. 7,176 (2008): 249–250.

12. For more on this, see Geraint A. Wiggins et al., "The Evolutionary Roots of Creativity: Mechanisms and Motivations," *Philosophical Transactions B* 370, no. 1,664 (2015).

13. Diana Deutsch et al. problematicized the belief that speech and music can be separated and defined by their acoustical properties. The authors begin with a phrase in English that, when repeated several times, listeners identify as music. They hypothesize that "during the process of repetition, the pitches forming the phrase increase in perceptual salience and that in addition they are perceptually distorted so as to conform to a tonal melody" (Diana Deutsch, Trevor Henthorn, and Rachael Lapidis, "Illusory Transformation from Speech to Song," *Journal of the Acoustical Society of America* 129, no. 4 [2011]: 2246).

14. Siu-Lan Tan, Peter Pfordresher, and Rom Harré, *Psychology of Music* (Hove: Psychology Press, 2010), 298.

15. Bruno Nettl, "Music," in *Oxford Music Online* (Oxford: Oxford University Press, 2007–2014), accessed 5 August 2012, http://www.oxfordmusiconline.com.

16. François-Bernard Mâche, *Music, Myth and Nature,* trans. Susan Delaney (Chur: Harwood Academic Publishers, 1983/1992), 73. While philosopher and sociologist Theodor Adorno found music not to be a language, he believed that music suffers from its inescapable similarity to it (Theodor W. Adorno and Susan Gillespie, "Music, Language, and Composition," *Musical Quarterly* 77, no. 3 [1993]: 401–414).

17. Elizabeth Hellmuth Margulis, *On Repeat: How Music Plays the Mind* (Oxford: Oxford University Press, 2014), 13.

18. Diana Raffman, *Language, Music, and Mind* (Cambridge, MA: MIT Press, 1993).

19. See Robert Walser, "The Body in the Music: Epistemology and Musical Semiotics," *College Music Symposium* 31 (1991): 117–126. Also see Mark Johnson, *The Body in the Mind: The Bodily Basis of Meaning, Imagination, and Reason* (Chicago: University of Chicago Press, 1987).

20. See Catherine Stevens, "Cross-Cultural Studies of Musical Pitch and Time," *Acoustical Science & Technology* 26, no. 6 (2004): 433; and W. Tecumseh Fitch, "The Evolution of Music in Comparative Perspective," *Annals of the New York Academy of Sciences* 1,060, no. 1 (2005): 3. Music *genres,* however, are consensual in their affirmation of the way certain music should sound and how we should behave with "our" music (e.g., we clap at the end of a jazz solo).

21. Daniel Margoliash and Howard C. Nusbaum, "Animal Comparative Studies Should Be Part of Linguistics," *Behavioral and Brain Sciences* 32 (2009): 459. Connections between music and language are explored in depth in Aniruddh D. Patel, *Music, Language, and the Brain* (Oxford: Oxford University Press, 2008); Nicholas Bannan, ed., *Music, Language, & Human Evolution* (Oxford: Oxford University Press, 2012); and Michael A. Arbib, ed., *Language, Music, and the Brain: A Mysterious Relationship* (Cambridge, MA: MIT Press, 2013).

22. Eduard Hanslick, *The Beautiful in Music: A Contribution to the Revisal of Musical Aesthetics* (London: Novello, Ewer and Co., 1891), 151; Igor Stravinsky, *Poetics of Music* (New York: Vintage Books, 1947), 23; Roger Sessions, *The Musical Experience of Composer, Performer, Listener* (Princeton, NJ: Princeton University Press, 1950), 11; Charles Seeger, "On the Tasks of Musicology (Comments on Merriam, 'Purposes of Ethnomusicology')," *Ethnomusicology* 7, no. 3 (1963): 215; Merriam, *The Anthropology of Music,* 6; Mieczyslaw Kolinski, "Recent Trends in Ethnomusicology," *Ethnomusicology* 11, no. 1 (1967): 1; Wilson Coker, *Music & Meaning: A Theoretical Introduction to Musical Aesthetics* (New York: Free Press, 1972), 24; Frank Harrison, "Universals in Music: Towards a Methodology of Comparative Research," *World of Music: Quarterly Journal of the International Institute for Comparative Music Studies and Documentation* 19, no. ½ (1977): 30; Bruno Nettl, *The Study of Ethnomusicology: Twenty-Nine Issues and Concepts* (Urbana: University of Illinois Press, 1983), 24; John Blacking, *How Musical Is Man?* (Seattle: University of Washington Press, 1995), 10; Wayne D. Bowman, *Philosophical Perspectives on Music* (New York: Oxford University Press, 1998), 69; Cook, *Music: A Very Short Introduction,* 4; Philip Tagg, "Towards a Definition of 'Music,'" accessed 5 August 2008, http://www.tagg.org/teaching/musdef.pdf; Ian Cross, "Music as a Biocultural Phenomenon," in *The Neurosciences and Music,* ed. Giuliano Avanzini et al. (New York: New York Academy of Sciences, 2003), 109–110; Borgo, *Sync or Swarm,* 65; Lawrence M. Zbikowski, "Musicology, Cognitive Science, and Metaphor: Reflections on Michael Spitzer's *Metaphor and Musical Thought,*" *Musica Humana* 1, no. 1 (2009): 99; Tan, Pfordresher, and Harré, *Psychology of Music,* 285; Ulrik Volgsten, "The Roots of Music: Emotional Expression, Dialogue and Affect Attunement in the Psychogenesis of Music," *Musicae Scientiae* 16, no. 2 (2012): 213; and Michael A. Arbib, "Five Terms in Search of a Synthesis," in *Language, Music, and the Brain,* 18.

23. Stravinsky, *Poetics of Music*, 24.

24. Steven Mithen, *The Singing Neanderthals: The Origins of Music, Language, Mind and Body* (London: Phoenix, 2006).

25. Steven Brown, "The 'Musilanguage' Model of Music Evolution," in *The Origins of Music*, ed. Nils L. Wallin, Björn Merker, and Steven Brown (Cambridge, MA: MIT Press, 2000), 271–300. Other chapters in this volume are also pertinent to our topic, as are Bannan, *Music, Language, & Human Evolution*; and Tomlinson, *A Million Years of Music*.

26. Herbert Spencer, "The Origin and Function of Music," in *The Works of Herbert Spencer*, vol. 14: *Essays: Scientific, Political, & Speculative*, vol. 2 (Osnabruck: Otto Zeller, 1857/1966), 420; and Richard Wallaschek, *Primitive Music* (London: Longmans, Green and Co., 1893), 230.

27. Charles Darwin, *The Descent of Man, and Selection in Relation to Sex* (Princeton, NJ: Princeton University Press, 1871/1981), 64.

28. See Laudan Nooshin, "Improvisation as 'Other': Creativity, Knowledge and Power," *Journal of the Royal Musical Association* 128, no. 2 (2003): 246.

29. Hanslick, *The Beautiful in Music*, 67, 68.

30. Edmund Gurney, *The Power of Sound* (New York: Basic Books, 1880/1966), 378.

31. Leonard B. Meyer, *Emotion and Meaning in Music* (Chicago: University of Chicago Press, 1961).

32. Fred Lerdahl and Ray Jackendoff, *A Generative Theory of Tonal Music* (Cambridge, MA: MIT Press, 1983), 2.

33. Author interview with Warwick Biggs, 14 November 2015.

34. Carroll C. Pratt, "The Design of Music," *Journal of Aesthetics and Art Criticism* 12, no. 3 (1954): 296. Coker acknowledges both syntax and reference in his semiotic-gestural theory of music and musical experience.

35. Coker, *Music & Meaning*, 145–146.

36. Deryck Cooke, *The Language of Music* (Oxford: Oxford University Press, 1959), 11.

37. See, for instance, Mithen, *The Singing Neanderthals*, 2. Contra this, see Eric F. Clarke, "Lost and Found in Music: Music, Consciousness and Subjectivity," *Musicae Scientiae* 18, no. 3 (2014): 354–368; and David Dunn, "Acoustic Ecology and the Experimental Music Tradition," *NewMusicBox*, 2008, n.p.

38. Plato worried about how the irrationality, seductiveness, and power of music fit into his idealized mathematical theory of harmony. Following Plato and his student Aristotle (who was more concerned with the specific than the ideal), a number of other eminent philosophers have deliberated on music and the aesthetic experience more broadly. Bowman's chapter "Music as Idea" surveys the legacy of thought from Kant, Schiller, Hegel, and Schopenhauer (*Philosophical Perspectives*, 69–132). Since it would be unfair to severely abridge these philosophers, I will not take stock of them here. Music in the context of cosmology, acoustical physics, and acoustical-numerological aesthetics extends beyond Greek natural philosophy and was also of great appeal to Chinese philosophers, with variations found in Japanese and Javanese traditions as well. See, for instance, Kenneth J. DeWoskin, *A Song for One or Two: Music and the Concept of Art in Early China* (Ann Arbor: Center for Chinese Studies, University of Michigan, 1982); and Sandra E. Trehub, Judith Becker, and Iain Morley, "Cross-Cultural Perspectives on Music and Musicality," *Philosophical Transactions B* 370, no. 1,664 (2015): 1–9. For an indigenous account, see Bernd Brabec de Mori and Anthony Seeger, "Introduction: Considering Music, Humans, and Non-humans," *Ethnomusicology Forum* 22, no. 3 (2013):

269–286. For an account of how music influenced the unfolding of science, see Peter Pesic, *Music and the Making of Modern Science* (Cambridge, MA: MIT Press, 2014).

39. For instance, the "free stochastic music" of Iannis Xenakis is indebted to probability, set, and game theories, while Jean-Philippe Rameau and Paul Hindemith based their theories in part on the overtone series as tied to universal principles.

40. See, for example, Lawrence Kramer, *Classical Music and Postmodern Knowledge* (Berkeley: University of California Press, 1995); Georgina Born and David Hesmondhalgh, eds., *Western Music and Its Others* (Berkeley: University of California Press, 2000); and Christoph Cox and Daniel Warner, "Music and Its Others: Noise, Sound, Silence," in *Audio Culture: Readings in Modern Music,* ed. Christoph Cox and Daniel Warner (New York: Continuum, 2007), 5–6.

41. Luigi Russolo, "The Art of Noises: Futurist Manifesto," in Cox and Warner, *Audio Culture,* 13.

42. Michel Serres, *The Five Senses,* trans. Margaret Sankey and Peter Cowley (London: Continuum, 2008/1985), 123.

43. Hillel Schwartz, *Making Noise: From Babel to the Big Bang & Beyond* (New York: Zone Books, 2011), 20–21. Also see Jacques Attali, *Noise: The Political Economy of Music,* trans. Brian Massumi (Minneapolis: University of Minnesota Press, 1985), 4; Jean-Jacques Nattiez, *Music and Discourse: Toward a Semiology of Music,* trans. Carolyn Abbate (Princeton, NJ: Princeton University Press, 1990), 48; Simon Reynolds, "Noise," in Cox and Warner, *Audio Culture,* 55–58; and Frances Dyson, *The Tone of Our Times: Sound, Sense, Economy, and Ecology* (Cambridge, MA: MIT Press, 2014).

44. Thomas Clifton, *Music as Heard: A Study in Applied Phenomenology* (New Haven, CT: Yale University Press, 1983), 1.

45. Gurney, *The Power of Sound,* 35.

46. Suzannah Clark and Alexander Rehding, introduction to *Music Theory and Natural Order from the Renaissance to the Early Twentieth Century,* ed. Suzannah Clark and Alexander Rehding (Cambridge: Cambridge University Press, 2001), 6. It should also be noted that Descartes acknowledged the emotional impact of music.

47. Chris Cutler, "Editorial Afterword," *ReRecords Quarterly Magazine,* 1988, 46–47.

48. Nicolas Collins, "Introduction: Sound Art," *Leonardo Music Journal* 22 (2013): 1.

49. Steven Connor, "Rustications: Animals in the Urban Mix," accessed 21 July 2013, http://www.stevenconnor.com/rustications/rustications.pdf, 4.

50. John Cage's 4'3" is the inevitable starting point for any discussion of silence. See, respectively, Prochnik, *In Pursuit of Silence*; and Claude Debussy, "Claude Debussy Quotes," accessed 22 July 2013, http://www.quoteland.com/author/Claude-Debussy -Quotes/1778.

51. Edgard Varèse, "The Liberation of Sound," in Cox and Warner, *Audio Culture,* 20, 19–20.

52. Christopher Small, *Musicking* (Hanover: Wesleyan University Press, 1998), 9.

53. "It is beauty but not a commodity. It seeks to dissolve the divisions within the aesthetic and so aestheticise the whole of society. This means creating a meaningful social life together. Seen from this perspective, art is no longer a specialised technique, an exclusive know-how but the universal ability to shape a worthwhile life, both personally and socially" (Heide Göttner-Abendroth, "Nine Principles of a Matriarchal Aesthetic," in *Feminist Aesthetics,* ed. Gisela Ecker [Boston: Beacon Press, 1985], 94).

54. This recent monograph grapples with definitions of music in the twenty-first century. A number express concern about the increasingly rare aspect of an authentic

experience, while others focus on themes of marketing and consumption, and a final node of activity speaks to our planet's health (Jon Rose, *Rosenberg 3.0: Not Violin Music* [Sydney: Rosenberg Museum, 2014], n.p.).

55. Susan McClary, afterword to Attali, *Noise*, 153.

56. See Robert Kraut, "Ontology: Music and Art," *Monist* 95, no. 4 (2012): 684–710.

57. Stephen Davies, "On Defining Music," *Monist* 95, no. 4 (2012): 535. A wide range of proposals have examined how music might correspond to our evolutionary interests; these would connect current practice to evolution, whether by adaptation, as a by-product, or some other explanation. For an overview, see Stephen Davies, *The Artful Species* (Oxford: Oxford University Press, 2012).

58. Morris Weitz, "The Role of Theory in Aesthetics," *Journal of Aesthetics and Art Criticism* 15, no. 1 (1956): 31, 32.

59. Howard Morphy, *Becoming Art: Exploring Cross-Cultural Categories* (Oxford: Berg, 2007), 17, 174. Also see Sally Price, *Primitive Art in Civilized Places* (Chicago: University of Chicago Press, 1989).

60. George Dickie, *Art and the Aesthetic: An Institutional Analysis* (Ithaca, NY: Cornell University Press, 1974), 40.

61. Sarah E. Earp and Donna L. Maney, "Birdsong: Is It Music to Their Ears?," *Frontiers in Evolutionary Neuroscience* 4, no. 14 (2012): 1.

62. Alfred Gell, "The Technology of Enchantment and the Enchantment of Technology," in *Anthropology, Art and Aesthetics*, ed. J. Coot and A. Shelton (Oxford: Clarendon, 1992), 46.

63. See Franco Fabbri, "A Theory of Musical Genres: Two Applications," in *Popular Music Perspectives*, ed. D. Horn and P. Tagg (Göteborg: International Association for the Study of Popular Music, 1982), 52.

64. See Philip V. Bohlman, "Musicology as a Political Act," *Journal of Musicology* 11, no. 4 (1993): 411–436.

CHAPTER 8

Facts to Suit Theories

"This is indeed a mystery," I remarked. "What do you imagine that it means?"

"I have no data yet. It is a capital mistake to theorise before one has data. Insensibly one begins to twist facts to suit theories, instead of theories to suit facts."

—Arthur Conan Doyle, *The Adventures of Sherlock Holmes*

CLERMONT, North Queensland, 9 November 2013: A tenant in the caravan park is sternly and repeatedly shouting the name of his town. What's wrong with Butch, Buddy, or Diesel? Scout and Bandit are also fine dog names. Maybe you could name a dog Clermont if you lived in Billings, Montana, or New York City, or even Paris—the name would likely roll off the tongue much easier in French. Yelling out a town's name—isn't that what a rock star would do at the end of a show, and then only once?

Clermont is a mining hub, and the caravan park here is laid out with mining history in mind. These days, mining means coal, but the town witnessed a gold rush in 1861. The back road, where I'm parked, is Prospector's Parade, which curves onto Johnny Cash Court. Speciman [*sic*] Drive becomes Fool's Gold Crescent (although both run dead straight), while Gold Rush Way cuts down the middle, and Detector Avenue is off to the side.

A pied butcherbird pair is actively singing duets, and as they fly around the park and the field behind, I follow them and record, getting a full tour as a bonus. A man drives twenty feet to drop off a small bag of trash and keeps the motor running as he gets out. The horse races blast from his speaker. In this neck of the woods, the radio network affords multiple opportunities to listen to racing twenty-four seven, both live and rebroadcast. Breathless announcers switch from track to track across the conti-

nent, as if it were breaking news. The races are compelling. I've warmed
to them as a music substitute. There's the rhythm and inflection of the
voice, not to mention the preposterous equine names: Ready, set, racing!
Take Me to Paris charges to an early lead, with Cash Strapped pushing
up. Temporary Home is showing pace. Farther back is Ready Reply, followed by Glass Harmonium. Big Weekend makes his move. Moment of
Excess lifting now. Who Shot the Barman presenting on the outside. And
it's Temporary Home by a nose![1]

She Devil—no, not a horse, but the name affixed to a Ford Falcon Ran-
chero parked on Johnny Cash Court where the birds have led me. You
know, the model with just the front seats. (Later, I go online to get the
correct color—vixen red or venom? I keep scrolling. Neither, as it turns
out—she's emperor red.) Next, the birds draw me to the temporary residents' side of the park, where two senior German couples with identical
rented vans have set to work cleaning their (to me) already immaculately
white vehicles with a squeegee and a bucket of soapy water. Meanwhile,
a young French couple is sullenly smoking at the campers' kitchen under
the NO SMOKING sign. Across from my campsite, someone dominates
a conversation. If the word "f—ing" is an intensifier, she is very intense
indeed. ("Remember when we—had to—mail the lotto in by—Saturday?
We put the same—numbers in every—week.")

Sixty-five people lost their lives in the 1916 Clermont flood. Among
the visible reminders of the flood's destructive force was a piano lodged
thirty-two feet up a tree. The tree is still here, and the piano is reputed to
be—it is not, but a replica is. I fantasized that a pied butcherbird would
sing in that tree this morning. No bird did. A bird in drought, a piano in
flood—it seemed a bit of serendipity that would make a terrific jumping-
off point for a (re)composition for violin and piano, *Up a Tree*. I planned
to take advantage of the ruined piano in our garage.

Is any of this human history, folly, and contradiction on subject? Yes,
and no. The cognitive dissonance that I often experience negotiating my
own species versus *Cracticus nigrogularis* gives me misanthropic pause.
Might we think about ourselves from an extremely limited, arrogant, and
skewed perspective? Who are we really? A hundred-piece symphony orchestra performing a masterwork of Western art music? A turbo-charged
jazz pianist improvising over the rapid onslaught of chord changes that

is John Coltrane's "Giant Steps"? Our pied butcherbird pair, Claire and Monty, if you will, knows nothing of what *those* humans are up to. Their interspecies encounter sounds different here in Clermont. The soundtrack to our and their real lives is first and foremost road traffic, airplanes, and generators. Add to the sonic basket that we are shouting at our dog, driving twenty feet to dump our garbage accompanied by the horse races, washing our van, listening to a talk show, and profanely gossiping. Music? Our piano is a fake one in a tree; meanwhile, we are blasting a three-chord tune from our old car about a new one: "It's a big day [guitar fill]; she's in the driveway."

I listen back to the morning's recording: eclectic duets are constantly changing and display skillful timbral variety; many are syncopated. Dovetailing hockets are so precise that I must announce after each delivery how the parts were divided. While Claire and Monty might be interested in human music, their opportunities are severely limited in Clermont. If they could be interviewed, their take on human sonic culture could be partial, deficient, and damning—much as ours is when we allow a cliché of birdsong to stand in for the full spectrum of songbirds' vocalizations. Just as Charles Hartshorne predicted, "Bird judgment of human music must indeed be hopelessly 'subjective' or, to invent a word, *ornithomorphic*."[2]

Is birdsong music? When I began my investigations, I felt no need for pied butcherbird vocalizations to cross an imaginary hurdle and be classified as such. The connection was obvious. It did not concern me that others were intent on keeping birdsong at a distance. However, in too many cases, the more I read and the more birds I heard, the less I could connect the two. I began a list.

My engagement here is to catalog and refute objections to the contention that birdsong is music and in so doing to reveal intra- and interdisciplinary "disconnects." I weave together threads from the sciences, social sciences, and humanities. While I cite certain books and articles, I might have drawn from a host of others. My spirited criticism is best read as a smorgasbord of typical arguments rather than as an appraisal or critique of any one scholar, many of whom are eminent. I have organized the arguments deployed to exclude birdsong from the category of *music* as follows: (1) the Humpty Dumpty objections; (2) the erroneous objections; (3) the illogical objections; and (4) the functional objections.[3] As we progress, many of the objections will show themselves to be a flawed assessment of both human music and birdsong.

THE HUMPTY DUMPTY OBJECTIONS

Humpty Dumpty announces in Lewis Carroll's *Through a Looking Glass*: "When I use a word, it means just what I choose it to mean—neither more nor less."[4] Carroll's ironic take on semantics and pragmatics pulls together our first group of objections for why birdsong is not music. The previous chapter's sweeping claims of human uniqueness typify the sizeable Humpty Dumpty category. These definitions and proclamations have the disadvantage of not being products of zoömusicological research. Instead, they rely on circular reasoning: defining music as "human" guarantees that only humans make it.

Still more references to the exclusionary zone pile up.[5] This includes Eduard Hanslick, who rejects all possibility of music in birdsong, writing: "Not the voices of animals, but their gut is of importance to us; and the animal to which music is most indebted is not the nightingale, but the sheep."[6] It is telling that the matter appears so cut and dried for these musicians and scholars. Inherent in their Humpty-Dumptyism is that our arrival on the planet is not marked by continuity but by a break from the past and a game-changing step up the ladder.

THE ERRONEOUS OBJECTIONS

After departing the blanket dismissals, we arrive at the piecemeal objections. The most common error is easily refuted: that birdsong is hardwired, innate, ready-made, automatic.[7] Western thought has suspected for centuries that songbirds learn their songs, and vocal learning in songbirds has been uncontested for over half a century. They are not bound to an inherited genetic program, and vocal learning remains a considerable and vibrant area of birdsong research. I admit I was unfamiliar with the great flexibility that vocal learning affords songbirds until I began my research, but this is not specialist knowledge that is difficult to come by: many book and article titles speak to this.[8] We also cannot ignore the "automatic" of player pianos and barrel organs, computer music, CDs, composer software, bands in boxes, drum machines, and other electronic music generators. Most music heard today requires little participation or skill other than to hit RETURN and PLAY.

Another fallacious argument is that only humans have culture.[9] Earlier, I reviewed how "cultural transmission" describes the passage of traits across generations of the same population outside of biological mechanisms of inheritance and how ethologists routinely refer to songbirds' complex song traditions as such.[10] Culture need not imply "high art." In some cases, survival hinges on it. Prehistoric bone flutes reveal instrumental music to be at least forty thousand years old, but this ignores a surely much older cultural tradition. Australia's critically endangered palm cockatoo (*Probosciger aterrimus*) is a cultural creature. In addition to developing a large and complex vocal repertoire, males drum with a large branch (chosen in a selection process) against a dead bough or tree while pirouetting with outstretched wings, creating a loud sound that can be heard up to a hundred yards away.[11] The alleged "nature/culture" separation of songbirds and humans modulates to "culture/culture": we both have it.

The lack of a regular beat is a common accusation, although a significant number of human music genres are not based on tactus-level periodicity and are instead free-rhythm genres.[12] Many scholars assumed that the capacity for music requires the ability to entrain to (or move in time to) a beat and that only humans could accomplish this.[13] Such sweeping statements on animal handicaps are common, and yet Frans de Waal insists that efforts to distinguish distinctly human competencies seldom hold up to scientific scrutiny for longer than a decade.[14] For instance, with millions of YouTube "hits" for Snowball, the dancing sulphur-crested cockatoo (*Cacatua galerita*), indications were that perhaps the (wo)man-in-the-street was well ahead of neuroscience. In a set of experiments, Aniruddh Patel and his colleagues played recordings of Snowball's favorite song to him at eleven different tempos and videotaped his response. Their subsequent article confirms that the cockatoo does entrain to the beat and even adjusts to a changing tempo, although not as well as an adult human (it seems a difficult test—I am partial to my favorite songs at their original tempo).[15]

Another correction: despite assertions to the contrary, it is well documented that birds *do* practice; neuroscientist Gisela Kaplan reports that many songbirds rehearse their phrases, and not just in the context of subsong, and will sing when no conspecific audience is nearby.[16] Juvenile birds must practice to advance their singing and somehow find gratification in this essential activity. In the preliminary stages of vocal learning, a songbird's practice efforts do not seem to be externally rewarded. There is great reluctance to admit that a songbird may enjoy singing. Perhaps, wary of anthropomorphism, scientists have vowed to struggle against the obvious: that birds do and must take pleasure in their essential activities. Sensitive to this paradox, neuroscientist Björn Merker introduced the concept of the "conformal motive," a motivational mechanism that seeks to explain how unreinforced practice is sustained at intermediate stages until mastery.[17] Likewise, a duetting pair must engage in rehearsals in order to craft their motif choices and perfect synchronization of delivery. For some humans, work and play are compartmentalized. This is not the case for me as a musician, because the richness of the experience of making music and the challenge to improve bring their own return, even in rehearsal and regardless of any external reward being offered. I want to leave open the possibility that it is much the same for pied butcherbirds.

A number of assessments of birdsong lump together other errata, including that only male birds sing loudly, that only small birds sing, that all good singers live in moderate climates, and that human music has clearly ordered phrases, whereas birdsong does not.[18] The comment that relative pitch is unique to humans was erroneous when published in 2010 and easily checked in articles from 1990 and 2004.[19]

Philosopher of music Peter Kivy would deny a songbird agency:

> For to say we hear bird songs as if they had syntactical properties is not to ascribe syntactical properties to them, any more than we are describing a monster when we say of someone that it is as if he had eyes in the back of his head. However, as soon as we take being able to hear bird noises as music to imply that therefore they are music, we are saying that they literally have syntactic properties; and that is a conceptual impossibility. A natural object cannot, as a matter of logic, have syntactic properties, whether it is a bird's "song" or anything else.[20]

Describing a bird's song as a "natural object" is wrong. Kivy cites no research that might have influenced his thinking, although elsewhere he writes on how Darwin built his evolutionary theory of music based on the songs of birds. We could thus expect Kivy to appreciate that Darwin, in acknowledging our continuity and connectivity, never used scare quotes.[21] Although "song" arrives partitioned off by Kivy, his *lack* of scare quotes around "noises" indicates that he feels no need to situate himself when issuing that personal verdict. It is highly problematic to apply this and other vague, complex concepts ("natural object" and "syntactic property") in arbitrary ways. He shores up his doctrine through a simplistic position: music is human, and birdsong is noise. Ultimately, Kivy's case comes to naught, for ethologists regularly credit birdsong with syntax.[22] His comments look ahead to the next section, just as a number of the coming illogical objections hark back to this erroneous collection.

The "Rules" of Music

A study of the pure whistled notes of the nightingale wren (*Microcerculus philomela*) discounts any parallel between birdsong and human music because this species (and thus, the article suggests, probably all birds) draws on a continuous range of sound intervals, rather than the discrete intervals of a Western scale based on twelve-tone equal-tempered or just intonation. Biologist Marcelo Araya-Salas pits the cultural bias of the human listener, who often finds the song of the nightingale wren to be musical, against the unassailable fact of the consonance of Western scales.[23] A biologist has seemingly grabbed the right to define music out of musicians' hands, and a prestigious, high-impact journal, along with its editors and peer-reviewers, has endorsed the article. It is difficult to imagine the reverse happening.

Since nightingale wren songs do not conform to Western scales, Araya-Salas concludes that they "are not organized by the same rules used in musical composition."[24] This view of the "rules" repackages medieval concepts of rationality and ratios in music while discounting the frequent appearance in human music of diverse tuning systems, blue notes, pitch bends, and portamentos. In fact, his "rules" are completely unrepresentative. For instance, I consulted ethnomusicologist William P. Malm's survey of music cultures in the Pacific, the Near East, and Asia, only to find it brimming with other scales and tuning habits, as well as amusing stories about Western scholars' surprise on encountering them. In the Asian music of the Soviet bloc, it was official policy that only certain music be collected and that it be made to fit twelve-tone equal-tempered scales. This caused considerable scholarly difficulty, since these "wrong notes" are inherent in the Islamic ornamented styles. Other genres and instruments that do not follow, or do not limit themselves to, twelve-tone equal-tempered scales include the music of just about every area of the globe.[25] Substantial human musical activity draws on a continuous range of sound intervals and idiosyncratic tunings, and what is presented as an exception turns out to actually be the norm.

Araya-Salas also hangs his argument on the consonance of human music versus the dissonance of birdsong. However, we do not hear and classify pitches in a universal way. Although some innate perceptual ability may affect our sense of dissonance, it is largely in the ear of the listener. Dissonance is a subjective quality, nuances of which are appreciated in many cultures, like singing in parallel seconds, which is central in the Solomon Islands, Lithuania, and elsewhere.[26] When looked at from multiple viewpoints, the dissonance of one period may be the consonance of another.[27]

In the same year as Araya-Salas's publication, an interdisciplinary article on scales, intervals, and patterns in the song of the musician wren (*Cyphorhinus arada*) confirms yet again that one songbird cannot stand in for all. Composer Emily Doolittle and behavioral biologist Henrik Brumm describe the musician wren's preference for discrete pitches, consonant over dissonant intervals, and perfect consonances over imperfect ones, with the octave being statistically favored.[28] The musician wren follows the "rules." Another study details how most hermit thrush songs favor simple frequency ratios found in Western and even many non-Western musical scales—scales Araya-Salas found lacking in the nightingale wren.[29] This protracted excursion is foundational to our topic. You could call this study a serious failure of policing by the review process.

When fallacies and illogical statements start piling up, especially from eminent journals and scholars, we are usually not far from a culture-specific and out-of-date concept of music. The emu in the room is, of course, the extraordinary importance accorded to Western art music, which makes up a very small class of musical phenomena, although its airs and graces take up a lot of space. The notion of the genre's unsurpassed sophistication and complexity is uninformed and deeply biased. Nevertheless, the cliché holds, and many judgments are marred by a partiality toward this music.

I could enumerate reasons why propping up the exception is culturally maintained, but we get closer to the problem that interests me if we upgrade birdsong. We need a turnabout list of why heritage Western art music does not reach the standards of pied butcherbird song: the timbral range of human participants is limited, the tuning system is monochromatic, the rhythm is often elementary, the ability and opportunity to compose are confined to just a few, and improvisation is (usually) lacking. If our list were to truly turn things about, it would read that these sounds "are not music" or "are not birdsong." However, whether the declared or undeclared yardstick, heritage Western art music is nonetheless the persistent point of reference. Going forward, at least some comparisons of birdsong must be struck with vocal music from the oral tradition, with contemporary music practices, and with music beyond the Western monoculture.

THE ILLOGICAL OBJECTIONS

It is crucial to keep in mind that even in the human domain, music practices form a broad church with no known universals. In this pluralistic scene, we could expect certain features to be transspecific, while others might be species specific or culture specific. It would therefore seem entirely illogical that should a bird's song sound musical to many human listeners and resonate with their core musical values but lack one attribute normally observed in, for instance, the street music of Havana in 1955 or the court music of Vienna in 1785 (not to mention the Communist Party music in Havana in 1955 or the street music in Vienna in 1785), that this one discrepancy or lack would be enough to discount the otherwise musical accomplishments of a species. This is the Wittgensteinian point. Although insisting on that lack would also invalidate many human activities that we routinely count as musical, a number of illogical objections demand one-on-one equivalency with "human" music. Seeking equivalents in sonic objects, however, usually impedes the discovery of deeper meanings.[30] In any case, pied butcherbird song is in no way a controversial example on the margins, so finding aspects in pied butcherbird tradition with overlap in other human cultures' music should be adequate.

In addition, an undue emphasis on the lack of song in primates other than humans violates the evenhandedness of the comparative method regarding homology/analogy.[31] Since we are the only primate species with the specialized cerebral capacity for vocal learning, it is illogical to expect music in our closest primate relatives. Instead, we must turn to the convergent evolution of vocal learners like songbirds.[32] Merker suggests how to frame our judgments: "If we abandon a homology-inspired focus on nonhuman primates and follow the comparative method wherever it leads us, we encounter true analogies of human music in birdsong."[33] As the reader knows, this is my strong sense as well—that we must judge by sonic phenomena and accompanying musical behavior.

Still other illogical objections stack up, for instance, that birdsong is competitive, while human music is not competitive but instead founded on sharing.[34] It seems entirely unreasonable to claim that the totality of every bird's song is a competition, but it is even more extreme to claim that human music is *not* competitive. The concept of a sharing environment is a romanticized view that ignores the life of actual musicians and the agents, managers, impresarios, sponsors, stage mothers, record company executives, club owners, small-time crooks, music teachers, and others who populate the cutthroat music industry. Think music competitions, pop charts, record awards, and self-competitive behavior.

Neither can we assume that while the periphery might be competitive, the actual moment of music making is not. Performers must contend with cutting sessions, trading fours, a tune called in a difficult key, an electric guitar player turning his amp up way too loud again tonight, a young sax player in a jam session who blows far too many choruses, a cellist who refuses to adjust her intonation to yours or even settle for a compromise, a first violinist in a string quartet who sets an unreasonably breakneck tempo, and any number of conductor anecdotes and jokes. All musicians have these stories: colleagues who do something to annoy, to one-up, or to manipulate for personal benefit—it is no different from any other workplace. In addition, a musician in front of an audience is competing for attention. A soloist must demand to be heard: I have arrived, and I am different. I allow that "sharing" is a part of the social experience of human music and avian ensemble singing. Noncompetitive? No.

HONEYMOON GAP, Bullen Road, Alice Springs, 10 September 2010, 5:00 AM: Neuroscientist Constance Scharff has arrived from Berlin for a week of recording and study. We pull off the road several miles out of town by a small, dry creek. I've never recorded here, but with the immense river red gums so favored by pied butcherbirds lining the creek and road, the place seems promising. Almost immediately, a bird begins to sing right where Scharff has pointed her microphone. We nod in silence, and I head off to record a more distant bird. When the nocturnal song and dawn chorus end, something spectacular happens: a frothy brown foam, a bit like an enormous latté, starts to flow right at my feet. Over the centuries, Roe Creek has carved a gap in the soaring red sandstone cliff, but in my years coming here, I've only ever seen the dry "creek" as a place-marker for water. With the dawn chorus complete, it's time for birds to feed—but no. Several species, including at least three pied butcherbirds, fly up to the few trees clinging to the cliff top and sing for ten minutes in an apparent jam session. It all works together. (I subsequently orchestrate this splendid exposition for six-part vocal ensemble.)

Birdsong endures critiques of being individualistic rather than the product of a group.[35] Earlier, I touched on examples of small-scale coordination: the ostinato of a pied butcherbird singing in the company of a grey shrike-thrush, the acoustic complexity of ensemble songs and the dawn chorus, and now the interspecies group at Roe Creek. My hunch on how to read these is consistent with the results of a recent study that found that "acoustic choruses can be fundamentally organized by social communication extending beyond species boundaries and that such communication networks are inherently clustered by increased stereotypy and synchrony among species."[36] The Roe Creek choir works together by more than happenstance. Other bird species have been documented performing in small ensembles, while Steven Feld describes how the Kaluli people perform no sounds in unison. Rather, their music involves extensive overlapping, alternation, and layering, much like the dawn chorus.[37] In addition, the monumental in music is a blip in human history. We know that much human music consists of an unaccompanied single line, and not all of it is on a grand scale: What of a one-man band or solo piano recital? Since any given territory will only support a handful of pied butcherbirds, there would never be an opportunity for a hundred-piece choir, even if the birds were predisposed to such an event.

Others claim that birdsong is less complex, diverse, innovative, and improvisatory.[38] This could be true—for some birds. It is difficult to know which of the ten thousand species of birds these writers refer to. Could they be comparing the simplest birdsong to the most complex human music? There is a hint here that human music follows a perpetual evolutionary path toward complexity, and yet we can trace the art of harmonic development in pop music's "evolution" from multichord swing jazz standards to simpler and simpler chord progressions. No matter the genre, art renews more than progresses. Much popular and folk music is simple, repetitive, and highly formulaic, and many human genres lack complexity in contrapuntal and harmonic realms.

On the other hand, the brown thrasher's (*Toxostoma rufum*) repertoire can run to thousands of song phrases, which are likely improvised, and brown thrashers are not alone in this ability. Nightingales (*Luscinia megarhynchos*) perform over two hundred different phrases formed from a thousand-plus song elements, while sedge warblers (*Acrocephalus schoenobaenus*) lack stereotyped phrases and instead compose "a seemingly endless stream of constantly varying, unique song types." Song sparrows (*Melospiza melodia*) also continually produce new song variants in "open-ended improvisations, in many cases unique utterances."[39] For the Australian magpie (*Gymnorhina tibicen*), unique motifs constitute 12–58 percent of the repertoire, with experimentation and improvisation rife in the nearly one thousand motifs in one study's sample.[40] Migratory marsh warblers (*Acrocephalus palustris*) borrow from up to seventy-six European and African birds encountered during their world travels to build up new motifs in a repertoire of mind-boggling variety; individuals are known to sing several hundred different note types for an hour or more without a break.[41] The blackbird (*Turdus merula*) is a compulsive improviser who "submits acquired themes to continuous experimentation and embroidery, eventually transforming many of them to such a degree that the originals are no longer recognizable," while the songs of starlings (*Sturnus vulgaris*) exist "at the very limits of human comprehensibility."[42] Given this partial listing of songbirds known to deliver highly versatile performances and incorporate new material in adulthood, I wonder why so many scholars settle on an impoverished conception of birdsong. I cannot claim that pied butcherbirds are unique in matters of complexity and innovation—they have competition.

Much discourse rakes over issues of intention, consciousness, and abstract thinking.[43] Even in the Middle Ages, when music required a rational human, there were those who considered birdsong to be music-like and worthy of imitation. In fact, one fourteenth-century poem set to polyphonic music by Jacopo da Bologna suggests that the song of a nightingale is preferable to some human music.[44] Must *intention* be the determining factor on what qualifies as music? If birdsong were music, then birds would be accorded the stature of musicians—a line that cannot be crossed, some would argue, until we have a theory of mind for animals. Since we have no general theory of human cognition, it is understandable that many scientists who study animal behavior avoid this vexed subject. Although it seems unscientific *not* to entertain the possibility of animal consciousness, my claim that birdsong can be fruitfully considered as music is not based on cognition.[45] To put sonic achievement through the prism of cognition is too blunt a procedure. I prefer to keep my ear on the song.

Further, the belief that birdsong cannot be the product of higher-order thought has a corollary: that every music performance is consciously theorized and could not take place without this thought. Through the lens of philosopher of mind Peter Carruthers, we discover an alternative route. He tackles why, in the final analysis, animal consciousness might not matter much in arguments on evolutionary and cognitive continuities between humans and other animals, believing many differences in mental processes could be trivial.[46] Echoing Carruthers's sense that jazz improvisation and free dance are not preceded by prior creative thoughts (assuming, of course, the many hours of preparation required to achieve expertise), musicologist Jeff Pressing describes how processing efficiency can coalesce so that minimal attentional resources are consumed.[47] The distinction between things automatic and conscious can scarcely be an absolute one. "Cognition" simply carries too much weight. It needs to be rehabilitated and revised, and a number of scholars are on this path. For instance, biologist-philosophers Humberto R. Maturana and Francisco G. Varela consider cognition to be an integral part of how a living organism interacts with its environment, suggesting that cognition need not involve a transfer of information or mental representations of an outside world; instead, they identify cognition with the full process of life—perceptions, emotions, and behavior.[48]

Some have criticized birdsong for lacking the hierarchical structure found in human music: "just a string of little bursts of sound: no more than one thing after another."[49] Although I pretend no competence in linguistics, I want to attempt to disentangle the relationship of language, music, and hierarchical structures vis-à-vis birdsong.

Recursion in Language

Language is a combinatorial system. According to linguist Noam Chomsky and his followers, all languages make use of recursion; that is, humans form extensions of sentences by embedding a clause within a clause, and this is unique to our species. A full discussion of recursion is a project much larger than I can undertake here, but let us begin with "pied butcherbirds are musical." This straightforward sentence is how animal communication systems are assumed to work, described by some as "finite state grammar." However, I might instead say, "Pied butcherbirds, who are known to recombine their motifs when they sing formal song, are musical." In this, I have recursively embedded a clause within a clause in what linguists call "context-free grammar." I follow a bird's song wherever it leads me, and here it leads me right to the limit of my expertise in linguistics. Perhaps in this way a bird's song provides us with a window onto how the erroneous and the illogical can slip by, even in academia, with what appear to be innocent generalizations.

My readings on recursion in language indicate additional ways to complicate the program. More importantly, however, while theories of syntax seem to have focused on English and other major world languages, recent linguistic work has challenged the assumption of universal recursion, showing that some human languages have a range of alternative strategies at their disposal without embedding. Thus, recursion appears to be neither a necessary nor a defining feature in a language.[50]

Is recursion in language relevant to a songbird? If birdsong were a language (which would assume the mapping of arbitrary symbols onto notes, which is not the case in human music, and which I am not arguing for in birdsong), and if it could also be proven that this bird language lacked recursion, then some would suggest that this lack would limit the sophistication and communicative ability of this supposed bird language—itself a recursive expedition. However, linguist James R. Hurford insists that the ability to manage a "primitive" language with only main clauses would also require significant brainpower.[51] Moreover, one recent study suggests that animal communication systems could contain more language-like structure than previously thought: an analysis of the vocalizations of various birds, whales, bats, orangutans, and hyraxes found unpredictable language-like complexities adhering to statistical processes similar to those in human language.[52]

Recursion in Music and Birdsong

The search for recursion in birds is currently fraught with disputation; it is not possible to make a simple declaration on whether birds do or do not have this capacity.[53] On a separate front, chestnut-crowned babblers (*Pomatostomus ruficeps*) have recently been found to have the ability to create new sound combinations by rearranging meaningless sounds, previously thought the preserve of humans, while evidence for abstract learning has been discovered in zebra finches (*Taeniopygia guttata*).[54] We do not need to read much small print before discovering that matters of hierarchy and other complexity are not so easily generalized and do not allow for broad strokes of dismissal concerning songbirds. As we return to the claim that birdsong lacks the hierarchical structure of human music, I will again take advantage of the many and serious critiques already in place.

First, is recursion relevant to and omnipresent in human music? The answer hangs on whether pitch and rhythm in works from Mozart to Brahms can stand in as equivalents for human music of all times and places. In *A Generative Theory of Tonal Music*, Fred Lerdahl and Ray Jackendoff acknowledge that dynamics, timbre, and motivic-thematic processes are not hierarchical.[55] Just as English cannot stand in for all languages, it seems reasonable to suppose that classical Western tonal works cannot stand in for all music. In addition, there is an inherent methodological problem with research that takes a small subset of music (or language) and develops theories, statistics, and analyses based on it. Successive work, however well intentioned, tends not to move to the edges but to continue with comparative studies that refer back to this small subset.

How we understand hierarchical "tree" structure and on what level we expend our analytical efforts have a history as a combat zone in musicology, and I am not alone in contesting the presumption of such structure in all, or even most, music.[56] Cyclic music seeks neither hierarchy nor closure—Susan McClary credits black pop music "for converting our collective sense of time from tortured heroic narratives to cycles of kinetic pleasure."[57] In addition, "the fact that groove carries enough weight to override other musical factors in certain kinds of musical experience suggests that the traditional linguistics-based viewpoint does not suffice in describing the entirety of music cognition," notes jazz pianist Vijay Iyer.[58] In short, although hierarchic structural devices are indeed a subset of musical relationships, since they do not generalize to music across cultures and are not even uniformly continuous in Western art music, nor are they ubiquitous, the application of linguistics' analytical models to music has failed to be an entirely fruitful one.[59]

Besides, the theoretical role that recursion plays in music is not easily available to the listener. In fact, it is highly difficult to give any full and adequate account of listening—perhaps this is the attraction of after-the-fact analysis, to try to get hold of what always seems to elude us in real-time listening. Must we struggle to connect linguistic analytical explanations to our musical encounter? Musicologist Robert Fink reasons that surface contentment best captures the fundamental listening experience; for me, what it is actually like much more closely resembles his account than any number of academic representations of what my listening *should* be like.[60] If we are not careful, the perspective that all the interesting analytical action takes place at higher hierarchical levels will obscure the enchantment of direct and immediate events. Linguistic comparisons and hierarchical theory neither describe the event of listening nor serve the music-analytical project well.

If we once again abandon the thought that birdsong is a language and are dealing with it as music, we arrive at the question of why birds might require recursion in their songs. For example, Two Tree's complex song is not recursive, but this takes nothing away from its musicality and combinatorial triumph. Clearly, birdsong has structure, which birds can vary and then build further on the variants, even if that structure is not hierarchical in nature. It simply does not suffice to state that because a bird's song is not complex in a certain manner, it is not music. Moreover, a work well organized along tree structure's hierarchical principles could nevertheless fail dismally for lack of elegance, groove, depth, or whatever other qualities it might require and strive for but fail to achieve.

The hostile hurdles some set up to shut out birdsong remind us that definitions are artifacts reflecting the culture of the definer—they are sites where values peek through the cracks. Many of this section's illogical objections can best be refuted if we simply keep in mind how few species have been canvassed; at this point, we are unable to say unequivocally what capacities songbirds might possess or lack.

THE FUNCTIONAL OBJECTIONS

To date, function carries the main explanatory burden of birdsong. The most common objection to birdsong being music is that birds only sing in order to acquire a territory and a mate, and in this birdsong is seasonal or hormonally driven.[61] Song is a real estate deed or a matchmaking ad. The nearly undisputed corollary is that human music is not functional.[62] For instance, neuroscientist Josh McDermott and evolutionary biologist Marc D. Hauser argue that while animal song is merely functional, human song is "produced *for pure enjoyment*."[63] Their assessment of human music as a leisure activity is ethnocentric, as well as outdated. There is no reason to consider instrumentality and aesthetics as mutually exclusive. Further, while male seasonal singing unquestionably occurs in many avian species, Kaplan reminds us that Australian magpie vocalizations do not fit such a conceptualization of birdsong. In that species, both sexes sing throughout the year, and one finds "no specific song for breeding enticements."[64] Blackbirds and willow warblers (*Phylloscopus trochilus*) develop their song long after securing a mate, suggesting that the song was developed and sung for its own sake—likewise for Wallace Craig's wood pewees and many other species, including pied butcherbirds, who deliver their ensemble songs abundantly and vigorously in the autumn.[65] In addition, pied butcherbird subsong often appears to be nondirected.

I find it impossible to reconcile comments preoccupied with a functionalist orientation of birdsong with the elaborateness and inventiveness found in chapters 4–6. There is so much variation from bird to bird that mere fidelity to a model is not sufficient. Culturally distinct patterns are violated, perhaps in order to surprise and satisfy the audience. The analogy of jazz musicians and other improvisers pertains: it would be bad form *not* to insert your own ideas into a performance. The aesthetic experience is specific, distinct, local, dynamic, and year-round. Since both males and females sing, they all know the repertoire and would know what it takes to craft subtle and not-so-subtle variations. Merker and I have speculated on whether truncated phrases in solo songs and mimicry could suggest, "I'm so laid-back and competent that I needn't bother to spell the whole thing out." In any case, the members of a pied butcherbird's conspecific audience would be hard-pressed to judge merely on the basis of musical traditions and appropriateness to genre—they would have to judge on aesthetics, even if some in the human audience refuse to.

The functional binary glosses over the fact that humans, like songbirds, affirm their territory, personal taste, identity, and group through music. My dizzying catalog of human music's uses and functions is too extensive to itemize here—they are, and for several scholars have been, a book unto themselves.[66] Existing in both sonic *and* social space, music has a long history of "worldly engagements," observes musicologist Lawrence Kramer.[67] Despite the continued insistence by some that function and music are an either/or proposition, our music making and responses to it are loaded with cultural meaning, embedded in other activities, and shaped by both biology and culture.

The argument that birdsong is not music because it is essentially a male activity fits in our functional inventory but also on the erroneous and illogical lists. This objection ignores the Western canon, men's compositions, all of them. On the other hand, the human male has dominated the way ethologists observe and interpret males of other species, sometimes resulting in flawed studies. Besides, uncovering an evolutionary function does not tell us about the experience of the singer (human or animal) or the listener. While the functions of territorial defense and mate attraction do a lot of the heavy lifting, too much sway has been given to them and not enough to investigating the fullness of avian lives. Other motivations are also likely candidates. For example, birdsong could serve as a diplomatic code. There is evidence that it could be a vehicle for various sorts of domestic communication and group consolidation. While birdsong is clearly an indicator of fitness and strength, we could also frame it as a challenge that provides a sense of accomplishment or as an aesthetic production. Proof of function at any level has no currency on how we judge the quality of a musical outcome.

In the natural sciences, many scholars allow that the functional and the aesthetic work in tandem. In 1871 Darwin credited birds with "strong affections, acute perception, and a taste for the beautiful."[68] While Henry Oldys understood human music and birdsong as evolutionary analogues and assumed aesthetic sensitivity on the part of both male and female birds, he felt Darwin did not go far enough in extolling birdsong's virtues. Oldys singled out certain songbirds' capacities that entitled them to "high rank as musicians," writing in 1917 that any explanation of how birds perceive their songs other than that they appreciate them as music would be "complicated, far-fetched, and altogether unsatisfactory."[69]

Likewise, Craig grappled with aesthetic issues in his 1943 study of the wood pewee:

> Bird songs are true music, they are esthetic art and we believe that this is the essence of the concept, because it is the characteristic which is found in all bird songs and is not found in the other utterances of the bird; also, it is the characteristic which is found in highest degree in the best singers and in those songs which are most distinctly songs and not mere calls.... One reason why biologists have never successfully defined bird song is that it is not a purely biological concept. In order to develop an adequate concept of bird song, we must make progress not only in ornithology but also in musical esthetics.[70]

Claiming to be the first scientist to write an essay on the musicology of birdsong, Craig never missed an opportunity to use the words "bird music."

W. H. Thorpe did not shrink from discussing musicality in bou-bou shrike duets (like pied butcherbirds, their tone sounds pure and flute-like and is relatively low pitched), claiming they transcended biological requirements. He marveled at cases of musical invention, especially songs outside the breeding season that display exceptional variety and richness, including the rearrangement of phrases and the invention of truly de novo material.[71] His colleague Joan Hall-Craggs penned a chapter entitled "The Aesthetic Content of Bird Song," noting the senseless addition of the qualifier "human" in definitions of music. In countering claims that Western classical music has no function, she writes: "If the form of art music should become totally divorced from function it will cease to communicate and will, therefore, cease to exist."[72] Those who would lob functional questions must be reminded that eminent scholars told a more complex version of the story. Songbirds enlist aesthetic qualities to fulfill a practical purpose, and the avian and human audience can take pleasure in how a bird's song performs its function. Moreover, one cannot assume that all structures in human or animal music serve an aesthetic purpose or a psychological function.[73] "Objects do not go into their concepts without leaving a remainder"—the auditory scene cannot be succinctly reduced, and function never serves as the sole explanatory tool.[74]

Paradigms and allegiances some scholars bring with them would deny the musical lives of birds and would do so without evidence. Authors purchase old and discredited generalizations at great cost, with many of the partial, distorted, mistaken, and/or misleading objections in this chapter based on glib reductionism of birdsong *and* human music. Their obsolete notions of music reveal the hegemony of Western culture and the bigotry of low expectations. The reality is exceedingly more nuanced. Despite numerous birdsongs achieving a high degree of complexity, many scholars look for only the types of complexity best known to them and, when not finding those, designate the unfamiliar as simpler or as not music.[75] They keep the story going. Still more depend on the "straw man" form of argumentation, with propositions inverted and obviously false premises defeated, like shifting the terms of discussion by substituting "language" for "music." Some discourse obscures as much as it reveals, with a sense of charity sorely lacking: an average pied butcherbird interrupts the broad generalizations and claims that some scholars make about humans and music—we need not rely on the most virtuosic songs. Birdsong survives its objectors.

In the midst of uncertain definitions, incomplete statistics, and unstudied species, and while some have moved on to vegetal and fungal "otherness" and even "vibrant matter," there are nevertheless those who rule out ever being surprised by an animal.[76] These dismissals narrow our understanding of ourselves and of whom we must become to survive. However, I believe we can successfully reframe the topic across the borders and binaries that dominate so many accounts. In these unsettled and irregular circumstances, music must be allowed to be in theory what it is in practice—an open concept constantly reworked and blurred at the edges by its practitioners, including songbirds.

NOTES

1. This moment of levity is balanced by the knowledge that in Australia thousands of overworked horses exit racing each year as "wastage."

2. Charles Hartshorne, *Born to Sing: An Interpretation and World Survey of Bird Song* (Bloomington: Indiana University Press, 1973), 8.

3. I also investigated this subject in Hollis Taylor, "Connecting Interdisciplinary Dots: Songbirds, 'White Rats,' and Human Exceptionalism," *Social Science Information* 52, no. 2 (2013): 287–306.

4. Lewis Carroll, "Humpty Dumpty," in *Through the Looking Glass*, accessed 15 August 2012, http://www.sabian.org/looking_glass6.php.

5. See John Andrew Fisher, "What the Hills Are Alive With: In Defense of the Sounds of Nature," *Journal of Aesthetics and Art Criticism* 56, no. 2 (1998): 176; Irving Godt, "Music: A Practical Definition," *Musical Times* 146, no. 1,890 (2005): 84; Josh McDermott and Marc D. Hauser, "Thoughts on an Empirical Approach to the Evolutionary Origins of Music," *Music Perception* 24, no. 1 (2006): 113; Martin Clayton, "The Social and Personal Functions of Music in Cross-Cultural Perspective," in *The Oxford Handbook of Music Psychology*, ed. Susan Hallam, Ian Cross, and Michael Thaut (Oxford: Oxford University Press, 2009), 38; Christian Lehmann, Lorenz Welker, and Wulf Schiefenhövel, "Towards an Ethology of Song: A Categorization of Musical Behavior," *Musicae Scientiae*, Special Issue, 2009–2010 (2009): 323; Sylvain Moreno, "Can Music Influence Language and Cognition?," *Contemporary Music Review* 28, no. 3 (2009): 335; Steven Brown and Joseph Jordania, "Universals in the World's Musics," *Psychology of Music* 41, no. 2 (2011): 230; Marcus Pearce and Martin Rohrmeier, "Music Cognition and the Cognitive Sciences," *Topics in Cognitive Science* 4 (2012): 469; Daniel Müllensiefen et al., "The Musicality of Non-musicians: An Index for Assessing Musical Sophistication in the General Population," *PLOS ONE* 9, no. 2 (2014): 1; and Laurel J. Trainor, "The Origins of Music in Auditory Scene Analysis and the Roles of Evolution and Culture in Musical Creation," *Philosophical Transactions B* 370, no. 1,664 (2015): 1.

6. Eduard Hanslick, *The Beautiful in Music: A Contribution to the Revisal of Musical Aesthetics* (London: Novello, Ewer and Co., 1891), 152. String players at this time performed on gut strings.

7. See G. Révész, *The Introduction to the Psychology of Music* (London: Longmans, Green and Co, 1953), 227; Ellen Dissanayake, *What Is Art For?* (Seattle: University of Washington Press, 1988), 119; and William Forde Thompson, *Music, Thought, and Feeling: Understanding the Psychology of Music* (New York: Oxford University Press, 2009), 38.

8. See, for example, W. H. Thorpe, "The Process of Song-Learning in the Chaffinch as Studied by Means of the Sound Spectrograph," *Nature* 173 (1954): 465–469; Peter Marler, "A Comparative Approach to Vocal Learning: Song Development in White-Crowned Sparrows," *Journal of Comparative and Physiological Psychology* 71, no. 2, pt. 2

(1970): 1–25; and Linda Wilbrecht and Fernando Nottebohm, "Vocal Learning in Birds and Humans," *Mental Retardation and Developmental Disabilities Research Reviews* 9 (2003): 135–148.

9. See Alan P. Merriam, *The Anthropology of Music* (Evanston, IL: Northwestern University Press, 1964), 21.

10. See, for example, Paul C. Mundinger, "Animal Cultures and a General Theory of Cultural Evolution," *Ethology and Sociobiology* 1, no. 3 (1980): 183–223; P. J. B. Slater, "The Cultural Transmission of Bird Song," *Trends in Ecology & Evolution* 1, no. 4 (1986): 94–97; Frans de Waal, *The Ape and the Sushi Master* (London: Allen Lane, 2001); Lestel, *Les origines animales*; the chapter "Culture in Animal Societies" in Zhanna Reznikova, *Animal Intelligence: From Individual to Social Cognition* (Cambridge: Cambridge University Press, 2007); and Lucy M. Aplin et al., "Experimentally Induced Innovations Lead to Persistent Culture via Conformity in Wild Birds," *Nature* 518, no. 7,540 (2015): 538–541.

11. G. A. Wood, "Tool Use by the Palm Cockatoo *Probosciger aterrimus* during Display," *Corella* 8, no. 4 (1984): 94–95.

12. Percy A. Scholes, *The Listener's History of Music* (London: Oxford University Press, 1954), 3–4. However, see Martin R. L. Clayton, "Free Rhythm: Ethnomusicology and the Study of Music without Metre," *Bulletin of the School of Oriental and African Studies, University of London* 59, no. 2 (1996): 323–332; and David Huron, *Sweet Anticipation: Music and the Psychology of Expectation* (Cambridge, MA: MIT Press, 2007), 201.

13. Aniruddh D. Patel, *Music, Language, and the Brain* (Oxford: Oxford University Press, 2008), 408.

14. Frans B. M. de Waal, "Darwin's Last Laugh," *Nature* 460 (2009): 175.

15. Aniruddh D. Patel et al., "Experimental Evidence for Synchronization to a Musical Beat in a Nonhuman Animal," *Current Biology* 19, no. 10 (2009): 1–4. Also see Hugo Merchant et al., "Finding the Beat: A Neural Perspective across Humans and Nonhuman Primates," *Philosophical Transactions B* 370, no. 1,664 (2015).

16. "An aesthetic factor . . . is extremely strong in humans but either weak or absent in animals. For instance, humans not only train others, they also train themselves," write David Premack and Ann James Premack, "Why Animals Have Neither Culture nor History," in *Companion Encyclopedia of Anthropology*, ed. Tim Ingold (London: Routledge, 1994), 359. However, see Gisela Kaplan, "Animals and Music: Between Cultural Definitions and Sensory Evidence," *Sign Systems Studies* 37, no. ¾ (2009): 77.

17. Björn Merker, "The Conformal Motive in Birdsong, Music, and Language: An Introduction," in *The Neurosciences and Music II: From Perception to Performance*, ed. Giuliano Avanzini et al. (New York: New York Academy of Sciences, 2005), 17–28.

18. See Willi Apel, "Bird Song," in *Harvard Dictionary of Music*, ed. Willi Apel (Cambridge, MA: Belknap Press, 1970), 96; and Stephen Davies, *The Artful Species* (Oxford: Oxford University Press, 2012), 32.

19. Josh H. McDermott et al., "Musical Intervals and Relative Pitch: Frequency Resolution, Not Interval Resolution, Is Special," *Journal of the Acoustical Society of America* 128, no. 4 (2010): 1949. For relative pitch, see Ron Weisman et al., "Absolute and Relative Pitch Production in the Song of the Black-Capped Chickadee," *Condor* 92 (1990): 118–124; T. Andrew Hurly, Laurene Ratcliffe, and Ron Weisman, "Relative Pitch Recognition in White-Throated Sparrows, *Zonotrichia abicollis*," *Animal Behaviour* 40, no. 1 (1990): 176–181; and Ronald Weisman and Laurene Ratcliffe, "Relative Pitch and the Song of Black-Capped Chickadees," *American Scientist* 92 (2004): 532–539.

20. Peter Kivy, *Music Alone: Philosophical Reflections on the Purely Musical Experience* (Ithaca, NY: Cornell University Press, 1990), 24–25.

21. Peter Kivy, "Charles Darwin on Music," *Journal of the American Musicological Society* 12, no. 1 (1959): 42–48.

22. See, for example, Evan Balaban, "Bird Song Syntax: Learned Intraspecific Variation Is Meaningful," *Proceedings of the National Academy of Sciences, USA* 85, no. 10 (1988): 3657–3660. Similarly, neuroscientists Marthaleah Chaiken, Jörg Böhner, and Peter Marler confirm that the acquisition of syntactic rules is a distinct process in normal song learning in European starlings ("Song Acquisition in European Starlings, *Sturnus vulgaris*: A Comparison of the Songs of Live-Tutored, Tape-Tutored, Untutored, and Wild-Caught Males," *Animal Behaviour* 46, no. 6 [1993]: 1079–1090).

23. Marcelo Araya-Salas, "Is Birdsong Music? Evaluating Harmonic Intervals in Songs of a Neotropical Songbird," *Animal Behaviour* 84, no. 2 (2012): 310.

24. Ibid., 313.

25. William P. Malm, *Music Cultures of the Pacific, the Near East, and Asia* (Englewood Cliffs, NJ: Prentice-Hall, 1977), 197, 21, 74, 91, 119.

26. See, for example, Trân Quang Hai and Nicholas Bannan, "Vocal Traditions of the World," in *Music, Language, & Human Evolution*, ed. Nicholas Bannan (Oxford: Oxford University Press, 2012), 159; and Daiva Račiūnaitė-Vyčinienė, "The Archaic Lithuanian Polyphonic Chant *Sutartinė*," *Lithuanus: Lithuanian Quarterly Journal of Arts and Sciences* 52, no. 2 (2006): n.p. African clawed frogs (in the three major clades of Xenopus) and dengue vector mosquitoes (*Aedes aegypti*) also produce consonant intervals.

27. "The idea that dissonance is a function of the timbre of the sound as well as the musical intervals also has important implications for the understanding of nonwestern musics, modern atonal and experimental compositions, and the design of electronic musical instruments," observes music theorist William A. Sethares, whose interests include algorithmic music composition and alternate tunings (*Tuning, Timbre, Spectrum, Scale*, 2nd ed. [London: Springer-Verlag, 1999], 5).

28. Emily Doolittle and Henrik Brumm, "O Canto do Uirapuru: Consonant Intervals and Patterns in the Song of the Musician Wren," *Journal of Interdisciplinary Music Studies* 6, no. 1 (2012): 55–85. Strict adherence to "the rules" is, however a fallacy even for humans, since pure-integer intervals are in practice modified.

29. Emily L Doolittle et al., "Overtone-Based Pitch Selection in Hermit Thrush Song: Unexpected Convergence with Scale Construction in Human Music," *PNAS* 111, no. 46 (2014): 16616–16621.

30. See Philip V. Bohlman, *World Music: A Very Short Introduction* (Oxford: Oxford University Press, 2002), 7.

31. For instance, Ray Jackendoff, "Parallels and Nonparallels between Language and Music," *Music Perception* 26, no. 3 (2009): 196; and Tomlinson, *A Million Years of Music*, 117.

32. Björn Merker, e-mail message to the author, 27 October 2015.

33. Björn Merker, "The Vocal Learning Constellation: Imitation, Ritual Culture, Encephalization," in *Music, Language, and Human Evolution*, ed. Nicholas Bannan (Oxford: Oxford University Press, 2012), 217.

34. Iain McGilchrist, *The Master and His Emissary: The Divided Brain and the Making of the Western World* (New Haven, CT: Yale University Press, 2009), 123.

35. David Kraft, "Birdsong in the Music of Olivier Messiaen" (PhD diss., Middlesex University, 2000), 63; Jeremy Mynott, *Birdscapes: Birds in Our Imagination and Experience* (Princeton, NJ: Princeton University Press, 2009), 176–177; and Scholes, *The Listener's History*, 3–4.

36. Joseph A. Tobias et al., "Species Interactions and the Structure of Complex Communication Networks," *Proceedings of the National Academy of Sciences, USA* 111, no. 3 (2014): 1020.

37. Steven Feld, "The Poetics and Politics of Pygmy Pop," in *Western Music and Its Others: Difference, Representation, and Appropriation in Music*, ed. Georgina Born and David Hesmondhalgh (Berkeley: University of California Press, 2000), 391.

38. Jeremy Mynott, *Birdscapes: Birds in Our Imagination and Experience* (Princeton, NJ: Princeton University Press, 2009), 176; Patel, *Music, Language, and the Brain*, 356; and P. J. B. Slater, "Animal Music," Oxford Music Online: Grove Music Online, accessed 5 August 2013, http://www.oxfordmusiconline.com.

39. See, respectively, Michael J. Boughey and Nicholas S. Thompson, "Species Specificity and Individual Variation in the Songs of the Brown Thrasher (*Toxostoma rufum*) and Catbird (*Cumetella carolinensis*)," *Behaviour* 57, no. 1–2 (1976): 65; Dietmar Todt and Henrike Hultsch, "How Songbirds Deal with Large Amounts of Serial Information: Retrieval Rules Suggest a Hierarchical Song Memory," *Biological Cybernetics* 79 (1998): 487; Clive K. Catchpole, "Temporal and Sequential Organisation of Song in the Sedge Warbler (*Acrocephalus schoenobaenus*)," *Behaviour* 59, no. 3–4 (1976): 226–246; Jeffrey Podos et al., "The Organization of Song Repertoires in Song Sparrows: Themes and Variations," *Ethology* 90, no. 2 (1992): 89, 104; and Gisela Kaplan, *Bird Minds: Cognition and Behaviour of Australian Native Birds* (Clayton South: CSIRO Publishing, 2015), 142.

40. Eleanor D. Brown, Susan M. Farabaugh, and Clare J. Veltman, "Song Sharing in a Group-Living Songbird, the Australian Magpie, *Gymnorhina tibicen*. Part I. Vocal Sharing within and among Social Groups," *Behaviour* 104 (1988): 22.

41. Françoise Dowsett-Lemaire, "The Imitative Range of the Song of the Marsh Warbler *Acrocephalus palustris*, with Special Reference to Imitations of African Birds," *Ibis* 121 (1979): 453–468.

42. Peter Marler, "Song Learning: The Interface between Behaviour and Neuroethology," *Philosophical Transactions: Biological Sciences* 329, no. 1,253 (1990): 109, 112; and David Rothenberg, "Interview with Peter Marler: Bird Song at the Edge of Music and Science: A Conversation between David Rothenberg and Peter Marler," *Terrain* (2014): n.p. Our local introduced blackbird scarcely sounds like his European cousins. Here is a zoömusicological project waiting to happen—the comparison and contrast in singing between blackbirds on two far-flung continents.

43. For instance, see Philip Ball, *The Music Instinct: How Music Works and Why We Can't Do without It* (London: Bodley Head, 2010), 160.

44. Elizabeth Eva Leach, *Sung Birds: Music, Nature, and Poetry in the Later Middle Ages* (Ithaca, NY: Cornell University Press, 2007), 274, 84.

45. See Donald R. Griffin, *Animal Minds* (Chicago: University of Chicago Press, 1992), 4.

46. Peter Carruthers, "Why the Question of Animal Consciousness Might Not Matter Very Much," *Philosophical Psychology* 17 (2004): 83. Also see David Clarke and Eric Clarke, preface to *Music and Consciousness: Philosophical, Psychological, and Cultural Perspectives*, ed. David Clarke and Eric Clarke (Oxford: Oxford University Press, 2011), xviii.

47. Jeff Pressing, "Psychological Constraints on Improvisational Expertise and Communication," in *In the Course of Performance*, ed. Bruno Nettl and Melinda Russell (Chicago: University of Chicago Press, 1998), 47–67. Neuroscientist Bernard J. Baars also concludes that our most proficient skills are usually those we are least conscious of (*A Cognitive Theory of Consciousness* [Cambridge: Cambridge University Press, 1988], 43–44).

48. Humberto R. Maturana and Francisco G. Varela, *The Tree of Knowledge: The Biological Roots of Human Understanding* (Boston: Shambhala, 1998).

49. Ball, *The Music Instinct*, 23.

50. Nicholas Evans and Stephen C. Levinson, "The Myth of Language Universals: Language Diversity and Its Importance for Cognitive Science," *Behavioral and Brain Sciences* 32 (2009): 443, 441.

51. James R. Hurford, "Human Uniqueness, Learned Symbols and Recursive Thought," *European Review* 12, no. 4 (2004): 551–565.

52. Arik Kershenbaum et al., "Animal Vocal Sequences: Not the Markov Chains We Thought They Were," *Proceedings of the Royal Society B: Biological Sciences* 281, no. 1,792 (2014): 1–9.

53. See Timothy Q. Gentner et al., "Recursive Syntactic Pattern Learning by Songbirds," *Nature* 440, no. 7,088 (2006): 1204. These results have been challenged—see Robert C. Berwick et al., "Songs to Syntax: The Linguistics of Birdsong," *Trends in Cognitive Sciences* 15, no. 3 (2011): 113–121. Also see Kazuo Okanoya, "Sexual Display as a Syntactic Vehicle: The Evolution of Syntax in Birdsong and Human Language through Sexual Selection," in *The Transition to Language*, ed. Alison Wray (Oxford: Oxford University Press, 2002), 48; Anna R. Parker, "Evolving the Narrow Language Faculty: Was Recursion the Pivotal Step?," paper presented at the 6th International Conference on the Evolution of Language, Rome, 12–15 April 2006, n.p.; and Kentaro Abe and Dai Watanabe, "Songbirds Possess the Spontaneous Ability to Discriminate Syntactic Rules," *Nature Neuroscience* 14, no. 9 (2011): 1067–1074—which is challenged in Gabriel J. L. Beckers et al., "Birdsong Neurolinguistics: Songbird Context-Free Grammar Claim Is Premature," *Neuroethology* 23, no. 3 (2012): 139–145.

54. See, respectively, Sabrina Engesser et al., "Experimental Evidence for Phonemic Contrasts in a Nonhuman Vocal System," *PLOS Biology* 13, no. 6 (2015): 1–16; and Caroline A. A. Van Heijningen et al., "Simple Rules Can Explain Discrimination of Putative Recursive Syntactic Structures by a Songbird Species," *PNAS* 106, no. 48 (2009): 20538–20543.

55. Fred Lerdahl and Ray Jackendoff, *A Generative Theory of Tonal Music* (Cambridge, MA: MIT Press, 1983), 9.

56. Musicologist Eugene Narmour argues that hierarchical melodic structures are perceptually much less significant to listeners than traditional analysts believe (*Beyond Schenkerism: The Need for Alternatives in Music Analysis* [Chicago: University of Chicago Press, 1977]). Also see Narmour, *The Analysis and Cognition of Basic Melodic Structures* (Chicago: University of Chicago Press, 1990), xi; Richard Cohn and Douglas Dempster, "Hierarchical Unity, Plural Unities: Toward a Reconciliation," in *Disciplining Music*, ed. Katherine Bergeron and Philip V. Bohlman (Chicago: University of Chicago Press, 1992), 156–181; and David Lidov, "Our Time with the Druids: What (and How) We Can Recuperate from Our Obsession with Segmental Hierarchies and Other 'Tree Structures,'" *Contemporary Music Review* 16, no. 4 (1997): 1–28.

57. Susan McClary, "Rap, Minimalism, and Structures of Time in Late Twentieth-Century Culture," in Cox and Warner, *Audio Culture*, 295.

58. Vijay Iyer, "Embodied Mind, Situated Cognition, and Expressive Microtiming in African-American Music," *Music Perception* 19, no. 3 (2002): 387, 388.

59. Leonard B. Meyer, *Music, the Arts, and Ideas: Patterns and Predictions in Twentieth Century Culture* (Chicago: University of Chicago Press, 1967), 259, 312.

60. Robert Fink, "Going Flat: Post-hierarchical Music Theory and the Musical Surface," In *Rethinking Music*, ed. Nicholas Cook and Mark Everist (Oxford: Oxford University Press, 1999), 103.

61. See Ball, *The Music Instinct*, 23.

62. See Ian Cross, "Music and Evolution: Consequences and Causes," *Contemporary Music Review* 22, no. 3 (2003): 83; Patel, *Music, Language, and the Brain*, 355; and McDermott and Hauser, "Thoughts on an Empirical Approach," 114.

63. Marc D. Hauser and Josh McDermott, "The Evolution of the Music Faculty: A Comparative Perspective," *Nature Neuroscience* 6, no. 7 (2003): 667, emphasis added.

64. Gisela Kaplan, "The Australian Magpie (*Gymnorhina tibicen*): An Alternative Model for the Study of Songbird Neurobiology," in *Neuroscience of Birdsong*, ed. H. Philip Zeigler and Peter Marler (Cambridge: Cambridge University Press, 2008), 51.

65. See Kaplan, "Animals and Music," 91; and Hollis Taylor, "Decoding the Song of the Pied Butcherbird: An Initial Survey," *Transcultural Music Review* 12, no. 12 (2008): 1–30; and Hollis Taylor, "Towards a Species Songbook: Illuminating the Vocalisations of the Australian Pied Butcherbird (*Cracticus nigrogularis*)" (PhD diss., University of Western Sydney, 2008) vols. 1 and 2.

66. See Lydia Goehr, *The Imaginary Museum of Musical Works: An Essay in the Philosophy of Music* (Oxford: Clarendon Press, 1992); and Tia DeNora, *Music in Everyday Life* (Port Chester: Cambridge University Press, 2000), xi, 163. Also see Martin Clayton, Trevor Herbert, and Richard Middleton, introduction to *The Cultural Study of Music: A Critical Introduction*, ed. Martin Clayton, Trevor Herbert, and Richard Middleton (New York: Routledge, 2003), 1–15.

67. Lawrence Kramer, "Musicology and Meaning," *Musical Times* 144, no. 1,883 (2003): 6.

68. Charles Darwin, *The Descent of Man, and Selection in Relation to Sex* (Princeton, NJ: Princeton University Press, 1871/1981), 2:108.

69. Henry Oldys, "The Meaning of Bird Music," *American Museum Journal* 17 (1917): 124–125. In his study of hermit thrush (*Catharus guttatus*) song, Oldys drew further comparisons between avian and human music. See Henry Oldys, "A Remarkable Hermit Thrush Song," *Auk* 30 (1913): 538–541.

70. Wallace Craig, *The Song of the Wood Pewee* Myiochanes virens *Linnaeus: A Study of Bird Music*, vol. 334 (Albany: University of the State of New York, 1943), 169, 172. An earlier article also took up the wood pewee's song and featured some notation: Craig, "The Music of the Wood Pewee's Song and One of Its Laws."

71. W. H. Thorpe, "Ritualization in Ontogeny. II. Ritualization in the Individual Development of Bird Song," *Philosophical Transactions of the Royal Society B: Biological Sciences* 251, no. 772 (1966): 357–358, 354.

72. Joan Hall-Craggs, "The Aesthetic Content of Bird Song," in *Bird Vocalizations: Their Relations to Current Problems in Biology and Psychology. Essays Presented to W. H. Thorpe*, ed. by R. A. Hinde, 367, 368, 380 (Cambridge: Cambridge University Press, 1969). Also see George Herzog, "Do Animals Have Music?," *Bulletin of the American Musicological Society* 5 (1941): 4; Edward A. Armstrong, *A Study of Bird Song* (New York: Dover Publications, 1973); and Rosemary Jellis, *Bird Sounds and Their Meaning* (Ithaca, NY: Cornell University Press, 1977), 196.

73. See Huron, *Sweet Anticipation*, 369.

74. Jane Bennett, *Vibrant Matter: A Political Ecology of Things* (Durham, NC: Duke University Press, 2010), 14.

75. Judith Becker, "Is Western Art Music Superior?," *Musical Quarterly* 72, no. 3 (1986): 346.

76. Dominique Lestel, *Les amis de mes amis* (Paris: Éditions du Seuil, 2007), 15. Lestel identifies as Cartesian thusly: "Le cartésien peut être justement caractérisé comme celui qui exclut a priori d'être surpris par un animal." See also Laura A. Ogden, Billy Hall, and Kimiko Tanita, "Animals, Plants, People, and Things: A Review of Multispecies Ethnography," *Environment and Society: Advances in Research* 4 (2013): 5–24; Anna Tsing, "Unruly Edges: Mushrooms as Companion Species," *Environmental Humanities* 1 (2012): 141–154; and Bennett, *Vibrant Matter*.

CHAPTER 9

Too Many Theories and
Not Enough Birdsong

> Logic will get you from A to B. Imagination will take you
> everywhere.
> —Albert Einstein

HORSESHOE BAY ROAD, Bowen, North Queensland, 28 October 2015,
4:13 AM: The moon is full and so is the throat of a pied butcherbird who
is perched high on a utility wire and facing the ocean. Set over me like a
numinous angel, the bird contrasts gymnastic upward vocal leaps with
steep downward frequency sweeps and delicate turns and whorls with
stationary syncopated notes. There's no competition except the crash of
waves and a distant conspecific's broken snatches wafting on the tropical
air. Surely our soloist deserves a better duet partner than the oscillating
mosquito whine that intrudes at 5:00 AM. Soon after, a willie wagtail adds
his agile soprano, and then an eastern koel (*Eudynamys orientalis*) ratchets
up a semitone with each rushed "koel-koel-koel-koel-koel."

Other birds, insects, and frogs gradually embellish the texture, and as
the sun rises, an active biophony provides orchestral accompaniment. Our
soloist is vigilant, glancing back and forth, yet apparently able to tune out
much of what goes on, like the long opening and closing envelope of a jog-
ger passing in one direction while a van rumbles in the other. They meet
under the bird, and of course I'm also standing right there—but nothing
disrupts the song's pace. When a magpie-lark lands on the wire just inches
away, the pied butcherbird delivers a few closing phrases and flies off.

Like all good artists, this soloist has conviction; s/he owns the stage. Without this bird, the chorus would still be substantial, but no individual would *demand* to be heard the way a pied butcherbird does. The raucous intermittent "laughing" of kookaburras in full chuckle mode is comparing apples and oranges. I can imagine the dawn chorus without a pied butcherbird; what I cannot imagine *is* this soloist—I am unable to match up what I used to expect from a bird's song with what I hear.

THEORETICAL AND METHODOLOGICAL CHALLENGES FOR ZOÖMUSICOLOGY

Will the musicality of sophisticated songbirds be championed? Will zoö-centric musicians participate in connecting the interdisciplinary dots in birdsong analysis? Will scientists forge a link with alternative ways of knowledge so that they and musicologists can swap stories? I believe they will. While no challenge to science's grip, zoömusicology is nonetheless an enthusiastic partner, one with the potential to alter contours of inquiry and complement scientific results with questions others are not bothering to pose. Thinking with Aldo Leopold, the natural sciences and musicology can be taught separately, but they cannot be deployed separately to solve issues of musicality in birdsong.

For those prepared to study birdsong as music, good recordings of good birdsong are not sufficient—zoömusicology needs good questions and methodologies. Ethologist Peter Marler speaks to this topic: "The whole phenomenon of the inventive potential of birds is understudied, very difficult to study, and I'm quite convinced that the possibilities are remarkable *if you could only document them convincingly.*"[1] With a mandate for broad explanatory principles and convincing methodologies, scientists are expected to sidestep troublesome details: "You have to pretend when you present a generalization, that things are much clearer than they really are," instructs Marler.[2] Some observations become data, while others become anomalies to be tidied up.[3] Complex birdsongs can be such anomalies.

This returns us to the pressure to study songbirds in a controlled setting. Many elaborate and complex songs come from those species least

suitable for laboratory housing. Although not useful for identifying nocturnal singers, especially those with multiple songposts, the banding
of wild birds will for some be an acceptable middle ground. Key for me
has been working ethically with animal partners and recognizing their
agency. While investigating them in their natural environment provides
rich results, such study is expensive, as mine has been (both personally
and institutionally), and may be met with the contention that the results
are not as reliable as laboratory findings. This argument goes both ways.
As I indicated at the outset, I am content to give up experimental control
and laboratory supervision with the confidence that if my research were
dependent upon birds singing in such a setting, my understanding of their
vocal world would be severely compromised.[4] In any case, these days a
wealth of precision recording and measuring devices is available to accompany researchers into the field.

Laboratory control is also pertinent in how we get our epistemologi-
cal bearings—whether we understand knowledge as situated or neutral,
subjective or objective, a product of the embodiment of our senses or one
unmarked by prejudice—the mythic "god trick of seeing [and hearing]
everything from nowhere."[5] Yet, despite our differences, the natural sciences and musicology can benefit by together thinking through issues
related to birdsong.

Another institutional stumbling block in moving the study of birdsong
forward is that very few species have been studied, not because ethologists are content with the body of knowledge obtained from a small pool
of songbirds but because the practicalities of introducing a new species
are considerable. Matters of time and dwindling funding make it nearly
impossible for researchers to choose to work on a heretofore-unstudied
songbird species. In some circles, it is considered a bad, even fatal, career
choice.

Into the bargain, despite accelerating scholarly interest in animals, a
number of obstacles and resistances inhibit the inclusion of animals in
disciplines traditionally theorized with an assumption of human uniqueness. Thus, as zoömusicologists take their place in academia and develop
nuances of approach in their respective animal studies, imagining how
the methodological models of a genuinely interdisciplinary approach
might look is only part of the task. We must ask if zoömusicology will in-

deed become a career option in musicology or any other humanities field and how such a change might be negotiated within current institutional frameworks. If birdsong is not music, then it will prove challenging for musicologists to make the case to study it, lecture on it, and win grants. Instead of asking the most interesting questions about animal music, zoö-musicologists will be asking, "Do you want fries with that?"[6]

Neither science nor art fully serves us in isolation. In pondering the prospects for interdisciplinary collaboration, I take up two challenging topics, one qualitative (or typically considered so) and the other quantitative (although, like technology, data are never neutral).

Musicality

Music is not a homogeneous reality—the human brain lacks a distinct music center. We process music throughout the brain, and we process components separately (as in vision), drawing on a suite of cognitive capacities. Music integrates diverse domains and motor skills, serves multiple functions, and shares key components with other systems, particularly speech.[7] Since musicking is a complex, multifarious ability, musicians who excel in one skill set may not in another. Although music is often referred to as an acquired competence based on the innate cognitive trait of musicality, the two are not so easily disentangled. A feedback loop makes it challenging for scientists to isolate the innate from the acquired. Nonetheless, new genomic technologies may allow us to pinpoint neural correlates and genes of specific features of musicality, including how we distinguish all manner of relationships, apprehend form and structure, and process expressive devices. Genetic syndromes and rare faculties associated with an altered musicality, like congenital impairments and absolute pitch, provide fascinating insights into musicality's biological basis.[8]

A comparative, multicomponent approach *across species*, preferably drawing on noninvasive procedures with animal volunteers (just as we do with humans) and not just across cultures, is essential in order to advance our understanding of musicality. Juxtapositions of human and animal music have in the past made for compelling reading, yet they have not been significantly enlarged upon, and many comparative studies concern themselves with birdsong and language. A recent transdisciplinary article by philosopher and musician David Rothenberg and colleagues calls instead for new descriptive models to compare birdsong and music, especially patterns of pitch and rhythm. This welcome plea for a more aesthetic approach to birdsong imagines embracing current studies in music theory relating to perception and cognition, like those of David Huron.[9] While other methods can be brought to bear on this task, and the authors employ one, many of the statistical analyses the authors propose would benefit from notations of birdsongs that are conducive to notation. After all, most comparative studies of human music are accomplished by means of notated music, even if the genre belongs to an oral tradition. The lack of available birdsong notations paired with a decreasing ability to read notation has held back vital work. Notation is readily exportable as a Music XML file, which can then be paired with various technologies and processes for analysis of sequential rules, levels of organization, and other structural matters. New descriptive models will also benefit from the informed speculation of zoömusicologists and their trained ear. Leonard Meyer's observations on human music also deserve a reply from zoömusicology and others vis-à-vis birdsong, like "the more exact the repetition of an event is, the more strongly we expect change," and "the greater the amount of change—in both rate and degree—in one parameter, the smaller must be the changes in other parameters if patterning is to be perceived."[10]

However, comparisons of birdsong with human music will be compromised if they focus on the current crop of laboratory songbirds. No one is more dogged about this shortcoming than Björn Merker, who is also a vocalist and informed listener with experience in a range of music.[11] I first met him when he paid us a visit in Berlin, bounding up the six flights three stairs at a time. Once inside, he was a nearly unstoppable bundle of energy and acumen. He leaped to his feet to sing and dance a vivid description of how he imagines vocal learning in human evolution at the interface of language and music—we were transported back 150,000 or more years to a savannah campfire. His interest in the motivational and evolutionary underpinnings of human music led him initially to study the innate songs of gibbons in both zoo environments and the rain forests of

Southeast Asia. (Gibbon songs propelled him back on his feet again to sing and mime.) Merker's later research focuses on the intersection of human music, language, and animal song, and his work occupies the vanguard of theorization on vocal learning.[12] My project has benefited from his encyclopedic knowledge across diverse fields, from his immersive listening to my catalog of pied butcherbird recordings, and from our ongoing discussions.

If we are going to truly examine issues of musicality, Merker believes, as do I, that zebra finches and other laboratory songbirds are not interchangeable with sophisticated songsters like the pied butcherbird. He claims that we are far from understanding the nuances of "emancipated singers"—birds not bound to a species-specific template but instead open-ended learners who incorporate new vocal material in adulthood and are able to disassemble and reassemble patterns into new acoustic constructs.[13] These vocalists and those who study them need to be represented around every table where scholars are deliberating on the origins, biological basis, evolution, and nature of musicality so that we have all the evidence we can muster.

The Lure of Numeracy

How we measure aspects of musicality is quite another challenge. As sociologist William Bruce Cameron famously observed, "Not everything that can be counted counts, and not everything that counts can be counted."[14] Numbers bridge ignorance of and between fields, but numbers can also disguise ignorance. They imply trust, impartiality, and objectivity—we speak of "statistical confidence," even though no pure measurement exists. Numbers do not passively describe; they also influence—they are power brokers in disguise. Birdsong may be expressed in the language of mathematics, although some numbers are more a product of technical possibility than of an interesting question. A surplus of data and byzantine detail produces noise, not music.

As tools of analysis have been sharpened, interdisciplinary discourse has shrunk. Citizen scientists in ornithology often cannot make sense of the numbers that clog current animal behavior articles. Weary and leery of specialist measurements, statistics, and graphs, several expert ornithologists have reported to me that obvious errors of understanding slip through in some articles. In essence, scholars can manage to publish short of a substantive history with and an understanding of a species as long as they have expertise in presenting their ideas in the numerical currency of the day. With retractions of scientific articles rising and the nonexpert or even close colleague struggling to fact check, we have a right to be prudent when it comes to data.

In 2012 zoölogist Ofer Tchernichovski invited me to deliver a paper on pied butcherbird song with him and several researchers from his New York–based Laboratory of Vocal Learning at the Music in Neuroscience conference in Monte Verità, Switzerland. The conference brought together neuroscientists who study hearing and music perception, the neural mechanisms of birdsong, and the algorithmic structure of music. The hosts especially encouraged attendance by neuroscientists "who love to play a musical instrument," as well as professional musicians interested in the topic.[15] By day we listened to reports of stimulating research into musicality, while evenings brought chamber music by stellar amateur musicians among the neuroscientists and lecture-concerts by professional musicians. In the end, I had to admit that most of the research was taking place at a level of numeracy that left me in the lurch—I had to take their word for it. Although in high school I relished mathematics, today's sophisticated calculations read like a foreign language. Perhaps I am typical of musicians; numbers do not always explain and instead need to be explained. I need to hear the song under discussion, no matter what the charts, graphs, and statistics purport. Still, we cannot hide from these circumstances; "the lure of numeracy" seems to increase each year.[16]

Should we disregard our methodological tradition and dive into other disciplines with the risk of appearing a naive participant? This issue has the potential to frustrate animal music research by humanities scholars, and each of us will have to come to terms with it in our own way: when to up our numeracy game, when to draw on our musicological toolbox (which more and more also involves sophisticated numeracy), and when to do both—not to mention when to simply rely upon our music-making experience. Interdisciplinary cooperation may be precisely what a project needs. In Monte Verità I came to see that science is not made simply by meticulousness and exhaustiveness; it is made by the scientific method and supported by sophisticated numeracy. Any contribution I could make to science would need to be a collaboration rather than a single-author effort, and I am disposed to make that compromise for some projects.

True to my initial instincts, I continue to seek out multiple points of entry. I want to champion some musical issues without the scientific method framing my investigations—to leave behind the essential and the typical and instead concentrate on an individual with all their peculiarities and asymmetries, or to leave behind a theory and simply be open to where a birdsong might take me. Science excels in the telling; music suggests. Facts can be deficient and can even mislead. Instruments, software, and experiments enumerate and explicate, but machine knowledge is partial and can miss nuances of relational meaning. We do not ask a machine to smell perfume, judge color, or taste wine. For now, at least, these and other complex evaluative judgments remain the domain of living organisms.

Animal music represents an expanded agenda for musicology, where exceptions are less of a concern than in science and findings need not be bound to a hypothesis or dullness, which all disciplines are susceptible to. After all, zoömusicology is not science—it is "stamp collecting" (Lord Rutherford's slur against anything not physics). Neuroscientific explanations of a bird's song will not render obsolete the explanatory role of zoömusicology; they are complementary. Some zoömusicologists may be interested in just one species, while others may delve into an entire assemblage of fauna at one site. The field is capacious. With most species yet unstudied, zoömusicology offers a ground-floor opportunity for musicologists, performers, and composers.

COMPOSERS' APPROPRIATION OF BIRDSONG

My tally of composers who have appropriated pied butcherbird song currently stands at twenty-one. My intent here is not to present an individual analysis of these works but merely to ask how pied butcherbird songs have inspired composers, to identify various strategies of appropriation, and to ask if new knowledge about avian vocalizations has arisen from these activities.[17]

While not all agree that birdsong can be cast as music, let alone that in it might lie the origins of music, birds have nonetheless been recurrent muses to composers. Registers of birdsong-inspired compositions abound, making it unnecessary to duplicate them here. Composers employ a range of appropriation strategies. Works may present an affinity for or an excursion into nature, and perhaps no sound is more evocative than that of songbirds, who are aural and visual markers of continents, localities, and seasons. When scored in compositions, audio recordings of birds also showcase a programmatic purpose. Imitation is popular, whether as direct quotation (with or without added accompaniment) or via poetic inspiration, and so is imitation revised as "improvement." Humor or vulgarity can be introduced by way of animal imitations. Composers have absorbed avian idioms beyond melody, especially in the twentieth and twenty-first centuries. Birdsongs are increasingly considered compelling models in multiple parameters and are called upon by some to evoke spirituality and mystery, as well as to provoke ecological reflection.

Few commercial recordings of pied butcherbirds are available, and most appropriations are drawn from four recordings. Recordists' liner notes detail the exhilaration of documenting these nocturnal songs. The first hails from David Lumsdaine (1931), whose music embodies his considerable experience in the Australian bush. In addition to penning musical scores, he has recorded environmental sounds for deployment as composition, including "Pied Butcherbirds of Spirey Creek." This 1983 track begins with insects, frogs, and a rushing creek; the pied butcherbird (Lumsdaine's "Buddha of Spirey Creek") enters at forty-five seconds in, much as a soloist in a classical concerto might. He appraises the song as follows:

> The Pied Butcherbird is a virtuoso of composition and improvisation: the long solo develops like a mosaic, through the varied repetition of its phrases. In the course of the song, some elements remain constant, some elements transform through addition and elimination. The bird is a virtuoso of decoration: there is an extraordinary delicacy in the way it articulates the harmonic course of its song with microtonal inflections, or places its cadences with a bird's equivalent of tremolandi and fluttertonguing. I've made a number of recordings of Pied Butcherbirds, and many of them are technically better than this set; but, beautiful as they may be, none of them matches the performance by these particular birds. Serendipity plays a large part in determining the musical quality of a soundscape—there are no retakes in the wild.[18]

I asked him for detailed directions and traveled to Spirey Creek in Warrumbungle National Park in the spring of 2005 and subsequent years as well. Lumsdaine's bird sang from a tall, isolated cedar tree not far from the creek, he told me, but on my trip, there was no "Buddha" there or anywhere within earshot. I managed to record soloists several miles away in both directions; those songs do not resemble the 1983 recording. Bushfires ravaged 80 percent of the park in 2013, and I have not yet returned to check how the birds have fared.

Mandala 4 is Lumsdaine's recasting of the Spirey Creek birdsong for string quartet, and the result is, like many in my survey, beholden to the composer's personal language.[19] The species call is emblematic of the pied butcherbird's voice and stands as a musical identity marker in the minds of those who have heard it. Lumsdaine is one of five composers who have chosen to represent the pied butcherbird via the species call.[20]

Another recording is from Andrew Skeoch, who writes in his liner notes:

> Ormiston Gorge, full moon, 3 AM. Our recording opens at one of the most spectacular locations in central Australia, and features the purest calls of any Australian songbird. The location is Ormiston Gorge, a huge valley carved through the ancient Macdonnell Ranges, west of Alice Springs. It acts like a cathedral, reflecting and echoing sounds off sheer rock walls. At the bottom of the chasm are permanent waterholes, with huge River Red Gums growing next to the water's edge. Crickets chirrup softly from dense grasses around the waterhole, and what may be a katydid can be heard later. . . . It is the early hours of the morning, and a full moon casts a silvery light with deep shadows. A Pied Butcherbird is roosting in a tree opposite the waterhole. Its calls are a succession of musical phrases, which are repeated and restated at intervals, forming a repertoire of over a dozen melodic fragments and variations. Here the Butcherbirds call intermittently, unhurried, their calls echoing up and down the gorge.[21]

The recording is exquisite, and the bird's song is an example of simple material being slowly reworked to bewitching effect over a four-hour spell. I have (re)composed based on this several times, with outcomes for solo recorder, for bass and violin, and for solo violin. Naturally, I asked for precise directions on where the recording was made, traveling there for the first time in 2006. The twenty-minute hike from the campground to

Ormiston Gorge is relatively easy to negotiate even in the dark. Not unlike Spirey Creek, though, Ormiston Gorge has been bereft of these choristers in all of the eight years I have gone there; singing pied butcherbirds can be found several miles down the road. I feel like a problem gambler, going back each year to the gorge without being rewarded.

Skeoch insists that he is not a composer: "I try to reveal the composition that is already there. I make choices of how to place the microphone and how to present the audio—you can call me an interpreter, or just a plain recordist," he told me. "People overlook how composed and musical birdsong is. Anything that can draw attention to it and blur the boundary I think is really good."[22]

Bird recordist Jean C. Roché's pied butcherbird track has seen the most appropriations, including those made by Emily Doolittle and Dario Martinelli. In yet another, after a few bird phrases, a jazz trio enters with punchy unison riffs matching the avian melodic contour and rhythm, followed by an up-tempo improvisation. The field recording continues at a reduced level. After several minutes, the field recording returns to full volume and interrupts the improvisation, a slow passage with the birdsong ensues, and a final section returns to unison riffs. These short motifs emulate the sound and then the silence of an interphrase interval.[23] Several seconds from the Roché recording also serve as audio for a pied butcherbird stuffed toy, which sounds when squeezed.[24]

In wildlife recordist Tony Baylis's pied butcherbird recording, the rapid-fire phrases of strong timbral contrast (with steep upward and downward portamentos abutting pure tones and hollow-sounding rattles) and swinging rhythms sit somewhere between the genres of Baroque and jazz. Baylis recalls:

> My wife Fiona and I had been travelling around Australia for about 10 months and found ourselves camped up for the night at China Wall, a vein of white quartz stretching across the remote landscape, near Halls Creek, Western Australia. It was one of those wonderfully balmy nights when the air is warm and welcoming. Predawn Fiona, who is a light sleeper, woke me up to this fluting ethereal sound that came out of the silence. We had only been in Australia about a year and my identification skills were still modest, so the author was a mystery at that time. I gathered my recording equipment and quietly scanned the area to discover where this stunning sound that demanded my attention was

coming from. The bird was hidden by shrubs, stunted trees and the low light level. I hardly dared to breathe, as for some considerable time the song poured down toward me; I was transfixed. Eventually, the singing finished, and I glimpsed two black and white birds fly away. Later that day I established the identity using playback: the Pied Butcherbird. Subsequently, I have recorded a number of these remarkable songsters, but that morning's performance, one of the most exquisite bird songs I have ever heard, is etched in our memory.[25]

It is no surprise that this outback encounter features on the British Library's *Beautiful Bird Songs from around the World*, as well as in my (re)composition *Hall's Creek* for recorder.

Other composers appropriated birdsong where I have no reference recording. In these cases, I must rely on texts (scores, transcriptions, letters, and interviews). I asked John Rodgers (1962) whether his bird model in "The Butcher-bird" for recorder was pied or grey. "I was trying to make music—not an ornithological document," he responded. "On the other hand, I didn't try too hard because they sounded pretty musical anyway."[26] His phrase lengths are conspicuously similar to those of butcherbirds, as are the contrasting timbres and alternation of phrases with pauses. For Rodgers, these avian solutions coincide with his sensibility, making him typical of those composers who find scant need to significantly rework pied butcherbird vocalizations.

Ron Nagorcka's (1948) inspiration came in part from the microtonality he heard in his pied butcherbird model; it is unclear how much his long-standing interest in just intonation influenced him to place the birdsong into this template.[27] One musician's "New Age" piano musings suggest a unity with nature and are consistent with works suitable for yoga classes or meditation.[28] We also find pied butcherbird song used as a wistful springboard, with no apparent avian material in any parameter of the composition.

Composers take highly personal voyages with their avian counterparts. The movement from mere melodic imitation and elaboration to a fuller exploration of avian idioms speaks to the appreciation of birdsong as more than a primitive commodity awaiting competent realization by a composer. In compositional design, pied butcherbird vocalizations have been sourced in matters of melody, rhythm, gesture, contour, dynamic envelope, and formal structure. The birds' phrase length and their balance of sound and silence have been honored to good effect, while some composers have appropriated what they perceived as a pied butcherbird scale, tuning system, or manner of repetition. Flute-like phrases have been assigned to piano and bass, clarinet and bassoon, xylophone and violin (and many more voices). While birdsong profoundly inspires some composers, for others it serves merely as a clichéd abbreviation. Some, but not all, composers trust the pied butcherbird material, including the interphrase interval. Inspiration and appropriation do not equate to formal research, however, and while there is no harm in composing based on limited research, there *is* a danger of drawing conclusions based on too small a sample.

As we saw in the case of Messiaen, a composer's avian transcription is less an ornithological artifact than a text that mediates between birdsong and the musical score, and as such it will always be conflicted in its tasks. No matter how accurate and perceptive their insights, the composers I surveyed have yet to work intensively or extensively enough with the species to add convincingly to new knowledge, or if they have, they have not published it.[29] The problem is that there is no single pied butcherbird song—there is one song after another delivered by one individual after another. Avian artists do not give up their secrets easily. Is capturing the jizz of one pied butcherbird song new knowledge? Yes, but I feel composers, with their deep sense of how music is put together, still have much more to give to this project of transcribing and analyzing birdsong, should they find the time to devote to it.

George List questions whether any *intra*species understanding is possible.[30] Perhaps I am too optimistic, but I believe we can approach in-group status. I appreciate that not everyone is prepared to mount a sustained, long-term engagement with a species. Nonetheless, when avian material is interrogated and worked by a composer, the resultant insights may at minimum point to what warrants further investigation by others.

(RE)COMPOSITIONS AND PERFORMANCES
OF PIED BUTCHERBIRD SONG

Inspiration rarely just comes to composers; more often, they must chase it down or even do without it and simply produce to demand. In what may seem paradoxical to some, composers both seek out material and choose rules that constrain their activity. I see myself as a sonic explorer, and I understand pied butcherbird song to be the manifestation of many tens of thousands (and perhaps millions) of years of culture. Similar to some composers I have surveyed, I do not set out to improve on pied butcher-bird songs—that is the birds' task—but rather to commend and showcase them. Thus, it is key that my (re)compositions of pied butcherbird vocal-izations maintain a close connection to the original.

Although I have penned pied butcherbird works for vocal and instru-mental ensembles and solo instruments other than violin, I concentrate here on pieces for solo violin that I perform myself. In them, I must "go out" the way a bird does, as a single voice. Of course, birds do not sing in a sound vacuum—the entire soundscape is unfolding, and space is, as in all music, an essential aspect in avian song. The music that humans at-tend to is typically continuous. In a concert setting, the quietest sections can find audience members coughing awkwardly, rustling programs, and squeaking chairs. In my DIY production, I wanted to minimize this sort of acoustic backdrop.

While an unaccompanied pied butcherbird transcription could surely sustain human interest, in pondering how I might encourage my audience to listen intently and comfortably without sacrificing the formal song aesthetic of an interphrase interval, I settled on performing with edited field recordings. These rarely incorporate the pied butcherbird and instead include the songs and sounds of other birds, insects, frogs, and mammals (like kangaroos and dingoes); the wind blowing through an outback fence (or even Jon and I bowing it); a livestock auctioneer; and an Australian Air Force helicopter taking off as I recorded on a remote Arnhemland airstrip—whatever I encounter on my trips. Some field recordings are spare, others dense. I make no attempt to create a pastoral character that romanticizes nature. One, for instance, draws from traffic sounds—trucks passing, horns honking, a car trundling across an old wooden bridge. My intent is simply to underline compelling aspects of places where I have recorded birds and in the process spark new ways to mediate human-animal relationships.

Since birdsong drives the compositional decisions, many of my pieces are almost direct transcriptions, although I do not bind myself to that rule. The most typical change is to shorten a song. Questions of range and timbre also arise—will a pied butcherbird phrase sound as compelling below its normal tessitura and on a violin? I struggle with how to reproduce such a diverse timbral palette, sometimes succeeding in approximating the tone color, other times choosing another sound that at minimum indicates a *change* in timbre. Playing pied butcherbird vocalizations on the violin may provoke new ways of hearing them, as did Webern's *Klangfarbenmelodie* arrangement of Bach's "Ricercar," a six-voice fugue from *The Musical Offering*.

As I began to internalize birdsong through composition and performance and to be in dialogue with the phrases, I knew when a piece did not work. Artists are not unique in this. Cytogeneticist Barbara McClintock urged us to "hear what the material has to say to you" and to "let it come to you"—we have to have "a feeling for the organism."[31] When in doubt, I went back to the recording. In the process, I was reminded of just how adroit, fluid, and consequent of movement pied butcherbird singing is. I needed to find a way to make my violin performance feel and sound just as spontaneous and organic. I had to listen to the minute details of pied butcherbird song more closely, imagine it more precisely, and match my physical gestures and kinetic processes to the sound. In essence, I had to foster a new physical vocabulary, one that perhaps I should have acquired much earlier and applied to all my repertoire. Thus, when I tried to insert and rework licks and tricks from the various genres that I have performed in, these never succeeded. Neither could I continue to write in my previous composer's style, where my works for strings focused on issues of rhythm and bowing, from dance forms and compound meter to how Classical players can appropriate extended techniques from nontraditional genres—all over. I had to start anew.

Music is a product of self-criticism on the part of the musician. I came to realize that birds spend much more time with their motifs than I do. Just as food plants and fiddle tunes have been winnowed down and refined by myriad trials, so too have the mercurial songs of pied butcherbirds seen numerous candidate solutions. Their results are never gimmicky. I learned to trust the material—to trust the birds—and to align and connect myself with their vocalizations as much as possible. If for a moment here and there I have the conceit that I have improved upon pied butcherbird phrases, I more often have the sense that it is they who have improved me as a musician.

Initially, nothing in my analytical work hinged on it being partnered with composition or performance—in fact, I did everything I could to keep them separate, lest my art should taint my science in the view of some. However, I became convinced that my ability to transcribe avian vocalizations improved with the back and forth of playing them on the violin—with me entering into the sheer materiality of the experience. I study avian vocalists, but I also study *under* them, so "pied butcherbird" became a performance practice, as well as an intellectual activity.

Some believe that if we can make music with songbirds—if there can be hybrids—then we are one musical community. Far from feeling detached from pied butcherbirds for want of making music with them, I feel thrilled just hearing them in situ. Avoiding performing in their company is not an attempt to hold myself in a zone of hygienic separation. Instead, the challenge reads like this: These birds are occupied in the spring with nocturnal formal song. We cannot underestimate the sheer athletic effort involved in squeezing out these vocalizations. Each phrase demands fluctuating body postures and gestures, and some songs go on for hours. Spring also involves nesting and nestlings. This is not the time for an interspecies recital. I understand my task to be much like an anthropologist's—"not to eliminate all disturbance but to disturb well."[32] While I believe there is a place for exploring the possibility of human–pied butcherbird interactions, animal welfare comes first.

Likewise, audio playback can stress birds, and even bird guides who use the technique have told me they dislike doing so, only employing it when clients demand it. I was once visiting a colleague who has a group of pied butcherbirds living on his property. They constantly come in for a feed, and he willingly obliges them with meat scraps. He had a speaker on his deck and encouraged me to plug my computer into it and play some pied butcherbird recordings. I hesitated, but I could see that if I did not do it, he would. I first played songs from other locations. Several birds flew in but did not sing. "Play them *their* songs," he encouraged, so I did, a couple of ensemble songs followed by several species calls from the previous year. They began to sing ensemble songs. When I stopped, so did they. I do not know how stressful playback via a recording or a human instrumentalist is, and my internal debate about infringing on their space—already so

Figure 9.1. Flapper in Maleny, Queensland. Photograph by Neil Boucher (2010). Used by permission.

disrupted and reduced by us—continues. I am more interested in chronicling what birds in the wild choose to sing without interference (except by chance—the Ross River birds in the trees around the amenities block chose me).[33] If I were around these birds in another season, I might attempt another such get-together.

Interspecies musician Jim Nollman applies the term "charged border" to his marine mammal encounters. He contrasts scientific methodology with his music making with whales, where no absolute meaning results "because everyone who experiences it gets to discover their own meaning." Nollman recommends that instead of trying to solve mystery, we simply esteem it.[34] Clarinetist David Rothenberg has also performed extensively alongside animal musicians and directed a keen ear to how animals might respond.[35] After spending four summers as a sound consultant on whale research vessels in Alaska and Hawaii, violinist Lisa Walker released the CD *Grooved Whale*, where she plays violin into underwater landscapes, capitalizing on the sounds of water and whales. She maintains that the whales in Hawaii occasionally sang back to her violin playing.[36]

Many think of birdsong as authentic, ancient, original, primitivist—as "other." The connotation of these words can be spun either way. Fortunately, the romanticization of birdsong is a superfluous scheme in the case of pied butcherbirds. Their vocalizations, whether delivered by the birds or appropriated by composers, are sufficiently robust and remarkable without program notes to prop them up and exoticize them. Nonetheless, I certainly do not hide that I am performing birdsong. Just as an anthropologist might organize an exhibition of artworks from the people she studies, my birdsong lecture/concerts—my *concerts des refusés*, if you will—have proved to be effective in disseminating my research findings to a broader public.

Ironically, as scientific consensus strengthens in matters of climate change, climate contrarians' distrust of the science increases. Sowing doubt via misinformation works against and cancels out respected research. If we understand the source of our problems to lie beyond science and technology, the solution will likely also lie there. Vibrant aesthetic encounters with pied butcherbirds in the concert hall have the potential to reset our perception of songbirds and how our practices impact them, as well as to reconfigure our feelings of stewardship for our lonely blue planet and all those who make their lives here. Mine is less an escape into nature than a petition for avian survival, a way to perhaps make a difference via small things. The hope is an audacious one—that with understanding comes empathy, and with empathy, engagement.

Currently, we have too many theories and not enough birdsong research by musicologists. Despite the long human history of our eavesdropping on birdsong, the movement of musicologists to document those songs is glacial. Since a musician's hunch is wasted without a rigorous response from zoömusicology, a handful of recent collaborative "boundary work" is a hopeful sign.[37] I look forward to zoömusicologists' direct engagement not only with theoretical arguments but with linking observation to conceptualization. Speculation, theorization, and argumentation have their place, but if the vast majority of researchers continue to be from the natural sciences, and few from musicology ever set foot in the field for a full sensorial experience, the field of zoömusicology will not develop, and our understanding of the musical capacities of other animals will be littered with blind spots. To leave birdsong, in particular, out of the scope of musicology is to impoverish the discipline.

Zoömusicologists can add a kind of boldness to the study of animal music. Their narratives may contest theory but also embrace, confirm, or ignore it. The field will bring together a number of skills and perspectives, whether in alliance or in tension, to tell a bigger and richer story than has yet been told about animals. Zoömusicologists will find nuance where others see black and white, exceptions where others see rules, and individuals where others see species. They will uncover an array of musical phenomena that others gloss over on their way to explicate function. They will nudge scientists to form productive collaborations on matters of musicality previously regarded as intractable. Zoömusicologists can claim a place in public discourse in a time of environmental crisis—the field has zoöpolitical work to do. When their accounts (and performances, lectures, recordings, videos, installations, and more) begin to flow in, other zoömusicologists will synthesize and connect them, so that our planet's dazzling panoply of musical capacities and activities will finally begin to be recognized and celebrated in all its impressiveness.

NOTES

1. David Rothenberg, "Interview with Peter Marler: Bird Song at the Edge of Music and Science: A Conversation between David Rothenberg and Peter Marler." *Terrain: A Journal of the Built + Natural Environment.* Accessed 15 December 2014. http://terrain .org/2014/interviews/peter-marler/.

2. Ibid., emphasis added.

3. Physicist Thomas Kuhn offers support for this, writing: "No part of the aim of normal science is to call forth new sorts of phenomena; indeed, those that will not fit the box are often not seen at all" (*The Structure of Scientific Revolutions*, 3rd ed. [Chicago: University of Chicago Press, 1962/1966], 24). Similarly, claims geo-ecologist Stan Rowe, "*Control* of phenomena, not *sensitivity* to them, is the goal of science" (*Home Place: Essays on Ecology* [Edmonton: NeWest Press, 1990/2002], 83).

4. I also investigate real-world contexts, minimizing distance, and increasing empathy in a chapter linking zoömusicology to participatory research ("Marginalised Voices:

Zoömusicology through a Participatory Lens," in *Participatory Research in More-Than-Human Worlds*, ed. Michelle Bastian, Owain Jones, Niamh Moore, and Emma Roe [London: Routledge, 2017], 38-53).

5. Donna Haraway, "Situated Knowledges: The Science Question in Feminism and the Privilege of Partial Perspective," *Feminist Studies* 14, no. 3 (1988): 581.

6. In addition, intense pressure exists to publish in high-ranking journals, yet these journals, and citation indices generally, tend to favor review articles over primary literature and theory articles over observational studies. Since funding agencies and academic institutions rely on journal-based metrics, theoretical majoritarian texts at the top of the pyramid structure may eclipse meaningful work at the "bottom." Zoömusicologists could at minimum be marginalized as second-class scholars, and some of birdsong's best stories could continue to be sidelined.

7. See Steven Feld, "Linguistic Models in Ethnomusicology," *Ethnomusicology* 18, no. 2 (1974): 197–217; Steven Feld and Aaron A. Fox, "Music and Language," *Annual Review of Anthropology* 23 (1994): 25–53; Nils L. Wallin, Björn Merker, and Steven Brown, eds., *The Origins of Music* (Cambridge, MA: MIT Press, 2000); Patel, *Music, Language, and the Brain*; and Nicholas Bannan, "Introduction: Music, Language, and Human Evolution," in *Music, Language, & Human Evolution*, ed. Nicholas Bannan (Oxford: Oxford University Press, 2012), 3–27.

8. I summarize in this section from a number of sources. See Ernst Terhardt, "Music Perception and Sensory Information Acquisition: Relationships and Low-Level Analogies," *Music Perception* 8, no. 3 (1991): 217–240; Josh H. McDermott and Andrew J. Oxenham, "Music Perception, Pitch, and the Auditory System," *Current Opinion in Neurobiology* 18 (2008): 1–12; Albert S. Bregman, *Auditory Scene Analysis: The Perceptual Organization of Sound* (Cambridge, MA: MIT Press, 1990); Steven Brown and Joseph Jordania, "Universals in the World's Musics," *Psychology of Music* 41, no. 2 (2011): 229–248; Henkjan Honing and Annemie Ploeger, "Cognition and the Evolution of Music: Pitfalls and Prospects," *Topics in Cognitive Science* 4 (2012): 513–524; Daniel J. Levitin, "What Does It Mean to Be Musical?," *Neuron* 73, no. 23 (February 2012): 633–637; Gary F. Marcus, "Musicality: Instinct or Acquired Skill?," *Topics in Cognitive Science* 4 (2012): 498–512; Andrea Ravignani, Daniel L. Bowling, and W. Tecumseh Fitch, "Chorusing, Synchrony, and the Evolutionary Functions of Rhythm," *Frontiers in Psychology* 5, no. 118 (2014): 1–15; W. Tecumseh Fitch, "Four Principles of Bio-musicology," *Philosophical Transactions B* 370, no. 1,664 (2015): 1–12; Bruno Gingras et al., "Defining the Biological Bases of Individual Differences in Musicality," *Philosophical Transactions B* 370, no. 1,664 (2015): 1–15; Henkjan Honing et al., "Without It No Music: Cognition, Biology and Evolution of Musicality," *Philosophical Transactions B* 370, no. 1,664 (2015): 1–8; and Tomlinson, *A Million Years of Music*.

9. David Rothenberg et al., "Investigation of Musicality in Birdsong," *Hearing Research* 308 (2014): 71–83.

10. Leonard B. Meyer, *Explaining Music: Essays and Explorations* (Berkeley: University of California Press, 1973), 5, 52.

11. Merker has written about a sleepless California night spent listening to "the rapturous strains of a mockingbird. . . . To follow his melodic lines constituted a challenge of the kind I am confronted with in listening to demanding music, and the effort was esthetically rewarding in the same human, musical terms." For more on this and other scholars and musicians with an interest in the field of zoömusicology, see http://www .zoömusicology.com, accessed 16 January 2016.

12. See, for example, Björn Merker, "Music: The Missing Humboldt System," *Musicae Scientiae* 6, no. 1 (2002): 3–21; Björn Merker, "The Conformal Motive in Birdsong, Mu-

sic, and Language: An Introduction," in *The Neurosciences and Music II: From Perception to Performance*, ed. Giuliano Avanzini et al. (New York: New York Academy of Sciences, 2005), 17–28; and Merker, "The Uneven Interface between Culture and Biology in Human Music," *Music Perception* 24, no. 1 (2006): 95–98.

13. Björn Merker, "The Vocal Learning Constellation: Imitation, Ritual Culture, Encephalization," in *Music, Language, and Human Evolution*, ed. Nicholas Bannan (Oxford: Oxford University Press, 2012), 222. In this chapter, Merker details his views on waste and frivolity in virtuoso avian song performances.

14. William Bruce Cameron, *Informal Sociology* (New York: Random House, 1969), 13.

15. Hollis Taylor, "The Australian Pied Butcherbird (*Cracticus nigrogularis*) and Huron's Psychology of Expectation," paper delivered at *Music in Neuroscience*, Monte Verità, 20 March 2012. See "Music in Neuroscience Monte Verità," accessed 3 January 2016, http://lcn1.epfl.ch/MV_Music_Neuroscience.

16. K. A. Gourlay, "Towards a Reassessment of the Ethnomusicologist's Role in Research," *Ethnomusicology* 22, no. 1 (1978): 26.

17. See Hollis Taylor, "Composers' Appropriation of Pied Butcherbird Song: Henry Tate's 'Undersong of Australia' Comes of Age," *Journal of Music Research Online* 2 (2011): 1–28, for a more in-depth discussion and analysis of these composers.

18. David Lumsdaine, "Pied Butcherbirds of Spirey Creek," on *Mutawintji* (CD, Wahroonga: Tall Poppies TP091, 1996), liner notes to track 1.

19. David Lumsdaine, *Mandala 4* for string quartet (York: University of York Music Press, 1996). Mark de Brito also appropriated this birdsong. See Taylor, "Composers' Appropriation," 14.

20. The other four composers who appropriated the pied butcherbird species call are Henry Tate (1873–1926) in *Dawn: A Symphonic Rhapsody* (1902), *Bush Miniatures* (1902–1924), and "Morning in the Gully" from *Suite Joyous* (1924); Freddie Hall (1948) in *The Pied Butcher-Bird* for B♭ clarinet and prerecorded tape (1987); Olivier Messiaen (1908–1992) in "Les étoiles et la gloire," movement 8 of *Éclairs sur l'Au-Delà* (1988–1992); and Hugh Dixon (1927) in *The Blue Wrens and the Butcher-Bird* for soprano voice and piano (2004).

21. Andrew Skeoch, "Ormiston Gorge, Full Moon, 3 am," *Spirit of the Outback* (CD, Newstead: Listening Earth LECD9902, 1999), liner notes to track 1. The individual was recorded at the main waterhole at the entrance to Ormiston Gorge, west of Alice Springs, Central Australia, at 2:30 AM on 4 October 1998 by Andrew Skeoch.

22. Andrew Skeoch, e-mail message to the author, 1 November 2010.

23. Yves Cerf, Frédéric Folmer, and Raúl Esmerode, "Corbeau flûteur-pie," track 9 on *Ornithologies: 10 pièces improvisées pour chants d'oiseaux* (CD, Altri Suoni AS067, 1999).

24. Jean C. Roché, *Les grands virtuoses: Les plus beaux chants d'oiseaux* (CD, Auvidis Tempo A6117, 1987). The bird was recorded near Lamington National Park in September 1974.

25. Tony Baylis, e-mail message to the author, 30 April 2014; track 9 on the *Beautiful Bird Songs from around the World*, disc 1 (CD, British Library NSACD 45, 2008).

26. John Rodgers, "The Butcher-Bird," track 7 on *Weaver of Fictions* (Genevieve Lacey) (CD, ABC Classics ABC 476 6439, 2006); John Rodgers, e-mail message to the author, 13 May 2009.

27. Ron Nagorcka, *Artamidae: A Suite of 5 Pieces Celebrating a Family of Australian Songbirds* for trombone, mandolin, clarinet, bass clarinet, flute, piccolo, sampler, and didjeridu (author, 2004); and Ron Nagorcka, e-mail message to the author, 23 September 2005.

28. Mark A. Hansen, "Pied Butcherbird" and "Pied Butcherbird 2," tracks 1 and 5 on *Australian Birdsong Improvisations* (CD, Plateau Road Records, 1997).

29. The field notes that David Lumsdaine paired with his pied butcherbird recordings greatly assisted me to get my bearings with this species. In addition (and encouragingly), composer Michael Hannan (1949) has a "butcherbird songlines" idea for the Northern Rivers area of NSW; he intends "to record pied butcherbirds in dozens of adjacent villages and map the similarities and differences in their calls," not unlike what I have done in Alice Springs and North Queensland (e-mail message to the author, 17 January 2016).

30. George List, "On the Non-universality of Musical Perspectives," *Ethnomusicology* 15, no. 3 (1971): 399.

31. Evelyn Fox Keller, *A Feeling for the Organism: The Life and Work of Barbara McClintock* (New York: W. H. Freeman and Company, 1983), 198.

32. Matthew Chrulew, "The Philosophical Ethology of Dominique Lestel," *Angelaki* 19, no. 3 (2014): 32. The *observer effect* in physics similarly describes how we cannot measure a system without a concomitant impact on it.

33. I cannot whistle. Ornithologist and artist Vicki Powys was able to provoke an interspecies "jam session" with a group of pied butcherbirds: "Many years ago, I was camped out at the Olgas [in Central Australia] on a painting expedition. Three pied butcherbirds were singing intermittent phrases while I was working on a painting. Each bird followed on from the last, just a few notes each. Every now and then I would whistle one of the parts and was amazed when the next bird chimed in on cue. The bird that missed out must have wondered what had happened!" (e-mail message to the author, 18 September 2008). Another person wrote to tell me: "I have been interested in birds all my life and often call to them by whistling their own calls. I had never seen or heard a pied butcherbird before and was utterly enchanted. I whistled back to it, and we carried on a duet for half an hour or so" (Gavan Bromilow, e-mail message to the author, 11 September 2012). Still another wrote: "One very rainy morning a Butcher Bird sheltered under my pergola and when I whistled to him he came and perched some 3 feet away from me on a ledge and gave a very fine musical performance for about 5 minutes" (Simon Green, e-mail message to the author, 5 October 2008).

34. Jim Nollman, *The Charged Border: Where Whales and Humans Meet* (New York: Henry Holt and Company, 1999), 66; and Jim Nollman, "Fowl Play: Creating Interspecies Music," *Orion* 16, no. 2 (1997): 14. Also see http://www.interspecies.com/.

35. See David Rothenberg, *Why Birds Sing: A Journey into the Mystery of Bird Song* (New York: Basic Books, 2005); Rothenberg, *Thousand Mile Song: Whale Music in a Sea of Sound* (New York: Basic Books, 2008); and Rothenberg, *Bug Music: How Insects Gave Us Rhythm and Noise* (New York: St. Martin's Press, 2013).

36. Lisa Walker, *Grooved Whale*, CD (EarthEar 696208010820, 2001).

37. See Emily Doolittle and Henrik Brumm, "O Canto do Uirapuru: Consonant Intervals and Patterns in the Song of the Musician Wren," *Journal of Interdisciplinary Music Studies* 6, no. 1 (2012): 55–85 ; David Rothenberg et al., "Investigation of Musicality in Birdsong"; W. Alice Boyle and Ellen Waterman, "The Ecology of Musical Performance," in *Current Directions in Ecomusicology: Music, Culture, Nature*, ed. Aaron S. Allen and Kevin Dawe (London: Routledge, 2016), 25–39; Emily L. Doolittle et al., "Overtone-Based Pitch Selection in Hermit Thrush Song: Unexpected Convergence with Scale Construction in Human Music," *Proceedings of the National Academy of Sciences, USA* 111, no. 46 (2014): 16616–16621; and Margaret Q. Guyette and Jennifer C. Post, "Ecomusicology, Ethnomusicology, and Soundscape Ecology: Scientific and Musical Responses to Sound Study," in Allen and Dawe, *Current Directions in Ecomusicology*, 40–56.

CHAPTER 10

Songbirds as Colleagues and Contemporaries

I am willing to contend that this capacity to hear the soundscape as music is simultaneously one of the most archaic ways of listening and the most modern.
—David Dunn, "Acoustic Ecology and the Experimental Music Tradition"

KINGS CREEK STATION, Central Australia, 30 September 2013: Wind, heat, and flies. It's like being at the beach: the end of every thought is punctuated with a grain of sand where my teeth meet. The flies are fast here, they work in marauding teams, and they bite. I couldn't do without my fly veil for even a moment. I watch four tourists wave their hands and scarves nonstop. They face a dilemma: Should three of them stand still and smile while the fourth takes their photo, knowing that the flies will briefly have their way with all of them? The tourists rise to the challenge: all movement except smile-and-click ceases for ten seconds.

In the course of my walks, I've found my pied scoundrel, much detested by the yellow-throated miners (*Manorina flavigula*). Let's hope they fit the species profiling and will sing with the voice of an angel. For the moment, the bird is up to much to-ing and fro-ing, generally causing a lot of yellow-throated miner consternation and even delivering a bit of mimicry in the afternoon heat and wind.

Ephemeral creekbeds and salt lakes are all that remain here of the large rivers and lakes of twenty-five thousand years ago. Verging on the art of bonsai, the stunted, contorted ghost gums (*Corymbia aparrerinja*) and native figs are relics from past times that have had to adapt to tough conditions. The biggest trees are river red gums, high-rise accommodation for a range of birds, insects, and reptiles. Although sand holds water long after the rain stops, during drought these gums drop both leaves and limbs with no apparent warning in order to survive—and thus their nickname, "widow maker." They are not ill; they are clever.

There aren't many campers here, but my neighbors are a colorful bunch. Ignoring the official Hill's Hoist, they have strung up their own rope with half a dozen fluorescent beach towels pegged and flapping in the wind, but nowhere near *their* camp—instead, on the edge of mine.[1] Heat and a long drive can magnify little irritations into full-blown issues. If one takes into account the flap factor, two of their towels are seriously encroaching into *my* camp. Any moisture in these towels was sucked out in fifteen minutes. My "view" is a towel television waving at me for attention, and as we do with any screen, I can't resist looking at it. Instead, my view could be what some forty films and documentaries have capitalized on at this very property—the rugged red sandstone domes of the George Gill Range, the majestic desert oaks, and the scraped red soil. For this and the birds I traveled six hours from Alice Springs.

Desperate for better scenery and three minutes of air conditioning, I drive to the far end of the campground with the fan on high, park at the sign Only Station Vehicles Past This Point, and go through the gate. Everyone else has sensibly opted for the café or the postage-stamp-size pool. My walk takes me up to Tank Hill Lookout. In desert country, one has no right to expect a spectacular view, although one is occasionally rewarded. I am not. The lookout delivers in a direct way all that its name promises: three water tanks on a hill with a 360-degree panorama. I have uncharacteristically left my water bottle behind, but—with a sensibility that surprises even me—when I get confused, I follow my boot prints in the soft, sandy earth back to the van. Still, I wince as I begin the drive back to my campsite: the place has no signs or markers, just a constant meandering of red tracks that are difficult for my brain to maneuver. I can't quite figure it out (I clench my teeth, locking onto a grain of sand). No sense looking for my camper van, since I am in it. (I admit it occurred to me, and for five seconds I had certain hope.) Suddenly, I spot the "Six Towels over Kings Creek" amusement park. I'm home.

At 3:00 AM I get up to the smell of my neighbor's drowned campfire, having retired before enjoying their lit one. A pied butcherbird is singing in the distance on the other side of a serious stock fence. I locate two other soloists, but all the pied singing is tardy and subdued, never mind how promising the basic material. This year, like last, I'm finding that the town birds are singing longer than the bush birds, if they sing at all. So, like some other creatures in times of drought, I head to town.

Musicologist Denise Von Glahn has asked provocatively how a warmer world might sound.[2] It sounds like Kings Creek Station.

This final chapter engages with real-world issues. I gather thoughts on how zoömusicology fits into understanding the current critical situation with respect to our planet's life support systems, and I turn to pragmatic concerns that link scholarship to citizenship.[3] My meditation on notions of environment, justice, and advocacy brings up issues of how we currently assess and esteem birds' lives, brains, and songs.

BIRDSONG AND THE UNFOLDING BIODIVERSITY CRISIS

The tenuousness of the planet's biodiversity is very much on my mind when I arrive every season at each field site. Will the birds still be present? Will they sing, and for how long? A bird's song goes right to the heart of our ethical responsibilities, our political institutions, our social relationships, and our self-understanding. Having avoided the yoke of ethnomusicologist Alan P. Merriam's "White Knight Concept," I nonetheless admit to his "Duty of Preservation Concept," *music* or not.[4]

Birds respond to fundamental environmental cues. Might the marked decrease in pied butcherbird nocturnal song, considerably shorter in duration and apparently delivered on far fewer days, be the result of cumulative human activity that keeps birds from devoting more attention and energy to song? Granted, the decade of my studies is just a twinkling. I remind myself to be patient with nature's cycles—but I cannot help wondering if this is a more major trend.

The music of nature has the potential to offer intriguing insights into the nature of music—but also into the nature of *nature*. Field recordings provide bioacoustic data whose use is beginning to be valued for estimating species health and richness and for tracking migration pathways and the cultural evolution of birdsong. Measurements from field recordings are powerful descriptors of animal diversity, with results potentially able to inform land management strategies and buttress grassroots conservation initiatives. When approached as rigorous data collection and documentation, field recording is a transgenerational project. I think of my field recordings as producing both discoveries and material for future discoveries.

Modern Australia has a shocking record of environmental degradation and species extinctions. The register of perils is full to overflowing. Habitat modification, fragmentation, and loss find many contributors, including mining, logging and land clearing, commercial (over)grazing, pesticide poisoning, fires of all persuasions, and monoculture farming and other simplifications of biodiversity. Building a new road into a wilderness area can be worse than its initial related project—the first cut inevitably spawns networks of secondary and tertiary roads.[5] These multiple factors result in interruptions of ecological processes and coevolved relationships. We stand to lose nature's free services.

Scientists at James Cook University have developed Edgar, a website for exploring the future impact of climate change on each species of Australian bird who, along with bats, may drop out of the sky in even *spikes* of hot weather.[6] Beginning with locations where a species has been observed, Edgar calculates and displays how well the climate across Australia will suit that species in the next seventy years. Edgar's climate suitability map shows potential gains and losses for pied butcherbirds—there will be change. A drier, hotter continent is in our future. What Edgar cannot predict is how successfully birds will find and move to areas of supposed habitat gain.

CROYDON, North Queensland, 15 October 2015: Lake Belmore, the "aquatic jewel of the Gulf Savannah," is almost empty. Engineers built it to supply the town's water but are now desperately searching for an alternative source. The annual fishing competition has been canceled—replaced by the Drought Breaker Project. Croydon and its surrounding cattle stations have not seen a good rain in four years. It's bleak.

The town's caravan park is back-to-basics. Trees are few and stingy with shade. The former manager has departed with his pet pig, replaced by a pet emu who until recently also roamed the park. The emu was subsequently banned for scaring backpackers by begging for food, and he is now confined to a fenced yard, where he sleeps with a dog. Dust and detritus blow about all day and into the night, giving me bloodshot eyes—and the left one is a bit swollen. I can't close the van windows because of the heat, so the inside gets powdered. My throat is scratchy, my lungs ache. Outside, someone's alto cough garnishes the struggling tenor drone of trailer air conditioners (not mine). I try to imagine how "wet" or even "not dry" would sound.

Five years ago I was here in the Wet. Again, I spent an entire day in my car, but under quite different circumstances. "Storm like being in a triple-powered car wash," I wrote in my notes. I only briefly cracked the window to record thunder threats and shudders amidst a hammering downpour. Afterward, I discovered the local bowerbird recovering from the devastation, clearing away large leaves from his theater and rearranging his collection. He decorates chiefly from what quenches our thirst—green bottle glass on one side, clear on the other, with red and white plastic bottle caps for pizzazz.

This year, I rise at 4:00 AM only to circle back and forth in the van between my five customary field sites as I desperately try to locate a singing bird. The cemetery has reverted to a place utterly for the dead; no sound graces the space except an Australian raven (*Corvus coronoides*), who declares "aah-aah-aah-aaaaaahh." Only one pied butcherbird vocalizes—for fifteen minutes right at dawn.

Exercise is limited to the perimeters of wakefulness—sunrise and sunset. On my walk, new tracks mark out the latest activity: swivels of kangaroo and wallaby tails and paws in the windswept dust compete with bird tracks. A large desiccated leaf skids along with me as I head to the amenities block to wash my hands. Before I can switch back to cold water, a slow, painful cry alerts me that a frog in the drain has likely just boiled to death.

Later, I stop by the tourist bureau to inquire about the drought. Marian has noticed a steep downturn in birdlife. The birds will sing and breed at the first rain, she tells me. When's that usually? "When He turns it on!" I thank her and depart, accompanied by the brittle rattle of dried seedpods shaken by the wind.

It sounds like Croydon.

Altogether common species can go extinct, and rapidly so. Many of Australia's birds are struggling, with steep declines of even iconic birds like the kookaburra. To lose a species or merely a local population is to narrow our concept of our planet and ourselves. Just to lose *lengthy* pied butcherbird nocturnal songs to significantly shorter ones is to diminish our understanding of these birds' musical capacity. In considering the challenges that we have placed in front of pied butcherbirds in their rough-and-tumble quest to survive and thrive, repercussions stretch beyond the global warming headline taken in by Edgar's calculations.

Ambient noise. We do not just want to protect a landscape for viewers; auditors want to hear a landscape without sound pollution. That landscape includes birds. A spate of recent articles has addressed how anthropogenic noise, especially from traffic, affects animals' communication systems. Alarm calls could be masked, increasing predation risk in both nestlings and mature birds. Foraging success could be impacted. Songs in noisy environments can fail to attract females, and some birds have resorted to pitching their songs higher, which scientists expect is stressful. Noise alone can affect overall body condition in birds.

Poison and introduced pests. While pied butcherbirds do not usually figure in the front line of decimation, they do disappear individually or in groups—poisoned, trapped, shot, or gone for reasons I cannot figure. Formerly abundant on Magnetic Island, today only two remain, in separate parts of the island. (The sound of a singing bird with no potential for a conspecific in the audience is a bittersweet song, indeed.) Delphine lost three of her pied butcherbirds in one day, the cause unknown. We both speculate poisoning, either by direct human means or by the birds sharing a cane toad (*Bufo marinus*). The giant South American cane toad was introduced into North Queensland in 1935 to control cane beetles. People optimistically expected them to be the latest thing in biological control. Unfortunately, the toads, who are not keen climbers, did not control the beetles, who live at the top of towering sugarcane stalks. The toads turned their omnivorous appetite elsewhere and now pose a serious threat to Australian biodiversity. Cane toads are known to eat birds, reptiles, rodents, and other amphibians, as well as dog food, pingpong balls, and their own young. Native frogs and toads cannot compete and are in decline. Cane toads are also threatening the existence of the valuable dung beetle, one of the most successful introduced species turned cane toad snack.

Of concern is not only what cane toads are eating but who is eating them. One scientist was an early critic of their introduction, warning that cane toads had the potential to be as great a pest as rabbits and prickly-pear cacti.[7] The toad and its tadpoles are highly poisonous, with toad ingestion and even toad licking reported to cause death in any number of species, including birds, goannas, snakes, quolls, freshwater crocodiles, and humans. Cane toads have now made their way onto Magnetic Island, and pied butcherbirds are vulnerable to them, although some species appear to be learning strategies for eating the nonpoisonous parts of the toad.

These amphibian invaders (granted, they arrived on a work visa) are highly mobile, and at present a "toxic cane toad slick rims northern Australia."[8] Efforts at their capture and disposal have not been straightforward. Travelers in the Top End are encouraged to "check your load for a toad," and sniffer dogs are in use in some areas. Locals have taken matters into their own hands, like the Kimberley Toadbusters, not to mention Toad Day Out, a pest-control festival of sorts run by town councils. Prizes are awarded to collectors of the most and the largest toads, after which the toads are killed and turned into fertilizer.[9]

Elsewhere, during a mouse plague in the 1980s in the arid opal-mining town of White Cliffs (New South Wales), pied butcherbirds disappeared after gorging themselves on poisoned mice:

> "Oh, I don't worry about snakes, I've had 'em comin' in here. All these snakes come through here. See, worse than snakes is bloomin' *mice*. Well, we had a mouse plague here, and—well, everybody else got it too, and they were worse than snakes. And then the tourists were comin' up here and camping up there at the caravan park. They'd poison the bloody mice, kick the mice out the door; and we had beautiful little butcherbirds and everything come round. The butcherbirds naturally are meat eaters, picked them up, took them off, and that was it. The birds and everything got poisoned. That's the tourists, because they

don't know any bloomin' better. They don't know any better. And now those magpies and everything are all gone."

"And the butcherbirds?"

"Yeah, they're gone. Yeah, poisoned 'em, yeah. Your little bloomin' hawks up there, black-shouldered kites up there. Yeah, they're all gone."[10]

Three decades on, most of these species have yet to return. In a place where intense heat prompts residents to live underground (opal-mining machinery doubles to dig troglodyte houses in the hillside), the distance to the next hospitable habitat for pied butcherbirds makes their reoccupation questionable. Glen Helen Resort similarly lost pied butcherbirds and magpies to poison after a mouse plague in 2011. These species have returned, contiguous habitat making for a short flight, and the manager is now trapping rather than poisoning mice in the aviary and hanging them up in a tree for the pied butcherbirds.

Traps and unexplained disappearances. An Internet video showed a quartet of singing pied butcherbirds. I wrote the filmmaker, Santi Acera, and we worked out a trade. I wanted to analyze the part singing, since a number of motifs are doubled, as clearly evidenced by the birds bowing and raising their beaks together. Acera wrote: "Watching it again, I realised that the butcher birds, when they compose their musical verses, not always is the friend beside them. Sometimes it is with some other bird that you can hear quite far away." These birds in the distance "don't appear in the performing area but are part of the orchestra—the audience popping in, everyone seated on the edge of their seats ready to prompt their musical verse."[11]

Acera and I exchanged several more e-mails about his astounding documentation. Whenever I play it for audiences, they are taken aback by the four birds sitting on a small table next to a birdcage in an open garage; two more are on the roof, and seemingly still others are in the trees. Acera's partner sent more details:

> Like everything beautiful there's a poignancy to the story. To the left of the table the birds sit on, hidden behind the bit of shed wall, was an injured young adult butcherbird in a big cage. I am a licensed wildlife carer, and some idiot had been feeding wild birds in his garden, then left a rat trap in the same area with food in it. This poor bird had been caught, at his lower back. The vet said to give him a chance, which I did,

for a couple of weeks, during which he steadily deteriorated physically and became sadder and sadder (no song at all), and I had to euthanise him, as he couldn't be successfully released, and clearly hated being in captivity. But that film was made almost immediately after he arrived, and I think they're welcoming him (they will accept an unknown young one, but not a new fully adult bird). They came two dusks in a row. . . .

Yes, it is pretty haunting. Have you been able to detect its little plaintive cry? Rhythmic, single pitch and with a gentle tone like a dove, very soft; nothing like the others' song. I can tell, maybe you can too, that it's responding to the other butcher birds. Very melancholic.[12]

I cannot pretend to understand this one-off event, although it has all the hallmarks of a distress call responded to by empathetic acquaintances. I visited the Aceras the next spring, and they showed me where the bird had been trapped. The injured bird could have been from the table musicians' immediate group or, if not, a neighbor known to them. People who watch the video often comment that it reminds them of a religious rite, even without having been told the story behind it. I recorded nocturnal song there for two springs. Since then, no pied butcherbirds have been seen or heard near the property.

Likewise, the group of eight to ten energetic singers from Esk, upon whom I based a string quartet, disappeared in 2012.[13] My extensive questioning of the locals failed to come up with any explanation for their disappearance, and no conspecifics have come in to claim the prime territory three years on. Also apparently gone—their superb singing tradition.

Protection versus collection. While the direct devastation of avian life has sometimes masqueraded under the name of "science," more often the actual motivation has been amassing a private collection, sport, target practice, cruelty, and/or the relief of boredom. In his 1928 presidential address to the Royal Australasian Ornithologists' Union, Edwin Ashby defined an ornithologist as "an 'all-round man' who is essentially a 'field worker'; one who knows the birds in their homes, an accurate observer. He must be a collector," he continued; "he must go through the drudgery of making skins after a day of long toil in the bush in which the stimulus of the search had made him unaware of his flagging energy."[14]

There was critique even at the time. Certain though Ashby was that shooting birds for their skins was formative for character development and that such collecting had absolutely no impact on birdlife, the outraged editor added these words: "Seeking to develop character in our boys, we will not present them with guns and skinning-knives for use on valuable birds; we will equip them with cricket bats and footballs by day and good books by night."[15] A. H. Chisholm was similarly adamant that protection and egg and skin collecting were incompatible, especially since most collections were held in private cabinets. He asked whether Ashby or anyone else could list half a dozen Australian birds whose complete life histories had been written, suggesting this as a much deeper, and less brutal, path to understanding.[16]

Peter Latz is a revered botanist in Australia's Red Centre. I met up with him at the Alice Springs Herbarium; now that he is "retired," he uses it as a home base between remote outback collecting trips. He recalls how the local birds where he grew up, in the Aboriginal community of Hermannsburg, southwest of town, were convenient moving targets devastated by young boys with slingshots and hunters with guns. Latz also remembers watching birds being slowly tortured to death. Throwing bits of meat for hawks to catch and then substituting a rock was another pastime.[17] It would be wrong to think that on account of our current understanding such activity has ceased. Our debt to birds is immense and mounting.

CAMERON ROAD, off the Flinders Highway, North Queensland, 1 November 2015, 4:15 AM: This place is normally teeming with pied butcherbird soloists, but four years of drought are having a devastating effect on song length, not to mention human and animal lives. I came to see and hear what the birds do, but as the sun rises, mostly what I see and hear is what *we* do: bottles and cans, shredded tires and plastic bags, and assorted building materials clog the roadside. The dawn chorus is a barking dog, a crowing rooster, a train, and, of course, traffic. A feral cat slinks by the car and heads into the parched field toward the fix of a ninety-second pied butcherbird song.

It sounds like Cameron Road.

Domestic and feral cats. Feral cats kill an estimated seventy-five million Australian animals *each night*—that's more than twenty billion birds, mammals, reptiles, amphibians, and insects annually. Feral cats also pose a global threat to wildlife.[18] Cats arrived with the British in about 1800, and it is now believed that some once-abundant mammal species that are only now being described went quickly extinct due to cat predation. Furthermore, cats have prevented attempts to reintroduce threatened Australian species. Pied butcherbirds are one of 123 bird species to be found in the stomach of feral cats, along with hundreds of other reptiles, marsupials, rodents, and frogs.[19] Since cats are active hunters, an inert kangaroo-chicken-poison sausage tends not to be successful, nor do cats willingly enter a cage. Innovative work on feral cats includes a sensor that can detect a passing feline, who is then squirted with poisonous paste. The cat subsequently ingests the paste when grooming. As a counterbalance, some have suggested bringing Tasmanian devils back to the mainland. Any optimistic future about cat control will almost certainly include the dingo, that top predator with whom Australia has a love-hate relationship.

STUART'S WELL, Stuart Highway, Northern Territory, 30 June 2004: We have an appointment with Jim Cotterill at his roadhouse south of Alice Springs. We tell the barmaid that Jim is expecting us, and a few minutes later here they come: Jim and, on a sturdy chain next to him, Dinky.

"Please don't approach him; let him approach you. Keep your hands to your sides and let him sniff around you; he'll breathe your breath and check your hair, but don't pet him."

I'm a dog person, but Dinky is special. He's a dingo, for starters. Jim got him through a local station owner who was running a dingo-baiting program and found some puppies. The horrid cruelty of 1080 poison bait, often used to target dingoes, is well documented; other species, including carnivorous birds, also take the bait or consume the poisoned dingo carcasses.

"My daughters both learned the piano. As Dinky was growing up, if the girls were practicing, he'd sing along—some people would say he's only howling, but that's not true, is it? He holds tones, pitching notes," Jim tells us. "You play low, he sings low; you play high, he sings high; you play in between, he goes in between. He waits for people to start, and when they stop, he stops. He gives a little yawn at the end."

This uncertain link in the food chain climbs on my lap on his way up to the keyboard of Jim's 1884 Thürmer piano. We exchange breaths from an inch away, Dinky making a thorough assessment with nose and eyes and who knows what else. The piano keys are dusty, not from lack of use but from the last paw performance.

Dinky takes his place, and I reach under him to thumb through the hymnal. He doesn't give me much room, but you don't really want to challenge him for space until you know where you fit in the pack. I stake out the unclaimed keys, not my preferred octaves, but I'll make do. As I pound out four or five hymns, like "Men of Old," Dinky delivers just as Jim promised. He's in top form. He even does an up-and-down paw cadenza, a very hip Cecil Taylor concept-driven note cluster, in the middle of "Lo, How a Rose E'er Blooming."

Dinky's vocalizations exceed theory. Our duet can be heard in 🔊 AUDIO 49. While I could specify what to listen for, I prefer each auditor to make a personal evaluation. Thinking with philosopher Kate Soper, "The culturalist would go by the achievement, not by the nature of the beast."[20]

A heightened existence in the face of crisis. The number of wild animals on the planet has halved in the last forty years and is set to halve again. As we take inventory and mull over ethical dilemmas, I draw together what some have described as peak moments that can scarcely be written about but only experienced:

> One fine sunny autumn afternoon a Pied Butcherbird in a sugar gum at the back of my house broke into the most beautiful song I have ever heard. (Yes, I've heard Nightingales). It was incredibly complex, flowing and melodic, did not include mimicry, but to the human ear was just so beautiful. I've never heard anything anywhere close from a Pied Butcherbird since. We have a pair here at the moment singing/duetting some nice phrases, but this bird on this particular day really did produce something extraordinary.

> "The pied butcherbird has ruined my response to the dawn chorus; if there is no pied butcherbird in it, it is just the dawn chorus. Other birds were singing, but as soon as the pied butcherbird started, it just made the morning," enthused Jane, to which Rob responded, "Yeah, they add

a little special something to the start of your day. It's just such a pure sound—it's almost like liquid crystal."

I listened to the pre-dawn song of a butcherbird, always one of the most profoundly moving experiences I've had. Once I heard a large population chanting a beautiful series of riffs together in the pre-dawn, and for me it was the ultimate "trance music" experience.

When I am on my deathbed, I hope I have the opportunity and wit to reflect on all of the joys I have experienced in my life. If I do, the call of this bird will be one that will give a special pleasure.... A group of birds at Woodgate in Queensland have developed a transcendingly beautiful series of notes that they use for their morning song. It is a lilting, skipping tune that, if scored for flute, could easily be mistaken for Mozart, such is its effortless grace and playful beauty. It will stay with me forever.

A Pied Butcherbird fluting on the desert air ... worth crossing the world for.[21]

The pied butcherbird has been our instrument for imagining not just birdsongs and bird lives but also our niche in the world. Animals create and enhance a conviviality of place, which our stories about them reinforce. We share a destiny. Their stories are *our* stories—they are narratives of connection. We respond to the sheer exuberance of birds and recognize our encounters with them as sites of exchange.

The delight is, however, bittersweet. On an almost weekly basis, evidence mounts of ... we might fill in the blanks with rising temperatures, rising sea levels, rising extinction rates, and our own rising sense of hopelessness. Given what is at stake in our fragile experiment on this planet, numbing numbers nonetheless require us to do what data cannot do: become part of a wider conversation on the unfolding biodiversity crisis. Taking my lead from Stephen Jay Gould's classic observation, "We will not fight to save what we do not love," my antidote to number fatigue is to communicate a palpable and lived experience in word and sound of what pied butcherbirds have accomplished and how our practices might threaten the accumulated experience of generations.[22] As the tinkling of just one alarm bell among many, I no doubt preach mainly to the converted about the consequences of policy inaction. I will not fabricate a sense of optimism, but I can say that my esteem for pied butcherbird songs has only been heightened a decade after I began to study them.

HUMAN EXCEPTIONALISM: OUR NARCISSISTIC PROJECT

We humans are a work in progress, a problematic species that has not been around that long. Scholars increasingly ask whether environmental fragmentation is the product of our fragmentary conception of the world. We are overdue for a rethink of our similarities and differences with animals. Although nature *or* nurture occasionally modulates to nature *and* nurture, we have witnessed how the default position of objections to birdsong being music depends on binary arrangements. Environmental philosopher Val Plumwood argues vigorously that "insights of continuity and kinship with other life forms (the real scandal of Darwin's thought) remain only superficially absorbed in the dominant culture, even by scientists."[23] Defining the human and the animal by their opposition rather than their complementarity is out of sync with our current challenges and bypasses more urgent and engaging modes of sense making.

The time has come to abandon our uncritical preference for human achievements—specifically for my purposes, to decenter the human in music—and instead to be open to the possibility of creativity and agency in animals. On many topics, to suggest human exceptionalism is highly premature, and any claims of our uniqueness in music or other domains must be considered provisional without comprehensive research. How acoustic results are shared across diverse taxa remains a matter for investigation and speculation. Structures long thought to have independent histories may derive from something more ancient and basic than a shared genetic toolkit and instead involve the regulatory circuits of early animals; some have suggested the term "deep homologies."[24]

The view that only humans make music expresses a wider proposition: that only humans dwell in worlds of meaning, that only humans act mindfully, and that only humans have and thrive by means of culture.

This view broadens to embrace human exceptionalism in all parameters and ways, or at least in those that matter most. The work of sustaining human uniqueness in music entails defining music in a way best suited to humans in classical Western culture, controlling the parameters of music that must be in place for sound constructs to pass into the hallowed realm of *music*, and offering smokescreens whereby evidence can be ignored or where the lack of seeking evidence is hidden. I am making the case to expand not just our understanding of what it is to be a songbird but also our understanding of humanness.

Another area of supposed human exceptionalism is the primacy of language to consciousness, or at least higher-order consciousness. Ethologist Jonathan Balcombe terms this "one of the most insidious and destructive ideas of all time: that you need language to think."[25] Iain McGilchrist agrees, insisting, "Language is necessary neither for categorization, nor for reasoning, nor for concept formation, nor perception: it does not itself bring the landscape of the world in which we live into being."[26] Arguments that without a concept for music, you cannot create it, and that only those with the word have the concept would lead us to believe that very few cultures have music.[27] Leonard Meyer attunes us to how "some of the most fundamental constraints governing aesthetic relationships may be unknown or not be explicitly conceptualized, even by those most accomplished and imaginative in their use, that is, creative artists," while ethnomusicologist Timothy Rice describes "highly sophisticated nonverbal musical understanding" that often exists despite an inability to translate it into verbal explanation.[28] As with humans, avian creativity does not depend on theory or language. Birds do communicate, even if they have no language, which we do not yet know. The stories we tell and are inclined to believe—about the arrival of human meaning; about genius, creativity, and originality; about music and language; about nature and culture; and about cognition and consciousness—these stories can amplify or diminish the perceived distance between us and animals.

THE BATTLEFIELD OF AVIAN COGNITION

I have focused on bird musicians and their musical artifacts and activities as I witnessed them. Dare I at this late moment claim that pied butcherbirds have certain cognitive competences and flaunt these as additional proof that their vocalizations are music? Although I will review pied butcherbirds' ostensible cognitive skills, I have not hung my argument on them for very good reason. For that, "You need a good anatomist," a zoölogist told me after I presented my work to his department. However, there must be several human lifetimes and more of what wild songs can tell us about pied butcherbirds' mental processes and musical sensibilities without the need for captivity or slaughter.

I had to overcome my caution about entering into an argument in this arena, which is at the limits of my expertise. I asked a lot of questions during the year I spent as a fellow at the Wissenschaftskolleg Institute for Advanced Study, which is located in Grünewald, an old Berlin quarter famous for its villas, forests, and small lakes. I heard my first nightingale, a midnight marvel, across the lake we lived beside. Forty international scholars from various disciplines share common meals, a weekly colloquium, and other regular symposia. I took seriously my "job" of having lunch with the other fellows, cornering almost everyone at some point to ask questions that might assist me to better imagine how pied butcherbirds fit into the scheme of things. Lunch might find me seated next to zoölogist Raghavendra Gadagkar as he relates how social insect societies resemble and surpass those of humans, with an aside on the tyranny of impact factor in journals. Meanwhile, someone at the end of the table is discussing the evolution of animal behavior in relation to sexual selection and communication; I discover shortly that it is the zoölogist Mike Ryan. At the next lunch, philosopher of science and polymath Philip Kitcher fields my questions about anthropomorphism, sociobiology, evolutionary theory, explanatory unification, game theory, and anything else I throw his way. On another day, I take a table with neuroscientist Constance Scharff to review the analyses we are undertaking of pied butcherbird song complexity.[29] And thus it went.

Between these impromptu conversations and industrial quantities of reading, I began to build up an understanding of the decidedly sophisticated cognitive abilities of animals, especially birds.[30] It becomes increasingly evident that animals are cleverer than we knew, and "current" understanding of animal cognition is in a state of feverish flux. Behavioral ecologist Zhanna Reznikova's unpacking of cognitive toolkits finds animals counting, using mirror images, creating cognitive maps, employing artificial intermediary languages to have a direct dialogue with experimenters, extracting and representing rules, and manipulating others with Machiavellian tricks.[31] In the grab bag of recent surprises are crows that give gifts (to humans), fish that decorate, newborn chicks that do arithmetic, horses that can read human emotions in a photograph, ravens that can imagine being spied upon (indicating abstract thought), a dingo pack's enduring response to the death of a pup, and yet more birds that use tools. We are perpetually surprised and delighted by our ignorance of animals. We do not know the half of it.

The cliché aside, a bird's brain is a complex structure that shares many similarities with ours; songbirds' brains underwrite cognitive capacities once thought to be the preserve of primates.[32] In addition, Australian birds appear to be more cooperative and bonded, longer lived, and perhaps even more intelligent than Northern Hemisphere temperate zone birds. Gisela Kaplan cites Australian songbirds' complexity of social life and communication, tool use, food versatility, proactive mobbing, and other attributes that, when considered together, suggest advanced cognition.[33] Like all living beings, birds are influenced and limited by their ecological niche, body mechanics, and neural architecture. Yet, birds' cognitive abilities likely *exceed* ours in some areas. For instance, food-caching skill allows some birds to remember the location of many hundreds of stored items; migrating birds fly for thousands of miles, navigating by way of the sun, the stars, and the earth's magnetic field, possibly via mental maps; and birds maintain a constant sensory connection to their environment, even when asleep.

Whether song in birds and humans is homologous, the process deriving from the genes of a mutual ancestor, or analogous, where unrelated genes are brought to bear for a similar result, is a subject broached by evolutionary biologist W. Tecumseh Fitch. "It was clear to Darwin," he posits, "and has remained unargued ever since, that bird song is analogous, not homologous, to human song (our common ancestor, a Paleozoic reptile, did not sing), and the same can be said for whale and seal song."[34] The difference between avian musical invention and "true" creativity implies (to some people) a cortex, but neuroscientist Onur Güntürkün has demonstrated that although birds lack a cerebral cortex, the forebrain structures in birds and primates converge in both neurobiological foundations and performance.[35] "There is cognition without cortex, and this cognition seems to miraculously be able to come out of these little brains," he marvels.[36] Yet another Wissenschaftskolleg alumnus who deftly fielded my questions over lunch, Güntürkün makes the case that similarities arrive from a common heritage, but they can also arise from a common selection pressure, without necessarily stemming from a common ancestor. (Dario Martinelli also pokes at the homology-analogy issue on several fronts, arguing that animals and humans hold in common an aesthetic sense.)[37] The highly structured avian brain is not a precursor to our brain nor a primitive form of it. In this revised understanding, it is function before form—it is not possible to predict cognition simply by examining brain structure. I *don't* need a good anatomist.

Today's ethologists generally agree that many species have conscious experiences.[38] While there is good reason to think that pied butcherbirds have some form of consciousness, since it is a process and not an object, we must look for it in action. I am an expert witness not as a neuroscientist but merely as a fellow musician. In that role, I would hazard that sonic achievements must surely tell us something about a songbird's capacity to recognize and denominate the basic principles of musical organization. Beautiful and well-crafted musical objects are *intended* to be so by their makers. Theirs is music as diplomacy and artistry. Pied butcherbirds could just screech, as they do in some of their loud, noisy calls.

Proficiency in the art of memory is essential for manipulating song elements, beginning in the sensitive learning period when a young bird is exposed to song and stores this auditory imagery for later rehearsal. In addition, the precise temporal synchronization found in the rapid interchanges of ensemble song speaks to "remarkable perception and information-processing abilities."[39] Combinatorial phrases suggest the ability to generate alternatives—this spontaneous arrangement of sound objects is an extravagant but exigent act for which Jeff Pressing has enumerated the real-time challenges: "sensory and perceptual coding, optimal attention allocation, event interpretation, decision-making, prediction (of the actions of others), memory storage and recall, error correction, and movement control."[40] While Pressing refers to human improvisers, a veritable

Figure 10.1. A pied butcherbird in Maleny, Queensland. Photograph by Hollis Taylor (2010).

suite of capacities could be similarly involved in birdsong production and reception.

Pied butcherbirds are not predictable or passive, so it would seem a very perverse course to insist that a detailed inherited program is at work guiding all their behavior. In navigating their physical and social landscapes, they plan ahead (stashing food in their larder) and remember (retrieving food from the larder, recalling a song). They express preferences. As a group-living species, they must have concepts of individuals and their qualities, as well as social expertise—they have themselves organized and have built a community via, amongst other things, music. This by no means exhausts the store.

Just as music exceeds the rational mind, cognition extends beyond our data. "I venture to suggest that if a rat's knowledge of the behaviour of other rats were to be limited to everything which behaviourists have discovered about rats to date," supposed psychologist N. K. Humphrey, "the rat would show so little understanding of its fellows that it would bungle disastrously every social interaction it engaged in."[41] Although pied butcherbirds seem somehow savvy in their application of musical expertise, thrashing out cognitive issues is best left to the professionals. Still, I cannot ignore how issues of cognition affect animal lives. Species and individuals hang precariously in the tensions, boundaries, and interplay between human empathy and apathy, between biophilia and biophobia.[42]

HOW IS BIRDSONG MUSIC?

In earlier chapters, I presented complex descriptions of the musical competences of a number of individual birds where their aspiration for novelty is central and the range of alternatives they draw on and invent is impressive. This vocal novelty has yet to be fully described via statistics and theories—the data have yet to confess and be smoothed. Again, I turn to Meyer, who ponders why some cultures severely restrict novelty, asking, "Does the need for novelty act as a correlate of value only when music becomes differentiated from other aspects of culture as a special, aesthetic object?"[43] This line of questioning, though fascinating, quickly breaks down. Meyer understands music-as-special to be a break, whereas I see the aesthetic *and* functional in music as a network that cannot be disentangled. His question goes right to the heart of how a better understanding of birdsong will improve our theoretical musings. Efforts to grapple with music's origins and foundations while maintaining that it is unique to human cognition, like theories that attribute music's origins to a specific form of Theory of Mind (Affective Engagement) or to bipedalism (to name just two of many) seem awkward in light of pied butcherbirds' musical lives.[44] If music were understood as transspecific, then such theories might benefit from recasting with a gain in explanatory power. I like to believe that an outback encounter by Meyer with pied butcherbird song would have affected how he crafted his question.

While not flattening the differences between human music and pied butcherbird song, I have presented the considerable overlap. Despite our incomplete knowledge of the role that vocalizations play in the lives of pied butcherbirds, the songs' surface qualities and the behaviors accompanying them invite descriptions in terms familiar both to everyday people and to musicologists. "Assignment is to write beautiful music in style of eighteenth century," a composer newly arrived from Eastern Europe used to tell our counterpoint class. Simply following the rules would not be rewarded with a top mark. Pied butcherbirds' artful combinatorics are on the same page: their songs exceed a rigid set of instructions. Such substantial scope for individual variation in this singing tradition, where repertoire can be pulled out of memory and performed in different circumstances and presumably under different motivational conditions and in different seasons, points to a capacity to manipulate to *musical* effect.

There are yet more reasons why musicology should pay attention to animal music. Of course, such a change in thinking ties in with my naturalist's concerns and my deep appreciation for avian vocalizations. Music is considered an ideal subject for cognitive studies, but the sample is being polluted and diluted by global exposure to Western music. Casting the net wider, a considerable number of musical traditions and sensibilities are currently at risk due to degraded, indifferent, or even hostile environments. In light of past and impending losses and the spreading drift into global homogeneity, David Huron and other researchers are concerned with whether we will be able to examine innate cognitive dispositions and auditory principles in humans in a globally mediated culture.[45] This makes the nearly untainted musical abilities of songbirds all the more precious to us.

I am not oblivious to the problematical nature of identifying how we might increase our debt to songbirds. I want to avoid giving the impression that they are only a utilitarian resource to us—a means to an end. Historian of science Donna Haraway understands the peripheral status that animals occupy: we imagine them as "plastic raw material of knowledge" for testing hypotheses in laboratories, on the one hand, and as natural objects of special status, entities capable of showing us our origin, on the other.[46] Animals matter in and of themselves, regardless of their "use factor." Their perspectives are under threat. What happens when those musical minds and traditions begin to fade away or disappear? We can say that birdsong is a local or a national resource, one that defines a place as much as climate or topography, but the story is part of a wider one that extends far beyond the shores of Australia. The symbolism of saving wildlife and habitat, whether in the deep Outback or in a suburban backyard, is an affirmation that we refuse to part with the fundamental category of wonder in our lives.

Selected by circumstance, I came early on to see that pied butcherbirds are not *my* bird—I'm their human. They are envoys into the very stuff of music. I want to see their vocalizations included in the roster of musical "must-hears." I also want, for me and for others, the possibility to listen to and contemplate what other bird musicians are up to in a deeper way than a short track on a nature CD can provide. I do not want to read about a magical song long gone—nor do I want to hear a pied butcherbird song from a speaker hanging from a tree or in an art gallery. Zoömusicology, not salvage musicology!

Previously, a small group of Western musicologists had the resources and clout to commandeer and map music; their world was flat, and they spent the bulk of their time driving around patches of familiar terrain. Ethnomusicologists rounded this world and broadened our understanding, followed by new musicologists, who taught us to hear and appreciate music from a much expanded discursive space that recognizes music's role in social formation. Likewise, up-and-coming zoömusicologists will push past old and tired narratives, past binaries and boundaries, and past gatekeepers to encounter in animal music the potential for new interdisciplinary approaches to and perspectives on music.

I call on musicologists, musicians, and others to dare to take their professional curiosity across the species barrier. Animal sounds have the potential to clarify *more* than perceptual principles. My creative practice has been extended by all the birds that I have heard. Far from being a challenge to the identity of music, songbirds and other creatures will offer new insights for us, reanimating the art and craft of music making and music analysis. Music (including birdsong) augments everything it comes into contact with: it energizes spaces and places. It transforms and celebrates and then transcends the moment.

One question I have not posed is, Do we find in birds the *origins* of music? The question can get more interesting. I am not thinking of birdsong as protomusic or "music," as the music of brutes or *musique brute*, but as music, or even Music. To withhold the label *music* from birdsong is outdated and arrogant. As we move beyond being quite obsessed with ourselves, although we could think of songbirds as distant, earthly, and substandard ancestors, we could instead consider them as world-forming colleagues and contemporaries—and I do.

MOUNT SURPRISE, North Queensland, 24 October 2013, 2:45 AM: A fellow musician once told me, "You have fifteen seconds to grab your audience." Rousted out of a dream by a pied butcherbird's clarion call, I force myself to sit up. I've been grabbed. I immediately turn on my recorder and give an "ident" (time, place, etc.) as I head out. The stage is awash in the light of a three-quarter moon. As clouds file past, it fades to dark. I've dragged my camp chair with me, so I take a seat in the nightclub, the only human audience in an unfolding spectacle of light and dark, sound and silence. The moonlight soon returns. Those sizeable birds flying regularly overhead—who are they, out at night? I expect the typical nocturnal ones, but some profiles match those of diurnal birds like kookaburras, kites, currawongs, black cockatoos, and straw-necked ibis.

The pied butcherbird takes four different songposts in the course of a nearly three-hour virtuoso performance, drawing a song circle around me. "Auditory space has no point of favored focus," wrote D. C. Williams.[47] He was right, but not about tonight. I'm in the middle, favored. Each scene has a different wash from our ancient luminaire. Even when the moonlight is at its most intense, the light is soft. My brain never gets enough information to be a reliable witness; it cannot confirm revelation of form, and I sometimes fall victim to shape-shifting objects. Attentive to the slightest detail, I'm riveted by the fluid theatricality. It's a free improv session, and anything could happen.

No cars, roosters, generators, or people disrupt. Crickets pulse, the one constant. Wallabies crash through the bush. A rabbit sneaks by me, provoking a large pair of wings to fly in the bunny's direction. Some bird silhouettes float noiselessly past like shadow puppets. A small grevillea tree drops an occasional flower, releasing a fragrance of honeysuckle blossoms set on a bale of herbaceous hay.

Swift descending *chip*/slow, ascending rattle.

Chip/*wow*/flutelike note/arabesque with a sudden octave drop/low bubbling note/species call-in-song.

Chip/rattle/*tik*.

At 5:15 AM, a mosquito jerks me out of my trance and warns that the nocturnal song is almost over. A kookaburra gives a forced laugh for a joke that didn't quite come off, then several mount a proper chuckle. Next are the "alarm" birds, who concoct frequency sweeps like car alarms—suddenly I'm in a raucous parking lot. A few new insects add pizzazz.

The pied butcherbird begins to fade out, truncating phrases and leaving longer and longer intervals of silence between them, while the chirpers, trillers, and squawkers come to dominate the sonic space. Sun's up, show's over.

NOTES

1. A Hill's Hoist is a height-adjustable rotary clothesline invented by South Australian Lance Hill in 1945. Artists often draw on this iconic backyard fixture to depict 1950s and 1960s Australian suburbia.

2. Aaron S. Allen, Jeff Todd Titon, and Denise Von Glahn, "Sustainability and Sound: Ecomusicology inside and outside the Academy," *Music & Politics* 8, no. 2 (2014): 12.

3. See David W. Orr, *Earth in Mind: On Education, Environment, and the Human Prospect* (Washington, DC: Island Press, 2004); and Steven Best, "The Rise of Critical Animal Studies: Putting Theory into Action and Animal Liberation into Higher Education," *Journal for Critical Animal Studies* 7, no. 1 (2009): 9–52.

4. Alan P. Merriam, "Purposes of Ethnomusicology, an Anthropological View," *Ethnomusicology* 7, no. 3 (1963): 207. Also see Alan P. Merriam, *The Anthropology of Music* (Evanston, IL: Northwestern University Press, 1964), 6, where he specifies his belief that only humans make music.

5. William F. Laurance et al., "Reducing the Global Environmental Impacts of Rapid Infrastructure Expansion," *Current Biology* 25, no. 7 (2015): R259.

6. "Edgar James Cook University," accessed 4 December 2014, http://spatialecology .jcu.edu.au/Edgar/. Also see "CSIRO Climate Change," accessed 2 December 2015, http://www.csiro.au/en/News/News-releases/2014/State-of-the-Climate-2014-A-clear -picture-of-Australias-climate.

7. Nigel Turvey, "Everyone Agreed: Cane Toads Would Be a Winner for Australia," *Conversation*, 8 November 2013, accessed 15 November 2014, http://theconversation. com/everyone-agreed-cane-toads-would-be-a-winner-for-australia-19881.

8. Ibid.

9. "Kimberley Toad Busters," accessed 15 November 2014, http://www.canetoads .com.au/.

10. Jane Ulman (ABC Radio National) interview with Jimmy, 5 September 2012.

11. Santi Acera, e-mail message to the author, 11 March 2008.

12. Linda Acera, e-mail message to the author, 13 March 2008, 21 June 2008.

13. Hollis Taylor, *Bird-Esk* for string quartet (Wollongong: Wirripang Press, 2009). *Bird-Esk* builds on pied butcherbird ensemble themes particularly suitable for rhythmic exploration: lively syncopations, phrase endings on weak beats, and a raw energy reminiscent of a bebop ensemble—these birds and their songs were special to me.

14. Edwin Ashby, "The Educational Value of the Study of Ornithology," *Emu* 28 (1928): 169.

15. Ibid., 172.

16. A. H. Chisholm, "Private Collecting—a Criticism," *Emu* 22, no. 4 (1923): 314.

17. Author interview with Peter Latz, 8 July 2014. Philosopher Freya Mathews offers a helpful way to frame this: a "focus on individuals is inconsistent with Aboriginal metaphysics. . . . individual beings are not exclusively individual: their identity is not exhausted by a specific spatiotemporal location" (Freya Mathews, "The Anguish of Wild-life Ethics," *New Formations* 76, no. 3 [2012]: 114–131, 127). Now that we are losing the equilibrium of ecosystems, compassion for individuals (a keystone of animal ethics) finds itself in conflict with the traditional understanding of the whole (ecological ethics).

18. "Feral Cats Australia," accessed 15 November 2014, http://www.abc.net.au/radionational/programs/backgroundbriefing/feral-cats-re-write-the-australian-story/5802204.

19. Tim S. Doherty et al., "A Continental-Scale Analysis of Feral Cat Diet in Australia," *Journal of Biogeography* 42, no. 5 (2015): 964–975.

20. Kate Soper, *What Is Nature? Culture, Politics and the Non-human* (Oxford: Blackwell, 1995), 53.

21. Simon Starr, e-mail message to the author, 5 April 2010; Hollis Taylor and Jane Ulman, *Bird Interrupted*, ABC Radio National, first broadcast 2 March 2014; Frankie Butler, e-mail message to the author, 31 October 2010; "Pied Butcherbird Image," accessed 16 December 2015, https://www.flickr.com/photos/richardhartphotography/5875964358; and Kay Milton in Mark Cocker and David Tipling, *Birds and People* (London: Jonathan Cape, 2013), 369.

22. Stephen Jay Gould, "Unenchanted Evening," *Natural History* 100, no. 9 (1991): 4–14. Also Thom van Dooren, *Flight Ways: Life and Loss at the Edge of Extinction* (New York: Columbia University Press, 2014).

23. Val Plumwood, "Nature in the Active Voice." *Australian Humanities Review* 46 (2009): n.p.

24. Neil Shubin, Cliff Tabin, and Sean Carroll, "Deep Homology and the Origins of Evolutionary Novelty," *Nature* 457 (12 February 2009): 818; and Scharff and Petri, "Evo-devo."

25. Jonathan Balcombe, *Second Nature: The Inner Lives of Animals* (New York: Palgrave Macmillan, 2010), 43–44.

26. Iain McGilchrist, *The Master and His Emissary: The Divided Brain and the Making of the Western World* (New Haven, CT: Yale University Press, 2009), 110.

27. See Stephen Davies, *The Artful Species* (Oxford: Oxford University Press, 2012), 29.

28. Leonard B. Meyer, *The Spheres of Music: A Gathering of Essays* (Chicago: University of Chicago Press, 2000), 193; and Timothy Rice, "Toward a Mediation of Field Methods and Field Experience in Ethnomusicology," in *Shadows in the Field: New Perspectives for Fieldwork in Ethnomusicology*, ed. Gregory F. Barz and Timothy J. Cooley (New York: Oxford University Press, 1997), 115.

29. "In our eagerness to prevent the problem of animal intelligence from becoming a stumbling block in the acceptance of our theories," he writes, "I think we all went overboard and ignored the possibility of animal intelligence" (Raghavendra Gadagkar, *Survival Strategies: Cooperation and Conflict in Animal Societies* [Cambridge, MA: Harvard University Press, 1997], 135). Also see "Mike Ryan," accessed 28 December 2014, http://www.sbs.utexas.edu/ryan/; "Philip Kitcher," accessed 19 December 2015, http://philosophy.columbia.edu/directories/faculty/philip-kitcher; and "Constance Scharff," accessed 3 January 2016, http://www.bcp.fu-berlin.de/en/biologie/arbeitsgruppen/neurobiologie_verhalten/verhaltensbiologie/team/scharff/index.html.

30. See, for example, Ann B. Butler, "Evolution of Brains, Cognition, and Consciousness," *Brain Research Bulletin* 75 (2008): 442–449; and the Avian Brain Nomenclature Consortium, "Avian Brains and a New Understanding of Vertebrate Brain Evolution," *Nature Reviews Neuroscience* 6 (February 2005): 151–159.

31. Zhanna Reznikova, *Animal Intelligence: From Individual to Social Cognition* (Cambridge: Cambridge University Press, 2007), 7.

32. Johan J. Bolhuis and Manfred Gahr, "Neural Mechanisms of Birdsong Memory," *Nature Reviews Neuroscience* 7, no. 5 (2006): 347.

33. Gisela Kaplan, *Bird Minds: Cognition and Behaviour of Australian Native Birds* (Clayton South: CSIRO Publishing, 2015), 194, 186–197.

34. W. Tecumseh Fitch, "The Biology and Evolution of Music: A Comparative Perspective," *Cognition* 100, no. 1 (2006): 183.

35. Onur Güntürkün, "The Convergent Evolution of Neural Substrates for Cognition," *Psychological Review* 76 (2012): 212–219.

36. "Cognition without Cortex: Onur Güntürkün at TEDx Jacobs University," accessed 1 November 2014, https://www.youtube.com/watch?v=nHTTVFDjQ1Q.

37. Dario Martinelli, *How Musical Is a Whale? Towards a Theory of Zoömusicology* (Hakapaino: International Semiotics Institute, 2002), 106–109.

38. Marian Stamp Dawkins, *Through Our Eyes Only? The Search for Animal Consciousness* (Oxford: W. H. Freeman, 1993), 2.

39. Christopher N. Templeton et al., "An Experimental Study of Duet Integration in the Happy Wren, *Pheugopedius felix*," *Animal Behaviour* 86 (2013): 821.

40. Jeff Pressing, "Psychological Constraints on Improvisational Expertise and Communication," in *In the Course of Performance*, ed. Bruno Nettl and Melinda Russell (Chicago: University of Chicago Press, 1998), 51.

41. N. K. Humphrey, "Nature's Psychologists," in *Consciousness and the Physical World*, ed. B. D. Josephson and V. S. Ramachandran (Oxford: Pergamon Press, 1980), 60.

42. For more on *biophilia*, see Edward O. Wilson, *Biophilia* (Cambridge, MA: Harvard University Press, 1984).

43. Leonard B. Meyer, "Universalism and Relativism in the Study of Ethnic Music," *Ethnomusicology* 4, no. 2 (1960): 53, emphasis added.

44. See, respectively, Steven Robert Livingstone and William Forde Thompson, "The Emergence of Music from the Theory of Mind," *Musicae Scientiae*, Special Issue, 2009–2010 (2009): 83–115; and Matz Larsson, "Self-Generated Sounds of Locomotion and Ventilation and the Evolution of Human Rhythmic Abilities," *Animal Cognition* 17 (2014): 1–14.

45. David Huron, "Lost in Music," *Nature* 453 (22 May 2008): 456–457.

46. Donna J. Haraway, *Simians, Cyborgs, and Women: The Reinvention of Nature* (London: Free Association Books, 1991), 11.

47. D. C. Williams, "Acoustic Space," *Explorations*, February 1955, 17.

ACKNOWLEDGMENTS

In researching and writing this book, I have benefited from the generosity, enthusiasm, and expertise of many humans. If I were limited to *one* thank-you, however, it would be to these explosive, inventive, unimaginable vocalists, beginning with Two Tree, the maestro of combinatoriality. Thank you to the Alice Springs virtuosos who reside at Palm Place, Emily Gap, Aurora, Gosse, Araluen Arts Centre, Todd, Milner Road, Irija, Newhaven, and the Racecourse. Temple Bar sang (and well) in 2014 from 12:10 AM to 6:20 AM with scarcely a break. Kempeana Crescent was a cellist in another life. The birds at Trephina Ridges Music Camps seem to run their own spring festival.

In North Queensland, a number of virtuosos in Bowen, Mount Surprise, and Charters Towers continue to sing despite the drought and shortened songs. I hope Cameron will return to the vocal facility I used to hear there. Greens Park (Georgetown) excelled in timbral tricks, delivered in the midst of other phrases straight out of Mozart, and I am grateful for five consecutive nights with this bird in 2015. The other Georges sing quite differently one from the other and very well indeed: George van Park, George Goldfields, and George Cumberland.

The Wogarno ensemble made it all happen. The duetists at Tibooburra were ace. I thank the Ross River Resort birds for briefly including me in their ensemble. The extended family of seven or eight birds in Esk developed a sense of rhythm and phrasing that would be the envy of jazz musicians. The ensemble songs of Sandstone Point were among my favorite until the birds evicted me in 2014. In Duaringa, I called him "Duaringa King" until this virtuoso mobbed me two years running with species calls and beak claps. I ran back to the car; he followed me the whole way, forcing me to acknowledge that he had quit the project.

Arthur (Bay, Magnetic Island) was the first bird to mimic as I stood underneath; other memorable soloists who appended mimicry include Il-parpa Road (thanks for the horse whinny), Wordsworth, Burke and Wills, South Terrace, and Heavitree Gap. Flapper in Maleny takes the award as the most photogenic bird. Thank you to Alice Springs Archery Summit for my elegant ringtone.

Early discussions with François-Bernard Mâche were crucial (Penny Allen and Charles Nemes facilitated this), as were those with Vicki Powys, former sound editor of the Australian Wildlife Sound Recording Group. Vicki rallied the group's members to share their extant pied butcherbird recordings with me: Tony Baylis, Jenny Beasley, Harold Crouch, Sydney Curtis, Stuart Fairbairn, Bill Flentje, Peter Fullagar, Gloria Glass, Andree Griffin, Helen Horton, Tony Howard, John Hutchinson, Gayle Johnson, David Lumsdaine, Howard Plowright, Vicki Powys, Bill Rankin, Andrew Skeoch, Dave Stewart, Bob Tomkins, and Fred Van Gessel contributed, as well as others who had deposited their recordings with the Australian National Wildlife Collection at the Commonwealth Scientific and Industrial Research Organisation (CSIRO). My work is indebted to their recordings, correspondence, and support. Vicki, Syd, and David were particularly devoted and thought-provoking correspondents who pushed this work to a higher level.

A great many other individuals shared insights and references as my research progressed, especially Dominique Lestel, Björn Merker, Debbie Bird Rose, and Constance Scharff. Other memorable conversations were with Jeffrey Bussolini, Matthew Chrulew, Vinciane Despret, Chris Herz-feld, Gisela Kaplan, Alan Marett, Susan McClary, Lesley Rodgers, and Gary Tomlinson. I am grateful to LJ and David Campbell from Wogarno Station, where I first heard pied butcherbirds; they welcomed my partner, Jon Rose, and me back multiple times with unequaled hospitality.

I met Dario Martinelli and David Rothenberg at the First (it was) Annual (it was, unfortunately, not) International Conference on Zoömusi-cology: "NightinGala," which they chaired. At this intimate event, along with Dario and David, other key people came into my life, including the scientists Henrike Hultsch, Constance Scharff, Ofer Tchernichovski, and Dietmar Todt. Henrike and Constance facilitated a brief residency at the Institute of Biology, Freie Universität (supported by a UTS International Researcher Development grant), where I studied nightingales. Dietmar took me to lunch while I was in Berlin, and we discussed our mutual work over a terrific asparagus pizza. Ofer invited me for a residency at his Hunter College Laboratory of Vocal Learning (where I also had conversations with Eathan Janney, Irene Pepperberg, and Diana Reiss) and to attend the Music in Neuroscience Conference in Monte Verità. I also enjoyed conversations at Columbia University with Darcy Kelley, Ana María Ochoa, and Douglas Repetto. The Cornell Lab of Ornithology invited me to speak, and I am grateful to their Raven team, especially Ann Warde.

In the decade of my research, I have been fortunate to have been supported by the following institutions, in reverse chronological order: Macquarie University (Julian Knowles); University of Technology Sydney (Anne Cranny-Francis); Laboratoire d'Eco-anthropologie & Ethnobiologie, Muséum national d'Histoire naturelle, Paris (Dominique Lestel); and the University of Western Sydney (Michael Atherton). My year as a fellow at Wissenschaftskolleg zu Berlin Institute for Advanced Study (2011–2012) was life-changing, and I thank Luca Giuliani and Constance Scharff for supporting my residency. Conversations on birdsong at Wiko with Alfred Brendel, Thomas Christensen, Avril Coghlan, Raghavendra Gadagkar, Jim Hunt, Philip Kitcher, Jacob Koella, Claudio Lomnitz, Maria Manjo, Mike Ryan, Steve Stearns, and Mark Viney were particularly helpful, as was my meeting there with Onur Güntürkün in 2015.

Still others who contributed to this project include Nicolas Bannan, Andrew Bell, Peter Carruthers, Neville Fletcher, Alan Gilanders, Andrew Horn, Aleks Kolkowski, Mary O'Kane, Alan Powers, Carol Probets, Robin Ryan, Carol Selle, Nick Shimmin, Cate Stevens, René van Peer, Corinne Vernizeau, Joe Wolfe, and Stephen Yezerinac. Peter Hill was more than generous in his support of my Messiaen research. "The pied butcherbird? Wonderful!" replied Meredith Wright in her permission to allow me to quote from a poem by her mother, Judith Wright. The Akademie der Künste, Berlin, Heinrich-Mann-Archiv no. 420 allowed me access to Heinz Tiessen's archives; Dr. Sonja Grund, head librarian at Wissenschaftskolleg zu Berlin, expedited this research; and Eva von Küglegen assisted me in German translation.

Jane Ulman from ABC Radio National accompanied me on several field trips to Alice Springs and was a boost to my studies (although some of our adventures must necessarily remain undocumented). Andrew Ford and Stephen Adams from ABC also programmed pied butcherbird performances. My appreciation goes to John Davis at the Australian Music Centre for suggesting that I pursue doctoral studies on my favorite bird.

I am also grateful to my many informants, both cited and anonymous. Lana and Jerry Cupper welcomed me to their home on the big island of Hawaii at the latter stages of this research, where I spent days reading about and pondering issues of climate change, environmental degradation, and sustainability. I could not have read these tracts from a city desk.

Debbie Bird Rose and the Environmental Humanities group at the University of New South Wales, Sydney, read an earlier draft of one chapter and are the source of ongoing inspiration, especially Eben Kirksey, Stephen Muecke, and Thom van Dooren. Michelle Bastian invited me to give a keynote lecture at an Environmental Humanities conference at Edinburgh College of Art, where I had stimulating conversations with Peter Nelson, Andrew Patrizio, Geoff Sample, and Françoise Wemelsfelder.

Thanks to the composers who assisted me in researching their works: Elaine Barkin, Charles Bodman Rae, Mark de Brito, Emily Doolittle, Michael Hannan, Mark Hansen, Freddie Hill, Ivan Kinny, David Lumsdaine, Christine Mercer (for Henry Tate), Ron Nagorcka, and John Rodgers. The Australia Council Inter-Arts Board supported my residency to study birdsong recording and sonographic analysis at SoundID, and I thank Neil and June Boucher for their ongoing hospitality and assistance. The Australia Council Music Board supported commissions for new works for The Song Company and for Genevieve Lacey based on pied butcherbird song.

On Magnetic Island, Chris Corbet, Andy Frost, Cecily MacAlpine, Charlie McColl, Delphine Turnbull, and Eric Vanderduys went out of their way to share their knowledge of the island's birds. On the mainland in Townsville, Kevin and Joyce Cameron and Jo Wienecke supported the project, and near Brisbane, Jenélle Dowling.

In Alice Springs, I was invited to speak and perform pied butcherbird compositions at the Desert Park Museum. In recent years, Nancy Hall and

Barbara McIlvain made it possible for me to sleep in an air-conditioned house rather than a hot car—and to watch their unstoppable bowerbird build, decorate, sing, and display atop the carport. The direct view just over my computer screen was better than a nest-cam. Thanks to Andrew Crouch, Tanya Hattingh, Percy Mudjan Jimba Jimba, Peter Latz, Lesley McDonald, Rod Moss, Sheleagh O'Brien, Uwe Path, Shane and Jodie Solczaniuk at Ross River Resort, Harry Stubbins, Jeannie Tahini, Myf Turpin, Chris Watson, and all the other ornithologists and everyday people who put me onto their local pied butcherbirds.

A number of photographers supported the project, no one more than the late Robert Inglis, who for several years running got out of bed in the middle of the night to find singing birds in the weeks before I arrived at Sandstone Point. Thanks also to Neil Boucher, Graeme Chapman, Duade Paton, and Chris Tate.

As a writer, I took inspiration from scholars like Dominique Lestel, Susan McClary, and Björn Merker, whose understanding of their subject is such that they write in a simple, straightforward manner, and I tried to emulate their good example. As an editor, Philip Kitcher has no peer, and his reading of an earlier draft greatly assisted me in this book's current organization and in avoiding dangerous paths where a novice has no right to trespass. The remnants of disorder and transgression are my own.

An enthusiastic and warm thank-you goes to the editors of the Music, Nature, Place series, Denise Von Glahn and Sabine Feisst; to IUP director Gary Dunham, assistant editor Janice Frisch, and lead project manager and editor David Miller; to copyeditor Mary M. Hill; and to Robert Fallon, whose peer review was comprehensive and meticulous. I have inevitably left someone out, but not for lack of gratitude. Visit www. zoömusicology.com for more on that subject and the diverse people and projects that inhabit this field.

Finally, one round of applause is not enough for the support I received from Jon Rose. Numerous curtain calls must recognize his incomparable, sage, and unflinching support, as well as his careful readings of several earlier drafts. My first six years of research were particularly challenging, including several when I had neither position, funding, nor (frankly) prospects. Go, he said—to Helsinki, to Sheffield, to Paris, to Berlin, and to Alice Springs and other far reaches of the Australian continent, all at great expense on self-employed musicians' shrinking finances (not to mention while he recovered from a bone marrow transplant). Never miss a year of fieldwork—it made both no, and absolute, sense. Jon's commitment became its own reward: I reckon he has heard more pied butcherbirds than anyone other than me, and together we applaud each resplendent bird musician who has lit up our lives.

NOTATION AND SUPPLEMENT
CONVENTIONS

Rattles (a rapid succession of short and harsh- or hollow-sounding notes) and other quickly iterated decorations are audible at their original speed, but I measure the number of iterations in the sonogram window and not by ear. I take advantage of the playback feature in my music notation software, reconfirming each phrase as I go in matters of pitch, rhythm, and metronome marking. For accidentals, I use only sharp signs (never flats). When I encounter a microtonal phrase, I place half-sharp accidentals above the notehead as needed. An already sharp note will be three-quarters sharp with the addition of a half-sharp sign, and even within the measure, the half-sharp sign applies only to that note unless tied. I designate an unusual sound or timbre with alphabet letters over the notehead, like R for a rattle, QR for a quasi rattle whose iterations fail to completely separate, and CH for a *chip* sound. If a note is noisy, thus lacking a clear pitch focus, I pick the closest apparent pitch (or pitches) and form the notehead(s) with an X, while I represent broad-spectrum notes that are less noisy with adjacent noteheads.

In notating a portamento, I draw a line between the beginning and end notes to connect them. If to my ear either end dominates, I use a normal notehead to indicate that end, while a grace note serves for the other end of the portamento. I do not know if the steepness or speed of a portamento is more significant for the bird than the pitch. The speed is usually swift and even, and I make no attempt to measure that aspect.

I set each phrase into one bar; thin double bar lines mark out phrases and indicate a momentary stop in singing. (I do not notate interphrase silence with rest signs—these silences are measured in my supplement.) I adjust time signatures on a measure-by-measure basis to allow all notes to fit, but for ease of visual inspection I then hide the time signature and any residual rests at the measure's end. (All hidden time signatures assume that a quarter note receives one beat in multiples like $\frac{2}{4}$, $\frac{3}{4}$, $\frac{4}{4}$, $\frac{5}{4}$, etc., rather than $\frac{6}{8}$ and the like.) I attempt to use one metronomic marking throughout an entire song unless this makes the notation prohibitively complex.

I treat virtually imperceptible variations of the same phrase as repetitions; it is difficult to do otherwise, since environmental conditions, a microphone or bird's (often changing) position, and discrepancies in recording technique from multiple recordists and a range of equipment (dating back to 1968) almost certainly introduce more variation into recordings than exists among the phrases as delivered. I also avoid indicating dynamics, which are subjective assessments under the best of conditions. Similarly, I limit articulations like an accent or staccato mark (the latter can be suggested by a rhythm of short duration) to the most extreme instances. For legibility, all transcriptions are written an octave below the pitch they were delivered on (as indicated by the treble clef with the 8 affixed above it).

In the supplemental summary sheet, for each song I tally the number of rattle types and rattle units, the rattle pulse rate, and average rattle frequency; the starting pitch of the species call-in-song; the lowest and highest frequencies in the song; the longest note in the song; whether there is a sense of a tonic or a major or minor key; whether the phrases fit twelve-tone equal-tempered reasonably well or not; whether the majority of notes are pure whistles or more broad spectrum sounds; the widest ascending and descending interval; the number of portamento types; the presence or absence of various timbral effects, a motif with repeated notes of the same pitch, a major or minor arpeggio, a double note, ostinato, transposition, and ascending or descending octaves; the total number of phrases; the average phrase duration and interphrase interval; and the number of main phrase types (if the song can be usefully understood in that way). I also log whether I have the entire song and the number of singers present.

LIST OF AUDIO TRACKS

AUDIO 1   A phrase from the pied butcherbird "Two Tree" with competing ambient sounds.

AUDIO 2   Basic pied butcherbird note types.

AUDIO 3   Complex, buzzy, or "noisy" notes.

AUDIO 4   A variety of short, repeated notes.

AUDIO 5   Notes that suggest mnemonic syllables.

AUDIO 6   Notes suggesting analog synthesizer signals.

AUDIO 7   A variety of pied butcherbird calls.

AUDIO 8   Species calls from ten individuals with varying pitch and melodic contour.

AUDIO 9   Species calls consisting of from one to five notes.

AUDIO 10   A variety of introductory notes in species calls.

AUDIO 11   Pied butcherbirds mobbing a flock of black kites.

AUDIO 12   The mobbing of an Australian raven.

AUDIO 13   The mobbing of a possum.

AUDIO 14   Beak claps and zips from a group of birds mobbing the author.

AUDIO 15   Four examples of a species call with a song phrase in response.

AUDIO 16   Two examples of a song phrase with a species call in
              response.

AUDIO 17   Species calls from six different sites as motifs in solo
              songs.

AUDIO 18   Species calls from five different sites as motifs in
              ensemble songs.

AUDIO 19   Species call notes incorporated in three phrases of a solo
              song.

AUDIO 20   Seven SLD2 variations from as many individuals.

AUDIO 21   Call and response with the author on violin at Ross
              River Resort campground.

AUDIO 22   "Wordsworth" abandons formal song with a coda of
              mimicry.

AUDIO 23   A supernumerary joins a duetting pair.

AUDIO 24   Two pied butcherbirds in duet with similar phrases.

AUDIO 25   Three pied butcherbird duets.

AUDIO 26   Two pied butcherbird duets.

AUDIO 27   A pied butcherbird duet.

AUDIO 28   Chimeric melody: appropriation of a peaceful dove
              motif followed by the model.

AUDIO 29   Chimeric melody: appropriation of a peaceful dove
              motif followed by the model.

AUDIO 30   Chimeric melody: appropriation of a noisy friarbird
              motif followed by the model.

AUDIO 31   Chimeric melody: appropriation of a grey butcherbird
              motif followed by the model.

AUDIO 32   Chimeric melody: appropriation of a reversing truck
              alarm followed by the model.

AUDIO 33   Six fanfares.

AUDIO 34   Phrases that emphasize octaves.

AUDIO 35   Scalar motion in a pied butcherbird duet.

AUDIO 36   A major chord outlined in the first three notes of a duet.

AUDIO 37   Two phrases boasting *Klangfarbenmelodie*.

AUDIO 38   A virtuoso's phrases with a kaleidoscope of tonal colors.

AUDIO 39   The timbral riches of a mimicking pied butcherbird.

AUDIO 40   Two one-pitch phrases from different birds.

AUDIO 41   As part of a duet, one individual repeats the first motif four times.

AUDIO 42   The harmonic convergence of a pied butcherbird ostinato and a grey shrike-thrush song.

AUDIO 43   Shape and balance in a formal song.

AUDIO 44   Shape and balance in a duet.

AUDIO 45   Two virtuosic solo phrases from different birds.

AUDIO 46   A virtuosic ensemble song.

AUDIO 47   Another virtuosic ensemble song.

AUDIO 48   The imperfect notes of a juvenile singer.

AUDIO 49   The dingo Dinky's obligato to "Lo, How a Rose E'er Blooming" with the author on piano.

LIST OF ABBREVIATIONS

AWSRG	Australian Wildlife Sound Recording Group
B	bubbly sound
BC	beak clap
BCE	before the Common Era
CE	Common Era
CH	a *chip* sound
CSIRO	Commonwealth Scientific and Industrial Research Organisation
DIY	do-it-yourself
FFT	fast Fourier transform
GPS	global positioning system
GST	grey shrike-thrush
H	*hollow* sound
HANZAB	*Handbook of Australian, New Zealand & Antarctic Birds*
kHz	kilohertz
NP	national park
NSW	New South Wales
NT	Northern Territory

PBB	pied butcherbird
QLD	Queensland
QR	quasi rattle
R	rattle
SA	South Australia
SC	species call
sec	seconds
SLD2	short-long descending second motif
VIC	Victoria
W or WOW	a *wow* sound
WA	Western Australia

GLOSSARY

absolute pitch The ability to identify a tone's pitch without an external reference pitch.

accelerando To gradually increase speed.

additive process The expansion and contraction of small musical cells or modules.

amplitude A measurement of the intensity of sound pressure, of which loudness (or volume) is the subjective assessment.

anacrusis One or more unstressed notes at the beginning of a piece or phrase. Also known as an "upbeat."

anthrophony Sounds produced by humans.

antiphonal song Two or more birds singing in alternation.

arpeggio, arpeggiated The notes of a chord sounded in succession rather than simultaneously.

biomarker An indicator of the condition of a living organism.

biophony The "voices of living organisms."[1]

call, call notes Usually short, simple avian vocalizations associated with general maintenance activities.

canon A polyphonic texture created by two or more voices performing the same or similar material at a temporal, spatial, or intervallic distance.

chimeric melody A melody formed by linking parts of two different melodies.

coda A short passage at the end of a piece of music that brings the work to a conclusion.

complex tone A sound with broadband energy in multiple frequencies.

compound melodic line A melody where separate melody lines are suggested by means of large pitch jumps (also referred to as implied polyphony or melodic segregation).

conspecific A living organism belonging to the same species as another.

continuous singer A bird who sings more or less nonstop.

contour The upward and downward pattern of a melody.

contrary motion When one line moves up and the other down.

counterpoint A texture formed by two or more individual melodic lines.

countersinging Two birds singing back and forth at one another.

crescendo A gradual increase in volume.

crystallized song The culmination of song development (after subsong and plastic song).

cultural transmission The passage of traits across generations of the same population outside of biological mechanisms of inheritance.

dawn chorus A period of high singing activity for a number of species of birds just before and at sunrise.

day song, daytime song Equivalent to diurnal song.

decrescendo A gradual decrease in volume.

diatonic Based on a seven-note major or minor scale or mode that spans an octave (as opposed to chromatic and microtonal intervals).

discontinuous singing A bird who sings with an interphrase interval that is as long as or longer than the phrase itself.

distributional analysis The labeling of phrases with letters and/ or numbers to assist in determining how they are delivered and organized.

diurnal song A song delivered during the daytime, including the dawn chorus (although the songs or phrases could differ between the dawn chorus and the rest of the daytime).

dominant The fifth note of the Western major or minor scale. When a chord is built on this scale degree, it is a dominant chord.

duet A coordinated vocal performance by two birds of the same species, whether synchronous, alternating, or overlapping.

eighth note A note that endures for half the value of a quarter note and twice the value of a sixteenth note.

ensemble song In pied butcherbirds, two or more birds singing together, either simultaneously or alternately.

ethologist A researcher who studies animal behavior with an emphasis on the behavioral patterns in natural environments.

eventual variety A pattern of singing in which a bird repeats a phrase multiple times before switching to another.

fast Fourier transform An algorithm used to compute a sonogram (also FFT).

formal song A discontinuous solo song of a pied butcherbird (usually sung nocturnally).

frequency A physical measurement of the number of cycles per second of a sound. One vibration per second equals 1 Hertz (Hz); 1,000 Hz equal 1 kHz. Pitch is the subjective assessment of frequency.

fundamental The lowest frequency at which a sound vibrates.

gap-fill The action of returning to notes that have been omitted in a sequence after a leap.

geophony Noncreature sounds, like thunder, rain, and wind.[2]

glissando A gliding effect performed by sliding one or more fingers rapidly over piano keys or harp strings.

harmonic overtones The sound energy produced simultaneously with and above a complex tone. The first harmonic in a complex tone is the fundamental.

hocket A sequential duet where singers alternate turns so rapidly and with such precision that a single melodic line is formed.

imitation Imitation, or mimicry, is the ability to reproduce, to a varying degree, sounds other than those of the species in question, including environmental sounds.

immediate variety A pattern of singing when successive phrases are different.

interphrase interval The silent period between birdsong phrases.

interval The distance between two consecutive pitches.

just intonation A tuning system built on the "pure" tones of simple ratios.

Klangfarbenmelodie German; a melody formed and perceived through timbral transformation, often of a single pitch.

leading tone The seventh (penultimate) scale tone in Western major or minor scales; it traditionally resolves to the tonic (eighth scale tone, an octave above the first).

leap An interval larger than three semitones (as opposed to a step).

lent French; "slow."

matched countersinging When two birds are singing formal song near one another and one preferentially sings a phrase from a common repertoire that best matches what the other is singing.

melisma Embellishment of one note of a melody by way of portamentos.

melodic contour The upward and downward pattern of a melody.

meter Periodic organization of musical time, relying on hierarchies formed by strong and weak beats and typically organized as duple or triple (or also quadruple).

microtonal A musical interval smaller than a semitone (like a quarter tone); the term can also point to the use of a tuning system other than twelve-tone equal temperament, as in just intonation.

mimicry Imitation, or mimicry, is the ability to reproduce sounds other than those of the species in question, including environmental sounds.

mobbing Harassment of a potential predator by a group, often by multiple species, via swooping and harsh calling.

monophonic Music for an unaccompanied single voice.

motif A clearly defined melodic or rhythmic idea that is a subsection of a phrase.

nonversatile singer A bird with a repetitious song.

note A discrete sound unit, whether modulated or not, represented by a continuous trace on the sonogram.

octave The intervallic relationship of two pitches where the higher is twice the frequency of the lower, they have an equivalent quality, and they are assigned the same note name.

octave generalization A special case of transposition where, in addition to contour, intervals and chroma (in essence, a note name of whatever octave) are also preserved.

oscines True songbirds, a suborder of passerines.

ostinato A simple, repeated, and unchanging pattern in the midst of other changing sounds.

passerines Perching birds (the order Passeriformes), which includes oscines and suboscines.

phrase In pied butcherbird song, a recognizable and orderly group of notes separated by silent pauses, which are generally of the order of several seconds.

piano, pianissimo Italian; "softly," "very softly."

pitch A subjective assessment of frequency that orders sounds from low to high.

plastic song The intermediate stage of song learning, where the notes are more structured than subsong yet still unstable and highly variable.

portamento Audibly connecting pitches by passing through all intervening tones, often mistakenly called glissando (which implies production on an instrument with fixed semitones, like the piano or harp).

post-skip reversal The tendency for melodic leaps to be followed by a change of direction.

quarter note A note that endures for half the value of a half note and twice the value of an eighth note.

quasi rattle A rattle where the pulses fail to completely separate to the ear and on the sonogram.

rattle A rapid succession of short and harsh- or hollow-sounding notes.

relative pitch The ability to identify a tone's pitch via a reference pitch.

repertoire size, song repertoire The total number of phrases, including variants, in a bird's vocabulary.

retrograde motion An inverted melody that proceeds from the last note to the first.

ring modulation A type of amplitude modulation where two sound signals combine to produce the sum and difference frequencies of the original carrier and modulation signals.

ritardando With a gradual decrease in speed.

rubato A (usually corresponding) shortening and lengthening of certain notes within a phrase.

sforzando, sforzandi (plural) A note with a strong attack transient (played emphatically and with force).

SLD2 A pied butcherbird motif with a short-long articulation on two pitches that are a descending second (major or minor) apart.

slur A sweeping curved line connecting two or more notes to suggest they be executed in a connected manner. Also used by ethologists as a synonym for portamento.

song A sustained singing performance.

song bout A clearly defined song delivered in its entirety.

songbirds Oscines, a suborder of passerines.

sonogram A graphic representation of sound that plots time on the horizontal x-axis, frequency on the vertical y-axis, and relative amplitude as a grey scale; contemporary applications allow for a color sonogram, but grey scale remains standard.

sotto voce Singing quietly or in less than full voice.

soundmark The auditory counterpart of a landmark.

species call A species-typical, multipurpose call of pied butcherbirds.

step The pitch distance between two consecutive tones (two or three semitones).

subsong The first tentative and structurally amorphous notes of learned birdsongs. Also, soft, rambling adult song bearing little or no resemblance to other song (formal or group).

syncopation In Western rhythmic contexts, a shift from note onsets and silence that emphasize a pulse and time signature to note onsets and silence that contradict the established pulse.

syrinx A bird's vocal mechanism, consisting of a valve in each primary bronchus just below the junction with the trachea.

tessitura The general pitch range of a voice or vocal part.

timbre The tone color or tonal quality of a sound; the key frequencies at related amplitude combine to give a sound a specific characteristic.

tonal center The reference (often also the final) pitch in a piece of music.

tonic The first degree (or root) of the Western major or minor scale.

transition versatility The likelihood of successive phrases being different.

transposition The raising or lowering of all the notes in a melody by the same interval, thus maintaining the contour.

tremolo A rapid repetition of the same or different pitches.

triad A three-note chord.

trill An alternation of two different, though near, pitches.

triplet A group of three notes in the time of two of the same length.

tritone An interval consisting of three whole tones. Also known as an augmented fourth or diminished fifth, a tritone divides an octave in half.

tuplet A grouping that divides the beat into a subdivision different from the time signature; the most common is the triplet.

twelve-tone equal temperament The standard Western temperament or tuning system. The ratio of each of the twelve semitones spanning an octave is nudged into position and made slightly impure in order to be divided uniformly, with the exception of the octave, which is acoustically pure.

unmatched countersinging When birds are singing back and forth at one another and one avoids repeating what the other just sang.

variant A modification of a phrase.

versatile singer A bird with several or many phrases in its repertoire that are often sung in no fixed order.

warbling A note that fluctuates widely in pitch.

x-axis The horizontal axis in a sonogram representing time.

y-axis The vertical axis in a sonogram representing frequency.

zoömusicology The study of music in animal culture.

NOTES

1. Bernie Krause, *The Great Animal Orchestra* (London Profile Books, 2012), 68.
2. Bernie Krause, *Wild Soundscapes Discovering the Voice of the Natural World* (Berkeley Wilderness Press, 2002), xii.

BIBLIOGRAPHY

Abe, Kentaro, and Dai Watanabe. "Songbirds Possess the Spontaneous Ability to Discriminate Syntactic Rules." *Nature Neuroscience* 14, no. 9 (2011): 1067–1074.

Abraham, Otto, and Erich M. von Hornbostel. "Suggested Methods for the Transcription of Exotic Music." *Ethnomusicology* 38, no. 3 (1994): 425–456.

Adamson, Robert. "Pied Butcher Bird Flute Solo." In *The Golden Bird*, 262–263. Melbourne: Black, 2008.

Adorno, Theodor W., and Susan Gillespie. "Music, Language, and Composition." *Musical Quarterly* 77, no. 3 (1993): 401–414.

Agawu, Kofi. "The Invention of 'African Rhythm.'" *Music Anthropologies and Music Histories* 48, no. 3 (1995): 380–395.

Alland, Alexander, Jr. *The Artistic Animal: An Inquiry into the Biological Roots of Art.* Garden City, NY: Anchor Books, 1977.

Allen, Aaron S. "Ecomusicology: Ecocriticism and Musicology." *Journal of the American Musicological Society* 64, no. 2 (2011): 391–394.

Allen, Aaron S., and Kevin Dawe. "Ecomusicologies." In *Current Directions in Ecomusicology: Music, Culture, Nature*, edited by Aaron S. Allen and Kevin Dawe, 1–13. London: Routledge, 2016.

Allen, Aaron S., Jeff Todd Titon, and Denise Von Glahn. "Sustainability and Sound: Ecomusicology inside and outside the Academy." *Music & Politics* 8, no. 2 (2014): 1–26.

Allen, Charles N. "Bird Music: Songs of the Western Meadow-Lark." *Century Illustrated Monthly Magazine* 36 (1888): 908–911.

——. "Songs of the Western Meadow Lark (*Sturnella neglecta*)." *Auk* 13, no. 1 (1896): 145–150.

Alyawarr Language Group. *Things That Birds Let You Know About.* Poster published by the Central Land Council, the Australian Institute of Aboriginal and Torres Strait Islander Studies, and the Alice Springs Desert Park, undated.

"Anathasius Kircher, *Musurgia universalis*." Accessed 20 January 2016. https://standrewsrarebooks.files.wordpress.com/2013/04/kircher-musurgia-bird-song.jpg.

Andersen, Johannes C. *Bird-Song and New Zealand Song Birds.* Auckland: Whitcombe & Tombs Limited, 1926.

Andrews, Edward R. G. "Bird Songs." *Musical Times* 71, no. 1,047 (1930): 446.

Anmatyerr Language Group. *Things That Birds Let You Know About.* Poster published by the Central Land Council, the Australian Institute of Aboriginal and Torres Strait Islander Studies, and the Alice Springs Desert Park, undated.

Apel, Willi. "Bird Song." In *Harvard Dictionary of Music*, 96. Cambridge, MA: Belknap Press, 1970.

——. "Cento." In *Harvard Dictionary of Music*, 140. Cambridge, MA: Belknap Press, 1970.

Aplin, Lucy M., Damien R. Farine, Julie Morand-Ferron, Andrew Cockburn, Alex Thornton, and Ben C. Sheldon. "Experimentally Induced Innovations Lead to Persistent Culture via Conformity in Wild Birds." *Nature* 518, no. 7,540 (2015): 538–541.

Araya-Salas, Marcelo. "Is Birdsong Music? Evaluating Harmonic Intervals in Songs of a Neotropical Songbird." *Animal Behaviour* 84, no. 2 (2012): 309–313.

Arbib, Michael A. "Five Terms in Search of a Synthesis." In *Language, Music, and the Brain: A Mysterious Relationship*, edited by Michael A. Arbib, 3–44. Cambridge, MA: MIT Press, 2013.

——, ed. *Language, Music, and the Brain: A Mysterious Relationship.* Cambridge, MA: MIT Press, 2013.

Armstrong, Edward A. *A Study of Bird Song.* New York: Dover Publications, 1973.

Ashby, Edwin. "The Educational Value of the Study of Ornithology." *Emu* 28 (1928): 169–173.

Asquith, Pamela J. "The Inevitability and Utility of Anthropomorphism in Description of Primate Behaviour." In *The Meaning of Primate Signals*, edited by Rom Harré and Vernon Reynolds, 138–176. Cambridge: Cambridge University Press, 1984.

Attali, Jacques. *Noise: The Political Economy of Music.* Translated by Brian Massumi. Minneapolis: University of Minnesota Press, 1985.

Australian Museum. "Birds in Backyards: Pied Butcherbird." Accessed 29 June 2011. http://www.birdsinbackyards.net/species/Cracticus-nigrogularis.

Avian Brain Nomenclature Consortium. "Avian Brains and a New Understanding of Vertebrate Brain Evolution." *Nature Reviews Neuroscience* 6 (February 2005): 151–159.

Axtell, Harold H. "The Song of Kirtland's Warbler." *Auk* 55 (1938): 481–491.

Baars, Bernard J. *A Cognitive Theory of Consciousness.* Cambridge: Cambridge University Press, 1988.

Balaban, Evan. "Bird Song Syntax: Learned Intraspecific Variation Is Meaningful." *Proceedings of the National Academy of Sciences, USA* 85, no. 10 (1988): 3657–3660.

Balcombe, Jonathan. *Second Nature: The Inner Lives of Animals.* New York: Palgrave Macmillan, 2010.

Ball, Philip. *The Music Instinct: How Music Works and Why We Can't Do without It.* London: Bodley Head, 2010.

Bannan, Nicholas. "Introduction: Music, Language, and Human Evolution." In *Music, Language, & Human Evolution*, edited by Nicholas Bannan, 3–27. Oxford: Oxford University Press, 2012.

——, ed. *Music, Language, & Human Evolution.* Oxford: Oxford University Press, 2012.

Baptista, Luis F. "Song Dialects and Demes in Sedentary Populations of the White-Crowned Sparrow (*Zonotrichia leucophrys nuttalli*)." *University of California Publications in Zoology* 105 (1975): 1–52.

Baptista, Luis F., and Robin A. Keister. "Why Birdsong Is Sometimes Like Music." *Perspectives in Biology and Medicine* 48, no. 3 (2005): 426–443.

Baptista, Luis F., and Donald E. Kroodsma. "Foreword: Avian Bioacoustics." In *Handbook of the Birds of the World*, edited by Luis F. Baptista and Donald E. Kroodsma, 11–52. Barcelona: Lynx Edicions, 2001.

Baptista, Luis F., and Pepper W. Trail. "The Role of Song in the Evolution of Passerine Diversity." *Systematic Biology* 41, no. 2 (1992): 242–247.

Bartók, Béla, and Albert B. Lord. *Serbo-Croatian Folk Songs*. New York: Columbia University Press, 1951.

Baylis, Jeffrey R. "Avian Vocal Mimicry: Its Function and Evolution." In *Acoustic Communication in Birds*, vol. 2, edited by Donald E. Kroodsma, Edward H. Miller, and Henri Ouellet, 51–83. New York: Academic Press, 1982.

Baylis, Tony. Track 9 on the *Beautiful Bird Songs from around the World*, disc 1. CD. British Library NSACD 45 (2008).

Becker, Judith. "Is Western Art Music Superior?" *Musical Quarterly* 72, no. 3 (1986): 341–359.

Beckers, Gabriel J. L., Johan J. Blolhuis, Kazuo Okanoya, and Robert C. Berwick. "Birdsong Neurolinguistics: Songbird Context-Free Grammar Claim Is Premature." *Neuroethology* 23, no. 3 (2012): 139–145.

Beecher, Michael D. "Birdsong Learning in the Laboratory and Field." In *Ecology and Evolution of Acoustic Communication in Birds*, edited by Donald E. Kroodsma and Edward H. Miller, 61–78. Ithaca, NY: Cornell University Press, 1996.

Bekoff, Marc. "But Is It Research? What Price Interdisciplinary Interests?" *Biology and Philosophy* 9 (1994): 249–252.

Belding, L. "Songs of the Western Meadowlark." *Auk* 13, no. 1 (1896): 29–30.

Bell, Alan. *Common Australian Birds*. 1956. Revised edition, Melbourne: Oxford University Press, 1969.

Bennett, Jane. *Vibrant Matter: A Political Ecology of Things*. Durham, NC: Duke University Press, 2010.

Bent, Ian D., David W. Hughes, Robert C. Provine, Richard Rastall, and Anne Kilmer. "Notation, I: General." In *Oxford Music Online* (Oxford: Oxford University Press, 2007–2014). Accessed 16 January 2014. http://www.oxfordmusiconline.com.

Berwick, Robert C., Kazuo Okanoya, Gabriel J. L. Beckers, and Johan J. Bolhuis. "Songs to Syntax: The Linguistics of Birdsong." *Trends in Cognitive Sciences* 15, no. 3 (2011): 113–121.

Best, Steven. "The Rise of Critical Animal Studies: Putting Theory into Action and Animal Liberation into Higher Education." *Journal for Critical Animal Studies* 7, no. 1 (2009): 9–52.

Bevis, John. *Aaaaw to Zzzzzd: The Words of Birds*. Cambridge, MA: MIT Press, 2010.

"BioMusic." Accessed 22 April 2014. http://www.biomusic.org/index2.html.

"Bird Instruments." In *Grove Music Online. Oxford Music Online*. Accessed 7 November 2014. http://www.oxfordmusiconline.com.

Blacking, John. *How Musical Is Man?* Seattle: University of Washington Press, 1995.

——. "Tonal Organization in the Music of Two Venda Initiation Schools." *Ethnomusicology* 14, no. 1 (1970): 1–56.

Blackwell, H. Richard, and Harold Schlosberg. "Octave Generalization, Pitch Discrimination, and Loudness Thresholds in the White Rat." *Journal of Experimental Psychology* 33, no. 5 (1943): 407–419.

Blainey, Geoffrey. *Triumph of the Nomads: A History of Ancient Australia*. Sydney: Sun Books, 1997.

Bohlman, Philip V. "Musicology as a Political Act." *Journal of Musicology* 11, no. 4 (1993): 411–436.

——. *World Music: A Very Short Introduction.* Oxford: Oxford University Press, 2002.

Bolhuis, Johan J., and Manfred Gahr. "Neural Mechanisms of Birdsong Memory." *Nature Reviews Neuroscience* 7, no. 5 (2006): 347–357.

Bondesen, Poul. *North American Bird Songs—a World of Music.* Klampenborg, Denmark: Scandinavian Science Press, 1977.

Borgo, David. *Sync or Swarm: Improvising Music in a Complex Age.* New York: Continuum, 2007.

Born, Georgina, and David Hesmondhalgh, eds. *Western Music and Its Others.* Berkeley: University of California Press, 2000.

Boucher, Neil J. "Understanding Avian Sound—It's Not What You Think!" *AudioWings* 15, no. 1 (2012): 7–14.

Boucher, Neil J., Michihiro Jinnai, and Hollis Taylor. "A New and Improved Spectrogram." Paper presented at the 19th Congress of the Australian Institute of Physics, Melbourne, Victoria, 5–9 December 2010.

Boughey, Michael J., and Nicholas S. Thompson. "Species Specificity and Individual Variation in the Songs of the Brown Thrasher (*Toxostoma rufum*) and Catbird (*Cumetella carolinensis*)." *Behaviour* 57, no. 1–2 (1976): 64–90.

Bowman, Wayne D. *Philosophical Perspectives on Music.* New York: Oxford University Press, 1998.

Boyle, W. Alice, and Ellen Waterman. "The Ecology of Musical Performance." In *Current Directions in Ecomusicology: Music, Culture, Nature,* edited by Aaron S. Allen and Kevin Dawe, 25–39. London: Routledge, 2016.

Brabec de Mori, Bernd, and Anthony Seeger. "Introduction: Considering Music, Humans, and Non-humans." *Ethnomusicology Forum* 22, no. 3 (2013): 269–286.

Brand, Albert R. "A Method for the Intensive Study of Bird Song." *Auk* 52 (1935): 40–52.

——. "Why Bird Song Can Not Be Described Adequately." *Wilson Bulletin* 49, no. 1 (1937): 11–14.

Brandily, Monique. "Songs to Birds among the Teda of Chad." *Ethnomusicology* 26, no. 3 (1982): 371–390.

Braverman, Irus. *Wild Life: The Institution of Nature.* Stanford, CA: Stanford University Press, 2015.

Bravery, Benjamin D., James A. Nicholls, and Anne W. Goldizen. "Patterns of Painting in Satin Bowerbirds *Ptilonorhynchus violaceus* and Males' Responses to Changes in Their Paint." *Journal of Avian Biology* 37, no. 1 (2006): 77–83.

Bregman, Albert S. *Auditory Scene Analysis: The Perceptual Organization of Sound.* Cambridge, MA: MIT Press, 1990.

Brown, Eleanor D., and Susan M. Farabaugh. "Song Sharing in a Group-Living Songbird, the Australian Magpie, *Gymnorhina tibicen.* Part III. Sex Specificity and Individual Specificity of Vocal Parts in Communal Chorus and Duet Songs." *Behaviour* 118, no. 3–4 (1991): 244–274.

Brown, Eleanor D., Susan M. Farabaugh, and Clare J. Veltman. "Song Sharing in a Group-Living Songbird, the Australian Magpie, *Gymnorhina tibicen.* Part I. Vocal Sharing within and among Social Groups." *Behaviour* 104, no. 1–2 (1988): 1–28.

Brown, Steven. "The 'Musilanguage' Model of Music Evolution." In *The Origins of Music,* edited by Nils L. Wallin, Björn Merker, and Steven Brown, 271–300. Cambridge, MA: MIT Press, 2000.

Brown, Steven, and Joseph Jordania. "Universals in the World's Musics." *Psychology of Music* 41, no. 2 (2011): 229–248.

Burton, Frederick R. *American Primitive Music.* New York: Moffat, Yard and Company, 1909.

Bussolini, Jeffrey. "Recent French, Belgian and Italian Work in the Cognitive Science of Animals: Dominique Lestel, Vinciane Despret, Roberto Marchesini and Giorgio Celli." *Social Science Information* 52, no. 2 (2013): 187–209.

Butler, Ann B. "Evolution of Brains, Cognition, and Consciousness." *Brain Research Bulletin* 75 (2008): 442–449.

Cameron, Alister. "Pied Butcher-Bird." *Sunbird: Journal of the Queensland Ornithological Society* 2 (1971): 78–79.

Cameron, William Bruce. *Informal Sociology.* New York: Random House, 1969.

Caro, T. M., and M. D. Hauser. "Is There Teaching in Nonhuman Animals?" *Quarterly Review of Biology* 67, no. 2 (1992): 151–174.

Carroll, Lewis. "Humpty Dumpty." *Through the Looking Glass.* Accessed 15 August 2012. http://www.sabian.org/looking_glass6.php.

Carruthers, Peter. "Why the Question of Animal Consciousness Might Not Matter Very Much." *Philosophical Psychology* 17 (2004): 83–102.

Carter, Thomas. "Birds Occurring in the Region of the North-West Cape." *Emu* 3 (1903): 89–96.

Catchpole, Clive K. "Temporal and Sequential Organisation of Song in the Sedge Warbler (*Acrocephalus schoenobaenus*)." *Behaviour* 59, no. 3–4 (1976): 226–246.

Cerf, Yves, Frédéric Folmer, and Raúl Esmerode. "Corbeau flûteur-pie." Track 9 on *Ornithologies: 10 pièces improvisées pour chants d'oiseaux.* CD. Altri Suoni AS067 (1999).

Chaiken, Martheleah, Jörg Böhner, and Peter Marler. "Song Acquisition in European Starlings, *Sturnus vulgaris*: A Comparison of the Songs of Live-Tutored, Tape-Tutored, Untutored, and Wild-Caught Males." *Animal Behaviour* 46, no. 6 (1993): 1079–1090.

Cheney, Simeon Pease. *Wood Notes Wild: Notations of Bird Music.* Boston: Lee and Shepard, 1892.

Chisholm, Alec H. *Bird Wonders of Australia.* 1934. 6th edition, Sydney: Angus and Robertson, 1965.

———. *Mateship with Birds.* Melbourne: Whitcombe & Tombs, 1922.

———. "Private Collecting—a Criticism." *Emu* 22, no. 4 (1923): 311–315.

Chrulew, Matthew. "The Philosophical Ethology of Dominique Lestel." *Angelaki* 19, no. 3 (2014): 17–44.

Clark, Suzannah, and Alexander Rehding. Introduction to *Music Theory and Natural Order from the Renaissance to the Early Twentieth Century*, edited by Suzannah Clark and Alexander Rehding, 1–16. Cambridge: Cambridge University Press, 2001.

Clarke, David, and Eric Clarke. Preface. In *Music and Consciousness: Philosophical, Psychological, and Cultural Perspectives*, edited by David Clarke and Eric Clarke, xvii–xxiv. Oxford: Oxford University Press, 2011.

Clarke, Eric F. "Lost and Found in Music: Music, Consciousness and Subjectivity." *Musicae Scientiae* 18, no. 3 (2014): 354–368.

Clayton, Martin R. L. "Free Rhythm: Ethnomusicology and the Study of Music without Metre." *Bulletin of the School of Oriental and African Studies, University of London* 59, no. 2 (1996): 323–332.

———. "The Social and Personal Functions of Music in Cross-Cultural Perspective." In *The Oxford Handbook of Music Psychology*, edited by Susan Hallam, Ian Cross, and Michael Thaut, 35–44. Oxford: Oxford University Press, 2009.

Clayton, Martin, Trevor Herbert, and Richard Middleton. "Comparing Music, Comparing Musicology." In *The Cultural Study of Music: A Critical Introduction*, edited by Martin Clayton, Trevor Herbert, and Richard Middleton, 1–15. New York: Routledge, 2003.

Clifton, Thomas. *Music as Heard: A Study in Applied Phenomenology*. New Haven, CT: Yale University Press, 1983.

Cocker, Mark, and David Tipling. *Birds and People*. London: Jonathan Cape, 2013.

Cody, Martin L., and James H. Brown. "Song Asynchrony in Neighbouring Bird Species." *Nature* 222, no. 5,195 (1969): 778–780.

Coffin, Lucy V. Baxter. "Individuality in Bird Song." *Wilson Bulletin*, June 1928, 95–99.

"Cognition without Cortex: Onur Güntürkün at TEDxJacobs University." Accessed 1 November 2014. https://www.youtube.com/watch?v=nHTTVFDjQ1Q.

Cohn, Richard, and Douglas Dempster. "Hierarchical Unity, Plural Unities: Toward a Reconciliation." In *Disciplining Music*, edited by Katherine Bergeron and Philip V. Bohlman, 156–181. Chicago: University of Chicago Press, 1992.

Coker, Wilson. *Music & Meaning: A Theoretical Introduction to Musical Aesthetics*. New York: Free Press, 1972.

Cole, Hugo. *Sounds and Signs: Aspects of Musical Notation*. London: Oxford University Press, 1974.

Collins, Nicolas. "Introduction: Sound Art." *Leonardo Music Journal* 22 (2013): 1–2.

"Constance Scharff." Accessed 3 January 2016. http://www.bcp.fu-berlin.de/en/biologie/arbeitsgruppen/neurobiologie_verhalten/verhaltensbiologie/team/scharff/index.html.

Cook, Nicholas. *Analysing Musical Multimedia*. Oxford: Clarendon Press, 1998.

———. *Music: A Very Short Introduction*. Oxford: Oxford University Press, 1998.

Cooke, Deryck. *The Language of Music*. Oxford: Oxford University Press, 1959.

Cousins, Geoffrey. *The Butcherbird*. Crows Nest: Allen & Unwin, 2007.

Covell, Roger. *Australia's Music*. Melbourne: Sun Books, 1967.

Cox, Christoph, and Daniel Warner. "Music and Its Others: Noise, Sound, Silence." In *Audio Culture: Readings in Modern Music*, edited by Christoph Cox and Daniel Warner, 5–6. New York: Continuum, 2007.

Craig, Wallace. "The Music of the Wood Pewee's Song and One of Its Laws." *Auk* 50, no. 2 (1933): 174–178.

———. *The Song of the Wood Pewee Myiochanes virens Linnaeus: A Study of Bird Music*. New York State Museum Bulletin no. 334. Albany: University of the State of New York, 1943.

Cramer, Alfred. "Schoenberg's 'Klangfarbenmelodie': A Principle of Early Atonal Harmony." *Music Theory Spectrum* 24, no. 1 (2002): 1–34.

Crease, Stephanie Stein. *Duke Ellington: His Life in Jazz with 21 Activities*. Chicago: Chicago Review Press, 2009.

Crist, Eileen. "Darwin's Anthropomorphism: An Argument for Animal-Human Continuity." *Advances in Human Ecology* 5 (1996): 33–83.

———. *Images of Animals: Anthropomorphism and Animal Mind*. Philadelphia: Temple University Press, 1999.

———. "'Walking on my page': Intimacy and Insight in Len Howards' Cottage of Birds." *Social Science Information* 45, no. 2 (2006): 179–208.

Cross, Ian. "Music and Evolution: Consequences and Causes." *Contemporary Music Review* 22, no. 3 (2003): 79–89.

———. "Music as a Biocultural Phenomenon." In *The Neurosciences and Music*, edited by Giuliano Avanzini, Carmine Faienza, Diego Minciacchi, Luisa Lopez, and Maria Majno, 106–111. New York: New York Academy of Sciences, 2003.

Crouch, Harold, and Audrey Crouch. *Bird Calls of the Inland*. Cassette. South Australian Ornithological Association (1977).

"CSIRO Climate Change." Accessed 2 December 2015. http://www.csiro.au/en/News/News-releases/2014/State-of-the-Climate-2014-A-clear-picture-of-Australias-climate.

Curtis, H. S. "The Albert Lyrebird in Display." *Emu* 72, no. 3 (1972): 81–84.

———. "Messiaen Meets Menura—Part 2." *AudioWings* 12, no. 1 (2009): 5–6.

Curtis, H. Sydney, and Hollis Taylor. "Olivier Messiaen and the Albert's Lyrebird: From Tamborine Mountain to Éclairs Sur L'au-Delà." In *Olivier Messiaen: The Centenary Papers*, edited by Judith Crispin, 52–79. Newcastle upon Tyne: Cambridge Scholars, 2010.

Cutler, Chris. "Editorial Afterword." *ReRecords Quarterly Magazine* 2, no. 3 (1988): 46–47.

Cynx, Jeffrey. "Auditory Frequency Generalization and a Failure to Find Octave Generalization in a Songbird, the European Starling (*Sturnus vulgaris*)." *Journal of Comparative Psychology* 107, no. 2 (1993): 140–146.

Dalziell, Anastasia H., Justin A. Welbergen, Branislav Igic, and Robert D. Magrath. "Avian Vocal Mimicry: A Unified Conceptual Framework." *Biological Reviews* 90, no. 2 (2015): 643–668.

Darwin, Charles. *The Descent of Man, and Selection in Relation to Sex*. 1871. Princeton, NJ: Princeton University Press, 1981.

Daston, Lorraine, and Gregg Mitman. "Introduction: The How and Why of Thinking with Animals." In *Thinking with Animals: New Perspectives on Anthropomorphism*, edited by Lorraine Daston and Gregg Mitman, 2–14. New York: Columbia University Press, 2005.

Davies, Stephen. *The Artful Species*. Oxford: Oxford University Press, 2012.

———. "On Defining Music." *Monist* 95, no. 4 (2012): 535–555.

Dawkins, Marian Stamp. *Through Our Eyes Only? The Search for Animal Consciousness*. Oxford: W. H. Freeman, 1993.

Debussy, Claude. "Claude Debussy Quotes." Accessed 22 July 2013. http://www.quoteland.com/author/Claude-Debussy-Quotes/1778.

de Gryys, Francy. "Butcher Birds." *Outrider* 3, no. 1 (1986): 147.

Dehaene, Stanislas. *Reading in the Brain*. New York: Viking, 2009.

Dennett, Daniel C. *The Intentional Stance*. Cambridge, MA: MIT Press, 1987.

DeNora, Tia. *Music in Everyday Life*. Port Chester: Cambridge University Press, 2000.

Descola, Philippe. *Beyond Nature and Culture*. Translated by Janet Lloyd. 2005. Chicago: University of Chicago Press, 2013.

———. *The Ecology of Others*. Translated by Geneviève Godbout and Benjamin P. Luley. Chicago: Prickly Paradigm Press, 2013.

Despret, Vinciane. *Que dirait les animaux, si. .. on leur posait les bonnes questions?* Paris: Éditions La Découverte, 2012.

Deutsch, Diana, Trevor Henthorn, and Rachael Lapidis. "Illusory Transformation from Speech to Song." *Journal of the Acoustical Society of America* 129, no. 4 (2011): 2245–2252.

de Waal, Frans. *The Ape and the Sushi Master*. London: Allen Lane, 2001.
——. "Are We in Anthropo-denial?" *Discover* 18, no. 7 (1997): 50–53.
——. "Darwin's Last Laugh." *Nature* 460 (2009): 175.
DeWoskin, Kenneth J. *A Song for One or Two: Music and the Concept of Art in Early China*. Ann Arbor: Center for Chinese Studies, University of Michigan, 1982.
Dickie, George. *Art and the Aesthetic: An Institutional Analysis*. Ithaca, NY: Cornell University Press, 1974.
Dingle, Christopher. *Messiaen's Final Works*. Farnham: Ashgate, 2013.
Dissanayake, Ellen. *What Is Art For?* Seattle: University of Washington Press, 1988.
Dixon, Hugh. *The Blue Wrens and the Butcher-Bird* for soprano voice and piano. Wollongong: Wirripang, 2004.
Dobkin, David S. "Functional and Evolutionary Relationships of Vocal Copying Phenomena in Birds." *Zeitschrift für Tierpsychologie* 50 (1979): 348–363.
Dobson, Charles W., and Robert E. Lemon. "Bird Song as Music." *Journal of the Acoustical Society of America* 61, no. 3 (1977): 888–890.
Doherty, Tim S., Robert A. Davis, Eddie J. B. van Etten, Dave Algar, Neil Collier, Chris R. Dickman, Glenn Edwards, Pip Masters, Russell Palmer, and Sue Robinson. "A Continental-Scale Analysis of Feral Cat Diet in Australia." *Journal of Biogeography* 42, no. 5 (2015): 964–975.
Dooling, Robert J. "Auditory Perception in Birds." In *Acoustic Communication in Birds: Song Learning and Its Consequences*, vol. 1, edited by Donald E. Kroodsma, Edward H. Miller, and Henri Ouellet, 95–130. New York: Academic Press, 1982.
——. "Perception of Complex, Species-Specific Vocalizations by Birds and Humans." In *The Comparative Psychology of Audition: Perceiving Complex Sounds*, edited by Robert J. Dooling and Stewart H. Hulse, 423–444. Hillsdale: Lawrence Erlbaum, 1989.
Doolittle, Emily, and Henrik Brumm. "O Canto do Uirapuru: Consonant Intervals and Patterns in the Song of the Musician Wren." *Journal of Interdisciplinary Music Studies* 6, no. 1 (2012): 55–85.
Doolittle, Emily L., Bruno Gingras, Dominik M. Endres, and W. Tecumseh Fitch. "Overtone-Based Pitch Selection in Hermit Thrush Song: Unexpected Convergence with Scale Construction in Human Music." *PNAS* 111, no. 46 (2014): 16616–16621.
Dowsett-Lemaire, Françoise. "The Imitative Range of the Song of the Marsh Warbler *Acrocephalus palustris*, with Special Reference to Imitations of African Birds." *Ibis* 121 (1979): 453–468.
Duggan, Francis. "The Pied Butcherbird." 8 January 2008. Accessed 20 June 2011. http://www.poemhunter.com/poem/the-pied-butcherbird.
Dunn, David. "Acoustic Ecology and the Experimental Music Tradition." *NewMusicBox*, 9 January 2008, n.p. Accessed 21 January 2008. http://www.newmusicbox.org /articles/Acoustic-Ecology-and-the-Experimental-Music-Tradition/.
Düring, Daniel N., Alexander Ziegler, Christopher K. Thompson, Andreas Ziegler, Cornelius Faber, Johannes Müller, Constance Scharff, and Coen P. H. Elemans. "The Songbird Syrinx Morphome: A Three-Dimensional, High-Resolution, Interactive Morphological Map of the Zebra Finch Vocal Organ." *BMC Biology* 11, no. 1 (2013): 1–27.
Dutton, Denis. *The Art Instinct*. New York: Bloomsbury Press, 2009.
Dyson, Frances. *The Tone of Our Times: Sound, Sense, Economy, and Ecology*. Cambridge, MA: MIT Press, 2014.
Earp, Sarah E., and Donna L. Maney. "Birdsong: Is It Music to Their Ears?" *Frontiers in Evolutionary Neuroscience* 4, no. 14 (2012): 1–10.

"Edgar James Cook University." Accessed 4 December 2014. http://spatialecology.jcu
    .edu.au/Edgar/.
"Edith Helena." Accessed 14 April 2014. http://www.tinfoil.com/cm-0503.htm.
Edwards, Scott V., and Walter E. Boles. "Out of Gondwana: The Origin of Passerine
    Birds." *Trends in Ecology & Evolution* 17, no. 8 (2002): 347–349.
Eggington, Timothy. "Anathasius Kircher." In "Anathasius Kircher, *Musurgia universa-
    lis*, 1650." Accessed 19 January 2016. https://www.reading.ac.uk/web/FILES
    /special-collections/featurekircher.pdf.
Elliott, Brian. "Jindyworobaks and Aborigines." *Australian Literary Studies* 8, no. 1
    (1977): 29–50.
Endler, John A., Lorna C. Endler, and Natalie R. Doerr. "Great Bowerbirds Create The-
    aters with Forced Perspective When Seen by Their Audience." *Current Biology* 20,
    no. 18 (2010): 1679–1684.
Engesser, Sabrina, Jodie M. S. Crane, James L. Savage, Andrew F. Russell, and Simon W.
    Townsend. "Experimental Evidence for Phonemic Contrasts in a Nonhuman Vocal
    System." *PLOS Biology* 13, no. 6 (2015): 1–16.
England, E. M. "A Butcherbird at Dawn." *Brisbane (QLD) Courier*, 3 May 1930, 20.
Ericson, Per G. P., Les Christidis, Alan Cooper, Martin Irestedt, Jennifer Jackson, Ulf
    S. Johansson, and Janette A. Norman. "A Gondwanan Origin of Passerine Birds Sup-
    ported by DNA Sequences of the Endemic New Zealand Wrens." *Proceedings of the
    Royal Society B: Biological Sciences* 269 (2002): 235–241.
Eureka. "Feathered Minstrels of the Bush: The Butcher Bird's Song." *Sydney (NSW)
    Morning Herald*, 13 February 1939, 18, Women's Supplement. Accessed 22 June 2011.
    http://nla.gov.au/nla.news-article17555296.
Evans, Nicholas, and Stephen C. Levinson. "The Myth of Language Universals: Lan-
    guage Diversity and Its Importance for Cognitive Science." *Behavioral and Brain Sci-
    ences* 32 (2009): 429–492.
Fabbri, Franco. "A Theory of Musical Genres: Two Applications." In *Popular Music Per-
    spectives*, edited by D. Horn and P. Tagg, 52–81. Göteborg: International Association
    for the Study of Popular Music, 1982.
Falconer, D. S. "Observations on the Singing of the Chaffinch." *British Birds* 35, no. 5
    (1941): 98–104.
Fallon, Robert Joseph. "Messiaen's Mimesis: The Language and Culture of the Bird
    Styles." PhD diss., University of California, Berkeley, 2005.
——. "The Record of Realism in Messiaen's Bird Style." In *Olivier Messiaen: Music, Art
    and Literature*, edited by Christopher Dingle and Nigel Simeone, 115–136. Alder-
    shot: Ashgate, 2007.
Farina, Almo. *Soundscape Ecology: Principles, Patterns, Methods and Applications*. Dor-
    drecht: Springer, 2014.
Feld, Steven. "Linguistic Models in Ethnomusicology." *Ethnomusicology* 18, no. 2
    (1974): 197–217.
——. "The Poetics and Politics of Pygmy Pop." In *Western Music and Its Others: Differ-
    ence, Representation, and Appropriation in Music*, edited by Georgina Born and David
    Hesmondhalgh, 254–279. Berkeley: University of California Press, 2000.
——. *Sound and Sentiment: Birds, Weeping, Poetics, and Song in Kaluli Expression*. Phila-
    delphia: University of Pennsylvania Press, 1990.
Feld, Steven, and Aaron A. Fox. "Music and Language." *Annual Review of Anthropology*
    23 (1994): 25–53.

"Feral Cats Australia." Accessed 15 November 2014. http://www.abc.net.au/radio
    national/programs/backgroundbriefing/feral-cats-re-write-the-australian-story
    /5802204.
Fink, Robert. "Going Flat: Post-hierarchical Music Theory and the Musical Surface." In
    Rethinking Music, edited by Nicholas Cook and Mark Everist, 102–137. Oxford: Ox-
    ford University Press, 1999.
Finlayson, H. H. *The Red Centre: Man and Beast in the Heart of Australia.* Sydney: An-
    gus and Robertson, 1943.
Fisher, John Andrew. "What the Hills Are Alive With: In Defense of the Sounds of Na-
    ture." *Journal of Aesthetics and Art Criticism* 56, no. 2 (1998): 167–179.
Fitch, W. Tecumseh. "The Biology and Evolution of Music: A Comparative Perspective."
    Cognition 100, no. 1 (2006): 173–215.
——. "The Evolution of Music in Comparative Perspective." *Annals of the New York
    Academy of Sciences* 1,060, no. 1 (2005): 1–21.
——. "Four Principles of Bio-musicology." *Philosophical Transactions of the Royal Soci-
    ety B* 370, no. 1,664 (2015): 1–12.
Fletcher, Neville. "Birdsong Science." *Australian Science* 27, no. 9 (2006): 35–37.
Fox Keller, Evelyn. *A Feeling for the Organism: The Life and Work of Barbara McClintock.*
    New York: W. H. Freeman and Company, 1983.
Frith, Clifford B., and Dawn W. Frith. *Bowerbirds: Nature, Art & History.* Malanda:
    Frith & Frith, 2008.
Gadagkar, Raghavendra. *Survival Strategies: Cooperation and Conflict in Animal Societ-
    ies.* Cambridge, MA: Harvard University Press, 1997.
Galison, Peter. *Image and Logic: A Material Culture of Microphysics.* Chicago: University
    of Chicago Press, 1997.
Gardiner, William. *The Music of Nature: An Attempt to Prove That What Is Passionate
    and Pleasing in the Art of Singing, Speaking, and Performing upon Musical Instru-
    ments, Is Derived from the Sounds of the Animated World.* London: Longman, Orme,
    Brown, Green and Longmans, 1832.
Garfias, Robert. "Transcription I." *Ethnomusicology* 8, no. 3 (1964): 233–240.
Garstang, Walter. *Song of the Birds.* London: John Lane the Bodley Head, 1923.
Gascoigne, Harold. "A Butcherbird Sings." In *Our Friends the Birds,* 18. Bribie Island:
    Bribie Laser Type & Print, 1991.
Gell, Alfred. "The Technology of Enchantment and the Enchantment of Technology." In
    Anthropology, Art and Aesthetics, edited by J. Coot and A. Shelton, 40–66. Oxford:
    Clarendon, 1992.
Gentner, Timothy Q. "Temporal Auditory Pattern Recognition in Songbirds." In *Neu-
    roscience of Birdsong,* edited by H. Philip Zeigler and Peter Marler, 187–198. Cam-
    bridge: Cambridge University Press, 2008.
Gentner, Timothy Q., Kimberly M. Fenn, Daniel Margoliash, and Howard C. Nusbaum.
    "Recursive Syntactic Pattern Learning by Songbirds." *Nature* 440, no. 7,088 (2006):
    1204–1207.
Gingras, Bruno, Henkjan Honing, Isabelle Peretz, Laurel J. Trainor, and Simon E.
    Fisher. "Defining the Biological Bases of Individual Differences in Musicality." *Philo-
    sophical Transactions of the Royal Society B* 370, no. 1,664 (2015): 1–15.
Godfrey, Reginald. "Poems & Rhymes: In the Bush." *Register* (Adelaide, SA), 17 Octo-
    ber 1925, 4.
Godman, Stanley, ed. *The Bird Fancyer's Delight.* 1717. Mainz: Schott, 1955.

Godt, Irving. "Music: A Practical Definition." *Musical Times* 146, no. 1,890 (2005): 83–88.

Goehr, Alexander, and Derrick Puffett. *Finding the Key: Selected Writings of Alexander Goehr.* London: Faber & Faber, 1998.

Goehr, Lydia. *The Imaginary Museum of Musical Works: An Essay in the Philosophy of Music.* Oxford: Clarendon Press, 1992.

Göttner-Abendroth, Heide. "Nine Principles of a Matriarchal Aesthetic." In *Feminist Aesthetics,* edited by Gisela Ecker, 81–94. Boston: Beacon Press, 1985.

Gould, John. *Birds of Australia.* 7 vols. London: Author, 1848.

——. *Handbook to the Birds of Australia.* 1865. Melbourne: Lansdowne Press, 1972.

Gould, Stephen Jay. "Unenchanted Evening." *Natural History* 100, no. 9 (1991): 4–14.

Gourlay, K. A. "Towards a Reassessment of the Ethnomusicologist's Role in Research." *Ethnomusicology* 22, no. 1 (1978): 1–35.

Gray, Patricia M., Bernie Krause, Jelle Atema, Roger Payne, Carol Krumhansl, and Luis F. Baptista. "The Music of Nature and the Nature of Music." *Science* 291, no. 5,501 (2001): 52–54.

Greenewalt, Crawford H. *Bird Song: Acoustics and Physiology.* Washington, DC: Smithsonian Institution Press, 1968.

Greer, Germaine. *White Beech.* London: Bloomsbury, 2013.

Griffin, Donald R. *Animal Minds.* Chicago: University of Chicago Press, 1992.

Gunther, R. T. *Early Science in Cambridge.* 1937. London: Dawsons of Pall Mall, 1969.

Güntürkün, Onur. "The Convergent Evolution of Neural Substrates for Cognition." *Psychological Review* 76 (2012): 212–219.

Gurney, Edmund. *The Power of Sound.* 1880. New York: Basic Books, 1966.

Guyette, Margaret Q., and Jennifer C. Post. "Ecomusicology, Ethnomusicology, and Soundscape Ecology: Scientific and Musical Responses to Sound Study." In *Current Directions in Ecomusicology: Music, Culture, Nature,* edited by Aaron S. Allen and Kevin Dawe, 40–56. London: Routledge, 2016.

Halafoff, K. C. "Musical Analysis of the Lyrebird's Song." *Victorian Naturalist* 75 (1959): 169–178.

Hall, Michelle L. "A Review of Hypotheses for the Functions of Avian Duetting." *Behavioral Ecology and Sociobiology* 55, no. 5 (2004): 415–430.

Hall-Craggs, Joan. "The Aesthetic Content of Bird Song." In *Bird Vocalizations: Their Relations to Current Problems in Biology and Psychology. Essays Presented to W. H. Thorpe,* edited by R. A. Hinde, 367–381. Cambridge: Cambridge University Press, 1969.

——. "The Development of Song in the Blackbird." *Ibis* 104, no. 3 (1962): 277–300.

Hansen, Mark A. "Pied Butcherbird" and "Pied Butcherbird 2." Tracks 1 and 5 on *Australian Birdsong Improvisations.* CD. Plateau Road Records (1997).

Hanslick, Eduard. *The Beautiful in Music: A Contribution to the Revisal of Musical Aesthetics.* London: Novello, Ewer and Co., 1891.

Haraway, Donna. *Primate Visions: Gender, Race, and Nature in the World of Modern Science.* London: Verso, 1992.

——. *Simians, Cyborgs, and Women: The Reinvention of Nature.* London: Free Association Books, 1991.

——. "Situated Knowledges: The Science Question in Feminism and the Privilege of Partial Perspective." *Feminist Studies* 14, no. 3 (1988): 575–599.

Harrison, Frank. "Universals in Music: Towards a Methodology of Comparative Research." *World of Music: Quarterly Journal of the International Institute for Comparative Music Studies and Documentation* 19, no. ½ (1977): 30–36.

Harting, James Edmund. *The Birds of Middlesex: A Contribution to the Natural History of the County.* London: John Van Voorst, 1866.

Hartshorne, Charles. *Born to Sing: An Interpretation and World Survey of Bird Song.* Bloomington: Indiana University Press, 1973.

———. "Musical Values in Australian Songbirds." *Emu* 53 (1953): 109–128.

———. "The Monotony-Threshold in Singing Birds." *Auk* 73 (1956): 176–192.

———. "The Relation of Bird Song to Music." *Ibis* 100 (1958): 421–445.

Hauser, Marc D., and Josh McDermott. "The Evolution of the Music Faculty: A Comparative Perspective." *Nature Neuroscience* 6, no. 7 (2003): 663–668.

Hecht, Julie, and Caren B. Cooper. "Tribute to Tinbergen: Public Engagement in Ethology." *Ethology* 120, no. 3 (2014): 207–214.

Herzog, George. "Do Animals Have Music?" *Bulletin of the American Musicological Society* 5 (1941): 3–4.

Higgins, P. J., J. M. Peter, and S. J. Cowling, eds. *Handbook of Australian, New Zealand & Antarctic Birds*, vol. 5. Melbourne: Oxford University Press, 2001.

———, eds. *Handbook of Australian, New Zealand & Antarctic Birds*, vol. 7A. Melbourne: Oxford University Press, 2006.

Hill, Freddie. *The Pied Butcher-Bird* for solo clarinet and audio tape. Sydney: Australian Music Centre, 1987.

Hill, Peter, and Nigel Simeone. *Messiaen.* New Haven, CT: Yale University Press, 2005.

———. *Olivier Messiaen: Oiseaux Exotiques.* Farnham: Ashgate, 2007.

Hindley, David. *Lifesong: Amazing Sounds of Threatened Birds.* Cassette Mankind Music, Cambridge (1992).

———. "The Music of Birdsong." *Wildlife Sound* 6, no. 4 (1990): 25–33.

Hindmarsh, Andrew M. "Vocal Mimicry in Starlings." *Behaviour* 90 (1984): 302–325.

Hold, Trevor. "Messiaen's Birds." *Music & Letters* 52, no. 2 (1971): 113–122.

———. "The Notation of Bird-Song: A Review and Recommendation." *Ibis* 112, no. 2 (1970): 111–172.

Honing, Henkjan, and Annemie Ploeger. "Cognition and the Evolution of Music: Pitfalls and Prospects." *Topics in Cognitive Science* 4 (2012): 513–524.

Honing, Henkjan, Carel ten Cate, Isabelle Peretz, and Sandra E. Trehub. "Without It No Music: Cognition, Biology and Evolution of Musicality." *Philosophical Transactions of the Royal Society B* 370, no. 1,664 (2015): 1–8.

Howard, Len. *Birds as Individuals.* London: Collins, 1952.

———. *Living with Birds.* London: Collins, 1956.

Huet des Aunay, Guillaume, Hans Slabbekoorn, Laurent Nagle, Floriane Passas, Pierre Nicolas, and Tudor I. Draganoiu. "Urban Noise Undermines Female Sexual Preferences for Low-Frequency Songs in Domestic Canaries." *Animal Behaviour* 87 (2014): 67–75.

Hulse, Stewart H., and Suzanne C. Page. "Toward a Comparative Psychology of Music Perception." *Music Perception* 5, no. 4 (1988): 427–452.

Hultsch, Henrike, and Dietmar Todt. "Learning to Sing." In *Nature's Music: The Science of Birdsong*, edited by Peter Marler and Hans Slabbekoorn, 80–107. Amsterdam: Elsevier Academic Press, 2004.

Humphrey, N. K. "Nature's Psychologists." In *Consciousness and the Physical World*, edited by B. D. Josephson and V. S. Ramachandran, 57–80. Oxford: Pergamon Press, 1980.

Hunt, Richard. "The Phonetics of Bird-Sound." *Condor* 25, no. 6 (1923): 202–208.

Hurford, James R. "Human Uniqueness, Learned Symbols and Recursive Thought." *European Review* 12, no. 4 (2004): 551–565.

Hurly, T. Andrew, Laurene Ratcliffe, and Ron Weisman. "Relative Pitch Recognition in White-Throated Sparrows, *Zonotrichia abicollis*." *Animal Behaviour* 40, no. 1 (1990): 176–181.

Huron, David. "Lost in Music." *Nature* 453 (22 May 2008): 456–457.

——. *Sweet Anticipation: Music and the Psychology of Expectation*. Cambridge, MA: MIT Press, 2007.

Huxley, Julian. Foreword. In *Birds as Individuals*, by Len Howard, 9–10. London: Collins, 1952.

Hyem, E. L. "Butcher Bird Notes." *Wildlife in Australia* 6, no. 1 (1969): 123.

Ingraham, Sydney E. "Instinctive Music." *Auk* 55, no. 4 (1938): 614–628.

Iyer, Vijay. "Embodied Mind, Situated Cognition, and Expressive Microtiming in African-American Music." *Music Perception* 19, no. 3 (2002): 387–414.

Jackendoff, Ray. "Parallels and Nonparallels between Language and Music." *Music Perception* 26, no. 3 (2009): 195–204.

James, Brian. "The Rhos Blackbirds—1980–89." *Wildlife Sound* 6 (1990): 42–45.

Janney, Eathan, Hollis Taylor, Constance Scharff, David Rothenberg, Lucas C. Parra, and Ofer Tchernichovski. "Temporal Regularity Increases with Repertoire Complexity in the Australian Pied Butcherbird's Song." *Royal Society Open Science* 3, no. 160,357 (2016): 1–15.

Jellis, Rosemary. *Bird Sounds and Their Meaning*. Ithaca, NY: Cornell University Press, 1977.

Johnson, Gayle. "Vocalizations in the Grey Butcherbird *Cracticus torquatus* with Emphasis on Structure in Male Breeding Song: Implications for the Function and Evolution of Song from a Study of a Southern Hemisphere Species." PhD diss., Griffith University, 2003.

Johnson, Mark. *The Body in the Mind: The Bodily Basis of Meaning, Imagination, and Reason*. Chicago: University of Chicago Press, 1987.

"Jon Rose." Accessed 7 November 2014. http://www.jonroseweb.com.

Jullien, François. *The Propensity of Things: Toward a History of Efficacy in China*. Translated by Janet Lloyd. New York: Zone Books, 1999.

Kaplan, Gisela. "Animals and Music: Between Cultural Definitions and Sensory Evidence." *Sign Systems Studies* 37, no. ¾ (2009): 75–101.

——. "The Australian Magpie (*Gymnorhina tibicen*): An Alternative Model for the Study of Songbird Neurobiology." In *Neuroscience of Birdsong*, edited by H. Philip Zeigler and Peter Marler, 50–57. Cambridge: Cambridge University Press, 2008.

——. *Bird Minds: Cognition and Behaviour of Australian Native Birds*. Clayton South: CSIRO Publishing, 2015.

Karkoschka, Erhard. *Notation in New Music: A Critical Guide to Interpretation and Realisation*. Translated by R. Koenig. 1966. London: Universal, 1972.

Kassler, Jamie C. *Music, Science, Philosophy*. Aldershot: Ashgate, 2001.

Kearns, Anna M., Leo Joseph, and Lyn G. Cook. "A Multilocus Coalescent Analysis of the Speciational History of the Australo-Papuan Butcherbirds and Their Allies." *Molecular Phylogenetics and Evolution* 66 (2013): 941–952.

Kelley, Laura A., Rebecca L. Coe, Joah R. Madden, and Susan D. Healy. "Vocal Mimicry in Songbirds." *Animal Behaviour* 76, no. 3 (2008): 521–528.

Kelley, Laura A., and John A. Endler. "Illusions Promote Mating Success in Great Bowerbirds." *Science* 335, no. 20 (January 2012): 335–338.

Kelly, Aileen. "Call Her Butcher Bird." *Poetry Monash* 36 (1992): 9.

Kennedy, John S. *The New Anthropomorphism*. Cambridge: Cambridge University Press, 1992.

Kershenbaum, Arik, Ann E. Bowles, Todd M. Freeberg, Dezhe Z. Jin, Adriano R. Lameira, and Kirsten Bohn. "Animal Vocal Sequences: Not the Markov Chains We Thought They Were." *Proceedings of the Royal Society B: Biological Sciences* 281, no. 1,792 (2014): 1–9.

Kidner, David W. "The Conceptual Assassination of Wilderness." In *Keeping the Wild: Against the Domestication of Earth*, edited by George Wuerthner, Eileen Crist, and Tom Butler, 1–15. Washington, DC: Island Press, 2014.

"Kimberley Toad Busters." Accessed 15 November 2014. http://www.canetoads.com.au/.

Kinsella, John. "Rapt." In *The Hierarchy of Sheep*, 72–74. Fremantle: Fremantle Press, 2001.

Kivy, Peter. "Charles Darwin on Music." *Journal of the American Musicological Society* 12, no. 1 (1959): 42–48.

———. *Music Alone: Philosophical Reflections on the Purely Musical Experience*. Ithaca, NY: Cornell University Press, 1990.

Knobloch, Eberhard. "*Musurgia Universalis*: Unknown Combinatorial Studies in the Age of Baroque Absolutism." *History of Science* 17 (1979): 258–275.

Koch, Ludwig. *Memoirs of a Birdman*. London: Country Book Club, 1956.

Koehler, O. "Der Vogelgesang als Vorstufe von Musik und Sprache." *Journal of Ornithology* 93, no. 1 (1951): 3–20.

Kolinski, Mieczyslaw. "Recent Trends in Ethnomusicology." *Ethnomusicology* 11, no. 1 (1967): 1–24.

———. "Transcription II." *Ethnomusicology* 8, no. 3 (1964): 241–251.

Kraft, David. "Birdsong in the Music of Olivier Messiaen." PhD diss., Middlesex University, 2000.

Kramer, Lawrence. *Classical Music and Postmodern Knowledge*. Berkeley: University of California Press, 1995.

———. "Musicology and Meaning." *Musical Times* 144, no. 1,883 (2003): 6–12.

Krause, Bernie. *The Great Animal Orchestra*. London: Profile Books, 2012.

———. *Wild Soundscapes: Discovering the Voice of the Natural World*. Berkeley: Wilderness Press, 2002.

Kraut, Robert. "Ontology: Music and Art." *Monist* 95, no. 4 (2012): 684–710.

Kroodsma, Donald E. "Ecology of Passerine Song Development." In *Ecology and Evolution of Acoustic Communication in Birds*, edited by Donald E. Kroodsma and Edward H. Miller, 3–19. Ithaca, NY: Cornell University Press, 1996.

Kuhn, Thomas S. *The Structure of Scientific Revolutions*. 1962. 3rd edition, Chicago: University of Chicago Press, 1966.

Kunst, Jaap. *Ethnomusicology*. The Hague: Martinus Nijhoff, 1974.

"Kurt Schwitters Ursonate." Accessed 26 December 2014. http://dangerousminds.net/comments/flipping_ursonate_the_greatest_sound_poem_of_the_20th_century_the_bird.

"Kurt Schwitters Ursonate." Accessed 26 December 2014. http://writing.upenn.edu /pennsound/x/Schwitters.html.

Langmore, N. E. "Functions of Duet and Solo Songs of Female Birds." *Trends in Ecology & Evolution* 13, no. 4 (1998): 136–140.

Larsson, Matz. "Self-Generated Sounds of Locomotion and Ventilation and the Evolution of Human Rhythmic Abilities." *Animal Cognition* 17 (2014): 1–14.

Laurance, William F., Anna Peletier-Jellema, Bart Geenen, Harko Koster, Pita Verweij, Pitou Van Dijck, Thomas E. Lovejoy, Judith Schleicher, and Marijke Van Kuijk. "Reducing the Global Environmental Impacts of Rapid Infrastructure Expansion." *Current Biology* 25, no. 7 (2015): R259–R262.

Leach, Elizabeth Eva. *Sung Birds: Music, Nature, and Poetry in the Later Middle Ages.* Ithaca, NY: Cornell University Press, 2007.

Leach, John Albert. *An Australian Bird Book.* Melbourne: Education Department of Victoria, 1911.

Lehmann, Christian, Lorenz Welker, and Wulf Schiefenhövel. "Towards an Ethology of Song: A Categorization of Musical Behavior." Special issue, *Musicae Scientiae* 13, no. 2, suppl. (2009–2010): 321–338.

Leopold, Aldo. *The River of the Mother of God and Other Essays.* Madison: University of Wisconsin Press, 1991.

Lerdahl, Fred, and Ray Jackendoff. *A Generative Theory of Tonal Music.* Cambridge, MA: MIT Press, 1983.

Lestel, Dominique. *L'animal est l'avenir de l'homme.* Paris: Fayard, 2010.

———. *Les amis de mes amis.* Paris: Éditions du Seuil, 2007.

———. *Les origines animales de la culture.* Paris: Flammarion, 2001.

Levine, George. *Darwin Loves You: Natural Selection and the Re-enchantment of the World.* Princeton, NJ: Princeton University Press, 2006.

Levitin, Daniel J. *This Is Your Brain on Music: The Science of a Human Obsession.* New York: Dutton, 2006.

———. "What Does It Mean to Be Musical?" *Neuron* 73, no. 23 (February 2012): 633–637.

Lidov, David. "Our Time with the Druids: What (and How) We Can Recuperate from Our Obsession with Segmental Hierarchies and Other 'Tree Structures.'" *Contemporary Music Review* 16, no. 4 (1997): 1–28.

List, George. "Ethnomusicology: A Discipline Defined." *Ethnomusicology* 23, no. 1 (1979): 1–4.

———. "On the Non-universality of Musical Perspectives." *Ethnomusicology* 15, no. 3 (1971): 399–402.

———. "Transcription III." *Ethnomusicology* 8, no. 3 (1964): 252–265.

Livingstone, Steven Robert, and William Forde Thompson. "The Emergence of Music from the Theory of Mind." Special issue, *Musicae Scientiae* 13, no. 2, suppl. (2009–2010): 83–115.

Lord, E. A. R. "*Cracticus nigrogularis* (Black-Throated Butcher-Bird) as Mimic." *Queensland Naturalist* 12, no. 6 (1945): 118–119.

Low, Tim. *The New Nature.* Camberwell: Penguin Books, 2003.

———. *Where Song Began: Australia's Birds and How They Changed the World.* Melbourne: Viking, 2014.

Lumsdaine, David. *Mandala 4* for string quartet. York: University of York Music Press, 1996.

———. "Pied Butcherbirds of Spirey Creek." Liner notes to track 1 on the CD *Mutawintji*. Wahroonga: Tall Poppies TP091 (1996).

Luther, David, and Jessica Magnotti. "Can Animals Detect Differences in Vocalizations Adjusted for Anthropogenic Noise?" *Animal Behaviour* 92 (2014): 111–116.

Lynch, Alejandro, Geoffrey M. Plunkett, Allan J. Baker, and Peter F. Jenkins. "A Model of Cultural Evolution of Chaffinch Song Derived with the Meme Concept." *American Naturalist* 133, no. 5 (1989): 634–653.

Mâche, François-Bernard. *Music, Myth and Nature.* Translated by Susan Delaney. 1983. Chur: Harwood Academic Publishers, 1992.

——. *Musique au singulier.* Paris: Éditions Odile Jacob, 2001.

——. "The Necessity of and Problems with a Universal Musicology." In *The Origins of Music,* edited by Nils L. Wallin, Björn Merker, and Steven Brown, 473–479. Cambridge, MA: MIT Press, 2000.

Madden, Joah R., Caroline Dingle, Jess Isden, Janka Sparfeld, Anne W. Goldizen, and John A. Endler. "Male Spotted Bowerbirds Propagate Fruit for Use in Their Sexual Display." *Current Biology* 22, no. 8 (2010): R264–R265.

Malm, William P. *Music Cultures of the Pacific, the Near East, and Asia.* Englewood Cliffs, NJ: Prentice-Hall, Inc., 1977.

Marcus, Gary F. "Musicality: Instinct or Acquired Skill?" *Topics in Cognitive Science* 4 (2012): 498–512.

Marett, Allan. *Songs, Dreamings, and Ghosts: The Wangga of North Australia.* Middletown, CT: Wesleyan University Press, 2005.

Margoliash, Daniel, and Howard C. Nusbaum. "Animal Comparative Studies Should Be Part of Linguistics." *Behavioral and Brain Sciences* 32 (2009): 458–459.

Margulis, Elizabeth Hellmuth. *On Repeat: How Music Plays the Mind.* Oxford: Oxford University Press, 2014.

Marian-Bălaşa, Marin. "Who Actually Needs Transcription? Notes on the Modern Rise of a Method and the Postmodern Fall of an Ideology." *World of Music* 47, no. 2 (2005): 5–29.

Marler, Peter. "Birdsong: The Acquisition of a Learned Motor Skill." *Trends in Neurosciences* 4 (1981): 88–94.

——. "A Comparative Approach to Vocal Learning: Song Development in White-Crowned Sparrows." *Journal of Comparative and Physiological Psychology* 71, no. 2, pt. 2 (1970): 1–25.

——. "The Instinct to Learn." In *Language Acquisition: Core Readings,* edited by P. Bloom, 591–617. Cambridge, MA: MIT Press, 1994.

——. "Song Learning: The Interface between Behaviour and Neuroethology." *Philosophical Transactions: Biological Sciences* 329, no. 1,253 (1990): 109–114.

——. "Three Models of Song Learning: Evidence from Behavior." *Journal of Neurobiology* 33 (1997): 501–516.

Marler, Peter, and Susan Peters. "Long-Term Storage of Learned Birdsongs prior to Production." *Animal Behaviour* 30, no. 2 (1982): 479–482.

——. "Structural Changes in Song Ontogeny in the Swamp Sparrow *Melospiza georgiana.*" *Auk* 99 (1982): 446–458.

Martinelli, Dario. *How Musical Is a Whale? Towards a Theory of Zoömusicology.* Hakapaino: International Semiotics Institute, 2002.

——. "Symptomatology of a Semiotic Research: Methodologies and Problems in Zoomusicology." *Sign Systems Studies* 29, no. 1 (2001): 1–12.

Mathews, F. Schuyler. *Field Book of Wild Birds & Their Music.* 1921. New York: Dover Publications, 1967.

Mathews, Freya. "The Anguish of Wildlife Ethics." *New Formations* 76, no. 3 (2012): 114–131.

Maturana, Humberto R., and Francisco G. Varela. *The Tree of Knowledge: The Biological Roots of Human Understanding*. Boston: Shambhala, 1998.

McClary, Susan. Afterword. In *Noise: The Political Economy of Music*, by Jacques Attali, 149–158. Minneapolis: University of Minnesota Press, 1985.

——. "Rap, Minimalism, and Structures of Time in Late Twentieth-Century Culture." In *Audio Culture: Readings in Modern Music*, 289–298. New York: Continuum, 2007.

McClary, Susan, and Robert Walser. "Start Making Sense! Musicology Wrestles with Rock." In *On Record: Rock, Pop, and the Written Word*, edited by Simon Frith and Andrew Goodwin, 277–292. New York: Routledge, 1990.

McDermott, Josh, and Marc Hauser. "The Origins of Music: Innateness, Uniqueness, and Evolution." *Music Perception* 23, no. 1 (2005): 29–59.

——. "Thoughts on an Empirical Approach to the Evolutionary Origins of Music." *Music Perception* 24, no. 1 (2006): 111–116.

McDermott, Josh H., Michael V. Keebler, Christophe Micheyl, and Andrew J. Oxenham. "Musical Intervals and Relative Pitch: Frequency Resolution, Not Interval Resolution, Is Special." *Journal of the Acoustical Society of America* 128, no. 4 (2010): 1943–1951.

McDermott, Josh H., and Andrew J. Oxenham. "Music Perception, Pitch, and the Auditory System." *Current Opinion in Neurobiology* 18 (2008): 1–12.

McGilchrist, Iain. *The Master and His Emissary: The Divided Brain and the Making of the Western World*. New Haven, CT: Yale University Press, 2009.

McIntyre, Emma, Marty L. Leonard, and Andrew G. Horn. "Ambient Noise and Parental Communication of Predation Risk in Tree Swallows, *Tachycineta bicolor*." *Animal Behaviour* 87 (2014): 85–89.

McLean, Mervyn. "A Preliminary Analysis of 87 Maori Chants." *Ethnomusicology* 8, no. 1 (1964): 41–48.

Merker, Björn. "The Conformal Motive in Birdsong, Music, and Language: An Introduction." In *The Neurosciences and Music II: From Perception to Performance*, edited by Giuliano Avanzini, Luisa Lopez, Stefan Koelsch, and Maria Majno, 17–28. New York: New York Academy of Sciences, 2005.

——. "Music: The Missing Humboldt System." *Musicae Scientiae* 6, no. 1 (2002): 3–21.

——. "The Uneven Interface between Culture and Biology in Human Music." *Music Perception* 24, no. 1 (2006): 95–98.

——. "The Vocal Learning Constellation: Imitation, Ritual Culture, Encephalization." In *Music, Language, and Human Evolution*, edited by Nicholas Bannan, 215–260. Oxford: Oxford University Press, 2012.

Merriam, Alan P. *The Anthropology of Music*. Evanston, IL: Northwestern University Press, 1964.

——. "Ethnomusicology Discussion and Definition of the Field." *Ethnomusicology* 4, no. 3 (1960): 107–114.

——. "Purposes of Ethnomusicology, an Anthropological View." *Ethnomusicology* 7, no. 3 (1963): 206–213.

Messiaen, Olivier. *Éclairs sur l'Au-Delà* for full orchestra, vol. 1. Paris: Leduc, 1998.

——. *Éclairs sur l'Au-Delà* for full orchestra, vol. 2. Paris: Leduc, 1998.

——. *The Technique of My Musical Language*. Translated by John Satterfield. 1944. Paris: Alphonse Leduc, 1956.

——. *Traité de rythme, de couleur, et d'ornithologie*, 7 vols. Paris: Leduc, 1994–2002. Vol. 1 (1994); vol. 2 (1995); vols. 3 and 4 (1996); vol. 5/1 (1999); vol. 5/2 (2000); vol. 6 (2001); vol. 7 (2002).

Messiaen, Olivier, and Claude Samuel. *Music and Color: Conversations with Claude Samuel.* Translated by E. Thomas Glasow. Portland, OR: Amadeus Press, 1994.

Meyer, Leonard B. *Emotion and Meaning in Music.* Chicago: University of Chicago Press, 1961.

——. *Explaining Music: Essays and Explorations.* Berkeley: University of California Press, 1973.

——. *Music, the Arts, and Ideas: Patterns and Predictions in Twentieth Century Culture.* Chicago: University of Chicago Press, 1967.

——. *The Spheres of Music: A Gathering of Essays.* Chicago: University of Chicago Press, 2000.

——. "Universalism and Relativism in the Study of Ethnic Music." *Ethnomusicology* 4, no. 2 (1960): 49–54.

"Mike Ryan." Accessed 28 December 2014. http://www.sbs.utexas.edu/ryan/.

Miller, Blanche E. "Some Birds of Mount Tambourine, South Queensland." *Emu* 23 (1928): 131–133.

Miller, Loye. "Songs of the Western Meadowlark." *Wilson Bulletin* 64, no. 2 (1952): 106–107.

Milligan, Alex. Wm. "Notes on a Trip to the Yandanooka District, Western Australia." *Emu* 4, no. 4 (1905): 151–157.

Milton, Kay. "Anthropomorphism or Egomorphism? The Perception of Non-human Persons by Human Ones." In *Animals in Person: Cultural Perspectives on Human-Animal Intimacy*, edited by John Knight, 255–271. Oxford: Berg, 2005.

Mithen, Steven. *The Singing Neanderthals: The Origins of Music, Language, Mind and Body.* London: Phoenix, 2006.

Moreno, Sylvain. "Can Music Influence Language and Cognition?" *Contemporary Music Review* 28, no. 3 (2009): 329–345.

Morphy, Howard. *Becoming Art: Exploring Cross-Cultural Categories.* Oxford: Berg, 2007.

Morris, Stanley. *Bird Song: A Manual for Field Naturalists.* London: Witherby, 1925.

Morton, Timothy. *Ecology without Nature: Rethinking Environmental Aesthetics.* Cambridge, MA: Harvard University Press, 2007.

Müllensiefen, Daniel, Bruno Gingras, Jason Musil, and Lauren Stewart. "The Musicality of Non-musicians: An Index for Assessing Musical Sophistication in the General Population." *PLOS ONE* 9, no. 2 (2014): 1–23.

Mundinger, Paul C. "Animal Cultures and a General Theory of Cultural Evolution." *Ethology and Sociobiology* 1, no. 3 (1980): 183–223.

Mundy, Rachel. "Nature's Music: Birds, Beasts, and Evolutionary Listening in the Twentieth Century." PhD diss., New York University, 2010.

"Music." In *Grove Music Online. Oxford/Grove Dictionary of Music.* Accessed 5 August 2012. http://www.oxfordmusiconline.com.

"Music in Neuroscience Monte Verità." Accessed 3 January 2016. http://lcn1.epfl.ch /MV_Music_Neuroscience.

Mynott, Jeremy. *Birdscapes: Birds in Our Imagination and Experience.* Princeton, NJ: Princeton University Press, 2009.

Nagorcka, Ron. *Artamidae: A Suite of 5 Pieces Celebrating a Family of Australian Song-birds* for trombone, mandolin, clarinet, bass clarinet, flute, piccolo, sampler, and didjeridu. Author, 2004.

Narmour, Eugene. *The Analysis and Cognition of Basic Melodic Structures*. Chicago: University of Chicago Press, 1990.

———. *Beyond Schenkerism: The Need for Alternatives in Music Analysis*. Chicago: University of Chicago Press, 1977.

Nattiez, Jean-Jacques. *Music and Discourse: Toward a Semiology of Music*. Translated by Carolyn Abbate. Princeton, NJ: Princeton University Press, 1990.

Nettl, Bruno. "Music." In *Oxford Music Online* (Oxford: Oxford University Press, 2007–2014). Accessed 5 August 2012. http://www.oxfordmusiconline.com.

———. "The State of Research in Ethnomusicology, and Recent Developments." *Current Musicology* 20 (1975): 67–78.

———. *The Study of Ethnomusicology: Twenty-Nine Issues and Concepts*. Urbana: University of Illinois Press, 1983.

Nicholls, James A., Michael C. Double, David M. Rowell, and Robert D. Magrath. "The Evolution of Cooperative and Pair Breeding in Thornbills *Acanthiza* (Pardalotidae)." *Journal of Avian Biology* 31, no. 2 (2000): 165–176.

Nollman, Jim. *The Charged Border: Where Whales and Humans Meet*. New York: Henry Holt and Company, 1999.

———. "Fowl Play: Creating Interspecies Music." *Orion* 16, no. 2 (1997): 12–15.

Nooshin, Laudan. "Improvisation as 'Other': Creativity, Knowledge and Power." *Journal of the Royal Musical Association* 128, no. 2 (2003): 242–296.

Norman, Janette A., Frank E. Rheindt, Diane L. Rowe, and Les Christidis. "Speciation Dynamics in the Australo-Papuan Meliphaga Honeyeaters." *Molecular Phylogenetics and Evolution* 42, no. 1 (2007): 80–91.

North, M. E. W. "Transcribing Bird-Song." *Ibis* 92 (1950): 99–114.

Nottebohm, Fernando. "The Neural Basis of Birdsong." *PLOS Biology* 3, no. 5 (2005): 759–761.

Odom, Karan J., Michelle L. Hall, Katharina Riebel, Kevin E. Omland, and Naomi E. Langmore. "Female Song Is Widespread and Ancestral in Songbirds." *Nature Communications* 5 (2014): 1–6.

Ogden, Laura A., Billy Hall, and Kimiko Tanita. "Animals, Plants, People, and Things: A Review of Multispecies Ethnography." *Environment and Society: Advances in Research* 4 (2013): 5–24.

Okanoya, Kazuo. "Sexual Display as a Syntactic Vehicle: The Evolution of Syntax in Birdsong and Human Language through Sexual Selection." In *The Transition to Language*, edited by Alison Wray, 44–64. Oxford: Oxford University Press, 2002.

Olds, W. B. "Bird-Music." *Musical Quarterly* 8, no. 2 (1922): 242–255.

Oldys, Henry. "The Meaning of Bird Music." *American Museum Journal* 17 (1917): 123–127.

———. "Parallel Growth of Bird and Human Music." *Harper's Monthly Magazine* 105 (1902): 474–478.

———. "A Remarkable Hermit Thrush Song." *Auk* 30 (1913): 538–541.

Orr, David W. *Earth in Mind: On Education, Environment, and the Human Prospect*. Washington, DC: Island Press, 2004.

Parker, Anna R. "Evolving the Narrow Language Faculty: Was Recursion the Pivotal Step?" Paper presented at the 6th International Conference on the Evolution of Language, Rome, 12–15 April 2006.

Patel, Aniruddh D. *Music, Language, and the Brain*. Oxford: Oxford University Press, 2008.

Patel, Aniruddh D., John R. Iversen, Micah R. Bregman, and Irena Schulz. "Experimental Evidence for Synchronization to a Musical Beat in a Nonhuman Animal." *Current Biology* 19, no. 10 (2009): 1–4.

Pearce, Marcus, and Martin Rohrmeier. "Music Cognition and the Cognitive Sciences." *Topics in Cognitive Science* 4 (2012): 468–484.

Pesic, Peter. *Music and the Making of Modern Science*. Cambridge, MA: MIT Press, 2014.

Peter, John M. *Some Indigenous Names of Australian Birds*. Hawthorn East: Birds Australia, 2006.

Petrovic, Milena, and Nenad Ljubinkovic. "Imitation of Animal Sound Patterns in Serbian Folk Music." *Journal of Interdisciplinary Music Studies* 5, no. 2 (2011): 101–118.

"Philip Kitcher." Accessed 19 December 2015. http://philosophy.columbia.edu /directories/faculty/philip-kitcher.

Phythian, Clare, Eleni Michalopoulou, Jennifer Duncan, and Françoise Wemelsfelder. "Inter-observer Reliability of Qualitative Behavioural Assessments of Sheep." *Applied Animal Behaviour Science* 144 (2013): 73–79.

"Pied Butcherbird Image." Accessed 16 December 2015. https://www.flickr.com/photos /richardhartphotography/5875964358.

Pieretti, N., A. Farina, and D. Morri. "A New Methodology to Infer the Singing Activity of an Avian Community: The Acoustic Complexity Index (ACI)." *Ecological Indicators* 11 (2011): 868–873.

Pijanowski, Bryan C., Luis J. Villanueva-Rivera, Sarah L. Dumyahn, Almo Farina, Bernie L. Krause, Brian M. Napoletano, Stuart H. Gage, and Nadia Pieretti. "Soundscape Ecology: The Science of Sound in the Landscape." *BioScience* 61, no. 3 (2011): 203–216.

Plumwood, Val. "Nature as Agency and the Prospects for a Progressive Naturalism." *Capitalism Nature Socialism* 12, no. 4 (2001): 3–32.

——. "Nature in the Active Voice." *Australian Humanities Review* 46 (2009): n.p.

Podos, Jeffrey, Susan Peters, Tamia Rudnicky, Peter Marler, and Stephen Nowicki. "The Organization of Song Repertoires in Song Sparrows: Themes and Variations." *Ethology* 90, no. 2 (1992): 89–106.

Powers, Alan. *Birdtalk*. Berkeley: Frog, Ltd., 2003.

Powys, Vicki, Hollis Taylor, and Carol Probets. "*A Little Flute Music*: Mimicry, Memory, and Narrativity." *Environmental Humanities* 3 (2013): 43–70.

Pratt, Carroll C. "The Design of Music." *Journal of Aesthetics and Art Criticism* 12, no. 3 (1954): 289–300.

Premack, David, and Ann James Premack. "Why Animals Have Neither Culture nor History." In *Companion Encyclopedia of Anthropology*, edited by Tim Ingold, 350–365. London: Routledge, 1994.

Pressing, Jeff. "Psychological Constraints on Improvisational Expertise and Communication." In *In the Course of Performance*, edited by Bruno Nettl and Melinda Russell, 47–67. Chicago: University of Chicago Press, 1998.

Price, J. Jordan, Scott M. Lanyon, and Kevin E. Omland. "Losses of Female Song with Changes from Tropical to Temperate Breeding in the New World Blackbirds." *Proceedings of the Royal Society B: Biological Sciences* 276 (2009): 1971–1980.

Price, Sally. *Primitive Art in Civilized Places*. Chicago: University of Chicago Press, 1989.

Prochnik, George. *In Pursuit of Silence: Listening for Meaning in a World of Noise.* New York: Doubleday, 2010.

Prum, Richard O. "Aesthetic Evolution by Mate Choice: Darwin's *Really* Dangerous Idea." *Philosophical Transactions of the Royal Society B* 367 (2012): 2253–2265.

Qureshi, Rugula Burckhardt. "Other Musicologies: Exploring Issues and Confronting Practice in India." In *Rethinking Music,* edited by Nicholas Cook and Mark Everist, 311–335. Oxford: Oxford University Press, 1999.

Račiūnaitė-Vyčinienė, Daiva. "The Archaic Lithuanian Polyphonic Chant *Sutartinė.*" *Lithuanus: Lithuanian Quarterly Journal of Arts and Sciences* 52, no. 2 (2006): n.p.

Raffman, Diana. *Language, Music, and Mind.* Cambridge, MA: MIT Press, 1993.

Ratner, Leonard G. "*Ars Combinatoria*: Chance and Choice in Eighteenth-Century Music." In *Studies in Eighteenth-Century Music: A Tribute to Karl Geiringer on His Seventieth Birthday,* edited by H. C. Robbins Landon and Roger E. Chapman, 343–363. New York: Oxford University Press, 1970.

Ravignani, Andrea, Daniel L. Bowling, and W. Tecumseh Fitch. "Chorusing, Synchrony, and the Evolutionary Functions of Rhythm." *Frontiers in Psychology* 5, no. 118 (2014): 1–15.

Read, Gardner. *Music Notation: A Manual of Modern Practice.* 1969. New York: Taplinger Publishing Company, 1979.

Reid, Donna Brink. *A Butcherbird Story.* Bassendean: Access Press, 2000.

Révész, G. *The Introduction to the Psychology of Music.* London: Longmans, Green and Co., 1953.

Reynolds, Simon. "Noise." In *Audio Culture: Readings in Modern Music,* edited by Christoph Cox and Daniel Warner, 55–58. New York: Continuum, 2007.

Reznikova, Zhanna. *Animal Intelligence: From Individual to Social Cognition.* Cambridge: Cambridge University Press, 2007.

Rhodes, Willard. "Transcription IV." *Ethnomusicology* 8, no. 3 (1964): 265–272.

Rice, Timothy. "Toward a Mediation of Field Methods and Field Experience in Ethnomusicology." In *Shadows in the Field: New Perspectives for Fieldwork in Ethnomusicology,* edited by Gregory F. Barz and Timothy J. Cooley, 101–120. New York: Oxford University Press, 1997.

Riebel, Katarina. "The Mute Sex Revisited: Vocal Production and Perception Learning in Female Songbirds." In *Advances in the Study of Behavior,* edited by Peter J. B. Slater, 49–86. Amsterdam: Elsevier Academic Press, 2003.

Riebel, Katharina, Michelle L. Hall, and Naomi E. Langmore. "Female Songbirds Still Struggling to Be Heard." *TRENDS in Ecology and Evolution* 20, no. 8 (2005): 419–420.

Robbings, Chandler S., Bertel Bruun, and Herbert S. Zim. *Birds of North America: A Guide to Field Identification.* New York: Golden Press, 1966.

Roberts, Helen H. "Melodic Composition and Scale Foundations in Primitive Music." *American Anthropologist,* n.s., 34, no. 1 (1932): 79–107.

Robinson, A. "Helpers-at-the-Nest in Pied Butcherbirds, *Cracticus nigrogularis.*" PhD diss., Griffith University, 1994.

Roché, Jean C. *Les grands virtuoses: Les plus beaux chants d'oiseaux.* CD. Auvidis Tempo A6117 (1987).

Rodgers, John. "The Butcher-Bird." Track 7 on *Weaver of Fictions* (Genevieve Lacey). CD. ABC Classics ABC 476 6439 (2006).

Rollin, Bernard E. "Anecdote, Anthropomorphism, and Animal Behavior." In *Anthropomorphism, Anecdotes, and Animals,* edited by Robert W. Mitchell, Nicholas S.

Thompson, and H. Lyn Miles, 125–133. Albany: State University of New York Press, 1997.

Rolston, Holmes, III. "Does Aesthetic Appreciation of Landscapes Need to Be Science-Based?" *British Journal of Aesthetics* 35, no. 4 (1995): 374–386.

Roper, Emma Rose. "Musical Nature: Vocalisations of the Australian Magpie (*Gymnorhina tibicen tyrannica*)." *Context: Journal of Music Research* 32 (2007): 59–72.

Rose, Deborah Bird. *Wild Dog Dreaming: Love and Extinction.* Charlottesville: University of Virginia Press, 2011.

Rose, Jon. *The Music of Place: Reclaiming a Practice.* Strawberry Hills: Currency House, 2013.

———. *Rosenberg 3.0: Not Violin Music.* Sydney: Rosenberg Museum, 2014.

Roseman, Marina. "Singers of the Landscape: Song, History, and Property Rights in the Malaysian Rain Forest." *American Anthropologist* 100, no. 1 (1998): 106–121.

Rothenberg, David. *Bug Music: How Insects Gave Us Rhythm and Noise.* New York: St. Martin's Press, 2013.

———. "Interview with Peter Marler: Bird Song at the Edge of Music and Science: A Conversation between David Rothenberg and Peter Marler." *Terrain: A Journal of the Built + Natural Environment.* Accessed 15 December 2014. http://terrain.org/2014/interviews/peter-marler/.

———. *Thousand Mile Song: Whale Music in a Sea of Sound.* New York: Basic Books, 2008.

———. *Why Birds Sing: A Journey into the Mystery of Bird Song.* New York: Basic Books, 2005.

Rothenberg, David, Tina C. Roeske, Henning U. Voss, Marc Naguib, and Ofer Tchernichovski. "Investigation of Musicality in Birdsong." *Hearing Research* 308 (2014): 71–83.Rowan, William. "A Practical Method of Recording Bird-Calls." *British Birds* 18, no. 1 (1924): 14–18.

Rowe, Stan. *Home Place: Essays on Ecology.* 1990. Edmonton: NeWest Press, 2002.

Russolo, Luigi. "The Art of Noises: Futurist Manifesto." In *Audio Culture: Readings in Modern Music,* edited by Christoph Cox and Daniel Warner, 10–14. New York: Continuum, 2007.

"Rustications: Animals in the Urban Mix." Accessed 21 July 2013. http://www.stevenconnor.com/rustications/rustications.pdf.

Rutherford, Kenneth M. D., Ramona D. Donald, and Alistair Lawrence. "Qualitative Behavioural Assessment of Emotionality in Pigs." *Applied Animal Behaviour Science* 139 (2012): 218–224.

Rutherford-Johnson, Tim, Michael Kennedy, and Joyce Bourne Kennedy. "Canon." In *The Oxford Dictionary of Music.* Accessed 5 April 2014. http://www.oxfordreference.com.

Sacks, Oliver. *Musicophilia: Tales of Music and the Brain.* New York: Alfred A. Knopf, 2007.

Sartre, Jean-Paul. "I Discovered Jazz in America." *Saturday Review of Literature,* 29 November 1947, 48–49.

Sasahara, Kazutoshi, Martin L. Cody, David Cohen, and Charles E. Taylor. "Structural Design Principles of Complex Bird Songs: A Network-Based Approach." *PLOS ONE* 7, no. 9 (2012): 1–9.

Saunders, Aretas A. *A Guide to Bird Songs: Descriptions and Diagrams of the Songs and Singing Habits of Land Birds and Selected Species of Shore Birds.* 1935. Garden City, NY: Doubleday & Company, 1951.

Scharff, Constance, and Jana Petri. "Evo-devo, Deep Homology and Foxp2: Implications for the Evolution of Speech and Language." *Philosophical Transactions of the Royal Society B* 366 (2011): 2124–2140.

Schmidt, Marc F., and Robin Ashmore. "Integrating Breathing and Singing: Forebrain and Brainstem Mechanisms." In *Neuroscience of Birdsong*, edited by H. Philip Zeigler and Peter Marler, 115–135. Cambridge: Cambridge University Press, 2008.

Schmidt, Rouven, Aoibheann Morrison, and Hansjoerg P. Kunc. "Sexy Voices—No Choices: Male Song in Noise Fails to Attract Females." *Animal Behaviour* 94 (2014): 55–59.

Schoenberg, Arnold. *Coherence, Counterpoint, Instrumentation, Instruction in Form.* Translated and edited by Severine Neff. Lincoln: University of Nebraska Press, 1994.

——. *Fundamentals of Musical Composition.* Edited by Gerald Strang and Leonard Stein. London: Faber and Faber, 1967.

Scholes, Percy A. *The Listener's History of Music.* London: Oxford University Press, 1954.

Schwartz, Hillel. *Making Noise: From Babel to the Big Bang & Beyond.* New York: Zone Books, 2011.

Seeger, Charles. "On the Tasks of Musicology." (Comments on Merriam, "Purposes of Ethnomusicology.") *Ethnomusicology* 7, no. 3 (1963): 214–215.

——. "Prescriptive and Descriptive Music-Writing." *Musical Quarterly* 44, no. 2 (1958): 184–195.

Serres, Michel. *The Five Senses.* Translated by Margaret Sankey and Peter Cowley. 1985. London: Continuum, 2008.

Sessions, Roger. *The Musical Experience of Composer, Performer, Listener.* Princeton, NJ: Princeton University Press, 1950.

Sethares, William A. *Tuning, Timbre, Spectrum, Scale.* 2nd edition. London: Springer-Verlag, 1999.

Shanahan, Daniel, and David Huron. "Interval Size and Phrase Position: A Comparison between German and Chinese Folksongs." *Empirical Musicology Review* 6, no. 4 (2011): 187–197.

Shiovitz, Kenneth A. "The Process of Species-Specific Song Recognition by the Indigo Bunting, *Passerina cyanea*, and Its Relationship to the Organization of Avian Acoustical Behavior." *Behaviour* 55 (1975): 128–179.

Shubin, Neil, Cliff Tabin, and Sean Carroll. "Deep Homology and the Origins of Evolutionary Novelty." *Nature* 457, no. 12 (February 2009): 818–823.

Skeoch, Andrew. "Ormiston Gorge, Full Moon, 3 AM." Liner notes to track 1 on the CD *Spirit of the Outback.* Newstead: Listening Earth LECD9902 (1999).

Slater, P. J. B. "Animal Music." Oxford Music Online: Grove Music Online. Accessed 5 August 2013. http://www.oxfordmusiconline.com.

——. "The Cultural Transmission of Bird Song." *Trends in Ecology & Evolution* 1, no. 4 (1986): 94–97.

——. "Sequences of Song in Chaffinches." *Animal Behaviour* 31 (1983): 272–281.

Small, Christopher. *Musicking.* Hanover: Wesleyan University Press, 1998.

Smith, Alexander Brent. "The Blackbird's Song." *Musical Times* 63, no. 953 (1922): 480–481.

Smith, W. John. "Singing Is Based on Two Markedly Different Kinds of Signaling." *Journal of Theoretical Biology* 152 (1991): 241–253.

Snedic, Michael. "Longing for Lyrebirds." *BBC Wildlife*, September 2008, 68–69.

Snow, C. P. *"The Two Cultures" and "A Second Look."* 1959. Cambridge: Cambridge University Press, 1964.

Snyder, Bob. *Music and Memory.* Cambridge, MA: MIT Press, 2000.

Snyder, Gary. *The Practice of the Wild.* New York: North Point Press, 1990.

Soper, Kate. *What Is Nature? Culture, Politics and the Non-human.* Oxford: Blackwell, 1995.

Sorce Keller, Marcello. "Zoomusicology and Ethnomusicology: A Marriage to Celebrate in Heaven." *2012 Yearbook for Traditional Music* 44 (2012): 166–183.

Sotavalta, Olavi. "Analysis of the Song Patterns of Two Sprosser Nightingales, *Luscinia*." *Annals of the Finnish Zoological Society "Vanamo"* 17, no. 4 (1956): 1–31.

Spector, David A. "Definition in Biology: The Case of 'Bird Song.'" *Journal of Theoretical Biology* 168 (1994): 373–381.

Spencer, Herbert. "The Origin and Function of Music." In *The Works of Herbert Spencer*, vol. 14: *Essays: Scientific, Political, & Speculative*, vol. 2, 400–451. 1857. Osnabruck: Otto Zeller, 1966.

Staal, Frits. "Mantras and Bird Songs." *Journal of the American Oriental Society* 105, no. 3 (1985): 549–558.

Stadler, Hans, and Cornel Schmitt. "The Study of Bird-Notes." *British Birds* 8, no. 1 (1914): 2–8.

Stainer, J. F. R. "Singing Birds." *Musical Times and Singing Class Circular* 40, no. 680 (1899): 671–672.

Stanyek, Jason. "Forum on Transcription." Special issue, *Twentieth-Century Music* 11, no. 1 (2014): 101–161.

Stevens, Catherine. "Cross-Cultural Studies of Musical Pitch and Time." *Acoustical Science & Technology* 26, no. 6 (2004): 433–438.

Stockmann, Doris. "Die Transkription in der Musikethnologie: Geschichte, Probleme, Methoden." *Acta Musicologica* 51, no. 2 (1979): 204–245.

Storr, Anthony. *Music and the Mind.* New York: Ballantine Books, 1992.

Stravinsky, Igor. *Poetics of Music.* New York: Vintage Books, 1947.

Strehlow, John. *The Tale of Frieda Keysser, Volume I: 1875–1910.* London: Wild Cat Press, 2011.

Suchoff, Benjamin. *Béla Bartók Essays.* Lincoln: University of Nebraska Press, 1976.

Suzuki, Toshitaka N. "Communication about Predator Type by a Bird Using Discrete, Graded and Combinatorial Variation in Alarm Calls." *Animal Behaviour* 87 (2014): 59–65.

Szőke, Péter. "Ornitomuzikológia." *Magyar Tudomany* 9 (1963): 592–607.

Szőke, Péter, and Miroslav Filip. "The Study Of Intonation Structure of Bird Vocalizations: An Inadequate Application of Sound Spectrography." *Opuscula Zoologica Budapest* 14, no. 1–2 (1977): 127–154.

Szőke, P., W. W. H. Gunn, and M. Filip. "The Musical Microcosm of the Hermit Thrush: From Athanasius Kircher's Naive Experiments of Musical Transcription of Bird Voice to Sound Microscopy and the Scientific Musical Representation of Bird Song." *Studia Musicologica Academiae Scientiarum Hungaricae* 11, no. 1/4 (1969): 423–438.

Tagg, Philip. "Towards a Definition of 'Music.'" Accessed 5 August 2008. http://www.tagg.org/teaching/musdef.pdf.

Tan, Siu-Lan, Peter Pfordresher, and Rom Harré. *Psychology of Music.* Hove: Psychology Press, 2010.

Tate, Henry. *Australian Musical Possibilities.* Melbourne: Edward Vidler, 1924.

Taylor, Hollis. "Anecdote and Anthropomorphism: Writing the Australian Pied Butcherbird." *Australasian Journal of Ecocriticism and Cultural Ecology* 1 (2011): 1–20.

——. "The Australian Pied Butcherbird (*Cracticus nigrogularis*) and Huron's Psychology of Expectation." Presented at *Music in Neuroscience*. Monte Verità, 20 March 2012.

——. *Bird-Esk* for string quartet. Wollongong: Wirripang Press, 2009.

——. "Blowin' in Birdland: Improvisation and the Australian Pied Butcherbird." *Leonardo Music Journal* 20 (2010): 79–83.

——. "A Call of the Pied Butcherbird." *AudioWings* 8, no. 2 (2005): 4–8.

——. "Can George Dance? Biosemiotics and Human Exceptionalism with a Lyrebird in the Viewfinder." *Social Semiotics*, 2016, 1–17. Accessed 18 September 2016. http://www.tandfonline.com/doi/abs/10.1080/10350330.2016.1223115?tab=permissions &scroll=top.

——. "Composers' Appropriation of Pied Butcherbird Song: Henry Tate's 'Undersong Of Australia' Comes of Age." *Journal of Music Research Online* 2 (2011): 1–28.

——. "Connecting Interdisciplinary Dots: Songbirds, 'White Rats,' and Human Exceptionalism." *Social Science Information* 52, no. 2 (2013): 287–306.

——. *Cumberdeen Dam V & T* for solo bassoon. Wollongong: Wirripang Press, 2009.

——. "Decoding the Song of the Pied Butcherbird: An Initial Survey." *Transcultural Music Review* 12, no. 12 (2008): 1–30.

——. *Lamington Plateau* for flute. Portland, OR: Twisted Fiddle, 2008.

——. "Marginalised Voices: Zoömusicology through a Participatory Lens." In *Participatory Research in More-Than-Human Worlds*, edited by Michelle Bastian, Owain Jones, Niamh Moore, and Emma Roe, 38–53. London: Routledge, 2017.

——. *Post Impressions: A Travel Book for Tragic Intellectuals*. Portland, OR: Twisted Fiddle, 2007.

——. *Riffingbirds* for solo violin. Wollongong: Wirripang Press, 2009.

——. "A Taste for the Beautiful." In *Esthétique et complexité—II: Neurosciences, evolution, epistémologie, philosophie*, edited by Zoï Kapoula, Louise-José Lestocart, and Jean-Paul Allouche, 181–187. Paris: Éditions CNRS, 2015.

——. "Towards a Species Songbook: Illuminating the Vocalisations of the Australian Pied Butcherbird (*Cracticus nigrogularis*)," vol. 1. PhD diss., University of Western Sydney, 2008.

——. "Towards a Species Songbook: Illuminating the Vocalisations of the Australian Pied Butcherbird (*Cracticus nigrogularis*)," vol. 2. PhD diss., University of Western Sydney, 2008.

——. "Whose Bird Is It? Messiaen's Transcriptions of Australian Songbirds." Special issue, *Twentieth-Century Music* 11, no. 1 (2014): 63–100.

Taylor, Hollis, and Andrew Hurley. "*Music* and *Environment*: A Snapshot of Contemporary and Emerging Convergences." *Journal of Music Research Online* (2015): 1–18.

Taylor, Hollis, and Dominique Lestel. "The Australian Pied Butcherbird and the Natureculture Continuum." *Journal of Interdisciplinary Music Studies* 5, no. 1 (2011): 57–83.

Taylor, Hollis, and Jane Ulman. *Bird Interrupted*. ABC Radio National (first broadcast 2 March 2014).

Tchernichovski, Ofer, and Josh Wallman. "Behavioural Neuroscience: Neurons of Imitation." *Nature* 451, no. 7,176 (2008): 249–250.

Templeton, Christopher N., Nigel I. Mann, Alejandro A. Ríos-Chelén, Esmeralda Quiros-Guerrero, Constantino Macías Garcia, and Peter J. B. Slater. "An Experimental Study of Duet Integration in the Happy Wren, *Pheugopedius felix.*" *Animal Behaviour* 86 (2013): 821–827.

Terhardt, Ernst. "Music Perception and Sensory Information Acquisition: Relationships and Low-Level Analogies." *Music Perception* 8, no. 3 (1991): 217–240.

Thelonius Monk: The Complete Riverside Recordings. Riverside RCD-022–2.

Thompson, N. S., K. LeDoux, and K. Moody. "A System for Describing Bird Song Units." *Bioacoustics* 5 (1994): 267–279.

Thompson, William Forde. *Music, Thought, and Feeling: Understanding the Psychology of Music.* New York: Oxford University Press, 2009.

Thorny. "Outdoor Australia: Songbirds of the Bush: A Varied Repertoire." *Sydney (NSW) Morning Herald*, 23 April 1940: 14 Supplement: Women's Supplement. Accessed 22 June 2011. http://nla.gov.au/nla.news-article17668184.

Thorpe, W. H. *Bird-Song: The Biology of Vocal Communication and Expression in Birds.* Cambridge: Cambridge University Press, 1961.

——. "Further Studies on the Process of Song Learning in the Chaffinch (*Fringilla coelebs gengleri*)." *Nature* 182 (1958): 554–557.

——. "The Learning of Song Patterns by Birds, with Especial Reference to the Song of the Chaffinch *Fringilla coelebs.*" *Ibis* 100 (1958): 535–570.

——. "The Process of Song-Learning in the Chaffinch as Studied by Means of the Sound Spectrograph." *Nature* 173, no. 4,402 (1954): 465–469.

——. "Ritualization in Ontogeny. II. Ritualization in the Individual Development of Bird Song." *Philosophical Transactions of the Royal Society of London. Series B, Biological Sciences* 251, no. 772 (1966): 351–358.

——. "Singing." In *A New Dictionary of Birds*, edited by A. Landsborough Thomson, 739–750. London: Nelson, 1964.

Threlfo, Glen. "Albert Lyrebird: Prince of the Rainforest." Canungra, QLD: O'Reilly's Rainforest Guesthouse, 2004.

Tiessen, Heinz. *Musik der Natur.* Passau: Atlantis Verlag, 1953.

Titon, Jeff Todd. "Economy, Ecology, and Music: An Introduction." *World of Music* 51, no. 1 (2009): 5–15.

——. "Music and Sustainability: An Ecological Viewpoint." *World of Music* 51, no. 1 (2009): 119–137.

——. "The Nature of Ecomusicology." *Música e cultura: Revista da ABET* 8, no. 1 (2013): 8–18.

Tobias, Joseph A., Robert Planqué, Dominic L. Cram, and Nathalie Seddon. "Species Interactions and the Structure of Complex Communication Networks." *Proceedings of the National Academy of Sciences, USA* 111, no. 3 (2014): 1020–1025.

Todt, Dietmar, and Henrike Hultsch. "How Songbirds Deal with Large Amounts of Serial Information: Retrieval Rules Suggest a Hierarchical Song Memory." *Biological Cybernetics* 79 (1998): 487–500.

Tomlinson, Gary. *A Million Years of Music: The Emergence of Human Modernity.* New York: Zone Books, 2015.

Trainor, Laurel J. "The Origins of Music in Auditory Scene Analysis and the Roles of Evolution and Culture in Musical Creation." *Philosophical Transactions of the Royal Society B* 370, no. 1,664 (2015): 1–14.

Trân Quang Hai and Nicholas Bannan. "Vocal Traditions of the World." In *Music, Language, & Human Evolution*, edited by Nicholas Bannan, 142–172. Oxford: Oxford University Press, 2012.

Transactions and Proceedings of the Royal Society of New Zealand 1868–1961. Accessed 14 July 2013. http://rsnz.natlib.govt.nz/.

Trehub, Sandra E., Judith Becker, and Iain Morley. "Cross-Cultural Perspectives on Music and Musicality." *Philosophical Transactions of the Royal Society B* 370, no. 1,664 (2015): 1–9.

Tsing, Anna. "Unruly Edges: Mushrooms as Companion Species." *Environmental Humanities* 1 (2012): 141–154.

Turvey, Nigel. "Everyone Agreed: Cane Toads Would Be a Winner for Australia." *Conversation*, 8 November 2013. Accessed 15 November 2014. http://theconversation .com/everyone-agreed-cane-toads-would-be-a-winner-for-australia-19881.

Ulman, Jane. ABC Radio National interview with Jimmy, 5 September 2012.

van Dooren, Thom. *Flight Ways: Life and Loss at the Edge of Extinction.* New York: Columbia University Press, 2014.

van Heijningen, Caroline A. A., Jos de Visser, Willem Zuidema, and Carel ten Cate. "Simple Rules Can Explain Discrimination of Putative Recursive Syntactic Structures by a Songbird Species." *PNAS* 106, no. 48 (2009): 20538–20543.

Varèse, Edgard. "The Liberation of Sound." In *Audio Culture: Readings in Modern Music,* edited by Christoph Cox and Daniel Warner, 17–21. New York: Continuum, 2007.

Voigt, Prof. Dr. A. *Exkursionsbuch zum Studium der Vogelstimmen.* Leipzig: Verlag Quelle & Meyer, 1950.

Volgsten, Ulrik. "The Roots of Music: Emotional Expression, Dialogue and Affect Attunement in the Psychogenesis of Music." *Musicae Scientiae* 16, no. 2 (2012): 200–216.

Wakin, Daniel J. "Musical Borrowing under Scrutiny." *New York Times,* 7 March 2012. Accessed 8 October 2013. http://www.nytimes.com/2012/03/08/arts/music/osvaldo -golijov-fracas-over-sidereus-overture.html?pagewanted=all.

Walker, Lisa. *Grooved Whale.* CD. EarthEar 696208010820 (2001).

Walker, Shirley. *Roundabout at Bangalow.* St. Lucia: University of Queensland Press, 2001.

Wall, Dorothy. "Blinky Bill Grows Up." A Project Gutenberg of Australia eBook, 1934. Accessed 30 June 2011. http://gutenberg.net.au/ebooks04/0400571h.html.

Wallaschek, Richard. *Primitive Music.* London: Longmans, Green and Co., 1893.

Wallin, Nils L., Björn Merker, and Steven Brown, eds. *The Origins of Music.* Cambridge, MA: MIT Press, 2000.

Walser, Robert. "The Body in the Music: Epistemology and Musical Semiotics." *College Music Symposium* 31 (1991): 117–126.

——. "The Polka Mass: Music of Postmodern Ethnicity." *American Music* 10, no. 2 (1992): 183–202.

Watson, Don. "Society of Birds." *Monthly,* December–January 2007–2008, 18–21.

W.C.T. "The Butcher Bird." *Cairns (QLQ) Post,* 27 September 1930: 9. Accessed 22 June 2011. http://nla.gov.au/nla.news-article41054145.

Weisman, Ronald G., Douglas J. K. Mewhort, Marisa Hoeschele, and Christopher B. Sturdy. "New Perspectives on Absolute Pitch in Birds and Mammals." In *The Oxford Handbook of Comparative Cognition,* edited by Thomas R. Zentall and Edward A. Wasserman, 67–79. Oxford: Oxford University Press, 2012.

Weisman, Ronald, and Laurene Ratcliffe. "Relative Pitch and the Song of Black-Capped Chickadees." *American Scientist* 92 (2004): 532–539.

Weisman, Ron, Laurene Ratcliffe, Ingrid Johnsrude, and T. Andrew Hurly. "Absolute and Relative Pitch Production in the Song of the Black-Capped Chickadee." *Condor* 92 (1990): 118–124.

Weiss, Michael, Henrike Hultsch, Iris Adam, Constance Scharff, and Silke Kipper. "The Use of Network Analysis to Study Complex Animal Communication Systems: A Study on Nightingale Song." *Proceedings of the Royal Society B: Biological Sciences* 281 (2014): 1–9.

Weitz, Morris. "The Role of Theory in Aesthetics." *Journal of Aesthetics and Art Criticism* 15, no. 1 (1956): 27–35.

Wemelsfelder, Françoise. "The Scientific Validity of Subjective Concepts in Models of Animal Welfare." *Applied Animal Behaviour Science* 53 (1997): 75–88.

White, Capt. S. A. *Into the Dead Heart: An Ornithological Trip through Central Australia.* 1914. Adelaide: Friends of the State Library of South Australia, 1914.

Wieneke, Jo. *Birds of Magnetic Island.* Queensland: Author, 2002.

Wiggins, Geraint A., Peter Tyack, Constance Scharff, and Martin Rohrmeier. "The Evolutionary Roots of Creativity: Mechanisms and Motivations." *Philosophical Transactions of the Royal Society B* 370, no. 1,664 (2015): 1–9.

Wilbrecht, Linda, and Fernando Nottebohm. "Vocal Learning in Birds and Humans." *Mental Retardation and Developmental Disabilities Research Reviews* 9 (2003): 135–148.

Williams, D. C. "Acoustic Space." *Explorations*, February 1955, 15–20.

Williams, Raymond. *Keywords: A Vocabulary of Culture and Society.* Glasgow: Fontana, 1976.

Wilson, Edward O. *Biophilia.* Cambridge, MA: Harvard University Press, 1984.

——. *Consilience.* New York: Alfred A. Knopf, 1998.

Witchell, Charles A. *The Evolution of Bird-Song, with Observations on the Influence of Heredity and Imitation.* London: Adam and Charles Black, 1896.

Wood, Ada. "A Friend in Need." *Queenslander* (Brisbane, QLD), 12 January 1928: 44. Accessed 22 June 2011. http://nla.gov.au/nla.news-article22942929.

Wood, G. A. "Tool Use by the Palm Cockatoo *Probosciger aterrimus* during Display." *Corella* 8, no. 4 (1984): 94–95.

Wright, Anthony A., Jacquelyne J. Rivers, Stewart H. Hulse, Melissa Shyan, and Julie J. Neiworth. "Music Perception and Octave Generalization in Rhesus Monkeys." *Journal of Experimental Psychology: General* 129, no. 3 (2000): 291–307.

Wright, Judith. *Birds.* Canberra: National Library of Australia, 2003.

Zbikowski, Lawrence M. "Musicology, Cognitive Science, and Metaphor: Reflections on Michael Spitzer's *Metaphor and Musical Thought.*" *Musica Humana* 1, no. 1 (2009): 81–104.

"Zoömusicology." Accessed 5 August 2013. http://www.zoömusicology.com.

INDEX

Page numbers in italics refer to figures and examples.

Aboriginal Australians, 14, 38–42, 179n38, 102, 200, 266, 281n17; Aboriginal song, 39–42; circular breathing technique in music, 144n8; music as aide-mémoire for, 199; names for pied butcherbirds, 40, 97–98, 110n8; sacred sites, 1, 112. *See also* Alyawarr language group; Anmatyerr language group; Luritja (Aboriginal) song

Abraham, Otto, 63

absolute (or perfect) pitch, 56, 72, 76, 155–156, 159, 238

accelerando, 150

accent, 154–155, 168, 290

Acera, Santi, 264–265

acoustemology, 9

"Acoustic Ecology and the Experimental Music Tradition" (Dunn), 257

additive process, 98–100, *100*, 105, 108, 132, 163. *See also* cells; combinatoriality

Adorno, Theodor, 205n16

Adventures of Sherlock Holmes, The (Doyle), 209

advertising calls and songs, 94, 125, 128. *See also* species call

"Aesthetic Content of Bird Song, The" (Hall-Craggs), 228

African music, 64, 161, 164

Afro-Cuban music, 11, 164

Agawu, Kofi, 64

Albert's lyrebird (*Menura alberti*), 53–55, 56, 142

Alice Springs, Australia, 12, 40, 101, 102, *102*, 104, 108, 125–126, 128, 135–136, 174, 200, 256n29; Araluen Arts Centre, 112; Desert Park, 106; Herbarium, 266; Honeymoon Gap, 219; Telegraph Station, 96–97

Alland, Alexander, Jr., 22

Alyawarr language group, 39

amphibians, 263, 267

amplitude, 27, 86, 91, 124

anacrusis, 150

Analysing Musical Multimedia (Cook), 53

Andersen, Johannes C., 68–69, *69*, 71

animals, 6, 13, 25, 26, 37, 38, 66, 176, 178n21, 185, 189, 191, 194, 199, 213, 228, 237, 238; as artists, 22, 230n16, 270; biodiversity crisis and, 260–270; in children's literature, 42; cognition and, 221, 271–276, 277; communication systems of, 222–223, 262; consciousness and, 221; definition of, 5, 270; didjeridoo impersonations of animal sounds,

40; ethnomusicology and, 8; humans as, 5, 36; as individuals, 5, 37, 38, 237, 270; kinship with, 42, 46, 52n82, 269, 270; music and the human/animal divide, 188, 189–191, 202, 225, 226, 228, 248, 271; musical notation and, 61; musical properties of animal sounds, 5, 6, 7, 40, 195, 278; performing with, 250–252; as teachers, 125, 152, 152, 173, 175–177, 178n8, 230n16; as utilitarian resource for humans, 212, 277–278; as whole sentient beings, 35–36; welfare and, 13, 237, 250

Anmatyerr language group, 39

Antarctic beech (Nothofagus moorei), 55

anthrophony, 77

anthropocentrism, 7, 190

anthropology/anthropologists, 17n28, 22, 60, 63, 201, 202, 250, 252

anthropomorphism, 35–38, 46–47, 52n82, 69, 165, 214, 272

antiphonal songs, 123, 125, 146n27. See also duet singing; ensemble songs; hocket

apostlebird (Struthidea cinerea), 183

Araya-Salas, Marcelo, 215–216

Archaeopteryx, 28

arpeggios, 83n74, 154, 155, 158, 183

art, definitions of, 200–203

Artamidae family, 28

Artistic Animal, The (Alland), 22

art music, Western, 62, 64, 161, 190, 193, 210; authority of, 202–203; concept of originality and, 185–186; hierarchical structure in, 223–225; as persistent point of reference, 217. See also classical music, Western

Ashby, Edwin, 265–266

Atherton Tablelands, 84

auctioneering, 187, 248

Australian Bird Book, An (Leach), 19

Australian magpie (Cracticus [Gymnorhina] tibicen), 28, 30, 34, 44, 45, 93, 115, 117, 120, 142, 264; sex of singing birds, 123, 225; unique motifs in repertoire of, 220; voice confused for pied butcherbird, 117, 142–143

Australian raven (Corvus coronoides), 97, 261

authenticity, recording technology and, 58

authorship, 186

avant-garde music, 62–63

Axtell, Harold H., 82n47

Bach, J. S., 149, 151, 185, 249

balance, 98, 99, 102, 134, 149, 152, 161, 164, 168–170, 169

Balcombe, Jonathan, 271

Banksy, 201

Bartók, Béla, 58, 60–61, 80n21, 83n59, 83n72; folksong and, 60, 109; on material and intellectual equipment, 76

Baylis, Tony, 245–246

beak claps, 31, 92, 93, 97, 284

Beautiful Bird Songs from around the World (British Library), 246

Beethoven, Ludwig van, 6, 36–37, 153, 201

Bell, Alan, 31

bell-bird (Anthornis melanura), transcription of song, 69

Bell Telephone Laboratories, 27

"Bemsha Swing" (Monk and Best), 166

Berio, Luciano, 161

Bevis, John, 66

Biber, Heinrich Ignaz Franz von, 151

bioacoustics, 9, 259

biodiversity crisis, 15, 259–270

biology/biologists, 5, 6, 19, 23–27, 37, 38, 71, 176, 204n4, 215, 216, 222, 225, 226, 227, 238, 240, 262. See also ethology/ethologists; neuroscience/neuroscientists; ornithology/ornithologists; science/scientists

BioMusic, 177n1

biomusicology, 9

biophony, 77

Bird Calls of the Inland (Australian birdsong recording), 59

Bird-Esk (Taylor), 281n13

Bird Fancyer's Delight, The, 24

Birds as Individuals (Howard), 36–37

Birds of North America: A Guide to Field Identification (Robbings, Bruun, and Zim), 72

birdsong, 4–5, 7, 10, 13, 109, 186, 187, 190–191, 192, 200, 202, 211, 237, 252; basic elements of, 23–28; biodiversity crisis and, 259–270; as biomarker, 24;

composers' appropriation of, 242–247, 255n20; female song, 25, 48n16, 117, 123, 156–157, 225, 226; language and, 189, 222–225; male birdsong, 24, 25, 54, 115, 117, 123, 124, 214, 225, 226–227; reasons for status as music, 203, 243, 276–280; recursion in, 223–225; sound art and, 161, 175, 198. *See also* notation, musical; songbirds

birdsong as music, objections to, 203, 211–212; erroneous, 212–215; functional, 225–229; illogical, 217–222; "rules" of music and, 215–217, 231n28. *See also* human exceptionalism; music, definitions of

black-backed butcherbird (*Cracticus mentalis*), 28

blackbird (*Turdus merula*), 71, 82n53, 220–221, 225, 232n42

black butcherbird (*Cracticus quoyi*), 28, 31

black-capped chickadee (*Poecile atricapillus*), 155, 156

black cockatoo, 180, 279

black-fronted butcherbird (*Cracticus nigrogularius*), 41, 210

Blacking, John, 63

black kite (*Milvus migrans*), 97

black-throated butcherbird, 29

black-throated crow-shrike, 29

bluegrass fiddling, 11

Blue Mountains, 11, 22, 104

blue notes, 2, 215

Blue Wrens and the Butcher-Bird, The (Dixon), 255n20

Blyth's reed warbler (*Acrocephalus dumetorum*), 6

Böhner, Jörg, 231n22

Boléro (Ravel), 164

Bondesen, Poul, 72–73, 82n57

boobook owl (*Ninox boobook*), 97, 106

Boucher, Neil, 88

bowerbirds, 20–22, 261

Brahms, Johannes, 186, 223

Brand, Albert R., 27, 82n47

break-o'-day-boy, 29

breeding songs, 53, 115, 118, 119, 122, 174, 225

Bregman, Albert S., 134, 151

bricolage, 185

bridge, 7

broad-spectrum (complex, buzzy, or "noisy") notes, 86–87, 88, 89, 90, 90, 93, 95, 108, 155, 161, 274

Brown, Steven, 190

brown thrasher (*Toxostoma rufum*), 220

Brumm, Henrik, 216

Bruun, Bertel, 72

budgerigars, 180

Burton, Frederick R., 83n72

Bush Miniatures (Tate), 109, 255n20

bush stone-curlew (*Burhinus grallarius*), 103

Busoni, Ferruccio, 186

"Butcher-Bird, The" (Rodgers, from *Weaver of Fictions*), 246

butcherbirds: black butcherbird, black-backed butcherbird, 28; 28, 31; black-fronted butcherbird, 41, 210; black-throated butcherbird, 29; grey butcherbird, 28, 31, 76, 117, 142–143, 153. *See also* pied butcherbird (*Cracticus nigrogularis*)

Cage, John, 78

call and response, 123, 161–162, 176

"Call Her Butcher Bird" (Kelly), 42–43

call-in-song. *See* pied butcherbird, notes and calls; species call

calls, distinguished from songs, 23, 25, 98, 227

camels, feral, 103, 110n14, 113

Cameron, William Bruce, 240

canaries, 24

cane toad (*Bufo marinus*), 262–263

canon, 161, 164–166

Caro, T. M., 176

Carrillo, Julián, 157

Carroll, Lewis, 212

Carruthers, Peter, 221

Carter, Thomas, 34, 116

casuarina tree (*Casuarina equisetifolia*), 141

cats, feral and domestic, 108, 266–267

cat-scolding calls, 93, 94

Cavalleria Rusticana (Mascagni), 173

Cavell, Stanley, 189

cells, 109, 161. *See also* additive process; combinatoriality

centonization, 153

Central Australia, 41, 108, 256n33, 257. *See also* Alice Springs, Australia; George Gill Range; Glen Helen Resort; Great Sandy Desert; Kings Creek Station; Nehwaven Wildlife Sanctuary; Ormiston Gorge; Ross River Resort
chaffinch (*Fringilla coelebs*), 69, 73
Chaiken, Marthaleah, 231n22
chanting, 187
chatter song, 124. *See also* subsong
chestnut-crowned babbler (*Pomatostomus ruficeps*), 223
China, musical notation in, 61
chip sound, 71, 91, 134, 141, 168, 176, 280
Chisholm, Alec H., 34–35, 91, 266
Chomsky, Noam, 222
Chopin, Frédéric, 138, 149, 170
chords, 75, 154, 155, 158, 159, 168, 183, 193, 210, 211, 220
"chromaticisms of duration," 6
citizen science/scientists, 35, 38, 43, 240
classical music, Indian, 11, 161, 164
classical music, Western, 7, 11, 49n24, 88, 170, 224; functionality in, 228; mimicry in, 186. *See also* art music, Western
Clifton, Thomas, 197
climate change, 252, 260
coastal taipan (*Oxyuranus scutellatus*), 121, 147
cockatiels, 180
cock-crow, 5
coda, 7, 108, 120, 121
Coker, Wilson, 192–193, 206n34
Collins, Nicolas, 198
Coltrane, John, 211
combinatoriality, 35, 40, 68, 115, 130, 132, 134, 135, 136, 143, 161, 163–164, 183, 222, 225, 274. *See also* additive process; cells
common blackbird (*Turdus merula*), 71, 72
Compendium Musicae (Descartes), 197
composition: agency in, 186; appropriation of birdsong in, 82n53, 162, 170, 242–250; by birds, 173; processes of, 132; rules of, 215; transcription and, 61; universe as, 194; Western canon and, 226. *See also* Messiaen, Olivier; Messiaen, Olivier, works of
conformal motive, 214

Connor, Steven, 199
consciousness, 22, 221, 271, 274
consonance, 215, 216, 231n26
contact calls, 94. *See also* species call
contour (melodic), 61, 65, 67, 77, 94, 95, 126, 128, 134, 138, 155–156, 193, 245; mnemonics and, 61
Cook, Nicholas, 53
Cook, Will Marion, 150
Cooke, Deryck, 193
cooperative breeding, 31
Corbet, Chris, 146n30
Corsaro, Il (Verdi), 173
Cotterill, Jim, 267
counterpoint, 120, 123, 164–165, 220. *See also* dawn chorus
countersinging, 119, 165, 166
Craig, Wallace, 25, 83n72, 225, 227
Crist, Eileen, 37
crystallized song, 24
currawongs, 28, 29, 97, 142, 175, 279
Curtis, Sydney, 53, 55–61, 79n6, 146n30
Cutler, Chris, 198, 203

Darwin, Charles, 38, 191, 215, 227, 270, 273
Davies, Stephen, 201
Dawn: A Symphonic Rhapsody (Tate), 255n20
dawn chorus, 106, 115, 120, 125, 170, 219; biodiversity crisis and, 268; contrapuntal events of, 120; human music compared to, 220; improvisation in, 174–175; sung by both sexes, 116
death adder (*Acanthophis laevis*), 141
Debussy, Claude, 6, 199
Dehaene, Stanislas, 176
Dennett, Daniel, 37
Descartes, René, 197
Descola, Philippe, 17n28
desert country, 12, 29
Despret, Vinciane, 52n82
Deutsch, Diana, 204n13
de Waal, Frans B. M., 37, 213
diatonic scale, 56
Dickie, George, 201
Dingle, Christopher, 76
dingoes, 40, 103, 105, 113, 248, 267–268
dinosaurs, 28–29
displacement patterns, 165

dissonance, 216, 231n27

diurnal (day) songs, 115, 122–125, 128–129; individual phrases of, 129–130, *131*, *132*, *133*, 134–136; sung by both sexes, 116. *See also* antiphonal songs; dawn chorus; duet singing; ensemble songs; hocket

Dixon, Hugh, 255n20

dominance calls, 94. *See also* species call

Doolittle, Emily, 216, 245

Dooren, Thom van, 49n33

double notes, 23, *86*, 88, 108, 127, 171

Doyle, Arthur Conan, 209

drinking songs, 162

drought, 1, 121, 258, 259, 260–262, 266

duet singing, 116, 123, 124, 136–138, 140, *137–140*; scalar motion in, 159, *159*; transposition and, 156. *See also* antiphonal songs; ensemble songs; hocket

Dukas, Paul, 5

Dunn, David, 257

Dutton, Denis, 22

"Duty of Preservation Concept," 259

dynamic envelope, 235, 246

Eastern brown snake, 147, 183

eastern koel (*Eudynamys orientalis*), 235

eastern whipbird (*Psophodes olivaceus*), 175

ecomusicology, 9

Edgar website, 260, 262

Einstein, Albert, 235

electronic music, 62–63, 64–65, 92, 213, 231n27

Elgar, Edward, 33

elimination, syntactical procedure of, 6

Ellington, Duke, 150, 199

Elliott, Brian, 40

Emotion and Meaning in Music (Meyer), 192

ensemble songs, 35, 104, 116, 122–125, 134, 136, 158, 161, 170, 175, 195, 219, 226, 250, 281n13; dawn chorus and, 106, 120; description and analysis of, 136–138, 140, *137–140*, 171; pitch in, 156; SLD2 motif in, 108; species call in, 98, *99*; structure of, 161–162; synchronization of, 274. *See also* antiphonal songs; duet singing; hocket

ethnocentrism, 7, 8, 225

ethnography, 4, 11

ethnomusicology/ethnomusicologists, 8, 9, 16n4, 39, 40, 60, 76, 77, 215, 259, 271, 278; Hungarian school, 83n59; musical notation in, 63–65; "statistical universals" and, 188

ethology/ethologists, 6, 23, 24, 25–26, 27, 37, 46, 51n59, 63, 72, 74, 78, 226, 236, 237; animal consciousness and, 271, 274; definition of song elements and, 98; syntax of birdsong and, 215; terms used for birdsong, 119, 123, 124, 165, 187, 213; Western music notation and, 75. *See also* biology/biologists; neuroscience/neuroscientists; ornithology/ornithologists; science/scientists

Europe, musical notation in, 61–62

European starling (*Sturnus vulgaris*), 155, 221, 231n22

Evolution of Bird-Song, with Observations on the Influence of Heredity and Imitation, The (Witchell), 66, 68

exposition, 7

Fabbri, Franco, 144

fair use, 186

Fallon, Robert, 57

fanfares, 65, 118, 125, 148, 154, *154*

fast Fourier transform (FFT), 73

Feld, Steven, 40, 219–220

Field Book of Wild Birds & Their Music (Mathews), 68

field guides, 20, 31, 32, 35, 66, 72, 82n51

field recordings, 57, 245, 248, 259–260

fieldwork, 9, 43, 46, 104, 135, 141, 182; fieldwork preparation, 11–13; recordings and, 64

Filip, Miroslav, 5, 73

Fink, Robert, 224

Fitch, W. Tecumseh, 273

flight calls, 94. *See also* species call

folk music/songs, 11, 40, 60, 109, 151

food-begging calls, 93, 94

fork-leaved corkwood (*Hakea divaricata*), 180

free forms, 161

friarbirds (leatherheads), 91

Gadagkar, Raghavendra, 272, 282n29

galah (*Cacatua roseicapilla*), 1–2

Galison, Peter, 27
gap-fill, 127. *See also* post-skip reversal
Gardiner, William, 66
Garstang, Walter, 68
Gell, Alfred, 202
Generative Theory of Tonal Music, A (Ler-
    dahl and Jackendoff), 223–224
geophony, 77
"George" (lyrebird), 53–55
George Gill Range, 258
gesture, 246
ghost gum (*Corymbia aparrerinja*), 257
"Giant Steps" (Coltrane), 211
gibbons, 23, 239–240
Glass, Gloria, 155
Glass, Philip, 163
Glen Helen Resort, 40–41, 264
gliding tones, 42. *See also* glissando;
    portamentos
glissando, 75, 76, 77. *See also* portamentos
Goehr, Alexander, 60
Goehr, Lydia, 185–186
Golijov, Osvaldo, 186
Gondwana, supercontinent of, 28
Gould, John, 29
Gould, Stephen Jay, 269
gramophone, 64
graphics, 27, 61, 63, 65, 66, 74, 75, 85
Gray, Patricia, 149
Great Barrier Reef, 12, 128
great bowerbird (*Chlamydera nuchali*), 21
great grey shrike (*Lanius excubitor*), 29
Great Sandy Desert, 121
Great Treatise on Supreme Sound, 61
Greer, Germaine, 92
Gregorian chant, 153
grey butcherbird (*Cracticus torquatus*), 28,
    31, 76, 117, 142–143, 153
grey shrike-thrush (*Collurincia harmon-
    ica*), 142, 143, 164, 165, 219
Grisey, Gérard, 161
Grooved Whale (Walker), 252
Grove Dictionary of Music, The, 188
Guido of Arezzo, 80n29
Güntürkün, Onur, 273–274
Gurney, Edmund, 191–192, 197

Hába, Alois, 157
Halafoff, K. C., 7

Hall, Freddie, 255n20
Hall-Craggs, Joan, 72, 149, 228
Hall's Creek (Taylor), 246
*Handbook of Australian, New Zealand &
    Antarctic Birds* (HANZAB), 115–116,
    118, 122
Hannan, Michael, 256n29
Hanslick, Eduard, 191, 212
Haraway, Donna, 84, 277
harmonics, 61, 88, 94, 95
"harmony of the spheres," 193
Hartshorne, Charles, 91, 149, 162, 211
Hauser, Marc D., 176, 225
Haydn, Joseph, 132
Heifetz, Jascha, 157
Helena, Edith, 173
Hendrix, Jimmy, 170
hermit thrush (*Catharus guttatus*), 73, 190,
    216, 234n69
Herzog, George, 60
Hill, Peter, 57
Hindemith, Paul, 207n39
Hindley, David, 74
hip-hop, 197
hocket, 123, 138, 151, 162, 211. *See also* an-
    tiphonal songs; duet singing; ensemble
    songs
Hoene-Wroński, Józef Maria, 199
hoop pine (*Araucaria cunninghamii*), 33,
    55, 141
Hornbostel, Erich M. von, 63
Howard, Len, 36–37
huia (*Heteralocha acutirostris*), 72
Hukwe song, in musical notation, 63–64
human exceptionalism, 10, 124, 203, 212,
    234, 237; narcissism of, 270–271
hummingbirds, 23
Humphrey, N. K., 276
Hunt, Richard, 71
Hurford, James R., 223
Huron, David, 127, 162, 277
Hutchinson, John, 153
Hymen, E. L., 117

imitation, 109, 185, 187, 243. *See also*
    mimicry
immature birds, 30, 78, 174; food-begging
    calls, 93; mimicry and, 142; nocturnal
    song and, 119; rehearsal singing by,

95; singing lessons for, 175–176, 177; species call and, 100, 110n11; subsong and, 116
improvisation, 26, 123, 161, 174–175, 217, 245
Ingraham, Sydney E., 27
interjections, 118, 122, 125
interphrase interval, 78, 118, 120, 124, 128, 141, 199, 245, 247, 248
intervals, 77, 81n45, 95, 100, 101, 126, 137, 138, 140, 151, 155, 158, 159, 167, 167, 215, 216, 231n27, 231n28. See also octave; perfect fifth; perfect fourth; semitone; tritone
intonation, 73, 157; absolute pitch and, 155; just intonation, 157–158, 215, 246
introduction, 7
Ives, Charles, 186
Iyer, Vijay, 224

Jackendoff, Ray, 192, 223–224
jackeroo, 29, 41
Jacopo da Bologna, 221
Japan, musical notation in, 61–62
jazz, 11, 15, 65, 124, 128, 149, 210–211; appropriation of birdsong and, 245; mimicry in, 185; ostinato in, 164
Johnson, Gayle, 146n30
juvenile birds. See immature birds

Kaluli people, 40, 219–220
kangaroos, 40, 84, 105, 113, 183, 248, 261, 267. See also wallabies
Kaplan, Gisela, 214, 225, 273
Karkoschka, Erhard, 59–60
keening, 187
Kelly, Aileen, 42–43
Kidner, David W., 18n31
Kings Creek Station, 257
Kircher, Athanasius, 5, 66, 73, 132
Kirtland's warbler (Dendroica kirtlandi), 81n47
Kitcher, Philip, 272
kites, butcherbird mobbing of, 97
Kivy, Peter, 214–215
Klangfarbenmelodie, 159–160, 160, 249. See also melody; pitch; portamento; timbre (tone color)
Kodály, Zoltán, 83n59

koel, 97, 235
kookaburras, 40, 129, 175, 236, 262, 279, 280
Korea, musical notation in, 61
Kramer, Lawrence, 226
Kroodsma, Donald E., 26
Kuhn, Thomas, 253n3
Kunst, Jaap, 64
kurbaru, 40

Lamington National Park (Queensland), 53, 168
landscape, 14, 15, 262
Langer, Susanne, 189
language: body, 35; consciousness and, 271; distancing humans from animals, 37–38; of mathematics, 240–242; music and, 187–189, 190, 193, 194, 204n13, 205n16, 205n21, 224, 225, 228, 239–240; music as the international language, 62; recursion in language, 222–223
Language of Music, The (Cooke), 193
Latz, Peter, 266
Leach, John Albert, 19
Leopold, Aldo, 10, 14, 236
Lerdahl, Fred, 192, 223–224
Levine, George, 38, 52n82
List, George, 8, 247
Liszt, Franz, 186
Living with Birds (Howard), 36
Ljubinkovic, Nenad, 40
Loriod, Yvonne, 55, 56
low-volume song, 124. See also subsong
Lumholtz's tree-kangaroo (Dendrolagus lumholtzi), 84
Lumsdaine, David, 10, 243–244, 256n29
Luritja (Aboriginal) song, 39–40
lyrebirds, 7, 53–56, 79n3, 79n5, 142, 184

MacDonnell Ranges, 102–103, 244
Mâche, François-Bernard, 5–7, 10, 188–189
Magnetic Island, 32, 33, 88, 128, 135; Arthur Bay, 140–141; cane toads as introduced pest on, 262–263; Magnetic Island National Park, 135; Nelly Bay, 164
magpie-lark (Grallina cyanoleuca), 156, 235
main theme, 7
Malm, William P., 215–16

mammals, 5, 84–85, 138, 155, 248; killed
by domestic and feral cats, 267; marine,
23, 251. *See also* cats, feral and domes-
tic; dingoes; gibbons; kangaroos; red-
necked pademelon (*Thylogale thetis*);
wallabies; whales
Mandala 4 (Lumsdaine), 244
mantras, 187
Marchesini, Roberto, 46
Marett, Allan, 39
Margulis, Elizabeth Hellmuth, 189
Marian-Bălașa, Marin, 77
Marler, Peter, 231n22, 236
marsh warbler (*Acrocephalus palustris*),
6, 220
Martinelli, Dario, 7, 245, 274
Mateship with Birds (Chisholm), 34–35
mathematics, 132, 134, 193, 194, 195,
206n38, 240–242
Mathews, Freya, 68, 281n17
Maturana, Humberto R., 222
McClary, Susan, 145n17, 200, 224
McClintock, Barbara, 249
McDermott, Josh, 225
McGilchrist, Iain, 22, 271
melisma, 152, *152*
melody, 33, 34, 134, 137, 138, 143, 149,
150–159, 204n13, 243, 246; chimeric,
152–153; compound melodic line,
151–152, *151*; iconic human melodies,
153–154, 178n13; melodic expectancies,
151; pitch and, 127, 138. *See also* accents;
contour (melodic); fanfares; gap-fill;
Klangfarbenmelodie; melisma; post-skip
reversal
memory, 66, 130, 132, 274, 277; birdsong
notation and, 71; mimicry and, 120;
muscle memory versus pitch memory,
156; sabotage of, 132
merengue, 11
Merker, Björn, 214, 218, 226, 239–240,
254n11
Merriam, Alan P., 259
Mersenne, Marin, 132
Messiaen, Olivier, 5, 79n6, 247; birdsong
recordings and transcriptions of, 55–61,
71, 75, 79n11; "chromaticisms of duration" of, 6

Messiaen, Olivier, works of: Éclairs sur
l'Au-Delà, 56, 75–76, 255n20; *Oiseaux
exotiques*, 57; *Réveil des oiseaux*,
57–58; *Traité de rythme, de couleur, et
d'ornithologie*, 57
meter, 54, 60, 149, 150, 155, 249
Meyer, Leonard B., 127, 151, 192, 239,
271, 276
microtones/microtonality, 77, 137, 157, 158
Miller, Loye, 71
Mills, Irving, 199
mimicry, 68, 83n74, 97, 117, 120, 122, 128,
143, 146n30, 184, 226, 257, 268; appended to formal song, 121–122; definition of music and, 184–187; description
and analysis of, 140–142; difference
identified and flattened by, 190; lyrebird, 53, 55; melody and, 152; scalar
passages in, 158; subsong with, 124–125,
135; timbre and, 161; virtuosity and,
170. *See also* imitation
Mithen, Steven, 190
mnemonics, 61, 68, 70, 82n51; birdsong
notation and, 66; for phrases in butcherbird song, 119; syllabic, 74; timbre and,
91, 92
mobbing calls, 43, 92, 94, 97, 173, 184, 273,
284. *See also* species call
Monk, Thelonius, 166
Moreton Bay fig (*Ficus macrophylla*), 55
"Morning in the Gully" (Tate, from *Suite
Joyous*), 109, 255n20
Morphy, Howard, 201
Morton, Timothy, 15
Mozart, W. A., 33, 88, 132, 138, 223
music, 4, 6, 100, 109, 118, 123, 127, 140,
144, 211, 212, 213, 224, 236, 238, 239,
241, 242, 243, 253, 257, 259, 270, 275,
276, 277, 278, 279; birdsong and whale
song linked to, 6, 149, 223; call-and-response in, 123, 161–162; combinatorial
games in, 132, 134; cultural practices
and, 9; evolution toward complexity,
220; interspecies, 251–252, 256n33;
materiality of the experience of, 4–5;
as mathematical art, 16n3; naming and
owning, 9, 17n19; natural sciences and,
82n57; nature-culture relation and, 13–

14; oral tradition and, 8, 11, 62, 217, 239; origins of, 6, 190, 204n4, 240, 243, 276, 279; recursion in, 223–225; religion and, 184–185; "rules" of, 215–217, 231n28; transmitted from birds to humans, 40

music, definitions of, 7, 8, 177, 199–200, 207n54, 212, 215, 225, 228; alterity and, 195–199; correlates in definitions of art, 200–203, 207n53; evocation of emotion and, 192–193; formalism in music and, 191–192; human/animal distinction and, 63, 189–191, 202, 271; language and, 187–189, 204n13, 205n16; as map of territorial disputes, 189–199; mimicry versus originality, 184–187; music and the superhuman, 193–195, 203, 206n38, 207n39; music/noise distinction, 195–197; music/nonmusic distinction, 197; music/silence distinction, 198–199, 207n50; music/sound distinction, 197–198. *See also* birdsong as music, objections to

Music, Myth and Nature (Mâche), 6

musicality, 7, 8, 10, 24, 26, 36, 42, 68, 91, 170, 174, 199, 225, 227, 241, 253; ethnomusicology and, 9; zoömusicology and, 236, 238–240

Musical Offering, The (Bach), 249

musician wren (*Cyphorhinus arada*), 216

Music in Neuroscience conference (Monte Verità, Switzerland), 241–242

Musicking (Small), 180

Music of Nature, The (Gardiner), 66

musicology/musicologists, 4, 5, 7, 8, 26–27, 36, 40, 57, 58, 59, 62, 64, 73, 75, 76, 77, 78, 123, 127, 144, 185, 187, 188, 189, 192, 193, 204n4, 221, 224, 226, 233n56, 238, 242, 252, 259, 277, 278; analysis as combat zone in, 224; ideology and, 199–200; natural sciences and, 236, 237, 253; "salvage musicology," 74, 278. *See also* biomusicology; ethnomusicology/ethnomusicologists; zoömusicology/zoömusicologists

Musik der Natur (Tiessen), 71

Musurgia Universalis (Kircher), 66, 67, 132

mutual recognition calls, 94. *See also* species call

Myall Lakes National Park (New South Wales), 65

Nagorcka, Ron, 246

natural sciences, 4, 38, 47, 82n57, 227; music notation and, 75; musicology and, 236, 237, 253. *See also* biology/biologists; ethology/ethologists; neuroscience/neuroscientists; ornithology/ornithologists; science/scientists

nature-culture relation, 13–16, 17n28, 18n31; human exceptionalism and, 270–271; songbird territories and, 24; songbirds' possession of culture, 213

Neanderthals, music and, 190

neuroscience/neuroscientists, 27, 100, 124, 138, 176, 213, 214, 219, 225, 231n22, 232n47, 272, 273, 274; Music in Neuroscience conference, 241–242. *See also* biology/biologists; ethology/ethologists; ornithology/ornithologists; science/scientists

Newhaven Wildlife Sanctuary, 121–22

New South Wales, 12, 65, 85, 263

New Zealand, 68, 69, 69, 71, 74, 115

nightingale (*Luscinia megarhynchos*), 24, 74, 74, 220

nightingale wren (*Microcerculus philomela*), 215

Noces, Les (Stravinsky), 6

nocturnal songs, 35, 101, 102, 104, 105, 106, 108, 115, 117–122, 125–128, 127, 136, 168, 169, 219, 250, 259, 262. *See also* solo singing

noise, music and, 195–197, 214–215

noise pollution, 77, 262

noisy friarbird (*Philemon corniculatus*), 153

Nollman, Jim, 251–252

North American Bird Songs—a World of Music (Bondesen), 73

Northern Territory, 3, 113, 267. *See also* Alice Springs, Australia

North Queensland, 12, 44, 120; Bowen, 114–115, 235; Clermont, 209; Croydon, 260–262; Cumberland Dam, 113; Etheridge Riverbed, 170; Gregory Downs, 113–114, 180, 183; Leichhardt River, 194; Mary Creek, 147; Mount Surprise,

279; Point Karumba, 172–173; Wills Developmental Road, 180; Yungaburra, 84, 94. *See also* Magnetic Island

notation, musical, 7, 28, 76–77, 78; automatic, 77; birdsong transcription (notation) and, 2, 5, 6, 7, 27, 58–60, 62, 65–66, 67, 68–75, 69, 70, 72–74, 77, 82n51, 135, 163–164, 190, 246–248, 250; as blueprint or report, 76; in ethnomusicology, 60–61, 63–65; mechanisms of, 61–63, 80n27, 80n29; music literacy and, 70; natural sciences and, 75. *See also* Messiaen, Olivier

Ntaria Ladies Choir, 41–42

octave, 83n74, 94, 97, 100, 110n6, 140, 143; ascending, 101, *139*, *151*, *157*, 164, 175, 216; descending, 138, *139*, 148, *157*, 168, 280; octave equivalence, 156–157; octave generalization, 138, 156, 178n22. *See also* intervals

ocularcentrism, 27

Oldys, Henry, 36, 227, 234n69

oral tradition, 8, 11, 62, 217

organ-bird, 29, 42

originality, 184–187, 202, 271

Ormiston Gorge, 244–245, 255n21

ornithology/ornithologists, 7, 8, 27, 28, 29, 36, 104, 115, 241, 265; Australian, 34, 38, 41, 79n6, 141, 146n30, 153, 155, 256; birdsong notation and, 68, 69, 71, 72, 81n44; citizen science and, 43, 240; collection versus protection, 265–266; definition of birdsong and, 25; numeracy and, 240–241; song types in ornithological literature, 115–117. *See also* biology/biologists; citizen science/scientists; ethology/ethologists; neuroscience/neuroscientists; science/scientists

ornithomusicology, 5, 9–10

ostinato, 161, 164, *165*, 219

Oxford Dictionary of Music, The, 188

Paganini, Niccolò, 170, 171

Page-Wood, Gladys, 81n45

palm cockatoo (*Probosciger aterrimus*), 213

Papua New Guinea, 20

parody, 185

parrots, 1, 23, 66. *See also* black cockatoo; cockatiels; galah (*Cacatua roseicapilla*); palm cockatoo (*Probosciger aterrimus*); rainbow lorikeet (*Trichoglossus moluccanus*); sulphur-crested cockatoo (*Cacatua galerita*)

Partch, Harry, 157

pastiche, 185

Patel, Aniruddh, 205n21, 213

peaceful dove (*Geopelia placida*), 153

percussion, 7

perfect fifth, 143. *See also* intervals

perfect fourth, 127–128, 168, *169*. *See also* intervals

Petri, Jana, 124

Petrovic, Milena, 40

phrase endings, 150, 161, 166–168, *166–167*, 281n13

physics, 206n38, 242, 256n32

pied butcherbird (*Cracticus nigrogularis*), 2–4, *3*, 8, *196*, 251, 275; Aboriginal people and, 39–42; alternative names for, 29, 40, 42–43, 97–98, 110n8; biodiversity crisis and threats to, 259–270; cognition and, 271–276; commercial recordings of, 3, 243–246; habitat, 11, 12, 30, 31, 49n33, 78, 112, 264; human musical compositions influenced by, 76, 109, 162, 170, 243–250, 252; listening to recordings of, 6, 204n4, 240, 250–251; nests/nestlings of, 30–31, *31*, 32, 42, 45–46, 93, 97, 116, 117, 120, 122, 250; in ornithological reportage, 28–33; stories of human interactions with, 1–2, 33, 34–35, 41–46, 70–71, 91, 92, 106–107, 117, 119, 150, 153–154, 155, 170–171, 174, 175–176, 178n13, 192, 195, 219, 235–236, 243, 244, 245–246, 250–251, 256n33, 263–265, 268–269, 279–280; study of birds in situ, 10, 12, 46, 250, 272; as teacher, 10–11; voice, 33–35

pied butcherbird, notes and calls, 2, 65, 75–79; basic note structure, 85–86, *86–87*, 88; calls, 92–98, *93*, *96*; calls in song, 98, *99*, 100–109, *100–102*; short, repeated notes, 88–91, *89*, *90*; timbre, 91–92. *See also* SLD2 (short-long descending second) motif; species call pied butcherbird, songs: "accent" (dialect) in, 117; conventions and preferences, 142–144, 144n7, 146n31; diurnal (day) singing, 122–125; ensemble song, 136–140, *137–140*; melody and pitch in, 150–159, *151–152, 154, 157–159*; musical activities and behaviors, 173–176; nocturnal singing, 117–122; (re)compositions and performances of, 247–253; rhythm and meter, 150; solo songs, 125–136, *127, 131, 133*; song types, 115–125; structure in, 161–170, *163, 165–167, 169*; virtuosity, 170–171. *See also* antiphonal songs; diurnal (day) songs, duet singing; ensemble songs; hocket; nocturnal songs; solo singing

Pied Butcher-Bird, The (Hall), 255n20

pied butcherbirds (nicknamed individuals): "Arthur," 141; "Buddha of Spirey Creek," 24; "Claire," 211; "Flapper," 251; "Monty," 211; "Ross Stuart," 126, 128, 129, 136, 163; "Two Tree," 129–130, *131, 132, 134–136, 152, 163,* 224

"Pied Butcherbirds of Spirey Creek" (Lumsdaine), 243–44

pied crow-shrike (*Cracticus picatus*), 29

pitch, 7, 77, 83n74, 88, 106, 134, 151, 157, 183, 204n13, 216, 223, 239; in birdsong notation, 65, 68, 69, 76; discrimination by birds, 88, 110n2, 155–157; fast Fourier transform (FFT) algorithm and, 73; melodic regression to the mean and, 127; in Messiaen's birdsong transcriptions, 59, 76; mimicry and, 142, 143; musical notation and, 61, 62, 63; one-pitch phrases, 150, 163, *163*; octave designations, 110n6; phrase endings and drop in, *166, 167*; pitch bends, 215; in SLD2 motifs, 101–102, *101, 102,* 126–127, 154; in species calls, 94–95, 110n11, 128; rattles and, 89–90; relative, 65, 155–156, 214, 230n19; sonograms and, 27, 86; structural versus ornamental, 138; timbre and, 91; "weak" beats and, 150. *See also* absolute (or perfect) pitch; blue notes; intervals; intonation; *Klangfarbenmelodie*; portamentos; tuning; twelve-tone equal temperament

plagiarism, 185, 186

plastic song, 24. *See also* immature birds; vocal (or song) learning

platypus, 85

Plumwood, Val, 270

poison, as threat to birds, 135, 260, 262–264

popular music, 11, 197, 220, 224

portamentos, 59, 77, 83n72, 95, 100, 128, 157–158, 183; ascending and descending, 168, 171, 245; in duets, 138, 140, *140*; *Klangfarbenmelodie* and, 160–161; in phrases of diurnal song, 130, 134, 135; "rules" of music and, 215; in singing lessons, 175. *See also* glissando

postmodern green theory, 15, 18n31

post-skip reversal, 127, 130. *See also* gap-fill

Power of Sound, The (Gurney), 191

Powys, Vicki, 146n30, 256n33

Premack, Ann James, 176

Premack, David, 176

Pressing, Jeff, 221, 274

prickly wattle (*Acacia victoriae*), 180

primates, 23, 100, 187, 218, 273, 274; primate exceptionalism, 100, 273

Primate Visions (Haraway), 84

Probets, Carol, 146n30

Prum, Richard O., 38

Pythagoras, 193

quadrivium, in ancient Greece, 16n3

Qualitative Behaviour Assessment, 35–36

Queensland, 12, 53, 91, 106, 175, 195, *196, 251, 269, 275. See also* Lamington National Park (Queensland); North Queensland; Witches' Falls National Park (Queensland)

quiet song, 124. *See also* subsong

Raffman, Diana, 189

rainbow lorikeet (*Trichoglossus moluccanus*), 86

Rameau, Jean-Philippe, 207n39

rapping, 187

rattles, 2, 76, 78, 89–91, *89–90,* 108, 127, 134, 171, 175, 176, 183, 245, 280; accent and, 155; in phrases of diurnal song, 130,

135; pulse rate of, 78, 150; quasi rattle, 89, *89*, 108, 134, 171; "scales" as, 158; in singing lessons, 175, 176
Ravel, Maurice, 164
Read, Gardner, 62, 64
recapitulation, 6, 7
recitative, 187
recordings, 64–65, 68, 74, 76, 77, 79n11, 110n6, 120, 126, 169, 200, 204n4, 236, 237, 243, 248, 249; as bioacoustic data, 259–260; playback of, 250–251
Red Centre, of Australia, 12, 266
red-necked pademelon (*Thylogale thetis*), 55
Reich, Steve, 163
repetition, 6, 109, 132, 161, *163*, 168, 189, 204n13, 239, 243, 247; monotony-threshold and, 162–163; short, repeated notes, 88–90, *89–90*; in stuck song syndrome, 162–163
reptiles, 258, 263, 267, 273. *See also* snakes
Révész, Géza, 40
"Revolutionary" Étude, op. 10, no. 12 in C minor (Chopin), 149
Reznikova, Zhanna, 272–273
rhythm, 6, 199, 210, 213, 217, 223, 239, 245, 246, 249; free rhythms, 161; musical notation and, 59–61, *61–63*, 66, 68, 71, 76, 77; in pied butcherbird song, 94, 130, 132, 134, 143, 150, 154, *163*, 164, *166*, 167, 168, 265, 281n13, 283. *See also* meter; tempo, of songs and calls
Rice, Timothy, 271
ritardando, 150
Rite of Spring, The (Stravinsky), 6
river red gum (*Eucalyptus camaldulensis*), 41, 107, 112, 174, 219, 244, 257–258
Robbings, Chandler S., 72
Roché, Jean C., 59, 245
rock-wallaby (*Petrogale assimilis*), 198
Rodgers, John, 246
rondo form, 161
Rose, Deborah Bird, 112
Rose, Jon, 16n2, 41, 121, 144n8
Ross River Resort, 102–108, *102*, 124, 251
Rothenberg, David, 239, 252
Rouse, Charlie, 166
Rowe, Stan, 253n3
rubato, 150
Russolo, Luigi, 196

Rutter, Jane, 33
Ryan, Mike, 272
Ryan, Robin, 40

salsa, 161
saltwater country, 12, 29
Samuel, Claude, 57, 58
Sartre, Jean-Paul, 15
satin bowerbird (*Ptilonorhynchus violaceus*), 20, 22
Saunders, Aretas, 69–70, *70*, 82n47
savannah country, 12, 29
scales, 77; canyon wren song and, 149; musician wren song and, 216; nightingale wren song and, 215; pied butcherbird song and, 109, 158–159, *158*, 247; Pythagoras and, 193; scales outside twelve-tone equal temperament, 215–216
Scharff, Constance, 124, 146n31, 219, 272
Schoenberg, Arnold, 159, 166–167, 186
Schwartz, Hillel, 196
Schwitters, Kurt, 68, 81n45
science/scientists, 4, 10, 23, 25–26, 36, 37, 38, 46, 49n24, 73, 134, 150, 176, 177n1, 185, 207n38, 214, 221, 227, 236, 238, 242, 253, 253n3, 262, 263, 265, 270; climate change and, 252, 260; philosophy of science, 272. *See also* biology/biologists; citizen science/scientists; ethology/ethologists; natural sciences; neuroscience/neuroscientists; ornithology/ornithologists
sea shanties, 161
sedge warbler (*Acrocephalus schoenobaenus*), 6, 220
Seeger, Charles, 76
semantics, 92
semitone, 77, 95, 140, 160, 168, 171, 235; deferred motion of, 170; octave leaps and, *157*; shape/balance and, 168, *169*. *See also* intervals
sequences, 89, 109
Serbo-Croatian Folk Songs (Bartók), 60
Serres, Michel, 196
sexual selection, 21, 38, 272
Shaggs, The (rock group), 202
shape, 161, 168–170, *169*
Shiovitz, K. A., 25
short-range song, 124. *See also* subsong

shrikes, 29, 31
signal diversity, 88
silence, 6, 28, 33, 78, 118, 150, 198–199, 245, 247
"Singing Lesson, The," 152, 178n8
singing lessons, 122, 125, 152, 173, 175–177. *See also* vocal (or song) learning
Skeoch, Andrew, 244–145, 255n21
skylark (*Alauda arvensis*), 6
SLD2 (short-long descending second) motif, 100–102, 104–106, 108, 126–127, *127*, 128, 136, 154, 155, 183; basic variants, *101*; in diurnal ensemble songs, 108; mapped in nocturnal songs, *102. See also* species call
slur, 77, 83n72. *See also* glissando; portamentos
Small, Christopher, 36, 180, 199
snakes, 11, 19, 32, 97, 105, 113, 121, 141, 147–148, 182, 183, 263
Snow, C. P., 4
Snyder, Gary, 185
"So-Called Bulgarian Rhythm, The" (Bartók), 60
sociobiology, 272
soft song, 124. *See also* subsong
solo singing, 33, 35, 98, *99*, *100*, 136, 156, 158, 163, 165, 166, 170, 171, 173, 175, 178n8, 226; diurnal, 116, 122–125, 128–136, *131*, *133*, 170; female, 25; mimicry appended to formal solos, 117, 120–122; nocturnal, 101, *102*, 103, 104, 106, 108, 112, 117–122, 125–128, *127*, 148, 174, 182, 183, 235–236, 243–244, 259; phrases in, 118, 144n7, 173, 199. *See also* nocturnal songs
song asynchrony, 165
songbirds, 7, 23–26, 28, 37, 68, 91, 123, 211, 216, 223, 236, 237, 239, 240, 243, 250, 252, 271, 278, 279; agency of, 214–215; brains of, 187, 273; capacities of, 149, 150, 155, 184, 203, 212, 218, 221, 223, 225, 227, 228, 273, 274, 277; culture possessed by, 213, 229; Gondwana as evolutionary birthplace of, 28; musical rehearsal by, 214; number of species, 23
song learning. *See* singing lessons; vocal (or song) learning
Songs of the Birds (Garstang), 68

song sparrow (*Melospiza melodia*), 220
song template, 23, 63
sonograms (spectrograms), 27–28, 58, 59, 70, 71, 72, 75, 76, 95, 120, 126; audio tracks paired with, 85; challenge to, 28, 49n26, 73; in field guides, 72, 82n57; of juvenile singers, 110n11, 174; of pied butcherbird notes, 85–86, *86*, *87*, 88, 89, *89*, *90*, *93*, 137, *160*; transcription compared with, 77; transcription paired with, 72, 78, 165; as universal graphic instrument, 75
Soper, Kate, 268
Sotavalta, Olavi, 72
sound art, 161, 175, 197, 198
soundmarks, 118, 122, 125
sound microscopy, 73
sound poetry, 187
soundscape, 9, 243, 248, 257
species call, 94–98, 135, 142–143, 184, 250; call-in-song, 98–100, *99*, *100*, 101, 102, 109, 125, 128, 136, 155, 156, 183, 280; compositions appropriating, 76, 109, 244, 255n20; as motifs in ensemble songs, *99*; sonograms and notation of, *93*, *96*, 110n11; transposed, 156. *See also* SLD2 (short-long descending second) motif
Spencer, Herbert, 190
spotted bowerbird (*Chlamydera maculata*), 21, 22
Sprechgesang, 187
Sprosser nightingale (*Luscinia luscinia*), transcription of song, 72, *72*
stage presence, 149, 171–172
starlings, 24, 155, 221
stasis, 161
Stefani, Gino, 203
stereotypy, 119, 219
Stravinsky, Igor, 6, 7, 186, 190
straw-necked ibis, 279
Strehlow, Carl, 39, 41
Strehlow, John, 41
structure, 34, 35, 39, 63, 109, 125, 161–170, 178n8; canon, 161, 164–166; combinatoriality, 161, 163–164; formal structure, 246; hierarchical structure, 223–225, 56n56; intonation, 73; macrostructure, 161; music notation and, 28, 63; ostinato

and, 161, 164, *165*; performance-as-a-whole and, 143; phrase endings, 161, 166–168, *166*, *167*; "plastic song" and, 24; repetition, 161, 162–163, *163*; shape and balance, 161, 168–170, *169*; syntax of bird calls and, 92

Stuart's Well, 267

stuck song syndrome, 162

subsong, 24, 115, 122, 144n3, 173, 226; diurnal, 124–125; immature birds and, 116; mimicry and, 135, 184; rehearsal and, 214

Suite Joyous (Tate), 109, 255n20

Suite No. 3 in D (Bach), 149

sulphur-crested cockatoo (*Cacatua galerita*), 129, 213

sunbirds, 32

superb lyrebird (*Menura novaehollandiae*), 7, 56, 142

Susskind, Walter, 171

Swainson's thrush (*Catharus ustulatus*), 26

swamp sparrow (*Melospiza georgiana*), 24

swing, 150, 177n3

Symphonic Rhapsody (Tate), 109

Symphonies of Wind Instruments (Stravinsky, 1920), 7

syncopation, 2, 148, 150, 211, 235, 281n13

syntax, 92, 206n34, 215, 222, 231n22

syrinx, avian, 23, 47n6, 127

Szeryng, Henryk, 171

Szőke, Péter, 5, 73, 83n59, 190

Tanami Desert, 121

Tasmania, 30

Tate, Henry, 109, 11n16, 255n17, 255n20

Taylor, Cecil, 268

Tchernichovski, Ofer, 241

Temiar people, 179n38

tempo, of songs and calls, 57, 59, 66, 94, 100, 150, 213–214

tessitura, 94, 100, 134, 156, 160, 249

theriomorphism, 46

Thorpe, W. H., 27, 72, 110n2, 121, 144n3, 227–228

Through the Looking Glass (Carroll), 212

Tiessen, Heinz, 71, 73, 82n53

timbre (tone color), 27, 28, 42, 57, 66, 68, 71, 74, 81n45, 104, 159–161, *160*, 197,

224, 246, 249; dissonance and, 231n27; in ensemble singing, 161; pied butcherbird vocal timbre, 29, 34, 42, 90, 91–92, 95, 109, 127, 134, 153, 154, 155, 159, 245, 249, 265; whisper songs and, 124. *See also* broad-spectrum (complex, buzzy, or "noisy") notes; *Klangfarbenmelodie*; mnemonics

Todd, Charles, 96

Tomlinson, Gary, 204n4

tonality, 7, 77, 91, 159, 168. *See also* microtones/microtonality

tonal languages, 187

tone quality, 95, 117, 119, 142, 174

tone/sound colors. *See Klangfarbenmelodie*; timbre (tone color)

Traité de rythme, de couleur, et d'ornithologie (Messiaen), 57

transcription. *See* notation, musical

transition versatility, 134–135, 163

transposition, 83n74, 100, 108, 110n11, 137, 138, *140*, 156, 290

tree-kangaroos, 84

trills, 33, 50n40, 78, 88, 89, 132, 134

triplets, 150

tritone, 101, 168. *See also* intervals

tropical bou-bou shrike (*Laniarius aethiopicus*), 72, 227

Trovatore, Il (Verdi), 173

truncation, 95, 100, 128, 161, 168, 169, 176, 183, 226, 280

tui (*Prosthemadera novaeseelandiae*), transcription of song, 69, *69*

tuning, 157, 178n8, 193, 215, 216, 217, 231n27, 247. *See also* blue notes; intonation; scales; twelve-tone equal temperament

twelve-tone equal temperament, 157, 215, *215*

twitter song, 124. *See also* subsong

Two Cultures, The (Snow), 4

undirected song, 124. *See also* subsong

unobtrusive signals, 124. *See also* subsong

Ursonate (Schwitters,), 68

Vanderduys, Eric, 146n30

Varela, Francisco G., 222

Varèse, Edgard, 199
variation, 68, 95, 101, 123, 130, 132, 138, 143, 155, 161, 162, 163, *163*, 186, 188, 226, 244, 277
Venda people, 63
ventriloquism, in song, 92, 116, 127, 172–173
Verdi, Giuseppe, 173
virtuoso/virtuosity, 115, 135, 160, 170–171, 183, 228, 243, 255n13, 279
vocal (or song) learning, 23–24, 26, 68, 187, 212–213, 214, 218, 231n22; cerebral capacity for, 218; in human evolution, 239; Laboratory of Vocal Learning (New York), 241; mimicry and, 187
Voigt, A., 82n51
Von Glahn, Denise, 259

Wagner, Richard, 154, 201–202
Walker, Lisa, 252
wallabies, 103, 180, 182, 198, 261, 279. *See also* kangaroos
Wallaschek, Richard, 190
Walser, Robert, 185
Wannga people, music of, 39
Warrumbungle National Park, 244
Watson, Chris, 146n30
Webern, Anton von, 161, 186, 249
Weitz, Morris, 201, 202
Wemelsfelder, Françoise, 35, 37
western bowerbird (*Chlamydera guttata*), 21
western meadowlark (*Sturnella neglecta*), 71
whales, 6, 149, 223, 251, 252, 273
whisper song, 115–116, 122, 124. *See also* subsong
whistling kite (*Haliastur sphenurus*), 97
White, S. A., 41
"White Knight Concept," 259
Wieneke, Jo, 32
Wild Dog Dreaming: Love and Extinction (Rose), 112
wilderness, 14–15
Williams, D. C., 279
Williams, Raymond, 13

willie wagtail (*Rhipidura leucophrys*), 120, 235
willow warbler (*Phylloscopus trochilus*), 225
Wilson, E. O., 8
winter wren (*Nannus hiemalis*), transcription of song, 70
Witchell, Charles A., 66, 68
Witches' Falls National Park (Queensland), 56, 57
Wittgenstein, Ludwig, 201, 217
wobulation, 88
Wogarno Station, Western Australia, 1, 3, 104
wood pewee, 225, 227
woodswallows, 28
work songs, African American, 161
wow sound, 91–92, 99, 108, 134, 137, *166*, 280
Wright, Judith, 43
Wyschnegradsky, Ivan, 157

Xenakis, Iannis, 207n39

yellow-breasted sunbird (*Nectarinia jugularis*), 32
yellow-faced whipsnake (*Demansia psammophis*), 105
yellow-throated miner (*Manorina flavigula*), 257

zebra finch (*Taeniopygia guttata*), 124, 223, 240
Zim, Herbert S., 72
zip calls, 93, 94, 95, 97, 110n11. *See also* species call
zoömusicology/zoömusicologists, 4–8, 10, 13, 14, 16n13, 47, 68, 85, 101, 103, 125, 140, 185, 202, 253n4, 278; anthropomorphism and, 165; biodiversity crisis and, 259–270; ethnomusicology and, 8–9; issues of musicality and, 238–240; numeracy and, 240–242; overreliance on theory, 252–253; position in academia, 237–238, 254n6; science and, 241–242; theoretical and methodological challenges for, 236–242

HOLLIS TAYLOR is a research fellow at Macquarie University. American by birth, she had enjoyed a thirty-year international career in classical, jazz, and world music when in 2002 she had an epiphany upon hearing the song of an Australian bird. A violinist/composer, ornithologist, and author, she confronts and revises the study of birdsong in her work, adding the novel reference point of a musician's trained ear. Her previous posts include fellowships at the Institute for Advanced Study in Berlin, the Muséum national d'Histoire naturelle in Paris, and the University of Technology Sydney.